NEURAL NETWORKS IN DESIGN AND MANUFACTURING

NEURAL NETWORKS IN DESIGN AND MANUFACTURING

Edited by

Jun Wang
University of North Dakota, USA

Yoshiyasu Takefuji
Case Western Reserve University, USA
Keio University, Japan

World Scientific
Singapore • New Jersey • London • Hong Kong

Published by

World Scientific Publishing Co. Pte. Ltd.

P O Box 128, Farrer Road, Singapore 9128

USA office: Suite 1B, 1060 Main Street, River Edge, NJ 07661

UK office: 73 Lynton Mead, Totteridge, London N20 8DH

NEURAL NETWORKS IN DESIGN AND MANUFACTURING

ISBN 981-02-1281-X

Printed in Singapore by Utopia Press.

To the memory of my father, Ching Hien (Jingxian) Wang, who passed away on the eve of the publication of this book.

Jun Wang

Editors

Dr. Jun Wang is an associate professor of industrial technology at the University of North Dakota, Grand Forks, ND. He received his B.S. degree in electrical engineering and his M.S. degree in systems engineering from Dalian University of Technology, Dalian, China. He received his Ph.D. degree in systems engineering from Case Western Reserve University, Cleveland, Ohio. Before joining the University of North Dakota, he held academic positions at Dalian University of Technology and Case Western Reserve University. Dr. Wang has been working in the field of neural networks for many years and has published twenty papers in various journals. His current research interests include theory and methodology of artificial neural networks, and their applications to decision systems, control systems, and manufacturing systems. Dr. Wang is a member of IEEE Circuits and Systems Society, Computer Society, Control Systems Society, Robotics and Automation Society, Systems, Man, and Cybenetics Society; International Neural Network Society; Institute of Industrial Engineers; Operations Research Society of America, and Decision Sciences Institute. He is also a member of Computer Integrated Manufacturing Technical Committee of IEEE Robotics and Automation Society.

Dr. Yoshiyasu Takefuji is a tenured associate professor in the Faculty of Environmental Information at Keio University since April 1992 and also in the Faculty of Electrical Engineering at Case Western Reserve University since 1988. Before joining Case, he taught at the University of South Florida for two years and the University of South Carolina for three years. He received his B.S. (1978), M.S. (1980), and Ph.D. (1983) degrees in electrical engineering from Keio University under the supervision of Professor Hideo Aiso. His research interests focus on neural network parallel computing for solving real-world problems. He is interested in VLSI applications and silicon architecture. He received the National Science Foundation/Research Initiation Award in 1989 and received the distinct service award from IEEE Transactions on Neural Networks in 1992 and has been an NSF advisory panelist. A member of the IEEE Computer Society, ACM, International Neural Network Society, and American Association for the Advancement of Science, he received the Information Processing Society of Japan's best paper award in 1980. He authored a book entitled *Neural Network Parallel Computing*, published by Kluwer Academic Publishers in January

1992 and coauthored two books *Digital Circuits*, (Ohm-Sha Publishers) in 1984 and *Neuro Computing*, (Baifukan Publishers) in 1992. He was an editor of *Journal of Neural Network Computing* and is currently an associate editor of *IEEE Transactions on Neural Networks*, *Neural/Parallel/Scientific Computations*, and *Neurocomputing*. He is also a guest editor of *Journal Analog Integrated Circuits and Signal Processing* for the special issue on analog VLSI neural networks and a guest editor of the special issue on neural network optimization in *Neurocomputing*. He has published more than 100 papers. He is included in *Who's Who in America*, *Who's Who in the Midwest*, *Who's Who in Science and Engineering*, *Men of Achievement*.

Contributors

Nirwan Ansari
New Jersey Institute of Technology

C. L. Philip Chen
Wright State University

Cihan H. Dagli
University of Missouri-Rolla

Edwin S. H. Hou
New Jersey Institute of Technology

Ram Huggahalli
University of South Carolina

Hung-Kang Jan
Industrial Technology Research Institute, Taiwan

Sagar V. Kamarthi
The Pennsylvania State University

Raju G. Khanchustambham
University of Maryland

Soundar R. T. Kumara
The Pennsylvania State University

C. Richard Liu
Purdue University

Young B. Moon
Syracuse University

Yoh-han Pao
Case Western Reserve University

Tep Sastri
Texas A&M University

Ramesh Sharda
Oklahoma State University

Rick L. Wilson
Oklahoma State University

Percy P. C. Yip
Case Western Reserve University

Guangming Zhang
University of Maryland

Zeeman Z. Zhang
New Jersey Institute of Technology

Preface

Over the past several years, there has been a reviving surge of research activities in neural networks. In application areas, although the major thrust was originally on pattern recognition, associative memory, combinatorial optimization, robotics and process control, neural networks have recently been applied to design and manufacturing. Despite the huge volume of publications in recent literature on neural network research, there is no single monograph addressing the roles of neural networks in design and manufacturing. This edited book is devoted to report the neural network research activities in design and manufacturing and to define and shape the academic and professional progress in these areas.

The focus of this book is on the applications of neural network concepts and techniques to design and manufacturing. The objectives of this book are to review the state of the art of the research activities, highlight the recent advances in research and development, and discuss the potential directions and future trends along this stream of research. This book is intended for a wide variety of readership. The potential readers of this book include, but are not limited to, beginners who are interested in the applications of neural networks to design and manufacturing, professionals who have been active in the areas of neural networks and design/manufacturing, and practitioners in industries who are applying neural networks to design and manufacturing.

This book is composed of ten chapters covering the applications of neural networks to various topics in design and manufacturing. The topics include group technology (Chapters 1 and 2), facility layout (Chapter 3), conceptual design (Chapter 4), a design case study (Chapter 5), feature sequencing (Chapter 6), scheduling (Chapter 7), system identification (Chapter 8), and machining processes (Chapters 9 and 10). The contributors of this book were invited and solicited among the active researchers in the fields of neural networks and design/manufacturing. All the contributed articles were peer-reviewed to ensure their quality and relevance to the theme.

Jun Wang would like to acknowledge the support of a research grant from the Advancing Science Excellence in North Dakota Program. The editors of this volume would like to thank Miss Catherine Roze, a graduate student at the University of North Dakota, for her editorial assistance. The editors would also like to thank World Scientific Publishing Company and its editors, Mr. Tony Moore and Mr. Chris Lee, for publishing this volume.

Jun Wang and Yoshiyasu Takefuji
September 1993

Contents

List of Figures

List of Tables

Chapter 1

A Neural Network Approach to Group Technology

Cihan H. Dagli
Engineering Management Department
University of Missouri-Rolla
Rolla, MO 65401 USA

Ram Huggahalli
Department of Electrical and Computer Engineering
University of South Carolina
Columbia, SC 29208 USA

1.1 Introduction

Group technology (GT) seeks to identify and exploit similarities of product design and manufacturing processes throughout the manufacturing cycle.[1,2] GT, a discrete-item production concept, is particularly applicable to batch production systems. These systems have evolved primarily to provide medium-sized lots of a small variety of products rather than large quantities of a single product (mass production) or small quantities of a great variety of products (job-shop production). Parts to be manufactured in such a system can be grouped into part families based on the similarities between them. Two types of part attributes can be used to observe similarities:[3]

1. Design attributes such as external/internal shapes, material, dimensions, and tolerances.

2. Manufacturing attributes such as machine tools, operation sequence, batch size, and production time.

The groups formed may be exploited in several ways. The greatest benefit is attained by designing the shop floor layout accordingly. Machines can be arranged into cells so that, parts in a part family can be maximally processed within a single cell. Since the parts processed in a cell are similar, the maximum possible degree of mass production ability is provided to batch production. The advantages are a reduction in material handling costs, lower set-up times, less in-process inventory, and lower manufacturing lead times.

Implementation of GT thus requires the recognition of resemblances between parts. There are three general ways of identifying common design and manufacturing attributes.[3] In *visual inspection*,[4] the physical attributes are compared manually and therefore it is the least accurate and most painstaking way of identifying groups. Machine vision, a research area of current interest is focused toward making visual inspection more efficient. In *classification and coding*, each part's attributes are comprehensively coded, and a classification is performed based on these codes. The main problems with this method are that of finding an optimal coding scheme for the given situation, and the time required for code assignment and comparison. The *production flow analysis* method simplifies recognition by considering only the manufacturing attributes derived from route sheets. A number of other analysis techniques (called machine-part family/cell formation techniques) based on manufacturing attributes have been developed since production flow analysis was proposed by Burbridge[5] in 1963. The subject of this paper is a new and an efficient analysis method directed toward machine-part family formation.

1.1.1 The Machine-Part Family Formation Problem

The assignment of a similar group of parts to a cell of machines having common processing characteristics results in *cellular manufacturing*. Machine-part family formation is necessary for the implementation of cellular manufacturing. The machine-part matrix represents the relations between machines and parts. It is the starting point for the development and implementation of most cell formation techniques. Hence, such a matrix must be made available from process plans and routing sheets. A 7 part, 5 machine example is shown in Table 1.1(a).

The objective of most algorithms is to rearrange the rows and columns of the machine-part matrix in such a way that the resultant matrix has all the '1' elements in the matrix clustered in groups in a block diagonal fashion. Each cluster in the rearranged form of the matrix would then indicate part groups and machine groups as shown in Table 1.1(b). According to Table 1.1(b), there must be two machine cells, the first containing machines 1 and 4, and the second containing machines 3, 2 and 5. Note that part 2 must be processed in both the machine cells. Such parts are called *exceptional parts* and the matrix element, represented by the (part, machine) coordinate (2, 3) is called an *exceptional element*. Our primary goal during classification is to minimize the number of exceptional elements. By doing so, we minimize the number of inter-cellular movements and therefore the material handling costs. An alternative solution to that shown in Table 1.1(b) is obtained by moving machine 3

Table 1.1: Machine-part family formation, (a) a 7-part, 5-machine, initial machine-part matrix, (b) a rearranged form of the matrix

		Parts						
		1	2	3	4	5	6	7
Machines	1		1		1	1	1	
	2	1		1				
	3	1	1					1
	4		1		1		1	
	5	1						1

(a)

		Parts						
		1	7	3	2	4	6	5
Machines	1				1	1	1	1
	4				1	1	1	
	3	1	1		1			
	2	1		1				
	5	1	1					

	Parts	Machines
Group 1:	1 7 3	1 4
Group 2:	2 4 6 5	3 2 5

(b)

to the first machine cell. However, this solution gives us two exceptional elements, (1, 3) and (7, 3) as compared to just one in the previous case. Exceptional elements are often depicted by an '*' or are encircled in the rearranged (or final) matrix.

The advantage of obtaining the block diagonal form of Table 1.1(b) can be realized when the numerical information in Table 1.1 is implemented on the shop floor. A cellular manufacturing implementation and its effect is pictorially shown in Figure 1.1. The matrices in Table 1.1 are used for this purpose.

Exceptional elements may be eliminated by duplicating *bottleneck* machines. Machine 3, in the example, is a bottleneck machine as it processes a part in both groups. By installing a duplicate of this machine in the first machine cell (as opposed to moving it to the first machine cell), two disjoint clusters are obtained. The resulting matrix takes the *pure* block diagonal form as shown in Table 1.2. Thus, a trade-off between material handling and machine duplication can be made.

In practical situations, very large matrices can be encountered. Several alternative solutions must then be evaluated to obtain optimal machine-part families. Several performance criteria by which a solution may be evaluated exist. Some of them are, total material handling cost, average machine utilization, average set-up time, and manufacturing lead time. Hence the need for techniques to obtain machine-

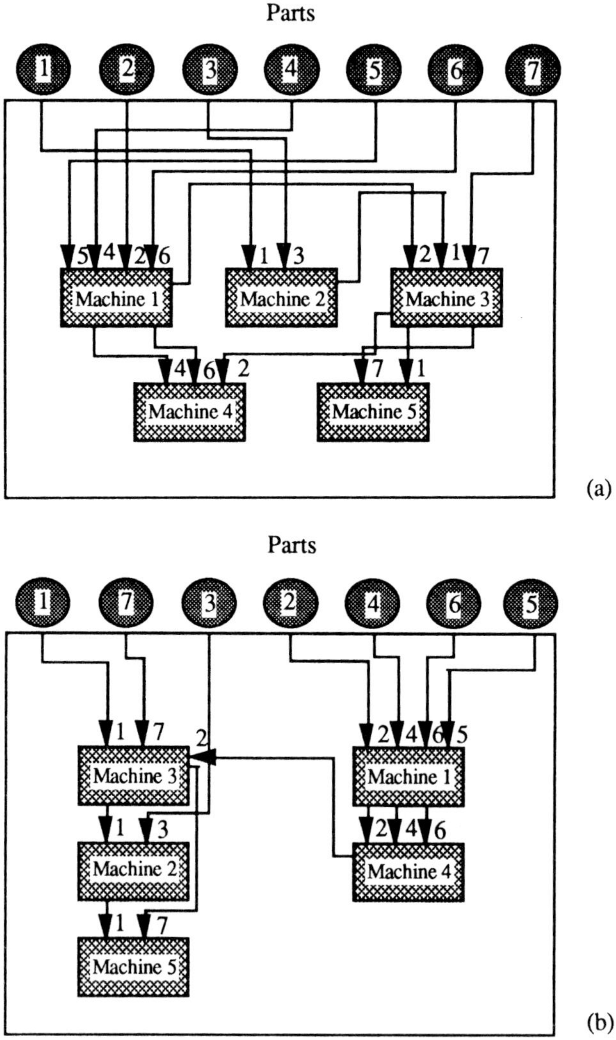

Figure 1.1: The effect of implementing the cellular manufacturing concept, (a) the traditional method for job routing and (b) the cellular manufacturing (GT) method

Table 1.2: A pure block diagonal form

		Parts						
		1	7	3	2	4	6	5
Machines	1				1	1	1	1
	4				1	1	1	
	3				1			
	3	1	1					
	2	1		1				
	5	1	1					

	Parts				Machines		
Group 1:	1	7	3		1	4	3
Group 2:	2	4	6	5	3	2	5

part clusters as efficiently as possible and also a set of heuristics to obtain at least close-to-optimal solutions.

1.1.2 Existing Approaches

To obtain an optimal solution in terms of a minimum cost, it is necessary for most algorithms to be iteratively implemented. Serial algorithms proposed in literature take significant time for each iteration. Highly parallel systems such as neural networks can be used, to be able to observe and compare different solutions in a short time. In light of the computational deficiencies of existing algorithms, even when implemented on hardware, the unmatched speed of neural networks must be considered for machine-part family formation problems where, large amounts of information must be processed in a short time. Moon proposed an interactive activation and competition model[6] in which a neural network is first established based on part similarities, machine similarities and the machine-part relations as obtained from the machine-part matrix. Then, parts and machines are grouped using the neural network which activates uniquely for each part group and machine group. Since this model requires the computation of similarities between every pair of parts and machines and very little information is known on the performance of the system, other methods of application of neural networks to the cell formation problem must be explored for achieving improved efficiency. Approaches to the cell formation problem are discussed in greater detail in Section 1.2.

1.1.3 Outline of the ART1 Approach

The paper proposes the use of a popular neural network paradigm called the binary Adaptive Resonance Theory paradigm (ART1) for machine-part family formation.

The essential function of an ART1 is to classify a set of binary vectors into groups based on a specified degree of similarity. Each group of similar patterns (or vectors) is represented by a pattern and the new patterns are compared with representative patterns before being classified into a certain group. Thus, it may be directly applied to classify the parts characterized by the column vectors, and the machines characterized by the row vectors in the machine-part matrix.

It is shown that the ART1 paradigm in its original form does not provide the expected results. The classification depends largely on the order in which vectors are sequentially applied. Also, a deficient learning policy that gradually diminishes the effectiveness of the representative pattern leads to a number of inappropriate classifications and a larger number of groups than necessary. The problems encountered with the basic ART1 can be attributed to, the high sensitivity of the paradigm to the heuristically chosen degree of similarity. This sensitivity can be reduced by applying the input vectors in the order of decreasing density (measured simply by the number of '1's in the vector) and by retaining only the vector with the greater density as the representative pattern. These modifications lead to a great improvement in the correctness of classification.

The method is then validated with test cases studied in literature, as well as with synthetically generated matrices. A procedure for obtaining the optimal cell formation solution is also proposed.

1.2 A Review of Existing Methods

Approaches to the machine-part family formation problem have been classified by King and Nakornchai[7] as,

1. similarity coefficient,
2. set theoretic,
3. evaluative,
4. other analytic approaches.

Significant contributions that fall under each of the above categories are discussed in this section. Kusiak[8] separated heuristic (most of items 1, 2, and 3 above) and enumerative approaches as matrix formulation and p-median formulation approaches respectively. Heuristic methods[8,9] attempt to rearrange rows and columns of the machine-part matrix to obtain the block diagonal form corresponding to a good low cost solution. The p-median formulation is an integer programming model of the machine-part family formation problem,[8] with the objective function of minimizing the total sum of distances in a cluster to the cluster median.

As observed by Wei and Gaither,[10] most algorithms found in literature are heuristic. Heuristic algorithms are in general faster than enumerative approaches. However, it is the enumerative approaches that assure one of an optimal solution.

1.2.1 Similarity Coefficient Method

In the similarity coefficient method (SCM)[7,11–14] proposed by Seifoddini the *similarity coefficient* between two machines is defined as,

$$\frac{\text{the number of components visiting both machines}}{\text{number of components visiting either of the two machines}}.$$

A similarity matrix containing the similarity coefficients between all pairs of machines is provided as the input to a clustering algorithm. The algorithm forms machine cells for various thresholds (degrees of similarity) and presents them in a tree-like diagram called a sl dendogram. The highest (or top) level of the dendogram corresponds to the lowest threshold; i.e., the threshold for which all machines come under a single group. At lower levels, as the threshold increases, machine pairs that have a similarity coefficient greater than the threshold are grouped together. Thus, higher thresholds correspond to machines that are more alike, and therefore a large number of small groups are formed. After the machines are classified and rearranged in the matrix, parts processed at each machine cell are moved closer together in the matrix to obtain the final block diagonal form. The bottleneck machines are then identified and duplicated as necessary. Efficient techniques to minimize data storage space in the algorithm's computer implementation make this approach attractive.

Since the threshold factor that determines similarity is usually arbitrarily chosen, a set of solutions are derived rather than a unique solution, and evaluated to determine the best solution. The arbitrariness could not be avoided although a number of methods were proposed for the proper selection of the threshold. These methods were reviewed by King and Nakornchai, and Seifoddini. Sahay and Seifoddini showed that, a lower threshold representing larger machine groups, leads to a smaller inter-cellular movement, and larger intra-cellular movement, while a larger threshold has an opposite effect. Both the costs can be summed for different threshold values and the threshold value corresponding to the minimum cost is chosen for the classification. Application of this method also results in the *improper machine assignment* problem.[12] This problem is solved simply by identifying such machines and by reassigning them appropriately.

1.2.2 Rank Order Clustering (ROC)

The Rank Order Clustering (ROC) algorithm of King[7] is an analytic method which, as a contrast, is not based on comparison of the vectors with respect to any degree of similarity. Here, first, each row entry is given a weight of $2n$ depending on its position in the row, with the first entry from the left (as a convention followed by King[7]) having the highest weight. The rows are then arranged according to their ranks, obtained on the basis of the sum of the weights in each row. The columns of the resultant matrix, are likewise rearranged to obtain the clustered form. The problem with this method is that, for large matrices, the computation of the weights can be beyond the scope of the computer. For example, in a 90×36 matrix, vectors of length 90 are encountered. If the most significant digit of such a vector is a '1', the corresponding weight would be 2^{90}, whose value far exceeds the maximum integer that can be stored in a conventional computer. To overcome this limitation, element by element comparisons for carrying out row or column ranking were proposed. The implementation of the algorithm needed a tremendous amount of memory and computation time. Its inefficiency in tackling large problems lead to the development of the ROC2 algorithm. The ROC2 eliminates the need for computing the binary rankings. It re-orders the rows and columns as follows:

1. For all columns, locate the rows with entries (1's). Move the rows with entries to the head of the row list, maintaining the previous order of the entries (1st iteration).

2. Repeat for all rows, re-ordering columns this time (2nd iteration).

The algorithm is a relatively efficient technique especially when powerful sorting algorithms such as Quicksort are used, in terms of memory requirement and computation time. Like the similarity coefficient method it is a heuristic technique that offers the flexibility to evaluate alternative solutions. If a pure block diagonal form exists, the algorithm obtains it within two iterations. However, if bottleneck machines are present, they are identified and duplicated to eliminate some or all exceptional element and more iterations of the ROC2 are performed. The final solution depends on the number of duplications allowed. It must be found by considering the cost factors involved and evaluating a set of solutions.

1.2.3 Integer Programming Method

Mathematical programming has been used for cell formation problems by several researchers such as Kusiak,[8] Wei and Gaither.[10] An optimal 0-1 integer programming model was developed by Wei and Gaither, to provide an analysis for the determination of machine-part cells. In their approach, the objective function is the total opportunity cost (cost of manufacturing exceptional parts). The approach minimizes the objective function subject to machine capacity constraints. Hence, given a machine-part matrix, an integer programming model consisting of the objective function and the constraints must be formulated. The model is then solved enumeratively by a software package with general integer programming facilities. The primary drawback of this method is the unpredictability of the time and computational effort to solve the problem. The run time is primarily determined by the problem structure, the number of variables and constraints and the ways in which the constraints are formulated. In large problems, where optimal solutions are not possible to obtain in a reasonable run time, Wei and Gaither suggest the use of a known solution to reduce the size of the problem. However, no method of integrating a known solution effectively into the approach was proposed. The model proposed is most useful when validating the solutions obtained from heuristic approaches.

1.2.4 Component Flow Analysis

Component flow analysis,[7,15] a variation of production flow analysis introduced by Burbridge[5], is an evaluative method that employs three stages of analysis. The first stage involves the identification and sorting of components or parts into groups based on their manufacturing requirements. The second stage groups machines using the lists of sorted components and constraint specifications. Groups are formed by observing combinations with the highest number of machines as the cores to which other ma chines are successfully added. In the third stage, groups thus obtained are analyzed to observe the loadings and flow patterns of the cells and based on the observations, groups are refined. Emphasis is on knowledge of local factors and analysis of data before and after group formation. The process is tedious requiring human judgement to be employed at every stage of the analysis.

1.2.5 Interactive Activation and Competition Model

Moon[6] proposed a neural network model whose architecture is directly derived from the machine part matrix. Neurons or processing units in the architecture are divided into three pools representing parts, machines and part instances. The initial weights of the connections between parts and between machines are computed as follows,

$$w_{ij} = \frac{s_{ij}}{n} - \text{threshold},$$

where w_{ij} is the weight of the connection between the ith and the jth neuron, s_{ij} is the similarity between the parts or the machines represented by the neurons, n is the number of parts or machines, and the threshold is typically 0.5. The similarity between two vectors (of the same length) is defined as the number of positions in which the vectors have the same value divided by the length of the vectors. The weights between the neurons in the part pool and the neurons in the machine pool are initially equal to 1.

Then, vectors representing parts and machines are applied to the neural network. Depending on the weights a particular neuron activates and suppresses other neurons, to indicate the part or machine group to which the input vector belongs. For a proper comparison, however, the results of the implementation of this recent approach are not known. However, the probable weaknesses of this model can be pointed out. First, the classifications may be too sensitive to the weight decay and the threshold parameters used. Second, the bottleneck machine identification is not addressed, although it is claimed that the approach simplifies the bottleneck machine problem without any further processing.

1.2.6 The ART1 Approach - the Difference

The ART1 approach[16,17] can be thought of as a direct mapping of the natural way of observing similarities. Most objects in the real world in the area of neural networks are represented as patterns. A pattern may be a 256×256 pixel image, or simply a binary vector. When humans encounter an object, an attempt is made to associate the current encounter with previous encounters - the effect is that of relating and classifying new experiences with old ones. Similarly, in the ART1 and several other neural networks, a new pattern is compared with a set of distinct stored patterns. The new pattern is then associated (or classified) with the stored pattern that is most similar to the new pattern.

In the machine-part family formation problem, the part patterns are given as column vectors, and the machine patterns are given as row vectors. The part patterns can first be classified by the ART1 to obtain part groups and then machine patterns can be classified to obtain machine groups. The machine-part matrix can be rearranged by placing parts within a part group adjacently and repeating the same for machines. The resulting matrix can be inspected for bottleneck machines and the number of exceptional cells to be minimized.

Analogous to the similarity coefficient in the similarity coefficient method, a degree of similarity (or similarity) between a new pattern and the stored pattern is used. However, similarity is defined as,

$$\frac{\text{number of `1's in the same position in both patterns}}{\text{number of `1's in the new pattern}}.$$

Thus, the similarity in this case is a measure to ensure whether the new pattern is properly classified or not. When an input pattern is applied to the network, stored patterns (each stored pattern representing a group) compete for it. The stored pattern closest to the input pattern is selected and the similarity between the two is computed. Once computed, the similarity is compared with a pre-specified threshold. A different threshold can be specified for the classification of parts and machines. Different degrees of clusters are obtained for different thresholds (as in the similarity coefficient method). If the similarity exceeds the threshold, a heuristic is used to change the stored pattern to be representative of its group. The performance of the ART 1 greatly depends on this heuristic.

In a hardware implementation of the ART1, the stored patterns compete for the input pattern in parallel resulting in major savings in time. Also, the parts and machines are classified after just a single application of each vector. Since the ART1 paradigm supports on-line learning, new parts and machines can be immediately classified and scheduled on the shop floor. Thus, besides being significantly different, the approach offers a greater efficiency of classification and can potentially form the core of an intelligent manufacturing system. The integration of ART1 with an expert system is proposed in Section 1.4.4.

1.2.7 Cost/Performance Analysis Methods

The existing approaches just discussed (except that of Section 1.2.3) can provide a final matrix consisting of fairly distinct clusters. Bottleneck machines also can be identified. However, to obtain an optimal cell formation solution, other methods that consider the performance criteria involved, the layout specifications such as maximum cell size, maximum number of cells allowed, cost factors, production volume and other parameters must be integrated with the clustering techniques. It is only after an analysis of a particular cell formation that bottleneck machinesmay be duplicated for an optimal solution.

Wei and Gaither's 0-1 integer programming approach[10] discussed in Section 1.2.5 is a general approach into which any type of a constraint (such as cost) can be incorporated. It was demonstrated that the approach provides a clustered final matrix with the cost of manufacturing exceptional parts outside the cellular system minimized. The method is more effectively used when a clustered matrix is obtained by a heuristic method (the faster, inaccurate option) and from the clustered matrix, the optimal duplication of bottleneck machines is made by enumeration. Integer programming models are however, tedious to formulate compared to simulation models. This analysis method is therefore not extensively used.

As Gupta and Tomkins[18] point out, one of the chief problems in evaluating a GT system is the lack of a single criterion of measurement. GT has an impact on both product design and production. Procurement, distribution policies and overall organization structure itself can be affected by GT. Several researchers, have concentrated on criteria such as maximizing machine utilization or minimizing material handling costs. According to Gupta and Tomkins, the objective of the GT practitioner is to achieve a balance of several criteria. Since this is an extremely complex problem, a mathematical analysis has never been attempted. The authors propose a flexible simulation model to observe the dynamic behavior of part families and for the analysis of a variety of cell formation structures. Flynn[19,20] also used simulation to study the effects of set-up time on output capacity. Simulation is the most popular performance analysis technique and its use in cell formation is inevitable.

In the following sections the ART1 approach introduced in Section 1.2.6 is discussed in detail. The ART1 system must be integrated with a decision support system that can perform cost/performance analyses to arrive at an optimal solution. The exact role of the ART1 system in such an integrated system is also discussed.

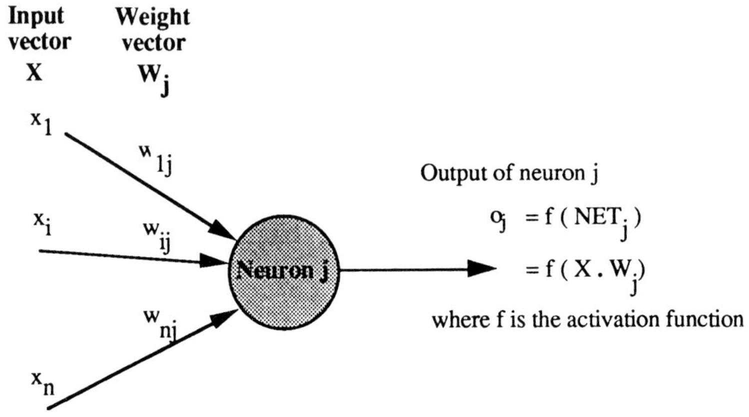

Figure 1.2: A neuron in artificial neural networks

1.3 The ART1 Model

Beginning with an overview of neural networks, this section explains the ART1 approach in detail. The defects of the basic ART1 paradigm is pointed out and some modifications that make ART1's performance more stable are suggested.

1.3.1 Neural Networks

Neural networks are massively parallelized computer systems[16,17] that have the ability to learn from experience and adapt to new situations, besides being extremely fast particularly when implemented in hardware. Since their inception, numerous applications have been introduced. Manufacturing is one of the areas in which extensive use of neural networks has been proposed.[21] In artificial neural networks, the basic processing element is the *neuron*. Every neuron has a set of inputs, each of which is associated with a weight. The values of the inputs are multiplied by the corresponding weights and all products are added to obtain a net value. The output of the neuron is a function of this net value. This function is called the *activation function*. Typical activation functions that are used are the step function and the sigmoid function. For example, in case of the step function, if the net value exceeds a threshold value, the output of the neuron is high, otherwise it is low. The artificial neuron with its activation function, are depicted in Figure 1.2.

A network is *trained* so that application of a set of inputs produces a desired set of outputs. Two types of training methods are used, *supervised* and *unsupervised*. Supervised training requires pairing each input vector to a target vector and iterative tuning of the network weights, to achieve the desired outputs for all input/target pairs. Examples of neural network paradigms that use this type of training are the perceptron and the backpropagation paradigms. In case of unsupervised training,

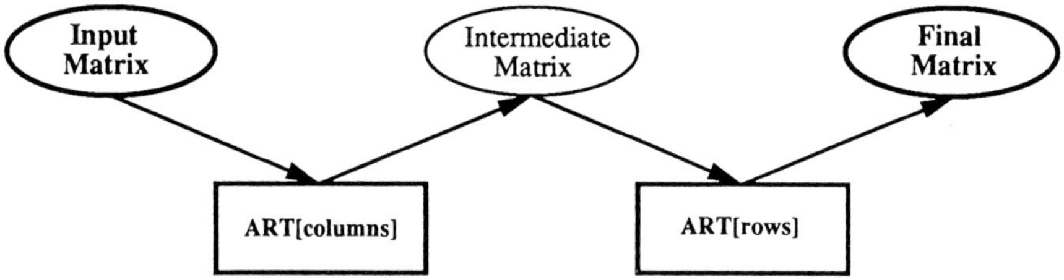

Figure 1.3: Cell formation with the ART1 paradigm

there are no predetermined desired outputs. If an input vector is detected to be similar to a stored pattern, the weights representing the stored pattern are adjusted such that the stored pattern is more like the input vector. The counter-propagation and the adaptive resonance theory networks implement unsupervised training.

A number of neural network paradigms can be used as classifiers. The most important feature of a neural network for this application is that it must be self-organizing. No desired output exists for each input vector, hence paradigms such as the backpropagation cannot be effectively used for this purpose. The counter-propagation and the ART paradigms can be applied directly to this problem. It is observed that the application of the ART1 (the binary ART) paradigm has a resemblance to the application of the similarity coefficient methods.

1.3.2 Group Technology Application

The columns and rows of the machine-part matrix, are binary vectors that can be applied as inputs to a neural network classifier. Column vectors can be first grouped to obtain an intermediate matrix and then, row vectors in this matrix can be grouped to obtain a final matrix. Figure 1.3 depicts this process. As the two groupings are independent, an efficient alternative is to group column vectors and row vectors simultaneously, reducing the total time by half. The disadvantages are that, additional memory will be required and additional effort will be needed to observe the final clustered form by combining the results of the two intermediate groupings formed. Note that the intermediate matrix serves only as an observation point and needs not be the input to either column grouping or row grouping.

ART1 at first classifies the column vectors (by convention), based on their similarity. In the intermediate matrix, the similar columns are placed next to each other. This achieves a degree of clustering of the '1' elements of the matrix. In the next step, the row vectors, are applied as inputs to the ART1 which likewise classifies them. Re-ordering the rows, such that similar rows are adjacent leads to the further clustering of the '1' elements resulting in a final matrix.

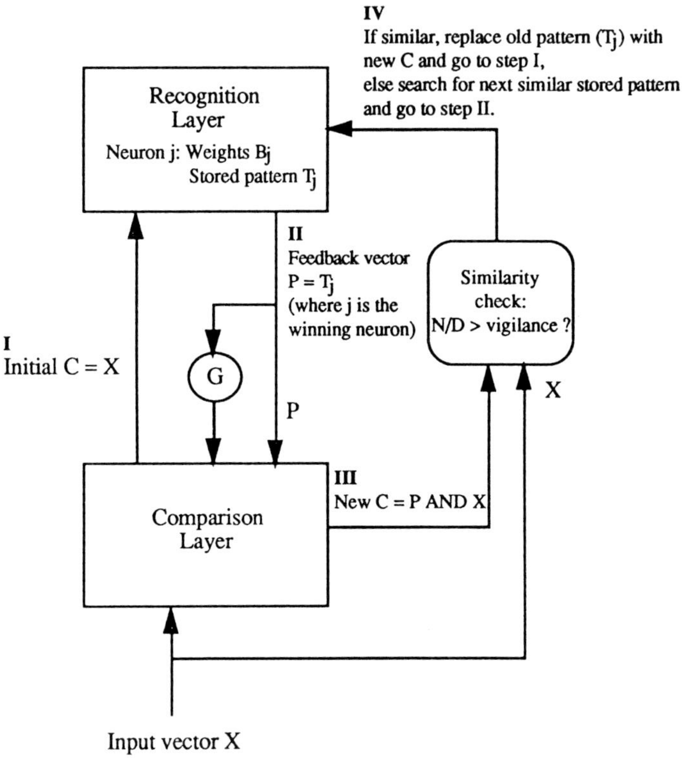

Figure 1.4: The ART1 model

1.3.3 The ART1 Paradigm

The ART1 architecture consists of two layers of neurons, the comparison layer and the recognition layer as shown in Figure 1.4.[17] In the comparison layer, each neuron has three inputs, a feedback signal from the recognition layer, an element p of the vector P, the gain signal G and an element x of the input vector X. The gain G is 0 if any element of the vector P is 1. The output of these neurons is 1, if any two of its three inputs is 1 (the two-thirds rule). Note that if G is 0, the output is simply the AND of x and p. The output of the comparison layer thus obtained is a vector C.

The binary input vector X is applied at the comparison layer and initially passes through the layer, unchanged as the binary vector C. This is because, initially G is set to 1 and all elements of vector P are zero. The vector C is the input vector to the recognition layer.

The weights corresponding to these inputs form the vector B_j at the j-th neuron.

For each neuron in the recognition layer, the dot product,

$$\mathrm{NET}_j = (B_j \cdot C), \tag{1.1}$$

is computed. The output of the neuron with the highest NET value becomes the *winning* neuron and all the other outputs of the recognition layer neurons are suppressed to 0.

Each neuron in the recognition layer is associated with a stored pattern. These patterns are stored in two forms, the weight vectors B_j which are not binary and the vector T_j, a binary vector. The elements of B_j are all typically initialized to the same low value, while all elements of T_j are initialized to 1. If the associated neuron wins, and a similarity check is satisfied, the weights are adjusted to the normalized values of the elements of the vector C as follows,

$$B_j = \frac{Lc_i}{L - 1 + \sum_k c_k} \tag{1.2}$$

$$t_j = \begin{cases} 1 & \text{if } b_{ij} > 0 \\ 0 & \text{otherwise} \end{cases} \tag{1.3}$$

where c_i is the i-th component of the comparison layer output vector C, j is the number of the winning recognition layer neuron, B_{ij} is the weight corresponding to the i-th component of vector C and L is a constant that is typically set equal to 2. The effect of doing so is that, the weights corresponding to the 1's in C are increased, while the other weights are forced to zero. This is done to increase the chance of a similar vector to be detected at this neuron, while decreasing the chance of accepting a dissimilar vector.

With each neuron in the recognition layer, there also exists a vector, T_j, the elements of which are one's for every non-zero value of the elements of B_j. If j is the winning neuron then the vector that is fed back to the comparison layer P equals T_j. Application of the two-thirds rule at this layer, G being forced to 0 if any element of P is 1, gives us the AND of the elements of vector P and the elements of the vector X, which is the new value of vector C. The number of ones in the resultant vector (N) divided by the number of ones in the input vector $X(D)$, gives us the similarity S, between the input vector and the vector to be stored at neuron j in the form of B_j and T_j. The value of S must exceed a pre-determined threshold value called the vigilance parameter, for the input vector to be classified into a specific category. The concept is similar to using thresholds in the similarity coefficient method. If the condition is satisfied, then Eqs. (1.2) and (1.3) is implemented, otherwise, the second layer neuron with the next highest NET is tested in the same manner. When an input vector is stored in conjunction with a recognition layer neuron for the first time, we say that an *exemplar* is created, also implying that a new category has been formed. Later when similar vectors are applied, they are *recognized* by comparison with this exemplar. If a sufficient match is attested by the similarity check, the two vectors are 'AND'ed and the resulting vector X' (new C) is stored in the form of the vector B_j and its binary version T_j. An example is given to demonstrate the working of the ART1.

1.3.4 ART1 Implementation - A Test Case

A 7 part, 5 machine matrix is shown in Table 1.3(a). From the matrix, the 7 column vectors and 5 row vectors must be applied to the ART1 for classification. The grouping of columns and rows are independent processes which can be run concurrently to save time. Here, only the working of the model of Figure 1.3 is explained. After the grouping of column vectors, an intermediate matrix as shown in Table 1.3(b) is formed. The groups are formed as the vectors are applied sequentially. Note at this point, that column vector 7 has not been grouped appropriately with vector 1. A vigilance parameter of 0.4 was used to obtain this matrix. Using the intermediate matrix, row vectors 1 to 5 are sequentially applied to the ART1 system, and once again with a vigilance of 0.4, the final matrix of Table 1.3(c) is achieved. The same process is repeated with vigilance of 0.3 for both column vector and row vector classification. This time, column vector 3 was not found to be similar to vector 1 unlike in the previous case. Also, in general, a higher vigilance implies a greater number of groups but with a greater similarity within the components of the groups. Note that, although, the number of part groups did not change, there are three machine groups in Table 1.3(c), while there are only two machine groups in Table 1.3(d).

For the classification of column vectors, columns 1 to 7 are applied sequentially to the ART network. The classification performed by the basic ART1 program on the column vectors is shown in Table 1.3(b). A vigilance parameter of 0.4 was used. When the first vector [0 1 1 0 1] is applied, an exemplar is first created at the first recognition layer neuron ($j = 1$). Using Eqs. (1.2) and (1.3) the new weights are computed to be $B_1 = [0\ 0.5\ 0.5\ 0\ 0.5]$, and the corresponding vector T_1 becomes [0 1 1 0 1] (i.e., equal to the input vector). No similarity check needs to be performed, as there is no pattern stored in the recognition layer. When the second vector [1 0 1 1 0], is applied, the NET value at neuron 1, is computed as, $\text{NET}_1 = B_1 \cdot C = 0.5$ There are two cases to be considered here.

Case 1: If initial b_{ij}'s are $\leq 0.5/3$, say 0.16, then, NET_2 =0.48 and neuron 1 wins. Now, at the comparison layer, $P = T_1 = [0\ 1\ 1\ 0\ 1]$, and the input vector X, with $G = 1$, produce new $C = X' = [0\ 1\ 1\ 0\ 1]$ AND $[1\ 0\ 1\ 1\ 0] = [0\ 0\ 1\ 0\ 0]$. The number of 1's in X', $N = 1$. The number of 1's in $T_1, D = 3$. Similarity, $S = N/D = 0.33$. This value is less than our vigilance 0.4. Hence, the vector X' is rejected and is not stored.

The second input vector is then stored as an exemplar at neuron 2, in the form of B_2 and T_2. The weights are computed once again with Eqs. (1.2) and (1.3), just as in the case of vector 1.

Case 2: If the initial values are 0.17, then $NET_2 = 0.51$ and neuron 2 wins. An exemplar is created at neuron 2 for the vector and weights are computed with Eqs. (1.2) and (1.3), as in the case of vector 1.

Thus, due to the lack of close resemblance in vector 1 and vector 2, they were classified into different groups. The determination of the winner in the recognition layer, and the similarity check at the comparison layer, contribute to the correct categorization of the input vectors. At the application of each input vector, either X' is stored or an exemplar is created. The same process, is repeated for the rest of the column vectors. Table 1.3(b) is the intermediate matrix shown in Figure 1.3. Table 1.3(c) shows, the result of applying the row vectors 1 to 5 of the intermediate matrix, in the same manner, to the ART network. Exactly the same type of classification process occurs. The vigilance for classifying rows may be different from the value used to classify columns.

1.3.5 Drawbacks of the Basic ART1

The results of applying the ART1 paradigm to the matrix of Table 1.3(a) for vigilances of (0.4, 0.4) and (0.3, 0.3) are shown in Table 1.3(c) and (d) respectively. These results are however far from the block diagonal form that we desire. Hence, the ART1 did not provide satisfactory results when applied in its basic form. Before modifications that drastically improve its performance are suggested, the drawbacks of the basic ART1 are stated.

The stored patterns grow sparser as more input vectors are applied. For example, assume that the first column vector has been stored. When the second vector is applied, and if the vigilance is equal to 0.3, it is classified into the same category as the first vector as shown in Table 1.3(d). The vector now stored at the first neuron will be $X' = (0\ 0\ 1\ 1\ 1)$ AND $(1\ 1\ 0\ 1\ 0) = 0\ 0\ 0\ 1\ 0$, a sparser vector. Thus the second vector has been absorbed into the stored pattern, and any further comparison with this vector is not possible. At a later stage, a vector such as column vector 4, that is similar to the second vector, will not be grouped with the second vector. Similarly, as other stored patterns get sparser during the early stages of classification, the input vectors that are applied later are improperly classified. This effect can be minimized by adjusting the vigilance for different runs of the program, to obtain a set of different solutions, however the classifications almost never result in the block diagonal form.

The classification process is completely dependent on the order in which the input vectors are applied. Supposing column vector 1 was applied after vectors 4, 5, 6, but before vectors 3 and 7. Then, a desired group (i.e., a group in which each vector satisfies the similarity check when compared to any other vector in the group), $\{2, 4, 5, 6\}$ is achieved even at low vigilances. Also, if vector 3 was applied last, another desired group $\{1, 7, 3\}$ will be achieved.

Table 1.3: Cell formation in a 7 × 5 matrix with the ART1, (a) input matrix, (b) intermediate matrix (vigilance = 0.4), (c) final matrix (Column and Row Vigilances = 0.4 and 0.4), (d) final matrix (column and row vigilances = 0.3 and 0.3).

		Parts						
		1	2	3	4	5	6	7
	1		1		1	1	1	
	2	1		1				
Machines	3	1	1					1
	4		1		1		1	
	5	1						1

(a)

		Parts						
		1	3	2	4	5	6	7
	1			1	1	1	1	
Machines	2	1	1					
	3	1		1				1
	4			1	1		1	
	5	1						1

Vigilance=0.4

	Parts			
Group 1:	1	3		
Group 2:	2	4	5	6
Group 3:	7			

(b)

		Parts						
		1	3	2	4	5	6	7
	1			1	1	1	1	
	4			1	1			
Machines	2	1	1					
	3	1		1				1
	5	1						1

Vigilance=0.4

	Parts	Machines
Group 1:	1 3	1 4
Group 2:	2 4 5 6	2
Group 3:	7	3 5

(c)

		Parts						
		1	2	7	4	5	6	3
	1		1		1	1	1	
	4		1		1		1	
Machines	2	1						1
	3	1	1	1				
	5	1		1				

Vigilance=0.3

	Parts	Machines
Group 1:	1 2 7	1 4
Group 2:	4 5 6	2 3 5
Group 3:	3	

(d)

The bottleneck machine problem is not solved. Even if a block diagonal form is achieved, the paradigm does not prescribe any method of dealing with exceptional elements.

A basic difficulty is encountered in the determination of the vigilance parameters. A higher vigilance parameter implies that the groups formed will be smaller with vectors that are more similar. At the same time, there is also an increase in the number of cells. This implies that the inter-cellular costs will increase while the intra-cellular costs will decrease. If the vigilance is low, larger groups are formed in fewer numbers and the costs are reversed. The vigilance value thus plays a critical role. But no obvious method of determining this value for an optimal machine-part cell formation exists. Other similarity coefficient methods had the same problem. These shortcomings of the ART1 make it unsuitable for the direct application of this paradigm to the classification problem.

1.3.6 Improving the Performance

For a much improved performance, a few modifications must be made. In this section, we propose two schemes to counter the first two drawbacks mentioned in Section 1.3.5. The other two are dealt with, using a larger example in Section 1.4.

For the first scheme, when a comparison between two vectors is successful, instead of storing X', the result of 'AND'ing vectors X and P, (when the two-thirds rule is applied), the vector having the higher number of one's must be stored. This ensures, that the store patterns become denser, rather than sparser as the classification progresses. If both vectors contain the same number of one's then, any of the vectors can be stored by convention. The chances of improper classification due to the comparison with sparse stored patterns which are not similar to any vectors applied until then, are minimized. In the example of Table 1.3(a), when column vector 1 is compared with vector 2, and the similarity between them is found acceptable, by convention, we could retain vector 1 as the stored pattern. Vector 2 will not be grouped with, 4, 5 and 6, but vectors 3 and 7 are rightly grouped with vector 1.

The second scheme involves the pre-processing of the machine-part matrix, to compensate for the dependency of the ART1 on the sequence of application of the vectors. The vectors are applied in a sequential manner, and if sparser vectors are encountered first, those vectors that group well with the denservectors that are to be applied later, will be classified improperly. This is the crux of the second drawback mentioned in Section 1.5. To avoid this, why not re-order the vectors according to the number of 1's in each vector, and apply them in order of descending number of 1's to the network? The effect of doing this is the *absorption* of the sparser vectors into the denser patterns that have already been stored. The advantages of these two schemes are clarified by solving the same example with the modified ART1.

1.3.7 Implementing the Modified Approach

The impact on the performance of the paradigm when the two schemes proposed in Section 1.3.6 are implemented is demonstrated using the same test case 7 × 5 matrix of Table 1.3(a). The results of each step are shown in Table 1.4 (a), (b), (c) and (d) respectively.

Step 1: Arrange the columns according the number of '1's in each column vector. This ensures that the denser vectors are grouped first.

Step 2: Group the column vectors, retaining the vector with the highest number of '1's as the stored pattern within each group. Note the correct clustering of vectors 1, 7 and 3 and vectors 2, 4, 6, and 5. A vigilance of 0.4 was used.

Step 3: Re-order rows according to the number of '1's in the rows.

Step 4: Group rows just as in Step 2, with a vigilance of 0.4.

A much more distinct block diagonal form has been obtained. The bottleneck machine is machine 3, since it processes a part (part 2) which is unlike the other parts that the cell formed by group 2 processes. This machine can be duplicated if the cost of moving part 2 from cell 1 to cell 2 is too high. It must be noted that buying a machine is a one-time cost, while inter-cellular movement occurs whenever the part is manufactured. Approaches to finding optimal vigilance values and to detect and automatic ally duplicate bottleneck machines in the matrix are discussed with larger examples in the following section.

1.4 Validation and Results

The results of application of the ART1 approach to some test cases are presented in this section. The observations are used to propose heuristics for finding the optimal machine-part family formation solution and to complement the capabilities of the ART1 paradigm itself.

The ART1 paradigm has been simulated with a *C* function in a program containing associated functions that load vectors from a file, pre-process the vectors, and create the final matrix. The functions and their relations are shown in Figure 1.5. The initial machine-part matrix is placed in a file in a specific format for access by the program. Hence, after classification of either columns or rows, the intermediate matrix is also created with the same format. Since the intermediate matrices contain shuffled rows or columns, the exact order of rows or columns must be saved before rearranging them again. Two different routines are called for loading column vectors and row vectors primarily to save the order of the machines and jobs respectively. These vectors a re loaded into an array which is provided to the function that models the ART1. This function calls a routine for checking the similarities between the current input vector and a stored pattern.

Table 1.4: Modified ART1 approach, (a) columns re-ordered in the input matrix (Table 1.3(a)), (b) column vectors grouped, (c) rows re-ordered in the intermediate matrix, (d) final matrix with row vectors grouped.

		Parts						
		1	2	4	6	7	3	5
	1		1	1	1			1
	2	1					1	
Machines	3	1	1			1		
	4		1	1	1			
	5	1				1		

(a)

		Parts						
		1	7	3	2	4	6	5
	1				1	1	1	1
	2	1		1				
Machines	3	1	1		1			
	4				1	1	1	
	5	1	1					

Vigilance=0.4

	Parts			
Group 1:	1	7	3	
Group 2:	2	4	6	5

(b)

		Parts						
		1	7	3	2	4	6	5
	1				1	1	1	1
	3	1	1		1			
Machines	4				1	1	1	
	2	1		1				
	5	1	1					

(c)

		Parts						
		1	7	3	2	4	6	5
	1				1	1	1	1
	4				1	1	1	
Machines	3	1	1		1			
	2	1		1				
	5	1	1					

Vigilance= 0.4

	Parts				Machines		
Group 1:	1	7	3		1	4	
Group 2:	2	4	6	5	3	2	5

(d)

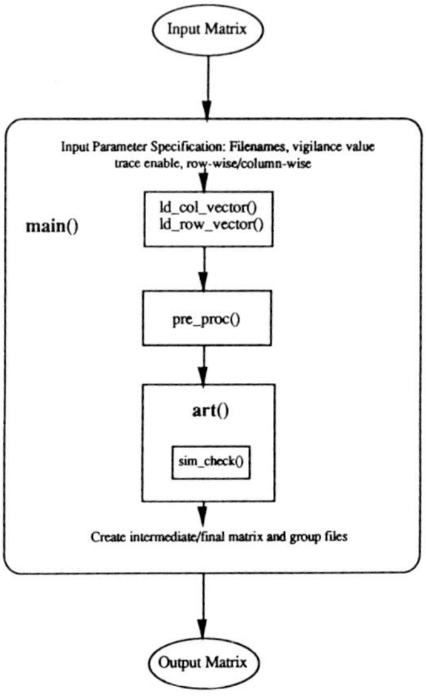

Figure 1.5: The structure of the program used to simulate the ART1

1.4.1 Formalizing the Cell Formation Procedure

Determination of Optimal Vigilances.

Consider the 43-part, 16-machine matrix shown in Table 1.5. This matrix has been adopted from King and Nakornchai's work and can also be found in the work of Sahay and Seifoddini and therefore is a good basis for comparison of the performance of the classifying system.

In order to determine the optimum vigilance values, the objective of the classification must be specified in another form. It is clear that the block diagonal form must be achieved to obtain proper distinct clusters of parts and machines. But what characterizes the block diagonal form from any other type of clustering, is the equal number of machine groups and part groups that are formed. That is, the number of part groups must be equal to the number of machine groups. Let us call our vigilances for column vector and row vector classification, ρ_1 and ρ_2 respectively. Let N be the number of part groups and M be the number of machine groups. N and M generally increase with ρ_1 and ρ_2 respectively. However, their rates of increase depend on the vector set. Also, there may be more than one set of ρ_1 and ρ_2 for which $N = M$.

It is difficult to test the matrix for very small increments in the vigilance parameter. However, the classification is not sensitive to very small increments. That is, satisfactory clusters can be obtained by varying the vigilances in large discrete step s. The results obtained in this way can be adjusted even manually, to obtain

Table 1.5: A 43-part, 16-machine matrix[5]

43 16

	1	2	3	4	5	6	7	8	9	10	11	12	13	14	15	16	17	18	19	20	21	22	23	24	25	26	27	28	29	30	31	32	33	34	35	36	37	38	39	40	41	42	43
1																																					1					1	
2		1								1																		1				1					1	1		1		1	
3							1										1																	1	1	1							
4					1				1					1					1		1		1						1														
5					1			1	1					1	1	1			1		1		1						1				1								1		1
6	1	1				1	1	1				1	1	1			1		1				1									1	1	1			1		1	1		1	1
7	1												1												1																		
8	1	1	1					1	1		1	1			1				1	1	1		1	1			1	1			1						1	1			1		1
9		1		1						1								1										1				1					1	1		1		1	
10	1											1	1												1	1					1								1				
11			1						1											1				1			1			1													
12											1											1		1			1			1													
13			1																					1																			
14		1				1											1																		1								
15					1									1					1		1												1								1		1
16		1					1			1								1														1					1	1				1	

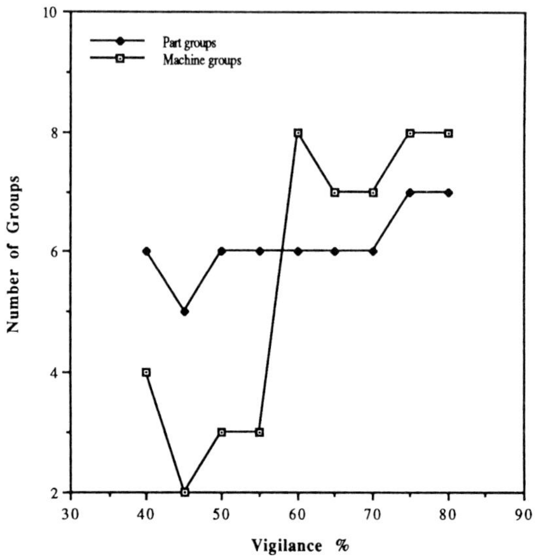

Figure 1.6: Variation of the number of clusters with vigilance - 43 $\times$ 16 matrix

distinct clustering. Figure 1.6 shows the effect of the vigilances on the number of groups formed. In the graphs, the groups obtained at higher vigilances (i.e., > 0.55) are not considered, because, due to their large number, they will not provide a cost effective cell formation. This is particularly so if the number of desired machine cells is initially specified. For smaller vigilances that are less than 0.55, the combination of, 5 part groups at 0.45, and 4 machine groups at 0.4, gives us the lowest difference in N and M. However, in the distribution of the number of machines in each of the 4 machine groups, a large variation occurred. Group 1, for example, had 8 machines, while group 4 had only 1 machine. Clearly, this is not a desirable grouping. If the vigilance for machine clustering is increased to 0.5, a much better distribution with respect to the evenness of the three groups formed, in the number of machines per group, is observed. The result shown in Table 1.6 shows us the cluster formation for vigilances of 0.45 for part groups and 0.5 for machine groups.

Simply by duplicating machines 6, 8 and 10, in Table 1.6, the final form of Table 1.7 was achieved. A total of 5 duplications were made. The result had 5 exceptional elements. Part 36 could not be grouped with even one of, parts 7, 17, 35 or 34 that have a '1' in the same position as part 36, because none of these parts had column vectors that had a higher number of 1's at any point. To see clearly why, there are four major part groups and the vector with the highest number of 1's in each group was the first vector to be stored (due to the pre-processing) at the neuron corresponding to the group. If these vectors do not have a 1 at the same position as the column vector corresponding to part 36, then part 36 will be grouped separately.

Table 1.6: Final matrix obtained with vigilances of (0.45,0.5)

43 16

	2	37	42	32	38	7	10	17	28	40	6	18	35	4	19	1	9	14	21	23	43	5	8	12	33	41	15	29	16	24	3	27	11	20	30	22	13	25	31	34	39	26	36
8	1	1			1				1						1	1	1		1	1	1		1	1		1	1			1	1	1	1	1					1				
5															1		1	1	1	1	1	1	1		1	1	1	1	1														
4															1		1	1	1	1		1						1															
11																	1													1	1	1		1	1								
12																														1		1	1		1	1							
13																														1	1												
6	1	1	1	1		1		1		1	1				1	1		1		1	1		1	1	1												1			1	1		
10																1								1													1	1	1		1	1	
15															1			1	1		1	1			1	1																	
3						1		1					1																											1			1
14	1							1			1		1																														
7																1																					1	1					
9	1	1	1	1	1		1		1	1		1		1																													
2	1	1	1	1	1		1		1	1																																	
16	1	1	1	1	1	1	1					1																															
1		1	1																																								

Program: art16.c

Part Groups: Vigilance: 45

GROUP 1 : 2 37 42 32 38 7 10 17 28 40 6 18 35 4
GROUP 2 : 19 1 9 14 21 23 43 5 8 12 33 41 15 29 16
GROUP 3 : 24 3 27 11 20 30 22
GROUP 4 : 13 25 31 34 39 26
GROUP 5 : 36

Machine Groups: Vigilance: 50

GROUP 1 : 8 5 4 11 12 13
GROUP 2 : 6 10 15 3 14 7
GROUP 3 : 9 2 16 1

Such classification s due to the drawbacks of the program can be called inappropriate classifications and the specific problem is a *representative vector problem*. However, since this happens only in case of very sparse vectors, the problem is ignored at this time. In any case, a number of simple methods can be implemented to eliminate such events. If part 36 is also classified as desired, the number of part groups for a vigilance of 0.45 will be only 4 groups which are fairly evenly distributed in the number of parts. This further justifies our selection of vigilance.

Duplication of Bottleneck Machines

The method divides the 43×16 matrix into smaller matrices, based on part groups. In case of Table 1.8 there are 4 part groups (ignoring part 36 for the moment). Hence, 4 smaller matrices with the same 16 machine numbers to identify their rows, but different part numbers are formed. Now, within the first matrix, from each machine group, the vector with the highest number of 1's (highest density) is identified. These vectors are compared with one another, and if they are similar to a reasonable degree, not only are the vectors grouped, but also the other members of their respective machine groups are clustered into one larger group. In our example, there are 3 machine groups. Machine 8, machine 6 and machine 9 have the highest density within each group. There is no other machine in the first machine group that processes parts in the first part group. Also, the row vector of machine 8 is similar to that of machine 9. Thus, machine 8 can be placed in machine group 3. Similarly, the row vector of machine 6 is similar to that of machine 9. Therefore, along with machine 6, other machines; i.e., 3 and 14 that are similar to machine 6 are clustered with machine 9. Alternatively, all members of a block need not be grouped if the vector with the highest density is found to be similar to another such vector. The process may be repeated for the remaining vectors in the block, thus grouping them only if they are similar with the highest density vector of another block. The second procedure produces more accurate results.

On repeating this procedure for the other three matrices, machine cells with duplicated machines are completely formed. Unnecessary duplications can be easily located and a few exceptional elements can be tolerated.

An algorithm for automatically duplicating bottleneck machines from the matrix of Table 1.6, can now be proposed in the following steps,

Step 1: Separate all part groups and machine groups. In this test case (Table 1.5) when the part groups are separated, four smaller matrices (a, b, c, d) are formed.

Step 2: For a smaller matrix, identify the vector with the highest density (representative vector) in each block.

Step 3: Compare all representative vectors with one another. (A degree of similarity must be chosen).

Table 1.7: Block diagram form after duplicating bottleneck machines

43 16	2	37	42	32	38	7	10	17	28	40	6	18	35	4	19	1	9	14	21	23	43	5	8	12	33	41	15	29	16	24	3	27	11	20	30	22	13	25	31	34	39	26	36
10																																					1	1	1		1	1	
7																1																					1	1					
6																																					1			1	1		
8																														1	1	1	1	1					1				
11																	1													1	1	1		1	1								
12																														1		1	1		1	1							
13																														1	1												
5															1		1	1	1	1	1	1	1		1	1	1	1	1														
4															1		1	1	1	1		1						1															
8															1	1	1		1	1	1		1	1		1	1																
6															1	1		1		1	1		1	1	1																		
10																1								1																			
15															1			1	1		1	1			1	1																	
8	1	1			1				1																																		
6	1	1	1	1		1		1		1	1																																
3						1		1					1																											1			1
14	1							1			1		1																														
9	1	1	1	1	1		1		1	1		1		1																													
2	1	1	1	1	1		1		1	1																																	
16	1	1	1	1	1	1	1					1																															
1		1	1																																								

Part Groups: Vigilance: 45

GROUP 1 : 2 37 42 32 38 7 10 17 28 40 6 18 35 4
GROUP 2 : 19 1 9 14 21 23 43 5 8 12 33 41 15 29 16
GROUP 3 : 24 3 27 11 20 30 22
GROUP 4 : 13 25 31 34 39 26
GROUP 5 : 36

Machine Groups: Vigilance: 50

GROUP 1 : 10 7 6
GROUP 2 : 8 11 12 13
GROUP 3 : 5 4 8 6 10 15
GROUP 4 : 8 6 3 14 9 2 16 1

Step 4: Group similar representative vectors. Each grouping results in the duplication of a bottleneck machine.

Step 5: Repeat Steps 2, 3, 4 for remaining members of each block.

Step 6: Repeat Steps 2, 3, 4, 5 for remaining smaller matrices.

The main advantage of this algorithm is that, the existing ART1 code itself can be used for Steps 3 and 4. A low vigilance may be used to allow machines in different groups to be classified in Step 4. However in this algorithm, the duplications are not justified by a cost/performance analysis (Section 1.2). A pure block diagonal form can be easily achieved, but the number of duplications needed for the pure block diagonal form can be extremely high. If the only criterion is performance then the number of exceptional cells must be minimized at any cost. In such a case, the pure block diagonal form is the optimal solution. In general, machine cost too is an important factor which restricts the number of duplications if it exceeds the cost saving due to lesser material handling. Other restrictions on the maximum allowable cell size and scheduling difficulties are also imposed. The simple algorithm just presented will not suffice. In the following section an algorithm for obtaining an optimal solution is presented. The details of cost/performance analysis are beyond the scope of this paper and were only reviewed in Section 1.2.

An Algorithm for Optimal Solution

The implementation of the following algorithm will complement the capabilities of the ART1 program and leads to an integrated system for optimal machine-part family formation solutions.

Step 1: Find optimal vigilances (as in Section 1.4.1).

Step 2: Obtain final matrix using the optimal vigilances.

Step 3: Separate part groups and machine groups (Table 1.8). Identify each block as $b_1, b_2, \ldots, b_{n\times m}$ where n is the number of part groups and m is the number of machines. n is also the number of sub-matrices formed due to the part groups.

Step 4: In each sub-matrix, find and mark blocks with the highest degree of clustering, where *degree of clustering* is defined as,

$$\frac{\text{number of `1's in a block}}{\text{dimension of the block}}.$$

This step can also be done manually as such blocks can be identified visually.

Step 5: In each block, except for the marked blocks in Step 4, identify machines corresponding to the highest number of exceptional elements within the block. Let the machines and the corresponding exceptional elements be

$$\begin{array}{cc} M_1 & e_1 \\ M_2 & e_2 \\ -- & -- \\ M_{n\times m} & e_{n\times m} \end{array}$$

It must be noted that by having exceptional elements in several part groups, some of $M_1, \ldots, M_{n\times m}$ may be the same.

Step 6: Check for cost/performance trade-offs through existing techniques (Section 1.2). Production volume, scheduling techniques, processing times, set-up times are some of the factors to be considered. Duplicate machine M_x corresponding to $e_x = \max\{e_1, \ldots, e_n\}$ if justified by the analysis.

Step 7: Remove M_x from the set $(M_1, \ldots, M_{n\times m})$ and replace this machine by a machine with the highest number of exceptional element in block x.

Step 8: Repeat Steps 6 and 7 until duplication of any other machine cannot be justified.

The algorithm facilitates the identification of bottleneck machines and the exceptional elements in the matrix. Thus it acts as an interface between the ART1 program and a decision making system that performs the cost/performance analysis. The algorithm has been implemented manually on the 43 × 16 matrix presented earlier as well as a 90 × 36 matrix discussed in the next section.

A 90 × 36 Matrix.

A 90 part, 36 machine matrix also adopted from King and Nakornchai's work[7] was used to further validate the function of the ART1 and the algorithm of just presented. The initial matrix is shown in Table 1.9.

Using the ART1, several classifications were obtained by varying the column and row vigilances. The variation of the number of clusters with the vigilance is shown in Figure 1.7. Once again the sparsity of the matrix leads to a number of inappropriate classifications (part 36 in the previous example). The numbers of part groups and machines are inflated owing to the such classifications. Part 18 (similar to part 73), parts 23 and 38 (similar to many other parts), parts 32 and 53 were incorrectly classified as separate groups. Therefore Figure 1.7 does not truly represent the cluster variation. If we consider only groups with at least three members, different but a more true cluster variation is obtained as shown in Figure 1.8. From the graph, the (column vigilance, row vigilance) combinations that need to be considered for further inspection are (0.25, 0.25), (0.25, 0.3), (0.3, 0.25), and (0.3, 0.3).

Table 1.8: Separation of parts groups and machines groups

43 16

	2	37	42	32	38	7	10	17	28	40	6	18	35	4	19	1	9	14	21	23	43	5	8	12	33	41	15	29	16	24	3	27	11	20	30	22	13	25	31	34	39	26	36
8	1	1			1				1						1	1	1		1	1	1		1	1		1	1			1	1	1	1	1					1				
5															1		1	1	1	1	1	1	1		1	1	1	1	1														
4															1		1	1	1	1		1						1															
11																	1													1	1	1		1	1								
12																														1		1	1		1	1							
13																														1	1												
6	1	1	1	1		1		1		1	1				1	1		1		1	1		1	1	1												1			1	1		
10																1								1													1	1	1		1	1	
15															1			1	1		1	1			1	1																	
3						1		1					1																											1			1
14	1							1			1		1																														
7																1																					1	1					
9	1	1	1	1	1		1		1	1		1		1																													
2	1	1	1	1	1		1		1	1																																	
16	1	1	1	1	1	1	1					1																															
1		1	1																																								

Program: art16.c

Part Groups: Vigilance: 45

GROUP 1 : 2 37 42 32 38 7 10 17 28 40 6 18 35 4
GROUP 2 : 19 1 9 14 21 23 43 5 8 12 33 41 15 29 16
GROUP 3 : 24 3 27 11 20 30 22
GROUP 4 : 13 25 31 34 39 26
GROUP 5 : 36

Machine Groups: Vigilance: 50

GROUP 1 : 8 5 4 11 12 13
GROUP 2 : 6 10 15 3 14 7
GROUP 3 : 9 2 16 1

Table 1.9: Initial 90 × 36 matrix

	1	2	3	4	5	6	7	8	9	10	11	12	13	14	15	16	17	18	19	20	21	22	23	24	25	26	27	28	29	30	31	32	33	34	35	36
1																																		1		
2																										1						1				
3																																1				
4						1																										1				
5																																1	1			
6																																1				
7																1																1				
8																									1		1	1		1						1
9					1																				1			1				1		1		1
10																															1					
11											1																				1	1	1	1		
12																																	1			
13																																1	1	1		
14					1																														1	
15																1						1			1			1		1						
16	1																																	1		
17																										1										
18															1																					
19																															1	1				
20																												1								
21																1						1			1		1	1		1						1
22																1						1			1		1	1		1						1
23						1																														
24					1																															
25																																1		1		
26																							1													
27																													1			1		1	1	
28											1																				1		1			
29						1																										1		1		
30																1												1								
31																																1	1	1		
32																																			1	
33																												1						1		
34	1																																			
35									1																	1										
36											1		1																		1	1	1			
37					1																											1				
38						1																														
39											1																									
40					1									1		1						1					1			1						
41	1										1														1						1	1	1	1		
42																										1						1				
43						1																										1		1		
44					1																															
45																																				1
46																																1	1			
47					1																														1	
48						1																				1										1
49						1																									1	1	1			
50	1																															1				
51																1						1														
52						1																			1		1									1
53																																			1	
54																																1	1	1		
55																			1							1					1	1			1	
56					1									1		1						1			1		1									
57																																		1	1	
58					1																											1				
59					1														1		1															
60																													1			1		1		
61																															1		1			
62																1					1															
63																1						1				1						1				
64					1									1		1						1			1		1									
65					1														1		1									1				1		
66					1																											1			1	
67					1														1			1														1
68																1						1			1											
69						1								1													1					1		1		
70																			1															1		1
71					1														1															1		1
72																																1	1	1		
73															1	1						1			1		1									
74						1																						1						1		
75													1																			1				
76														1		1						1			1		1			1						
77	1													1					1			1			1	1				1						
78																				1						1	1					1				
79																	1					1				1	1			1		1		1		1
80																		1												1					1	
81					1		1									1				1								1			1					1
82																		1												1					1	1
83					1	1														1	1							1			1					
84									1												1					1						1	1	1		
85					1		1									1				1								1			1					1
86						1											1			1	1						1							1		
87					1														1			1				1	1									
88																			1	1		1			1	1	1									
89					1														1		1				1		1			1						
90		1																	1			1			1	1	1			1		1				

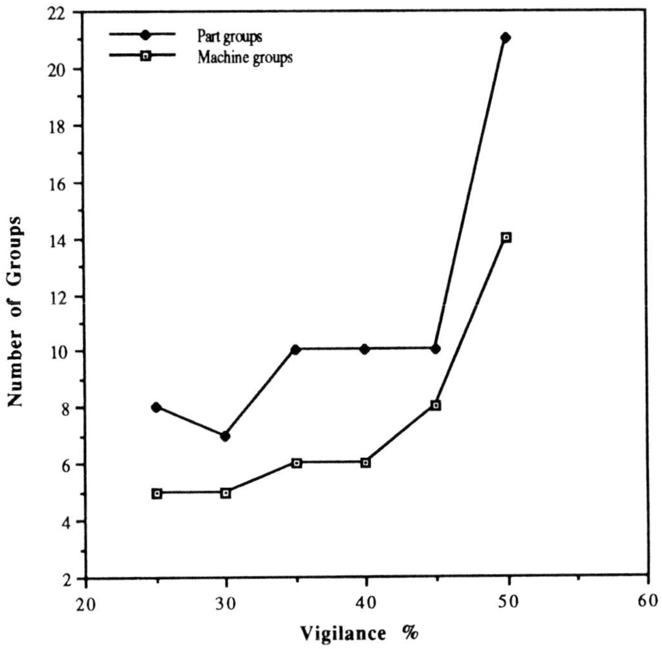

Figure 1.7: Variation of the number of clusters with vigilance - 90 × 36 matrix

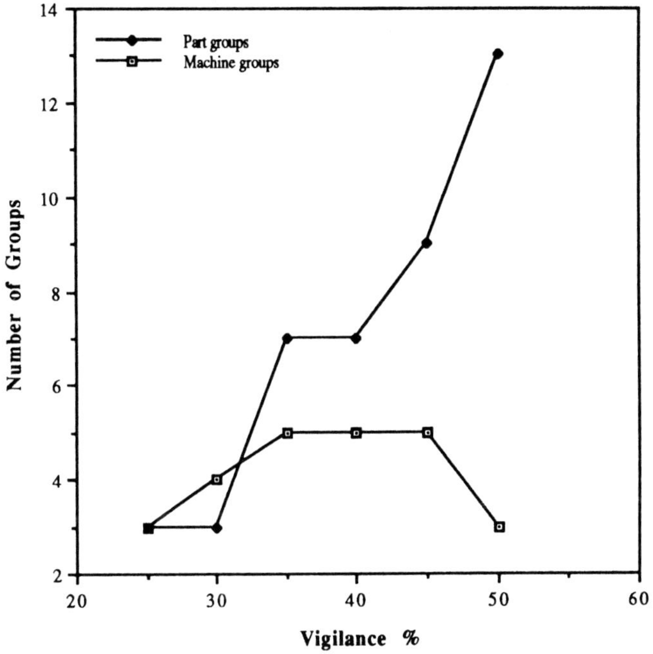

Figure 1.8: Variation of the number of clusters with vigilance - 90×36 matrix

The combination (0.3, 0.3) results in the least number of inappropriate classifications and is therefore chosen. The final matrix obtained with these vigilances is shown in Table 1.10. The part groups and machine groups are separated giving 3 sub-matrices A, B, and C, shown in Tables 1.11(a), (b) and (c) respectively (the inappropriate classifications are included in sub-matrix C) and total of 12 blocks. The blocks were then numbered (Step 3) as follows,

Sub-matrix A: B_1, B_2, B_3 and B_4
Sub-matrix B: B_5, B_6, B_7 and B_8
Sub-matrix C: B_9, B_{10}, B_{11} and B_{12}
(Blocks numbered from top to bottom in each sub-matrix).

The degree of clustering for each block is computed and the following three blocks are marked (Step 4), Marked blocks: B_3, B_5 and B_{10}

In Step 5, in all but the marked blocks, the machines with the highest number of exceptional elements in a block are identified as (32, 36, 35, 5, 25, 35, 31, 25, 35) and the corresponding exceptional elements are, (7, 8, 2, 4, 3, 4, 3, 8, 2).

With the simple criterion that a machine must be duplicated if within a block, it introduces more than 2 exceptional elements, Step 6 is implemented by duplicating machine 36 (having the highest number of exceptional elements - 8). In Step 7, machine 36 is then replaced by in the set by machine 19 which has the next highest number of exceptional elements - 7, in the block. Steps 6 and 7 are repeated until no other machine has more than 2 exceptional elements in the block. The final result is shown in Table 1.12. A listing of part groups and machine groups for various vigilances is also given in Table 1.12.

Comparison

The modified ART1 performs extremely well producing results that are very much comparable to the ROC2 algorithm and similarity coefficient methods. The ROC2 algorithm produced, for the matrix of Table 1.5, a solution that used 5 additional machines and had only one exceptional element.[7] The method employed by Sahay and Seifoddini,[11] produced 6 additional machines and 8 exceptional elements. The result of Table 1.7 shows that the application of the modified ART1 algorithm produced, 5 additional machines and 4 exceptional elements (ignoring part 36's claim to exclusiveness).

For the 90 $\times$ 36 matrix, ROC2's solution had 18 duplications with 6 remaining exceptional elements, while the solution shown in Appendix B has 21 duplications and 10 exceptional elements. Thus, speed apart, the ART1 shows sufficient classification accuracy.

1.4.2 A Synthetic Matrix Generator

A synthetic matrix generation (SMG) program facilitates the validation and refinement of this approach. Two main ways in which synthetic matrix generation is

Table 1.10: Final matrix (vigilances = 0.3 and 0.3)

[illegible]

Program: art16.c

Part Groups: Vigilance: 30

GROUP 1 : 79 80 21 22 77 60 76 [illegible] [illegible] 89 8 65 [illegible] 73 87 52 [illegible] 78 82 48 70
80 2 35 42 17
GROUP 2 : 41 9 [illegible] 11 36 55 [illegible] 49 13 28 29 31 43 54 [illegible] [illegible] [illegible] 72 74 4 5 7
16 19 25 33 37 46 50 57 58 [illegible] 75 1 3 6 10 12 34 39
GROUP 3 : [illegible] 85 56 [illegible] 83 15 67 71 59 14 30 47 51 [illegible] 20 [illegible] 44 43
GROUP 4 : 18
GROUP 5 : 23 38
GROUP 6 : 26
GROUP 7 : 32 53

Machine Groups: Vigilance: 30

GROUP 1 : 32 34 33 4 31 1 11 9 13 3 4 8 10 12 24
GROUP 2 : 5 36 [illegible] 19 21 20 7
GROUP 3 : 22 27 16 [illegible] 26 30 14 15 17 2
GROUP 4 : 35 18 29
GROUP 5 : 23

Table 1.11: Separation of part groups and machine groups - 90 $\times$ 36 matrix, (a) submatrix A, (b) submatrix B, (c) submatrix C

90 36

	79	90	21	22	77	40	76	86	88	89	8	65	69	73	87	52	63	78	82	48	70	80	2	35	42	17
32	1	1											1				1	1					1		1	
34	1							1				1	1								1					
33																										
6								1					1			1				1						
31																										
1					1																					
11																										
9																								1		
13																										
3																										
4																										
8																										
10																										
12																										
24																										
5						1				1		1			1											
36	1		1	1							1					1			1	1	1					
28			1	1							1															
19		1			1				1	1		1			1						1					
21								1		1		1														
20								1	1									1								
7																										
22	1	1	1	1	1	1	1		1					1	1		1									
27	1	1	1	1		1	1	1	1	1	1		1	1	1	1		1								
16			1	1		1	1							1			1									
25		1	1	1	1		1		1	1	1			1		1										
26	1	1			1				1						1		1	1		1			1	1	1	1
30	1	1	1	1	1	1	1			1	1	1							1			1				
14					1	1	1						1													
15														1												
17	1							1																		
2		1																								
35																			1			1				
18																			1			1				
29																										
23																										

(a)

90 36

	41	9	84	11	36	55	27	49	13	28	29	31	43	54	60	66	68	72	74	4	5	7	16	19	25	33	37	46	50	57	58	61	75	1	3	6	10	12	34	39
32	1	1	1	1	1	1	1	1	1		1	1	1	1	1	1		1		1	1	1		1	1		1	1	1		1		1		1	1				
34	1	1	1	1			1		1		1	1	1	1	1			1	1				1		1	1				1				1						
33	1		1	1	1			1	1	1		1		1				1			1							1				1						1		
6								1			1		1						1	1																				
31	1			1	1	1		1		1														1								1					1			
1	1																						1						1										1	
11	1			1	1					1																														1
9			1																																					
13					1																												1							
3																																								
4																																								
8																																								
10																																								
12																																								
24																																								
5		1														1											1				1									
36		1																																						
28		1																	1							1														
19						1																																		
21			1																																					
20																																								
7																																								
22																	1																							
27																																								
16																	1					1																		
25	1	1															1																							
26			1			1																																		
30																																								
14																																								
15																																								
17																																								
2																																								
35						1	1									1														1										
18																																								
29							1								1																									
23																																								

(b)

90 36

	81	85	56	64	83	15	67	71	59	14	30	47	51	62	20	24	44	45	18	23	38	26	32	5
32																								
34								1																
33																								
6					1															1	1			
31	1	1			1																			
1																								
11																								
9																								
13																								
3																								
4																								
8																								
10																								
12																								
24																								
5	1	1	1	1	1		1	1	1	1		1				1	1							
36	1	1					1	1										1						
28	1	1			1	1					1				1									
19							1	1	1															
21					1				1					1										
20	1	1			1																			
7	1	1																						
22			1	1		1	1						1											
27			1	1																				
16	1	1	1	1		1					1		1	1										
25			1	1		1																		
26																								
30						1																		
14			1	1																				
15																			1					
17																								
2																								
35										1		1											1	1
18																								
29																								
23																						1		

(c)

Table 1.12: Block diagram after duplication

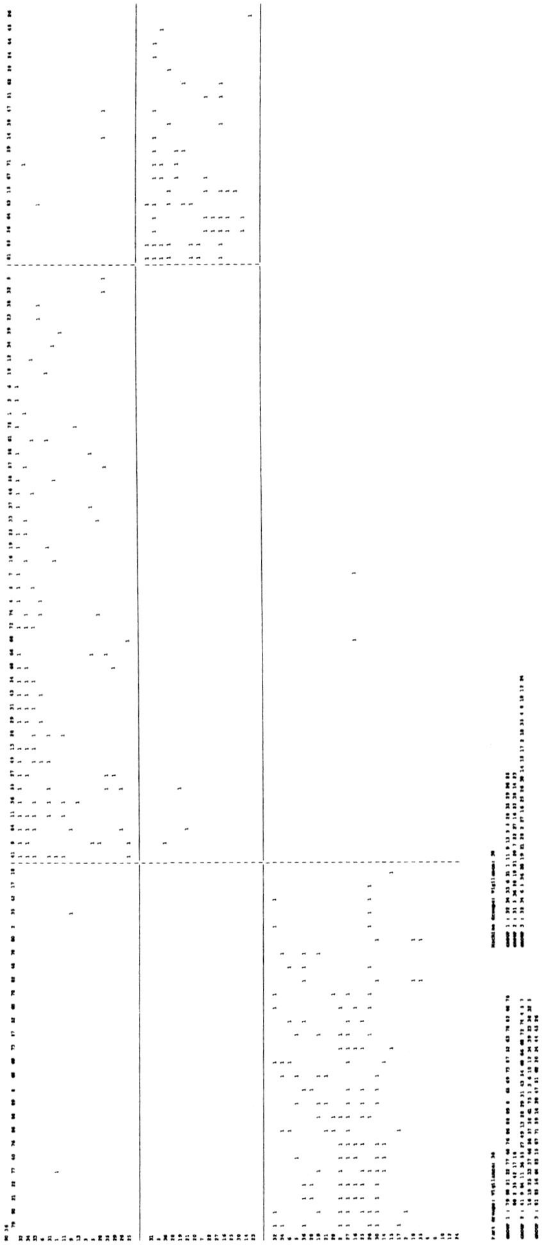

beneficial are:

1. Large matrices can be automatically generated. Typing a matrix of size 200 × 100 into the computer can take days!

2. Special cases can be simulated easily. This advantage renders debugging and refinement easier tasks to accomplish.

The program uses the standard random number function, rand() extensively. The user is given control over the density of specific regions in the matrix through a set of control parameters. The program is briefly explained in the following. The results of simulating two specific cases of a 200 × 100 matrix are then presented.

The Program

The structure of the program is shown in Figure 1.9. The type of input information to be provided to the program is indicated in Figure 1.10. The execution of the program produces a file called *Result* that contains the pure block diagonal form and a file called *Input* that contains the jobs and machines in the correct order. The *Input* file is provided to the ART1 program (Figure 1.5) for classification of column and row vectors. The final matrix obtained from the ART1 program can be compared with the original block diagonal form in the *Result* file.

The program as of now provides control over the probabilities of an element in the clusters of the block diagonal form, of an element in the row vector corresponding to the bottleneck machine and of any other element in the sparser regions. Therefore, reasonably realistic situations can be created by the SMG. Note that parts that have been grouped together by the SMG need not actually be similar although the '1' elements of their column vectors are clustered into a single block. The ART1 program will then not classify such parts into a group although they appear to be so in the *Result* file. Therefore the creation of a block of clustered '1's must involve a technique that relates the vectors that form a clustered block. The technique used in the SMG creates the first row of each block as follows:

For each element in the first row of each block,
if rand() mod 10 > dense_factor then element =1.

Then, for the remaining rows, if first row element (in the corresponding column) = 1 and if rand() mod 50 > sparse_factor - 10, then element = 1; If a low dense_factor is used, then the probability of an element in the first row being a '1' is high. The values of the elements in the remaining rows depends probabilistically on the values of the elements in the same column in the first row.

Matrix without Bottleneck Machines

The SMG was used to generate a 200 part, 100 machine input matrix for which the final matrix is a pure block diagonal form. The final matrix and the input (initial) matrix obtained by ordering the rows and columns of the final matrix are given in Tables 1.13 and 1.14 respectively. The control parameters used are

dense_factor (Maximum = 9) = 4
bneck_dense_factor (Maximum = 9) = 9 (zero probability)
sparse_factor (Maximum = 49) = 49 (zero probability)

The definitions of the above parameters are implicit in Figure 1.9. By assigning maximum values for the bneck_dense_factor and the sparse_factor, it is ensured that the result matrix is a pure block diagonal matrix as shown in Table 1.13.

The classifications obtained through the ART1 program for the vigilance combinations of (0.4, 0.4) and (0.2, 0.2) are shown in Tables 1.15 and 1.16 respectively. The final matrices obtained show that if a pure block diagonal form exists, it can be obtained with a higher probability with lower vigilance values. The final matrix obtained using (0.2, 0.2) shows 10 distinct clusters. The representative vector problem explained in section 1.1 produces 5 inappropriate exceptional elements.

Matrix with Two Bottleneck Machines

As a second special case, two bottleneck machines (machine 16 and 26 as in the user specifications shown in Figure 1.10) were introduced into the 200 × 100 matrix (Table 1.17 shows the original matrix, and Table 1.18 shows the input matrix). The control parameters used were,

dense_factor (Maximum = 9) = 4
bneck_dense_factor (Maximum = 9) = 7
sparse_factor (Maximum = 49) = 49 (zero probability)

Decreasing the bneck_dense_factor results in the (pseudo) exceptional elements shown in the result matrix. The objective of this experiment was to use the ART1 to correctly identify the bottleneck machines.

The bottleneck machines had a drastic effect on the classifications. Since the row vectors corresponding to the bottleneck machines can be expected to have a greater density the ART1 makes them the representative vectors. At lower row vigilances, many row vectors tend to group with these representative vectors leading to a number of inappropriate classifications. However, especially if the bottleneck machines are few in number, they can be separated from the other machines at higher vigilances as shown in Figure 1.11. In the final matrix the bottleneck machines can be expected to collect at the top of the rows as shown in Table 1.19 (vigilance combination of (0.2, 0.5)). The classification can be performed after removing the bottleneck machines for accurate results.

1.4.3 Summary of Results

The ART1 program, with the modifications discussed in Section 1.2, produces reasonably accurate classifications. The functionality of the ART1 approach has been verified with several test cases, including those obtained from a synthetic matrix

Table 1.13: Original block diagonal matrix (or result matrix)

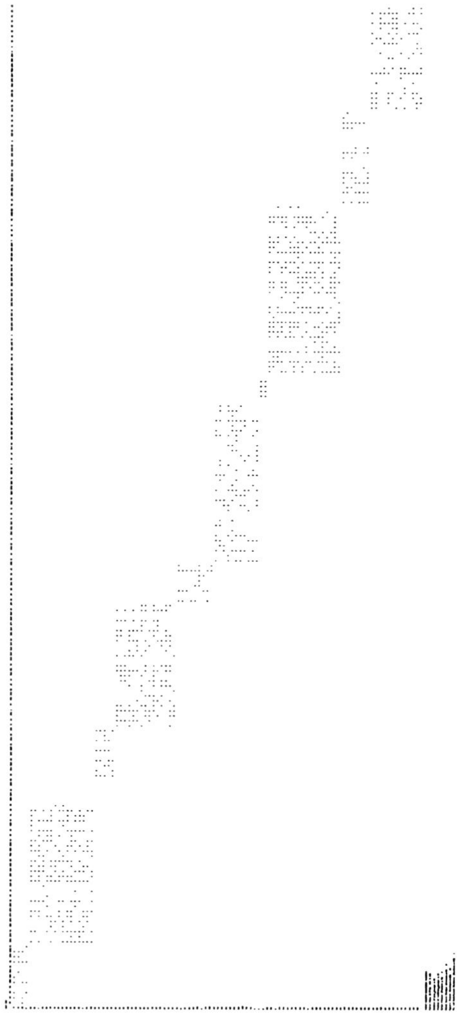

Table 1.14: Initial 200 × 100 matrix

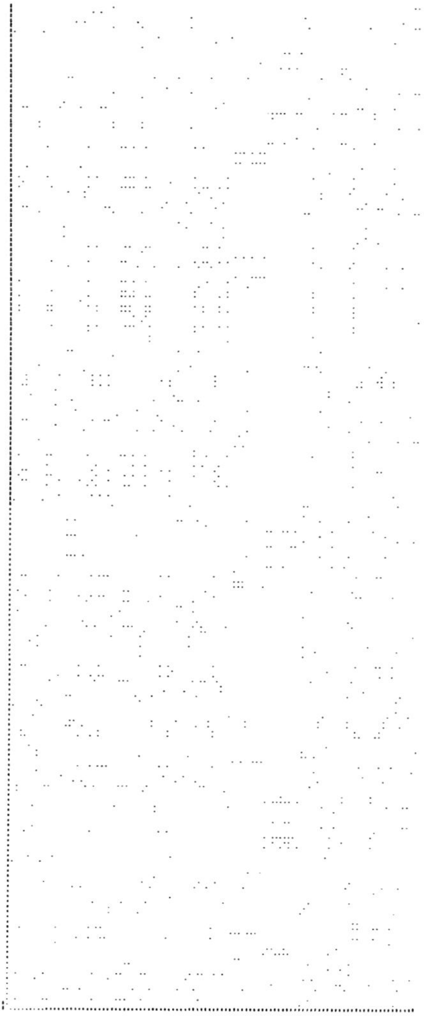

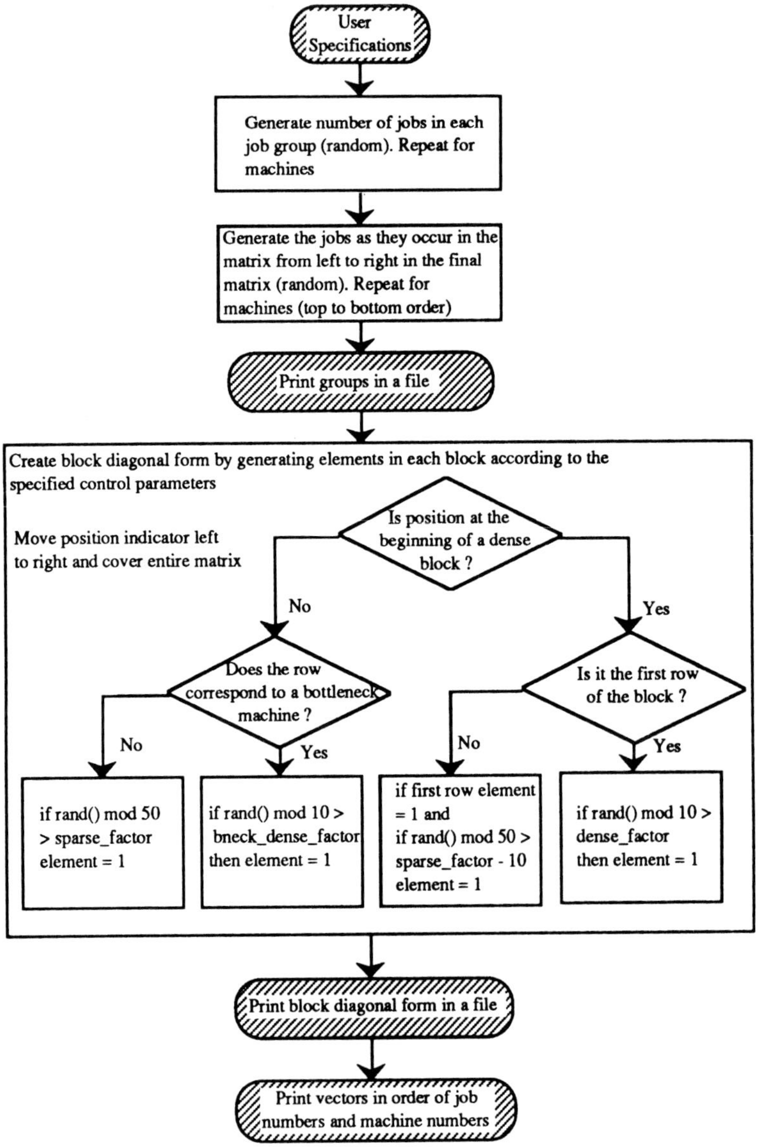

Figure 1.9: Structure of the synthetic matrix generator program

Table 1.15: Final matrix from the ART1 program (vigilances = 0.4 and 0.4)

Table 1.16: Final matrix from the ART1 program (vigilances = 0.2 and 0.2)

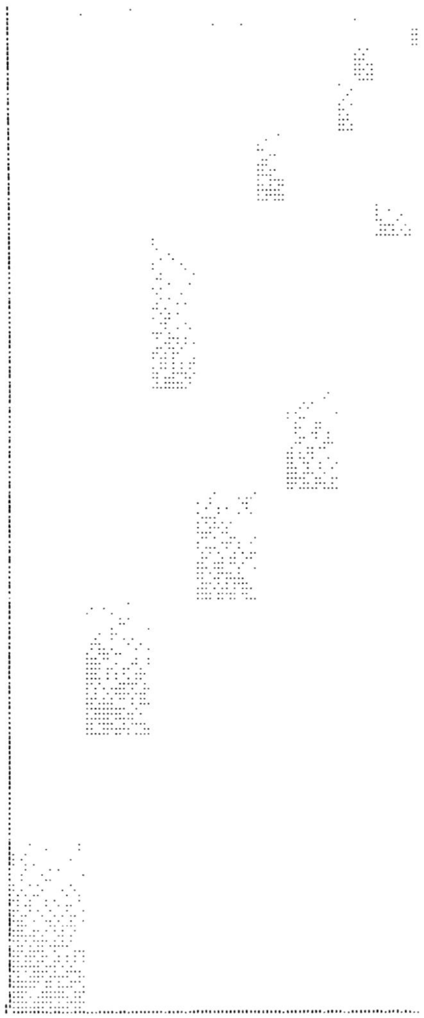

Table 1.17: Original block diagram matrix (or result matrix, with two bottleneck machines)

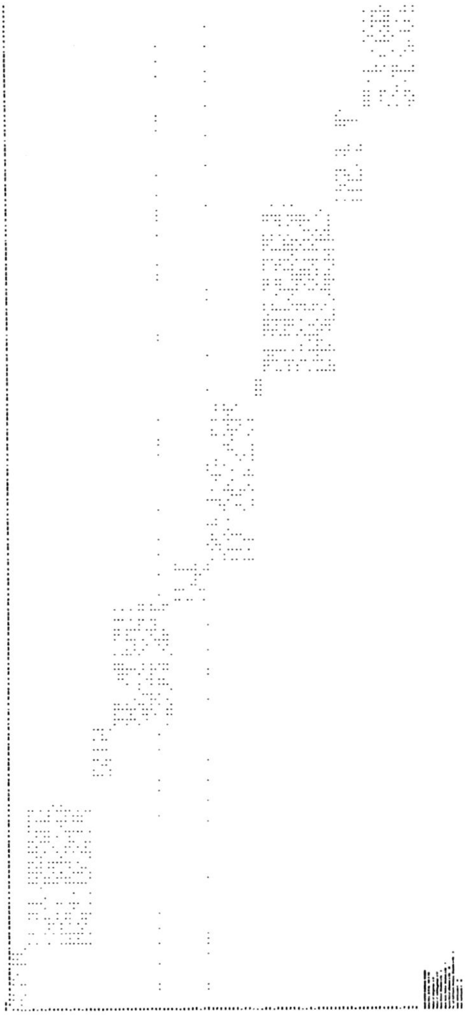

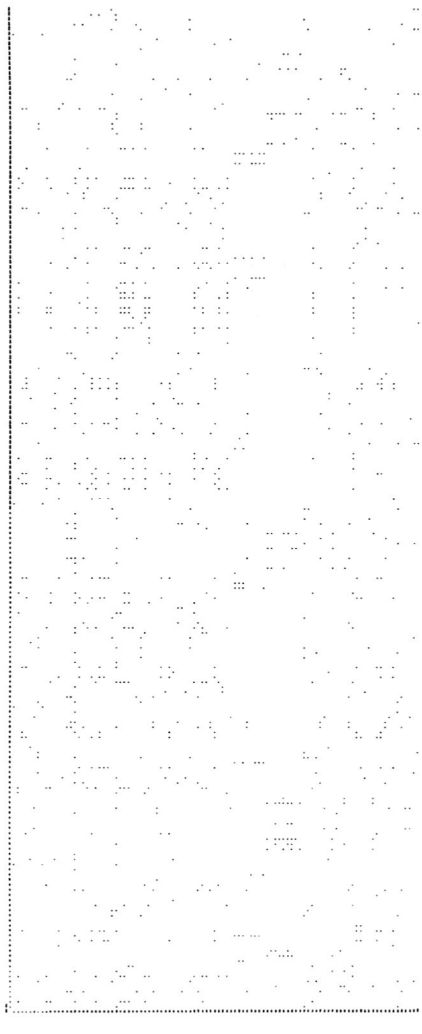

Table 1.18: Initial 200 × 100 matrix (with two bottleneck machines)

Table 1.19: Final matrix from the ART1 program (vigilances = 0.2 and 0.5; with two bottleneck machines)

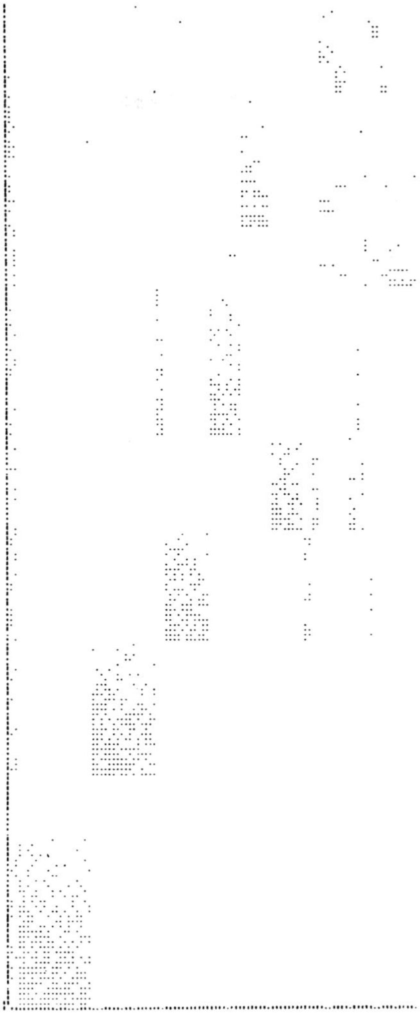

```
INPUT MATRIX GENERATOR PROGRAM
Enter Size (A × B): 200 × 100
Number of jobs = 200
Number of machines = 100
Number of job_groups = 19
Reassign?  (y/n)y
job_groups = 10
Number of machine_groups = 10
Reassign?  (y/n)n
Dense Factor (Maximum = 9):  4
Bneck Dense Factor (Maximum = 9):  7
Sparse Factor (Maximum = 49):  49
No.  of Bottleneck Machines (Maximum = 20):  2
Print Bottleneck 0:  16
Print Bottleneck 1:  26
Printing Input Matrix in Input ....
Printing Block Diagonal Form in Result....
DONE
```

Figure 1.10: User interaction with the SMG

generator. The formation of part groups and machine groups are sensitive to the vigilance parameter. A technique for limiting the possible values of the vigilance parameter has been proposed and tested. The final matrix is obtained for an optimal column vigilance and row vigilance combination. An algorithm to identify bottleneck machines for duplication has also been implemented successfully.

The performance of the simulation program is comparable to the performance of other algorithms in terms of computational effort and time and therefore the software itself can be used for cell formation. The time taken for processing matrices of various sizes is shown in Figure 1.12. Further reduction in computational time can be achieved by performing part grouping and machine grouping in parallel at the cost of an extra memory requirement. The program is user-interactive, and offers flexibility, in choosing the vigilance parameters, accepting matrices of very large order, obtaining traces of the classification process, and in easy modification of the ART1 to test new schemes. Implementation of this program is thus straightforward.

At this stage, it must be emphasized that the ART1 program is only a simulation of a neural network. The software can be definitely used to obtain optimal machine-part cell formation solutions, but true advantage of the method will be realized only when implemented on hardware.

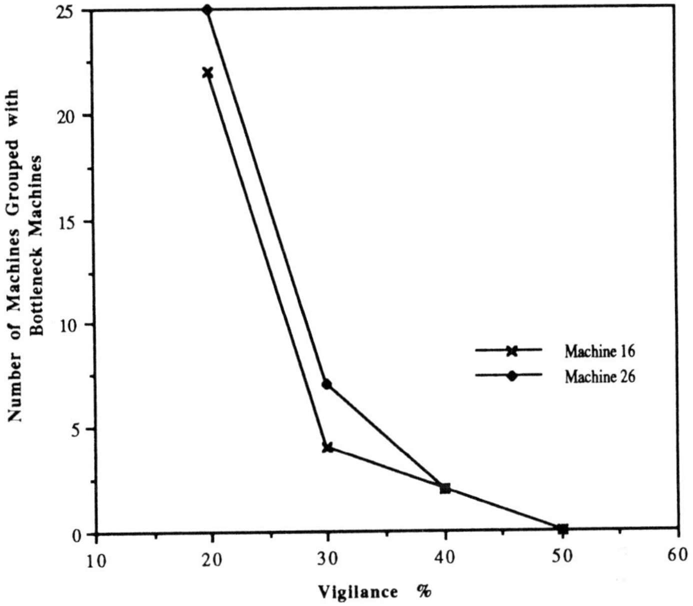

Figure 1.11: Separation of the bottleneck machines from other machines

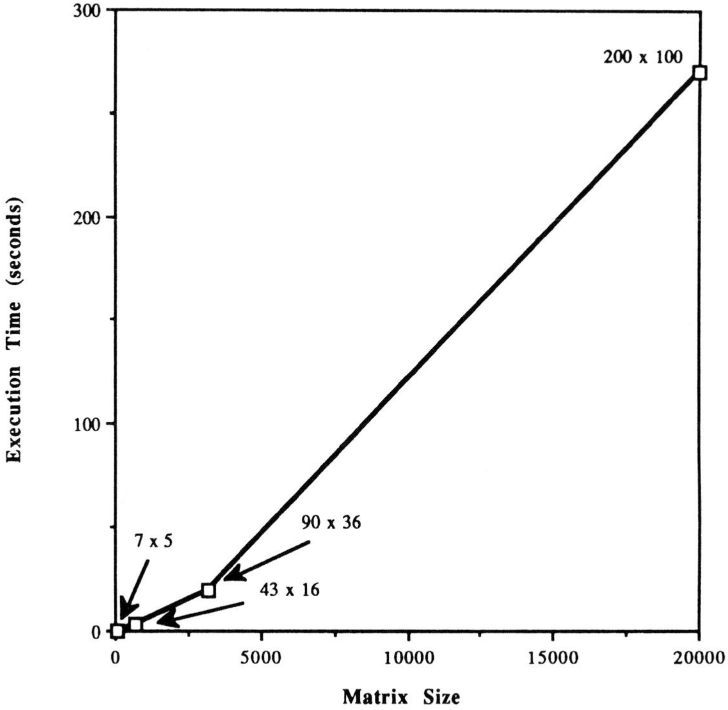

Figure 1.12: Execution time of the ART1 program

1.4.4 Future Work

Several improvements to the ART1 paradigm and enhancements for building an integrated group technology support system are possible as part of further research work. The overall problem posed by cellular manufacturing is very large and complex. The scope of this thesis is restricted to a facility that encourages the formal implementation of the cellular manufacturing in real time. Some of the issues that must be addressed before actual implementation are discussed in this section.

An Integrated Group Technology Support System.

The ART1 provides us an excellent classification methodology, particularly when the schemes proposed in Section 1.3.6 and Section 1.4.1 are used. However, the problem of finding the minimum cost solution, cannot be solved by the ART1. The ART1 provides the flexibility of considering various options for cell formation, but leaves the decision to a cost/performance analysis system. Integrating an expert system, with the ART1 can facilitate the automatic identification of the optimum solution. The ART1 performs the clustering with low initial vigilance parameters and provides the part and machine groups formed, to the expert system. The groups thus formed are evaluated in terms of cost by the expert system. Vigilances are changed by suitable increments and a new classification is again obtained and evaluated. The expert system then compares the cost figures of various cell formations and recommends an optimal solution. Sufficient range of the vigilance parameters can be covered so that the global minimum is not missed. Trade-offs needed between duplication of bottleneck machines and material handling costs are made automatically by the expert system. The expert system itself must be integrated with simulation software (since no known efficient analytic method for computing optimal solutions exists) for assessment of a cell formation and the scheduling involved. The expert system together with the simulation software forms a decision support system to be integrated with the ART1 program. The integrated system is depicted in Figure 1.13.

Improvements to the ART1 Paradigm

The only significant weakness of the ART1 paradigm is that of the *representative vector*. The original paradigm used a heuristic that results in the gradual decay of the density of the representative vector. The poor classification accuracy was corrected by retaining the highest density vector as the representative vector at each comparison. The new heuristic though relatively very accurate, has the effect of introducing a few additional exceptional parts typically having one or two exceptional elements. Such parts may be eliminated very easily (by proper classification), particularly as they tend to collect toward the extreme right corner of the final matrix.

1. *Fast Learning vs. Slow Learning.* The type of learning employed in this implementation of the ART1 is called fast learning. In fast learning, the application

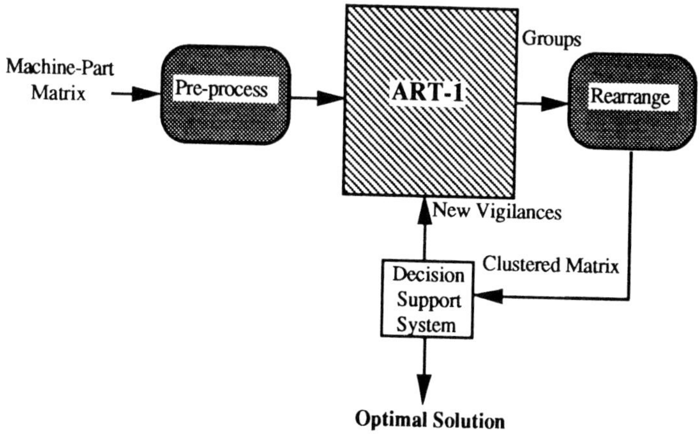

Figure 1.13: An integrated group technology support system

of an input pattern has an immediate effect on the weight vector particularly in the original heuristic. More specifically, the weights are changed according to Eqs. (1.2) and (1.3) in Section 1.3, where for unmatched positions, the weights become zero. As a contrast, in slow learning, when there is a pattern match, the weights are incremented and decremented by small amounts to make the stored pattern slightly more similar to the input pattern. Slow learning if properly implemented can eliminate the representative vector problem, since the representative vector has a resemblance to all input patterns experienced until the time of concern. Slow learning has a stability problem because the classification will be extremely sensitive to the initial weight values, the increment and decrement values used. Most of the other binary, unsupervised, feedback recall paradigms employ learning schemes similar to slow learning and have varying stability characteristics. The efficiency of other neural network paradigms for this classification problem must therefore be determined.

2. *Improving the Software.* The bottleneck machine duplication algorithm was implemented manually so far. Additional *C* routines that automate the entire procedure can be developed.

An important issue when building the integrated group technology support system is that of *isualization.* Efficient visualization techniques are extremely important not only for user-interactiveness but also for easy manipulation of large matrices. Currently the program is implemented on an Apollo workstation wherein the windows allow both vertical (row-wise) as well as horizontal (column-wise) scrolling. Few window systems provide for column-wise scrolling, resulting in the wrap-around of the row vectors. In any case, inspection and manipulation of large matrices is extremely tedious. Even if the entire procedure is automated, it is necessary to provide for manual intervention as well through a good graphical user interface.

Hardware Implementation of the ART1

A hardware implementation of the ART1 can be used as a co-processor in computers dedicated to group technology. The classification process then depends essentially only on the time needed to sequentially apply all the input vectors. The neural network itself will be extremely fast and its time delay is negligible compared to other delays. The possibility of integrating other neural networks such as the Hopfield net for obtaining the global minimum of the total cost, must be explored. This would alleviate the intensive need for an expert system, whose interaction with the neural network will be much slower.

Use in Real Time

In batch manufacturing systems, when new parts are to be made, or when the manufacture of some parts is to be stopped, the optimal cell formation solution can be quite different and inefficient for the current situation, compare d to the original solution. Provided we have a fairly flexible manufacturing system, it may be possible to regularly re-adjust the shop floor to suit our current needs without incurring excessive overhead expenses. In such a case, a neural network system can greatly facilitate the identification and evaluation of the numerous options that must be considered to obtain optimal layouts for the manufacturing system. Even if the plant layout cannot be changed, the new parts can be correctly classified and various scheduling possibilities can be tested. If not optimal, the best possible schedule under the restrictions can be employed.

1.5 Conclusions

The ART1 neural network paradigm has been successfully implemented for cell formation problems. The results compare favorably with popular existing algorithms such as King's ROC2 and similarity coefficient based algorithms. Modification of the original paradigm and preprocessing of input vectors obtained from the machine-part matrix, were necessary to obtain drastic improvements in clustering. The paradigm and associated processing modules were simulated with a program and tested with several test cases. The ART1 can be used to obtain several part and machine classifications by varying the threshold parameters called column vigilance and row vigilance respectively. Vigilances that lead to approximately equal number of part groups and machine groups are used to obtain the final matrix. An algorithm for identifying bottleneck machines from the final matrix has been proposed and tested using matrices studied earlier in literature. A synthetic matrix generator has also been developed to facilitate further validation and refinement of the existing ART1 system. The work presented in this thesis is expected to lead to an integrated group technology support system.

1.6 References

1. N. L. Hyer, *Group Technology at Work,* (Society of Manufacturing Engineers, 1984).

2. N. L. Hyer and U. Wemmerlov, "Group technology in the US manufacturing industry: a survey of current practices," *International Journal of Production Research,* **27** (8) (1989) 1287-1304.

3. M. P. Groover, *Automation, Production Systems and Computer Integrated Manufacturing*, second edition (Prentice Hall, Englewood Cliffs, NJ, 1987).

4. K. G. Banerjee and A. H. Redford, "Visual inspection of components for mechanized assembly," *International Journal of Production Research*, **20** (5) (1982) 545-553.

5. J. L. Burbridge, "A manual method of production flow analysis," *The Production Engineer*, **56** (1977).

6. Y. B. Moon, "Interactive activation and competition model for machine-part family formation," *Proceedings of the International Joint Conference on Neural Networks*, Washington D.C., **II** (January 1990) 667-670.

7. J. R. King and V. Nakornchai, "Machine-component group formation in group technology: review and extension," *International Journal of Production Research*, **20** (2) (1982) 117-133.

8. A. Kusiak, A. Vannelli and K. R. Kumar, "Clustering analysis: models and algorithms," *Control and Cybernetics*, **15** (2) (1986) 139-154.

9. K. R. Kumar and A. Vannelli, "A method of finding minimal bottleneck cells for grouping part-machines families," *International Journal for Production Research*, **24** (2) (1986) 387-400.

10. J. C. Wei and N. Gaither, "An optimal model for cell formation decisions," *Decision Sciences*, **21** (2) (1990) 243-257.

11. A. K. Sahay and H. Seifoddini, "An algorithm for forming machine-component cell in group technology," *Proceedings of the 9th International Conference on Production Research*, **I** (1987) 1314-1321.

12. H. Seifoddini, "A note on the similarity coefficient method and the problem of improper machine assignment in group technology applications," *International Journal of Production Research*, **27** (2) (1989) 1161-1165.

13. H. Seifoddini, "Duplication process in machine cells formation in group technology," *IIE Transactions* (December 1989) 382-388.

14. H. Seifoddini and P. M. Wolfe, "Application of the similarity coefficient method in group technology," *IIE Transactions* (September 1986) 271-277

15. I. F. K. El-Essawy and J. Torrance, "Component flow analysis - an effective approach to production systems design," *Production Engineer*, **51** (1972).

16. P. K. Simpson, *Artificial Neural Systems - Foundations, Paradigms, Applications and Implementations* (Pergamon press, NY, 1990).

17. P. D. Wasserman, *Neural Computing - Theory and Practice* (Van Nostrand Reinhold, 1989).

18. R. Gupta and J. A. Tomkins, "An examination of the dynamic behavior of part families in group technology," *International Journal of Production Research*, **20** (1) (1982) 73-86.

19. B. B. Flynn, "The effects of setup time on output capacity in cellular manufacturing," *International Journal of Production Research*, **25** (12) (1987) 1761-1772.

Chapter 2

Neuro-Clustering for Group Technology

Young B. Moon
Department of Mechanical, Aerospace and Manufacturing Engineering
Syracuse University
Syracuse, NY 13244 USA

2.1 Introduction

Group Technology (GT) is a manufacturing principle based on the assumption that a higher level of efficiency and productivity can be achieved by grouping similar parts and similar machines together. The principle has been adopted in many fields including machining, part design, variant process planning, manufacturing cell design, facility layout and scheduling.[1,2]

By applying the GT concept, the manufacturing companies can achieve various improvements such as reduced setup changes, shortened lead time, reduced work-in-progress, reduced inventory level, high throughput rate, less material handling cost, better space utilization, less variety of tools, less variety of jigs and fixtures, reduced scrap, and simplified product design varieties.

Two engineering problems in implementing GT are part family/machine group formation and part classification. These problems are investigated in various contexts. The part classification and coding system (such as Optiz, KK-3, MICLASS, etc.) aids the operator in assigning a unique code to each part. The assigned codes are used to form part families by using numerical taxonomy,[3] a goal programming-based clustering analysis,[4] or a hierarchical structure inherent in some coding systems. However, despite some advantages such as efficient design retrieval and easy classification of new parts, the adoption of the coding system requires a considerable amount of effort and time. This strong commitment required in the early stage of implementation has been a stumbling block in employing GT in many companies.

Production Flow Analysis was proposed by Burbidge as a simpler alternative to the part classification and coding system. These approaches are concerned primarily with the processing methods already being used in manufacturing plants. The production flow analysis is carried out in three successive analyses: (1) factory flow analysis, (2) group analysis, and (3) line analysis. Most of the necessary information is obtained from the existing route cards (or process plans) so that additional efforts may be minimized in implementing the GT principle. The information from the route cards is typically represented as a matrix in which elements assume the value of 0 or 1. An element of value 1 indicates that the corresponding part type needs an operation on the corresponding machine type. As a result of applying one of the part family/machine group formation approaches, the final arrangement of the matrix will have a block diagonal form. In the final matrix, each block may represent a part family and the associated machine group.

Despite the sizable literature suggesting a variety of methods for computers to find part families/machine group,[5] there are no published reports of any successful applications of such method starting from original company data.[6] A possible reason is that the researchers have not taken into account various practical factors. This chapter presents new approaches to address these problems using neuro-computing models which are inspired by the way brain neuronal systems perform to generate intelligent decisions.

2.2 Part Family/Machine Group Identification: Standard Family Formation

Most of the approaches developed for part family/machine group formation are concerned with 'how to form' the families as opposed to 'how to identify' the families. However, since the production flow analysis is exploiting the practices which already exist rather than suggesting new ones, the nature of the solution technique should be one which identifies 'naturally occurring' families and groups. Inappropriately forced formations may have detrimental effects.[7] The difficulty lies in finding a method which provides such identification capabilities which a human is good at, through pattern recognition, experience and intuition, and still solves a large problem typically with hundreds of parts and machines.

This section presents a neurocomputing model which exploits the interactive activation and competition model of neural networks to identify natural part families and machine groups.

Notation

$P = \{p_1, p_2, \ldots, p_r\}$: a set of part types
p_r: the number of parts (rows)

$M = \{m_1, m_2, \ldots, m_s\}$: a set of machine types
m_s: the number of machines (columns)
$T = [a_{ij}]$: a machine-part matrix,
$a_{ij} = 1$, if the machine i is required for part j, otherwise $a_{ij} = 0$
$SP = [b_{mn}]$: a similarity matrix for part types
$SM = [c_{mn}]$: a similarity matrix for machine types
act(k): the activation value of a unit k
w_{kl}: a connection weight between unit k and unit l
netinput(k): the net input value to a unit k
output(k): the output value from a unit k
extinput(k): the external input value to a unit k
max: the maximum activation value allowed
min: the minimum activation value allowed
rest: the resting activation level
decay: the decay rate which determines how fast the resting level is reached

2.2.1 Processing Units

Three different pools of processing units are used in the approach; each pool representing part types, machine types, and part instances respectively. The pools for the part types and the machine types primarily contain the similarity information among their units through excitatory and inhibitory connections. The part instances link both part types and machine types and play the role of a buffer. Each processing unit has an activation value which is determined by the external input value and output values from other connected processing units.

2.2.2 Connection Weights

There are two kinds of connections involved in this network. One is based on the machine-part matrix, and the other is based on the similarity matrices derived from the machine-part matrix.

The weights between part instances and part types, and between part instances and machine types are given as a maximum value if there is a connection, and otherwise given as 0. The null weight means that there is no significant connection between the two processing units. Normally, the maximum value is chosen as 1.

The weights among part types and among machine types are determined by the similarity matrices. The similarity matrix for part types ($SP = [b_{mn}]$) is constructed by counting the number of machines in common between two part types, while the similarity matrix for machine types ($SM = [c_{mn}]$) is constructed by counting the number of parts in common between two machine types. Diagonal values are given as the number of components.

$$b_{mn} = \sum_{j=1}^{m_s} b_{mnj} \tag{2.1}$$

where $b_{mnj} = 1$ if $a_{mj} = a_{nj}$, $b_{mnj} = 0$ otherwise;

$$c_{mn} = \sum_{i=1}^{p_r} c_{mni} \tag{2.2}$$

where $c_{mni} = 1$ if $a_{im} = a_{in}$, $c_{mni} = 0$ otherwise.

The weights between unit i and unit j for either part types or machine types are calculated using the following formula:

$$w_{ij} = \frac{s_{ij}}{n} - \text{adjustment} \tag{2.3}$$

Here, s_{ij} is the value from the similarity matrix, and n is the number of components. A negative weight means that there is inhibitory activity between the two processing units. The weights emphasize the dissimilarity between units by having negative values unlike other similarity coefficients approaches.[8,9]

2.2.3 Updating Rules

Each processing unit receives an external input and/or outputs a signal from/to the connected units. A combined input to the processing unit, i, is calculated as follows:

$$\text{netinput}(i) = \sum_j w_{ij}\text{output}(j) + \text{extinput}(i) \tag{2.4}$$

where $\text{output}(j) = [\text{act}(j)]^+$, $[\text{act}(j)]^+ = \text{act}(j)$ if $\text{act}(j) > 0$, $[\text{act}(j)]^+ = 0$ otherwise.

The activation values are updated according to the following equation:

If ($\text{netinput}(i) > 0$),

$\text{act}(i) = \text{act}(i) + \text{netinput}(i)\ (\max - \text{act}(i)) - \text{decay}\ (\text{act}(i) - \text{rest})$

otherwise,

$\text{act}(i) = \text{act}(i) + \text{netinput}(i)\ (\text{act}(i) - \min) - \text{decay}\ (\text{act}(i) - \text{rest})$

where $\max = 1, \min \leq \text{rest} \leq 0,\ 0 < \text{decay} < 1$.

The decay rate (decay) determines how fast the stable condition is reached. The stable condition is when the activation values of all the processing units do not vary more than 0.1% of the previous cycle. If the decay rate is decreased, the execution of the neural network slows down. On the other hand, an excessively high decay rate may result in an oscillatory situation in which the resting level is never achieved. This is because it introduces abrupt changes in the activation values of the processing units. For example, several units in a pool may become suddenly active owing to the high decay rate in the beginning of the execution. In the next cycle, these active units send strong inhibitory signals to each other. This causes the activation values of the

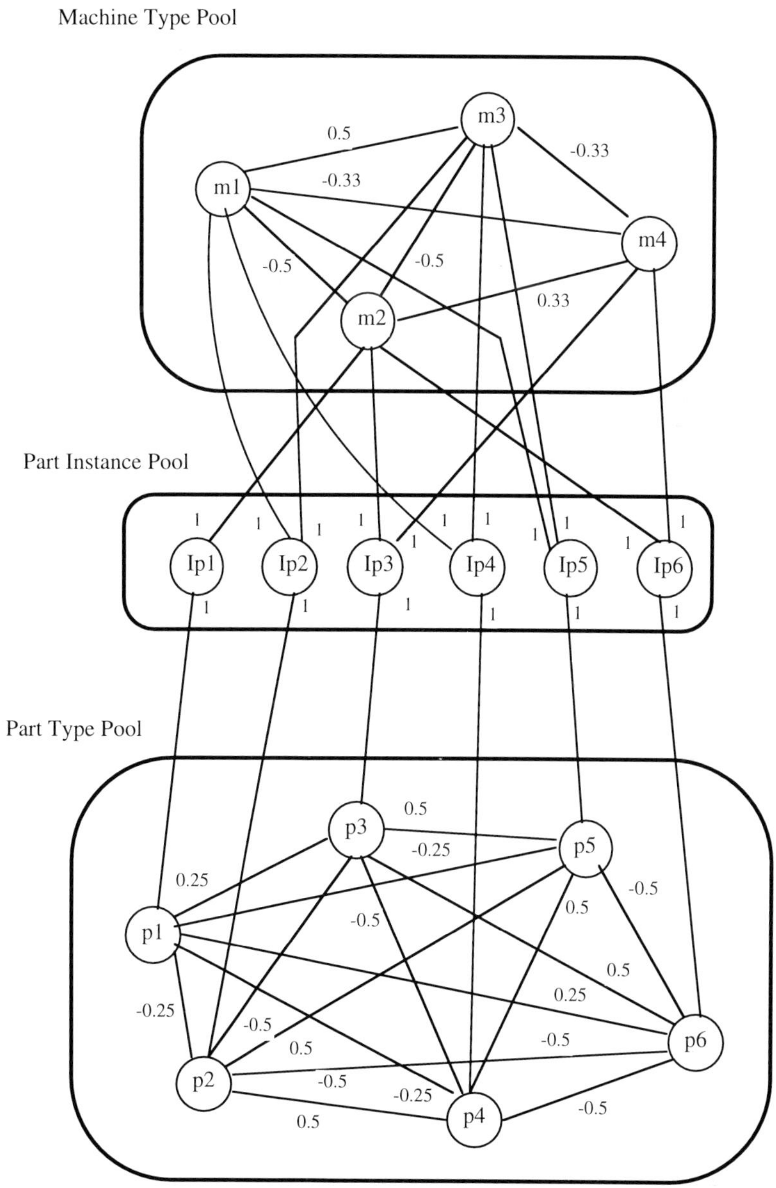

Figure 2.1: An example of the neural network

involved units to approach a minimum level. Since the units still receive excitatory signals, they become active again. Therefore, the stable condition will never be reached. Even though there is no optimal algorithm to determine the decay rate, the values between 0.05 and 0.2 are usually chosen.

2.2.4 Procedure

The first step is to construct a neural network using Eqs. (2.1), (2.2), and (2.3). Once the network is established, a unit from either the part type pool or the machine type pool is arbitrarily chosen. The updating procedure starts by clamping the chosen unit, that is, by giving an external input to the unit. After reaching a stable condition, the units with activation values greater than a *similarity threshold* are grouped together and deleted from the part type set (P) or the machine type set (M). The *similarity threshold* determines the number of part families. For example, if the *similarity threshold* value is equal to the minimum activation value allowed (min), all of the parts and machines are grouped as one family. On the other hand, if the *similarity threshold* value is equal to the maximum activation value allowed (max), each part or machine will represent each family. Also, the *similarity threshold* value should be greater than the resting level (rest) which is the most natural activation value of processing units. Therefore, users should determine the *similarity threshold* value by considering a desirable number of families to be formed.

Then, the next available unit is chosen and clamped. The procedure continues until there is no component left in both the part type set and the machine type set. The whole procedure is depicted in Figure 2.2.

2.3 Generalized Family Formation

In this generalized family formation, more manufacturing factors and production constraints are considered. Additional manufacturing factors that have been considered include different process plans for each part, sequence of operations in part production routing, part production cost, part processing time, and lot size. In this section, only three factors are considered.

The first is the sequence of operations which has a significant effect on material handling costs and time. In clustering approaches used for standard family formation, the operations of a part are performed on a corresponding group of machines regardless of the sequence of operations. It might happen that the machines performing the first and the last operations of a part form a cell, while the machines performing the intermediate operations form another cell. Although the within-cell layout problem can be considered after the cell configurations are determined, it is more desirable to solve the layout problem before the cells are formed.

The second factor is lot size. In the standard family formulation, the lot size of every part is considered to be the same. However, the required quantity of each part

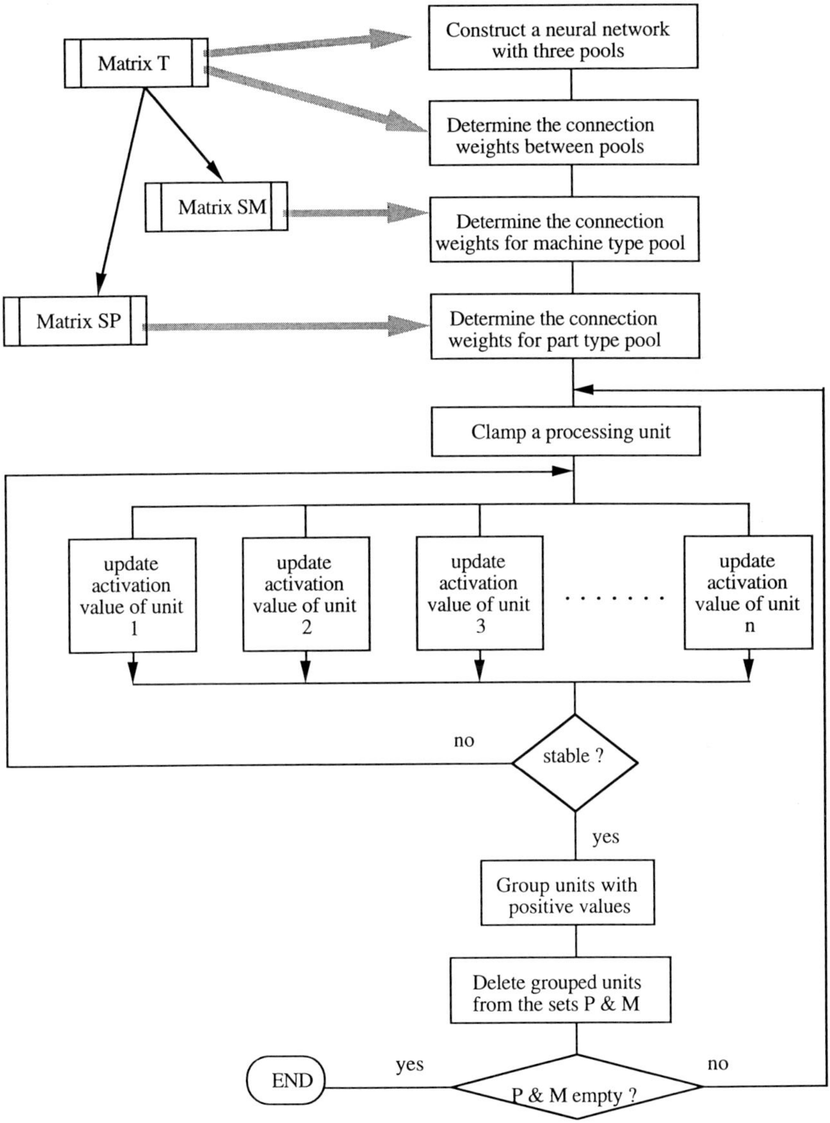

Figure 2.2: A summary of the process

is varied in actual situations. The degree of importance of each part is proportional to its lot size. For example, we may want to gather two large size part types into a family which perhaps only uses some similar machines rather than two smaller size part types which use more of the same machines. To improve the effectiveness of our approach, the data of lot size is added to generate proper part families and machine cells in order to reduce the actual intercellular moves.

The third extension is the involvement of multiple process plans. Each part can be manufactured by more than one process plan. A process plan needs to be assigned to each part such that the overall performance is optimal.

2.3.1 Sequence of Operations

The sequence of operations for a part is an ordered list of machines which process the part. This information is also adopted from route sheets. The setup of the network system for involving the sequence of operations is the same as in the standard family formulation except for the weights between the machine units in the machine pool. The strengths between part units are derived from the Jaccard coefficient formula based on the machine-part incidence matrix. However, the strengths between machine units in the machine pool are developed from the Jaccard coefficient formula and a sequence coefficient. The new formula used for machine unit connection is:

$$d(i,k) = \frac{a_{11}}{d - a_{00}} \tag{2.5}$$

$$S(i,k) = d(i,k) + \frac{Ct(i,k)}{N} \tag{2.6}$$

$$A = \frac{\sum_i \sum_k S(i,k)}{m(m+1)} \tag{2.7}$$

$$W_{ik} = \begin{cases} 0 & \text{if } i = k \\ S(i,k) - A, & \text{otherwise} \end{cases} \tag{2.8}$$

where $k = 1, \ldots, n;\ i = 1, \ldots, n$.
$d(i,k)$: Jaccard similarity coefficient between unit i and unit k.
a_{11} (or a_{00}): the number of entries shown by value 1 (or 0) at the corresponding position in units i, k.
d: the number of entries in a pattern.
n: the number of entries in each pattern.
W_{ik}: the strength of the connection between machine unit i and machine unit k.
$S(i,k)$: the similarity value between machine unit i and machine unit k.
C: An experimental constant.
$t(i,k)$: the consecutive times of machines i and k, in the operation sequence of all the part types.

N: the maximum of $t(i,k); i,k = 1,\ldots,m$.
m: the number of machine types.

A sequence coefficient can be added to the Jaccard similarity coefficient, with a higher priority value, in terms of the number of any consecutive two machines. That is, because the activations of highly related units are excited not only from their partners in the same pool, but also from the related pool. For example, a family of similar parts is generated by the main excitations from all related parts as well as by indirect excitations from the machine pool. Therefore, the parts operated most by the same consecutive machines will be more easily organized together than the parts processed just by the same required machines. Furthermore, since the consecutive machine units have stronger relations, they tend to be assigned to the same cell. After the machine units are excited, the corresponding part units will also be strongly excited.

The constant C determines how fast a stable condition is reached. If C is small, the execution of the neural network slows down. On the other hand, C being too high may result in an oscillatory situation, in which the resting level is never achieved. This is because it introduces abrupt changes in the activation values of the units. Usually, the value of C can be fixed after several experimental runs with the network.

2.3.2 Lot Sizes

For the cases of different lot sizes, the quantitative analysis of the interrelations between part types is developed from the Jaccard similarity coefficient formula. The similarities between machines are derived by multiplying the quantity of each part type to its corresponding entry. The formula for calculating the similarities between machines is as follows:

$$S(i,k) = \frac{\sum_u X_i(u)X_k(u)Q(u)}{\sum_u [X_i(u) + X_k(u) - X_i(u)X_k(u)]Q(u)} \tag{2.9}$$

where $u = 1,\ldots,n$,
n: the total number of the machine types,
$S(i,k)$: the similarity coefficient between machine type i and k,
$X_i(u)$: the entry on the position of machine type i to part type u in incidence matrix; $X_i(u) = 0$ or 1,
$Q(u)$: the lot size of part type u.

The collection of forecasted demand for each part is the first step to be computed before the similarity coefficients between machine types are calculated. The calculation of the strengths of the connections between part units and between the other units remains the same as in standard family formulation.

2.3.3 Multiple Process Plans

Kusiak[10] proposed a method for the generalized Group Technology concept within which each part type has one or more process plans and a specific process plan has to be chosen for each part type. His method is an integer programming method, called the p-median model. The advantage of this integer programming method is that the optimal solution can be obtained. However, the computations involved are so extensive that the larger size cases cannot be dealt with efficiently. Furthermore, it is unreasonable to assume that the number of part families (clusters) can be determined in advance. This family formation problem with multiple process plans can be restated as one to find the optimum solution for grouping specific parts into families processed by a group of machines. The constraint is that only a single process plan should be assigned to a part type while all the part types are assigned with a process plan.

In our approach, only one specific process plan is assuredly chosen for each part type because we set strong inhibitory connections among the process plans of a part. If there are three process plans designed for a part type, the strength of the connection between either two is set to be strongly inhibitory. Eventually, only one of the process plans will be activated.

In standard family formulation, the strengths among the machine units are developed from the similarity coefficients in order to promote "default assignment." However, in the multiple process plan case, the same methodology is not valid because the number of process plans for each part varies. This value, minimizing the influences of the machine units, was obtained through many experimentations.

2.4 Unified GT Implementation

The part family formation and part classification are closely related, and usually the same approach is used for both problems in most applications. Regardless of the approach adopted for the formation and classification, a critical problem is how to maintain consistency. The consistency problem can be addressed most effectively if the formation and classification are a single procedure rather than two separate procedures. This section presents an approach for using the learning ability of the backpropagation learning algorithm[11] to automate the process of new family formation during the classification process. We divide this task into four phases: seeding phase, mapping phase, training phase, and assigning phase. The flow chart of the classifying procedure is shown in Figure 2.3.

2.4.1 Seeding Phase

The initial part family formation is not required for this approach. At the initial stage when there is no initial part family formed, we choose three to five apparently distinctive parts from the part pool as part family representatives (seed parts) and assign a family ID number to each seed part for classification purpose.

In order to form a set of training patterns used as input to the network, a customized coding system based on part feature descriptions has been constructed. The

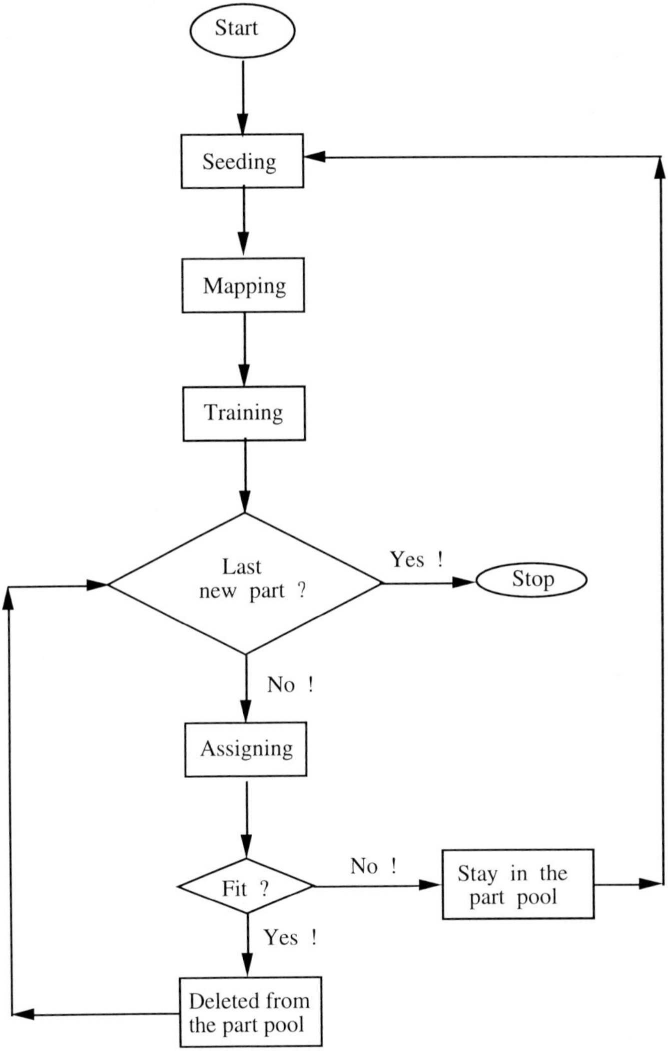

Figure 2.3: Flowchart of new part classification.

part features may be design features or manufacturing features. For example, in designing a cellular manufacturing cell, the part features are defined in terms of manufacturing attributes such as surface finish, required tools, tolerances, etc. The chain type code is adopted so that each digit of the code represents an independent feature. Currently only binary digits are used for the code.

2.4.2 Mapping Phase

Using this feature-based coding system, we assign a code to each seed part as the input patterns. We also map the predetermined family numbers to binary codes that are used for the target patterns. In this manner, a set of part families is mapped to a set of training pattern pairs, and each of them consists of an input pattern (part code) and a target pattern (family code). Those parts left in the part pool are coded by the same coding system. However, a relevant part family for each part is not known yet.

A neural network is then constructed. The number of input units is equivalent to the number of features contained in a classification code system. The number of output units is decided by the number of output pattern digits. If there are n output units, then $2n$ part families can be considered. As to the number of hidden units, there exists no formula to decide how many hidden units are suitable for the network. It is decided by trial and error. Generally speaking, if the number of the hidden units is not sufficient, it needs a longer time to train the network to get the same learning result. If the number of hidden units is too many, a redundant computing burden is required. The weight values of the unit connections are randomly assigned in the initial stage and will be modified due to the network mapping of the knowledge to the internal representation.

2.4.3 Training Phase

The next phase is the training phase. A set of training pattern pairs are presented to the network. The input patterns are received by the input units and the target patterns are associated with the output units. The results of the forward learning procedure are compared with the target patterns. The obtained errors are used to push the system to execute the backpropagation learning procedure. In the meantime, these errors are also viewed as performance measures of the network. We set a threshold value as the desired error level. The lower the threshold value is, the longer the training time and the better the learning results are, but the larger the computational burden. After each cycle of presenting the whole set of training pattern pairs, the sum of the squared errors of each training pattern (tss) is computed. When the tss value is less than the threshold value, the obtained activations of the output patterns are close enough to the target patterns, therefore the training procedure is finished. At this moment, the well-trained network is ready for the final task, classifying the rest of the parts to the most appropriate part families.

2.4.4 Assigning Phase

The last phase is the assigning phase. This phase utilizes neural networks' capabilities of spontaneous generalization and fault tolerance. Suppose we present a pattern that is similar to one of the training pattern sets. The trained network extracts the features of this pattern and compares these features with stored internal representations in order to find the nearest part family. The target patterns are not given in the pattern set in this phase while the input patterns and target patterns are both contained in the training pattern set.

There are two possible answers as a result of this phase. If the features of the input pattern are similar to the generalized features of any existing part family representative, then the output pattern will be the same part family number. If there exist no significant similarities between the test part and any of the part family representative, the activation values of the output units will not indicate any existing family code. That means a new part family should be set up for this part.

After the assigning phase, the first classification cycle is over. Those family members selected in the first cycle are eliminated from the part pool and we choose another three to five new seed parts from the remaining parts in the part pool as new family representatives. These new representatives are added into the seed pool in order to retrain the neural network. The new trained neural network will find the similar parts for each predetermined families. Note that, for the neural network, the stored memories learned in the first cycle will be erased or modified in the second cycle. This procedure is repeated until every part is classified into its proper part family. The algorithm of this heuristic method is summarized below.

Notation

F_n: The nth family.
I: The iteration cycle number.
m: The maximum digit number in the target pattern code.
N : The number of new family seeds (also called family representatives).
NF_n : The number of new family members in F_n.
NP : The number of parts in the part pool, P.
NS : The number of seeds in S, i.e., the number of existing families.
$P = \{p_1, p_2, \ldots, p_i\}$, the part pool.
$S = \{s_1, s_2, \ldots, s_j\}$, the seed pool, also the training set.
T_i : The activation value of a digit in a target pattern code, $T_i = 1$ or 0.
X_i : The activation value of a digit in an output pattern code, $|X_i| < 1$.
TT: The threshold value.

Algorithm

Step 0:

$$\begin{aligned} I &= 1 \\ NS &= 0 \\ NP &= NP \\ S &= \{\,\} \\ P &= \{p_1, p_2, \ldots, p_{NP}\} \end{aligned}$$

Step 1: Determine the value of N.
$N > 2$ and $N < 6$ or 7
(The maximum value of N depends on the number of apparently distinctive parts.)

Step 2: Choose N seed parts from part pool.

Step 3: Assign predetermined family ID numbers to each seed part.
These input-target pattern pairs form the training set, S.
Add these seed parts into the seed pool.
$NS = NS + N$, a new set S
Eliminate the training parts from the part pool.
$NP = NP - N, P = P - \{p_i | p_i \; S\}$

Step 4: Present the training set to the backpropagation network for training it.

Step 5: Present the remaining parts in the part pool for the assigning phase.
For a part, if $|T_i - X_i| < TT \quad i = 1, 2, \ldots, m$
then the part belongs to the corresponding family;
otherwise this part is not assigned to any family yet.
After the assigning phase, each family seed is associated with its family members.

Step 6: Eliminate family members chosen in this cycle from the part pool.
$NP = NP - \sum NF_n \quad n = 1, \ldots, NS$
The Ith cycle is finished.

Step 7: If $NP > 0$, then $I = I + 1$ and go to Step 2;
otherwise, stop.

2.5 Automatic Generation of GT Families

The consistency problem addressed in Section 4 is reconsidered. This time, an unsupervised learning neural network, ART (Adaptive Resonance Theory) is adopted.[12] The classification operation and the learning operation are two basic components of our approach. The classification operation consists of three major phases: recognition, comparison, and search. The learning operation is subdivided into two phases: training and new family formation. The modified ART model has been based on the ART1 model. However, the process control tools, such as the two-thirds rule, Gain 1, Gain 2, and reset were simplified or modified. This makes the modified ART model more suitable for GT applications. For brevity, ART is used to refer the modified ART1 network in the following description.

2.5.1 New Family Formation Phase

In order to form a set of input patterns which will be fed into the network, a customized coding system based on part feature descriptions has been constructed. The part features may be design or manufacturing features. The chain type code is adopted so that each digit of the code represents an independent feature. According to this feature-based coding system, we assign a code as an input pattern to each part. Since there is no family formed in the beginning, any one of part vectors, P_k, may be destined to belong to the first part family, $F(1)$.

Then a two-layer neural network is constructed. The number of neurons in Layer 1 is fixed and equal to the number of part pattern digits. Each neuron in Layer 2 stands for a part family. There are two kinds of connection weights in the network, the bottom-up weight vector, B, and the top-down weight vector, T. The bottom-up weights work for the recognition phase, while the top-down weights are used for the comparison phase. The formulas for bottom-up and top-down weights are presented as below:

$$b_{ij} = \frac{X_i}{1+A}$$

$$t_{ji} = X_i$$

where
A: the number of attributes of input vectors,
X_i: component i of input vector P_k,
b_{ij}: component i of bottom-up weight vector B_j
T_{ji}: component i of top-down weight vector T_j.

As a result, the weight vector T_j is equal to the input part vector, P_k. For the first part family, j is equal to 1.

During the classification process, when the new part cannot be matched with any family prototype, a new family neuron will be created in the network. Once the new family neuron F_j and its own links are constructed, the network has learned the features of this new part.

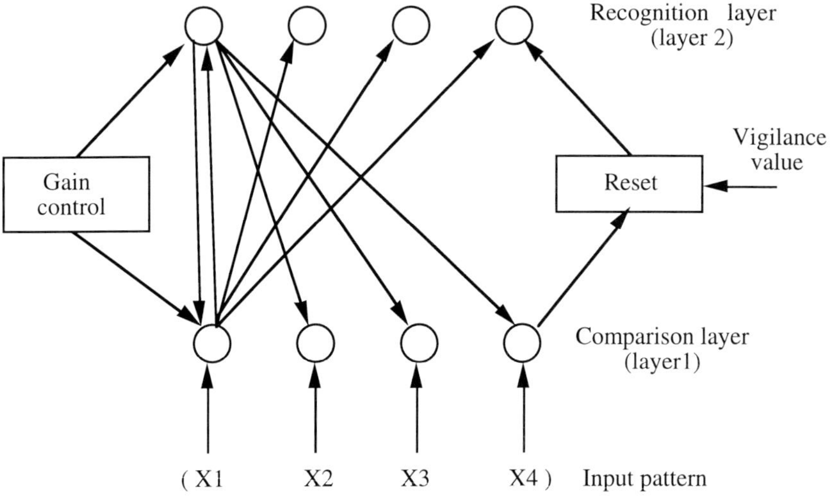

Figure 2.4: Architecture of an ART network.

2.5.2 Recognition Phase

After the initial network is constructed, we present the other part vectors to the network one by one. The recognition and comparison phases are devised to address the problem of how the ART model judges whether a new part belongs to one of the existing families. The recognition phase is the prejudging process, while the comparison phase does the actual examination. In both phases, the dot product of the two vectors is used to indicate the similarity between them.

In the recognition phase, each family neuron has a dot product value named BSUM which is a weighted sum of a new part vector and its own bottom-up weight vector. The formula of BSUM is given:

$$\text{BSUM} = b_{1j}X_1 + b_{2j}X_2 + \ldots + b_{nj}X_n.$$

Among these family neurons, only one of them which BSUM is the largest will be selected as the winner and has the right to accept a more precise examination in the comparison phase.

This winner-take-all phenomena can be explained by a feedforward lateral-inhibition network. Each neuron in the third layer connects a positive weight to itself and is linked with other neurons by negative weights. Thus, if a neuron has the largest bottom-up dot product value, it will suppress other neurons' outputs and augment itself. At the end of competition, only the winner in layer 3 will send a feedback to the corresponding neuron in layer 2 in order to initiate the comparison phase. In the real network architecture, the third layer will not be shown up and the winner-take-all response is implemented by the algorithm.

2.5.3 Comparison Phase

The recognition phase is a kind of bottom-up process. In contrast, the term *top-down process* describes the process of the comparison phase. As shown in the Figure 2.3, each neuron in layer 2 has a top-down weight vector T_j that is also the family's representative. T_j, which is a binary vector, is used for comparison with the new part vector to verify that the part truly belongs to the jth family by computing the top-down weighted sum, TSUM:

$$\text{TSUM} = t_{j1}X_1 + t_{j2}X_2 + \ldots + t_{jn}X_n.$$

Vector B_j determines which prototype is most similar to the input vector . However, regardless of whether minimum distance functions or maximum dot product is adopted, the bottom-up processing does not guarantee that input vector P truly belongs to family $F(j)$ For instance, three different vectors A, B and C may have the same dot product values of (AB) and (CB) but these three vectors in reality belong to different categories respectively. Therefore, it is necessary to verify that the new part vector actually belongs to a specific family neuron whose bottom-up weighted sum is the largest one. This verification is performed by the top-down process in comparison phase.

The similarity coefficient and the vigilance parameter play important roles in this phase. It is worthwhile studying the nature of different similarity measures and their discrimination capabilities before choosing one of them as the similarity coefficient formula. There are eleven different similarity measures discussed in the literature such as simple matching similarity and Jaccard similarity. In our work, the formula of similarity coefficient is defined as follows:

$$S_{jk} = \frac{\text{TSUM}_j}{\text{number of ones of vector } P_k}$$

The higher similarity coefficient means that the part vector P is more similar to the winning family prototype. Therefore, the similarity coefficient measure provides an objective analysis of the relationship between existing families and new parts. Nevertheless, we need to set up a threshold value to decide whether a new part belongs to the winner part family or not. This step is a rather subjective judgement, that is, the users themselves should decide the constraints of the maximum number of parts in a family and the final number of part families. We define this threshold value as the vigilance threshold (VI).

$$\begin{aligned} S_{jk} &> VI, \text{ succeed} \\ S_{jk} &< VI, \text{ fail} \end{aligned}$$

If S_{jk} is larger than VI, then the kth new part will be grouped into the jth family; otherwise, we regard this winning family prototype as unqualified one. Hence, if the value of vigilance is set high, the classification resolution is high and the parts are likely to be split up into a large number of separate families. When the value of vigilance is set low, the classification sensitivity becomes obtuse so that a couple of families could be merged into a large family. This kind of behavior provides a very convenient way to adjust the final number of families as the users wish.

2.5.4 Search Phase

In the comparison phase, if the similarity coefficient is larger than the vigilance, no search is needed and the training phase will be initiated; otherwise a backtracking search method will be executed. In other words, if the part fails to be grouped into the winning family, the current winner will be eliminated from further consideration by a single failure and other stored exemplars will be considered in the order of decreasing BSUM value.

This is because another prototype may give a better match even when the most similar winner to the new part fails to be qualified. That is, other prototype's corresponding similarity coefficient may exceed the vigilance value, even if its BSUM is lower than the previous winners'.

The current winner family neuron will be inhibited from firing again if it fails to match. Then the network goes back to the recognition phase to choose the second winner to see if it is qualified. This process repeats, prototype by prototype, until one of them can match the input vector. Otherwise, a new family should be formed because no stored family prototype can fit this novel part. In the former case, the network will enter a training cycle to modify the weight vectors T_j and B_j, both associated with the neuron of the latest winning family.

2.5.5 Training Phase

When a family neuron succeeds in the top-down processing, the ART algorithm will implement the training phase to adjust the weight values of vector B and vector T in order to obtain a new prototype that is a compound of the new part and the prototype of the winning family.

Vector B_j and vector T_j are all prototypes used to represent the same part family $F(j)$ but serve different purposes. The bottom-up weight vector has a "self-scaling" property, while the top-down weight vector possess a "matching" property. Because the properties and functions between bottom-up weights and top-down weights are different, their learning formulas are also different. Due to the self-scaling property, the bottom-up weights are real numeral vectors while the top-down weights are integer vectors due to the matching property. The weight adjustment formula for new bottom-up weight vector, B', and top-down weight vector, T', are given below:

$$t'_{ji} = t_{ji}X_i \tag{2.10}$$

$$b'_{ij} = \frac{t'_{ji}}{1 + \text{TSUM}_j} \tag{2.11}$$

where TSUM_j in the denominator stands for the number of coincidences of 1's between the jth family prototype and the input part. If this number is large, i.e., there are more common features between the input part and the winner family prototype, the value of b'_{ij} is smaller. On the other hand, if this number is small, it will produce larger weight values for b'_{ij}. This "self-scaling" property makes the network separate two vectors where one is a subset of another. Hence the network with this property has a higher pattern resolution than the network without this property.

The top-down weight adjustment formula is given in Eq. (2.10). This formula can be explained by an AND logic or intersection. The result of computing is the intersection of unit-valued features between weight vector T and new part vector P. The procedure of training may be viewed as a process of retaining components of the stored prototype vectors that match the new part vector. Note that this process is irreversible. If one of components of vector T_j is adjusted from one to zero, the network can never restore this weight value to one. In this way, the basic features of the jth part family will be preserved by the latest weight vector of T_j'. Thus, T_j' represents the newest jth family prototype.

2.6 Conclusion

The neuro-computing models are suggested as flexible and powerful alternative to the part family/machine group formation and part classification processes. Research demonstrates that the developed neural network can address the GT family formation problem efficiently. Furthermore, it shows that the extensions with the involvement of other manufacturing information can be done easily within the same unified structure. More detailed descriptions of the models presented here can be found in several papers.[5,13,14,15]

2.7 References

1. N. L. Hyer and U. Wemmerlov, "Group Technology and Productivity," *Harvard Business Review*, (July-August 1984) 140-149.

2. N. L. Hyer and U. Wemmerlov, "Group Technology in the US Manufacturing Industry: A Survey of Current Practices," International *Journal of Production Research*, **27** (8) (1989) 1287-1304.

3. A. S. Carrie, "Numerical Taxonomy Applied to Group Technology and Plant Layout," *International Journal of Production Research*, **11** (4) (1973) 399-416.

4. C. Han and I. Ham, "Multiobjective Cluster Analysis for Part Family Formations," *Journal of Manufacturing Systems*, **5** (4) 223-230.

5. Y. B. Moon, "Establishment of a Neurocomputing Model for Part Family/Machine Group Identification," *Journal of Intelligent Manufacturing*, **3** (1992) 173-182.

6. J. L. Burbidge, *Production Flow Analysis,* (Oxford Science Publications, 1989).

7. C. T. Mosier, "An Experiment Investigation the Application of Clustering Procedures and Similarity Coefficients to the GT Machine Cell Formation Problem," *International Journal of Production Research*, **27** (10) (1989) 1811-1835.

8. J. McAuley, "Machine Grouping for Efficient Production," *The Production Engineer*, (1972) 53-57.

9. H. Seifoddini and P. M. Wolfe, "Application of the Similarity Coefficient Method in Group Technology," *IIE Transactions*, **18** (3) 271-277.

10. A. Kusiak, "The Generalized Group Technology Concept," *International Journal of Production Research*, **25** (4) (1987) 561-569.

11. D. E. Rumelhart, G. E. Hinton and R. J. Williams, "Learning Internal Representations by Error Propagation," *Parallel Distributed Processing: Explorations in the Microstructure of Cognition,* **1**, (MIT Press, Cambridge, MA, 1986) 318-362.

12. G. A. Carpenter and S. Grossberg, "A Massively Parallel Architecture for a Self-Organizing Neural Pattern Recognition Machine," *Computer Vision, Graphics and Image Understanding*, **37** (1987) 54-115.

13. Y. Kao and Y. B. Moon, "A Unified Group Technology Implementation using the Backpropagation Learning Rule of Neural Networks," *Computers and Industrial Engineering*, **20** (4) (1991) 425-437.

14. Y. B. Moon and U. Roy, "Learning Group-Technology Part Families from Solid Models by Parallel Distributed Processing," *International Journal of Advanced Manufacturing Technology*, **7** (1992) 109-118.

15. Y. B. Moon and S. C. Chi, "Generalized Part Family Formation using Neural Network Techniques," *Journal of Manufacturing Systems*, **11** (3) (1992) 149-159.

Chapter 3

A Parallel and Distributed Processing Algorithm for Facility Layout

Percy P. C. Yip and Yoh-han Pao
Department of Electrical Engineering and Applied Physics
Case Western Reserve University
Cleveland, Ohio 44106, USA

3.1 Introduction

In this chapter, we advocate a new type of parallel and distributed processing approach to searching for optimal solutions. The new search technique is called "Guided Evolutionary Simulated Annealing" (GESA). We demonstrate the GESA technique with the facility layout problem. The GESA technique is certainly parallel, because a number of solution candidates are evaluated in parallel. It is distributed in the following sense: the search strategy depends not on the objective value of a particular candidate, but on the set of objective values of the entire population of solution candidates. That means, the search decision is distributed onto the entire population. The GESA algorithm can be easily mapped onto a massively parallel machine; the algorithm works on an entire population, and each individual in the population can be processed by a separate processor, with the processing proceeding independently in parallel most of the time.

Our algorithm can also be viewed as a hybrid technique involving both simulated evolution,[7,8,9] genetic algorithms,[13,18] and simulated annealing.[19] A new idea of "regional guidance" is implemented into the GESA technique.[26] By regional guidance, we mean that the algorithm has a mechanism for measuring the qualities of many regions, and automatically focuses the search onto regions with higher chances of attaining the global optimum.

The GESA algorithm is also related to neural-net computing. It provides a new tool for training networks with quite general connections.[26]

In this chapter, we demonstrate the GESA algorithm with the facility layout problem. In Section 3.2, we describe the problem and the current heuristic procedures used for solving the problem. The GESA approach is described in Section 3.3. Simulation results for the eight benchmark problems are presented and compared with other techniques in Section 3.4. We then conclude our discussion in Section 3.5.

3.2 Facility Layout Problem

Facility layout problem is one of the classic NP-complete problems.[10] The task of the facility layout problem is to assign n facilities to n locations. For each pair of facilities, a non-negative weight is associated with the activity between them. We want to place each facility in a location in such a way as to minimize the sum of weights times distances between pairs of facilities.

We demonstrate the GESA algorithm with the facility layout problem, not only because of the complexity of the problem, but also because of its significance in manufacturing. Many actual problems in a plant can be converted to layout problems. To illustrate that, we consider a manufacturing plant with n departments. There are materials flowing between these n departments. One of the problem is to locate these n departments so as to minimize the total cost of the material flow. This problem is readily converted to a layout problem by setting the weights associated with each pair of facilities as the average cost of material flow per unit distance between the departments. Tompkins and White[24] claimed that between 20-50% of the total operating expense in manufacturing were attributed to material handling. A good layout can reduce operating expense significantly.

The facility layout problem that we deal with here is to assign n equally-sized facilities to n homogeneous fixed locations so as to minimize the total cost y defined as follows :

$$y = \sum_{i=1}^{n} \sum_{j=i+1}^{n} f_{ij}\, d_{kl} \quad \text{(for facility } i \text{ in location } k \text{ and facility } j \text{ in location } l\text{)}$$

where f_{ij} is the cost of material flow per unit distance between facilities i and j ($f_{ij} = 0$ for $i = j$) and d_{kl} is the distance between locations k and l ($d_{kl} = 0$ for $k = l$).

In actual cases, there may be more locations than facilities or the facilities may require different amounts of space. The former problem may be solved by using dummy facilities in the formulation, the latter by dividing facilities into subfacilities each requiring a standard amount of space and using large values for the interfacility weights between the component parts.[21] Therefore, we only need to consider the assignment of n equally-sized facilities to n homogeneous locations.

In devising algorithms, an assumption that the distances between spaces are rectangular and measured "center-to-center" is made. This corresponds to the factory floor application where movement takes place along a rectangular grid of aisles.

Several optimal procedures[11,12,20] are available for dealing with this problem, but these procedures are impractical for all but small-sized problems. These approaches are basically derivatives of branch and bound techniques computational complexity of this task has motivated the development of many heuristic algorithms.[1,4,5,14–17,22,23] Since 1968, the eight problems offered by Nugent[22] have become the standard benchmark for comparing different techniques.

Heuristic procedures can basically be classified as improvement methods and construction methods. In improvement methods, an initial solution is randomly generated. Systematic exchanges between facilities are made and the results are evaluated. The exchange that produces the best solution is retained and the procedure continues until the solution cannot be improved further. The H63,[16] H63-66,[17] and CRAFT[1] are the most popular improvement methods. In construction methods, such as FATE and, TAA,[15] a facility is assigned to a location, one at a time, based on some analysis, until all facilities have been assigned. Many hybrid techniques, such as FLAC,[15] start with a construction procedure to get a trial initial solution, and then continue with an improvement method to obtain a better solution.

In this chapter, we demonstrate the GESA approach using the 8 benchmark problems offered by Nugent[22] and compare the results with other heuristic procedures. The plant shapes, cost matrices, and distance matrices of these 8 problems are given in Figures 3.3 and 3.4, Tables 3.6-3.13.

3.3 Guided Evolutionary Simulated Annealing Approach

The GESA search technique starts out with a guess of N likely candidates, actually chosen at random in the solution search space. These candidates are the so-called parents. Initially each parent can generate a number of children, say M. The GESA algorithm is given in Figure 3.1. The basic mechanisms are similar to those of the simulated evolution procedure.[6] However, GESA differs from simulated evolution in the competition process. In GESA, there are two levels of competition. One is the local competition: the children in the same family (i.e., generated from the same parent) compete with each other and only the one with the lowest objective value survives. The best child then competes with its parent to find the parent for the next generation. If the best child is better than its parent, then it is accepted as the parent for next generation. If the best child is worse than its parent, we have a Boltzmann probability that the child be accepted. It means, we accept the best child as the parent for next generation if

$$y_1 < y_2 \quad or \quad \exp(-\frac{y_1 - y_2}{t}) > \rho$$

where

y_1 is the objective value of the best child
y_2 is the objective value of its parent
t is the temperature coefficient
ρ is a random number uniformly distributed between 0 and 1.

The second level of competition is the competition among the families. The number of children that should be generated in the next generation depends on the results of the second level competition. This second level competition actually provides the measure of the fitness of each family. Instead of using the objective value of a single point, that may be biased, we use all the children for that measure. Each child has an objective value that is compared to the lowest objective value ever found for all solution candidates in the entire evolution process, and the number of acceptance is calculated according to the algorithm given in Figure 3.2.

The number of children for the next generation is proportional to that acceptance number so that there are still a total of MN points. We fix the total number of children generated in each generation because of hardware considerations. In a massively parallel machine, the number of processing elements is fixed. Each individual in the population is handled by a processing element, and so the number of populations should be fixed.

The procedures continue until a certain number of iterations have been reached or until an acceptable solution has been found. It is the effect of the second level competition that gives a measure of the regional information. The acceptance number actually provides the information of how good the region is. If a region is believed to have better likelihood of attaining the optimal solution (as measured by a higher acceptance number), we focus more intently on search in that region.

The algorithm starts with a higher initial temperature. The temperature is decreased after each generation until it reaches the freezing temperature at which the temperature stops decreasing.

We can also view the algorithm as parallel simulated annealing with competition. Each family can be thought of as a multiple-trial-parallel simulated annealing machine with the children contributing the trials in parallel. In the GESA algorithm, we have N families, that means, we have N parallel simulated annealing machines. These N machines compete with each other, and the better one will have more trials and the worst one will have fewer trials. In simulated annealing theory, we know that we should increase the trials with decreasing temperature. The competition among the families (second level competition) actually provides such a mechanism that the number of trials for the best parallel simulated annealing machine (i.e., the number

Step 1	Set initial temperature t
Step 2	Randomly select N parents
Step 3	Generate children from the parents
Step 4	Find the best child for each parent (first level competition or local competition)
Step 5	Find the parents for the next generation. (selection) For each family, we accept the best child as the parent for next generation if $y_1 < y_2 \quad \text{or} \quad \exp(-\frac{y_1 - y_2}{t}) > \rho$ where y_1 is the objective value of the best child y_2 is the objective value of its parent t is the temperature coefficient ρ is a random number uniformly distributed between 0 and 1.
Step 6	Find the number of children that will be generated from the parents of the next generation (second level competition). The details of this step are given in Figure 3.2
Step 7	Decrease the temperature coefficient t
Step 8	Repeat Step 3 to Step 7 until an acceptable solution has been found or until a certain number of iterations has been reached

Figure 3.1: The guided evolutionary simulated annealing algorithm

Step 1	Repeat Step 2 to Step 5 for each family; Goto Step 6
Step 2	count = 0
Step 3	Repeat Step 4 for each child; Goto Step 5
Step 4	Increase count by 1 if

$$y_1 < y_2 \quad or \quad \exp(-\frac{y_1 - y_2}{t}) > \rho$$

where

y_1 is the objective value of the child

y_2 is the lowest objective value ever found

t is the temperature coefficient

ρ is a random number uniformly distributed between 0 and 1.

Step 5	Acceptance number of the family is equal to count
Step 6	Sum up the acceptance numbers of all the families
Step 7	For each family, the number of children generated can be calculated according to the following formula

$$M = \frac{T \times A}{S}$$

where

M is the number of children that will be generated for that family

T is the total number of points

A is the acceptance number for that family

S is the sum of the acceptance number

Figure 3.2: Algorithm for determining the number of children in each family in the next generation

Table 3.1: GESA parameters used

Number of facilities n	Initial temperature	No. of parents	Total no. of children in each generation
5	100,000	5	5×5
6	100,000	6	6×6
7	100,000	7	7×7
8	100,000	8	8×8
12	100,000	12	12×12
15	500,000	15	15×15
20	1,000,000	20	20×20
30	4,000,000	30	30×30

of children generated from the best family) increases with decreasing temperature or with increasing iterations.

Using the GESA technique for the facility layout problem, the total cost is the objective function. The search space is the set of all valid assignments. Each valid assignment is represented by a n-dimensional vector $\underline{x}$ with the following properties:

$\underline{x} = (x_1, x_2, x_3, \ldots, x_k, \ldots, x_n)$ such that

$\forall i \in [1, n], \exists k \in [1, n]$ such that $x_k = i$.

The physical interpretation of such a vector $\underline{x} = (x_1, x_2, x_3, \ldots, x_k, \ldots, x_n)$ is as follows:
The first facility is assigned to location x_1; the second facility to location x_2; the kth facility to location x_k. The nth facility is assigned to location x_n.

A simple random mutation is used for the reproduction of the children from their parents. A child is generated from its parent by a random mutation between 2 assignments of the parent (i.e., the children vectors are generated by a random switch between 2 elements in the parent vector). For instance, the vector (1, 2, 6, 4, 5, 3, 7) is a possible child of (1, 2, 3, 4, 5, 6, 7).

3.4 Simulation Results

For each problem, fifty trials were conducted using different initial assignments. The parameters used for these 8 problems are given in Table 3.1.

The temperature was decreased by a factor of 0.99 after each generation. The program terminates when the optimal solutions had been found or when five hundred iterations had been reached. The results are given in Table 3.2.

For $n = 5, 6, 7$ and 8, the optimal costs were found in all these 50 trials. For higher n, the system might converge to one of the sub-optimal costs because we terminated the process after 500 iterations.

Table 3.2: Summary of results obtained with use of the GESA approach

n	Iterations				Final cost				Average time
	min	max	average	standard deviation	min	max	average	standard deviation	t
5	1	51	6.52	9.19	25	25	25	0	0.06 sec.
6	1	20	4.94	4.52	43	43	43	0	0.04 sec.
7	1	64	13.56	15.11	74	74	74	0	0.12 sec.
8	1	54	14.62	10.73	107	107	107	0	0.16 sec.
12	13	500	165.56	165.52	289	293	289.36	1.05	8.26 sec.
15	27	500	177.76	138.10	575	580	575.18	0.56	19.20 sec.
20	500	500	500	0	1285	1297	1287.38	3.31	2.72 min.
30	500	500	500	0	3062	3102	3079.32	9.55	13.20 min.

For n <= 15, the best known costs are the global minimum costs;
Average time t is the average time required to find a solution in one trial; 50 trials were made for each problem.

Our results are compared with those obtained from other techniques in Tables 3.3 and 3.4. Table 3.3 gives a comparison of the average final costs obtained with different techniques, and Table 3.4 gives the comparison of the best final costs obtained with different techniques. These 2 tables indicate that our technique is the best among the techniques listed here. Table 3.5 gives the best layout solutions obtained by GESA to these 8 test problems. The actual layout of facilities corresponding to the best layout vectors are given in Figure 3.3.

3.5 Conclusion

A new type of parallel and distributed processing algorithm has been applied to the facility layout problem. Eight versions of benchmark problem were used for comparison. The GESA approach was found to compare favorably with other heuristic techniques. The GESA technique is of general applicability and that it can be used to deal with many different decision problems, especially for those problems where satisfactory heuristic procedures are not known.

3.6 References

1. E. S. Buffa, G. C. Armour, and T. E. Vollmann, "Allocating facilities with CRAFT," *Harvard Business Review,* **42** (1964) 136-158.

2. S. Bharitkar, K. Tsuchiya, and Y. Takefuji, "Neural computing for the facilities layout problem," *Proceedings of World Congress on Neural Networks*, Portland, Oregon, (July 11-15, 1993).

Table 3.3: Comparison of the average costs obtained

n	H63	H63-66	CRAFT	Biased Sampling	FLAC	DISCON	FATE	TAA	GESA	best known
5	27.6	29.4	28.2	26.8	25	N.A.	26	25	25	25
6	44.2	44.2	44.2	43.6	43	47.5	50.6	43	43	43
7	78.8	78.4	79.6	74.8	74	N.A.	78	74	74	74
8	114.4	110.2	113.4	107	107	118.8	126.7	116	107	107
12	317.4	310.2	296.2	293	289	322.2	326.2	314	289.36	289
15	632.6	600.2	606	580.2	585	630.8	660.8	596	575.18	575
20	1400.4	1345	1339	1313	1303	1416.4	1436.3	1414	1287.38	1285
30	3267.2	3206.8	3189.6	3189.6	3079	3436.4	3390.6	3326	3079.32	3062

(a) Results of H63, H63-66, CRAFT, Biased Sampling are obtained from Nugent et al.[22]
(b) Results of FLAC are obtained from Scriabin and Vergin [23]
(c) Results of DISCON are obtained from Drezner [5]
(d) Results of FATE and TAA are obtained from Heragu and Kusiak [15]
(e) The first four of the best known results (n = 5-8) are global optimal solutions obtained from Nugent et al.[22]; the last four of the best known results (n =12, 15, 20, 30) are obtained from Burkard and Bonniger [3]

Table 3.4: Comparison of the best final costs obtained

n	H63	H63-66	CRAFT	Biased Sampling	FLAC	DISCON	FATE	TAA	TTB	GESA	best known
5	25	29	25	25	25	N.A.	26	25	25	25	25
6	43	43	43	43	43	43	50.6	43	43	43	43
7	87	77	74	74	74	N.A.	78	74	74	74	74
8	109	107	107	107	107	107	126.7	116	107	107	107
12	301	304	289	289	289	295	326.2	314	289	289	289
15	617	578	583	575	585	597	660.8	596	575	575	575
20	1384	1319	1324	1304	1303	1376	1436.3	1414	1290	1285	1285
30	3244	3161	3148	3093	3079	3330	3390.6	3326	3106	3062	3062

(a) Results of H63, H63-66, CRAFT, Biased Sampling are obtained from Nugent et al.[22]
(b) Results of FLAC are obtained from Scriabin and Vergin [23]
(c) Results of DISCON are obtained from Drezner [5]
(d) Results of FATE and TAA are obtained from Heragu and Kusiak [15]
(e) Results of TTB are obtained from Bharitkar, Tsuchiya and Takefuji [2]
(f) The first four of the best known results (n = 5-8) are global optimal solutions obtained from Nugent et al.[22]; the last four of the best known results (n =12, 15, 20, 30) are obtained from Burkard and Bonniger [3]

Table 3.5: Layout vectors corresponding to the best solutions obtained

n	best cost	best layout vector
5	25	(3, 4, 5, 1, 2)
6	43	(3, 2, 1, 6, 5, 4)
7	74	(1, 2, 5, 3, 4, 7, 6)
8	107	(3, 4, 8, 2, 1, 5,6, 7)
12	289	(8, 4, 12, 5, 1, 2, 10, 6, 11, 3, 7, 9)
15	575	(1, 2, 7, 6, 14, 13, 9, 4, 5, 11, 10, 15, 3, 8, 12)
20	1285	(17, 9, 2, 10, 19, 16, 18, 12, 1, 3, 7, 8, 11, 4, 14, 6, 20, 5, 15, 13)
30	3062	(17, 26, 3, 7, 30, 28, 15, 16, 21, 22, 10, 29, 27, 2, 6, 9, 18, 5, 14, 1, 25, 11, 12, 23, 13, 24, 4, 19, 20, 8)

3. R. E. Burkard and T. Bonniger, "A heuristic for quadratic boolean programs with applications to quadratic assignment problems," *European Journal of Operational Research,* **13** (1983) 374-386.

4. Z. Drezner, "DISCON: A new method for the layout problem," *Operations Research,* **28** (1980) 1375-1384.

5. Z. Drezner, "A heuristic procedure for the layout of a large number of facilities," *Management Science,* **33** (1987) 907-915.

6. D. B. Fogel, "An evolutionary approach to the traveling salesman problem," *Biological Cybernetics,* **60** (1988) 139-144.

7. D. B. Fogel, *System Identification through Simulated Evolution: A Machine Approach to Modeling,* (Ginn Press, 1991).

8. L. J. Fogel, "On the organization of intellect," Ph.D. Dissertation, University of California at Los Angeles, 1964.

9. L. J. Fogel, A. J. Owens, and M. J. Walsh, *Artificial Intelligence through Simulated Evolution,* (John Wesley, New York, 1966).

10. M. R. Garey and D. S. Johnson. *Computers and Intractability: A Guide to the Theory of NP-Completeness,* (W. H. Freeman, New York, 1979).

11. J. W. Gavett and N. V. Plyter. "The optimal assignment of facilities to locations by branch and bound," *Operations Research,* **14** (1966) 210-232.

12. P. C. Gilmore, "A solution to the module placement problem," *IBM Research Report,* **RC-430** (April 1961).

13. D. E. Goldberg, *Genetic Algorithms in Search, Optimization & Machine Learning* (Addison-Wesley, Reading, MA, 1989).

14. C. H. Heider, "An N-step, 2-variable search algorithm for the component placement problem," *Naval Research Logistics Quarterly,* **20** (1973) 699-724.

15. S. S. Heragu and A. Kusiak, "Machine layout problem in flexible manufacturing systems," *Operations Research*, **36** (1988) 258-267.

16. F. S. Hiller, 11Quantitative tools for plant layout analysis," *Journal of Industrial Engineering*, **14** (1963) 33-40.

17. F. S. Hiller and M. M. Conners, "Quadratic assignment problem algorithms and the location of indivisible facilities," *Management Science*, **13** (1966) 42-57.

18. J. H. Holland, *Adaptation in Natural and Artificial Systems* (University of Michigan Press, Ann Arbor, MI, 1975).

19. S. Kirkpatrick, C. D. Gelatt, Jr. and M. P. Vecchi, "Optimization by simulated annealing," *Science*, **220** (May 1983) 671-680.

20. E. L. Lawler, "The quadratic assignment problem," *Management Science*, **9** (1963) 586-599.

21. R. F. Love, J. G. Morris, and G. O. Wesolowsky, *Facilities Location: Models and Methods*, (North-Holland, NY 1988).

22. C. E. Nugent, T. E. Vollmann, and J. Ruml, "An experimental comparison of techniques for the assignment of facilities to locations," *Operations Research*, **16** (1968) 150-173.

23. M. Sciabin and R. C. Vergin, "A cluster analysis approach to facility layout," *Management Science*, **31** (1985) 33-49.

24. J. A. Tompkins and J. A. White, *Facilities Planning*, (Wiley, New York, 1984).

25. P. P. C. Yip, "The role of regional guidance: The guided evolutionary simulated annealing approach," Ph.D. dissertation, Department of Electrical Engineering and Applied Physics, Case Western Reserve University (1993).

26. P. P. C. Yip and Y. H. Pao, "A fast universal training algorithm for neural networks", *Proceedings of World Congress on Neural Networks*, Portland, Oregon, July 11-15 (1993).

Labels of the 5 locations

1	2	
3	4	5

Labels of the 6 locations

1	2	3
4	5	6

Labels of the 7 locations

1		
2	3	4
5	6	7

Labels of the 8 locations

1	2	3	4
5	6	7	8

Labels of the 12 locations

1	2	3	4
5	6	7	8
9	10	11	12

Labels of the 15 locations

1	2	3	4	5
6	7	8	9	10
11	12	13	14	15

Labels of the 20 locations

1	2	3	4	5
6	7	8	9	10
11	12	13	14	15
16	17	18	19	20

Labels of the 30 locations

1	2	3	4	5	6
7	8	9	10	11	12
13	14	15	16	17	18
19	20	21	22	23	24
25	26	27	28	29	30

Figure 3.3: The shapes of the plants and the labels for the locations

Best layout of the 5 facilities

3	4	
5	1	2

Best layout of the 6 facilities

3	2	1
6	5	4

Best layout of the 7 facilities

1		
2	5	3
4	7	6

Best layout of the 8 facilities

3	4	8	2
1	5	6	7

Best layout of the 12 facilities

8	4	12	5
1	2	10	6
11	3	7	9

Best layout of the 15 facilities

1	2	7	6	14
13	9	4	5	11
10	15	3	8	12

Best layout of the 20 facilities

17	9	2	10	19
16	18	12	1	3
7	8	11	4	14
6	20	5	15	13

Best layout of the 30 facilities

17	26	3	7	30	28
15	16	21	22	10	29
27	2	6	9	18	5
14	1	25	11	12	23
13	24	4	19	20	8

Figure 3.4: The best layout of facilities corresponding to the best layout vectors in Table 3.5

Table 3.6: Cost matrix and distance matrix for the 5-facility-problem

(a) Cost matrix (with elements f_{ij})

	1	2	3	4	5
1	0	5	2	4	1
2	5	0	3	0	2
3	2	3	0	0	0
4	4	0	0	0	5
5	1	2	0	5	0

f_{ij} = cost of material flow per unit distance between facility i and facility j

(b) Distance matrix (with elements d_{kl})

	1	2	3	4	5
1	0	1	1	2	3
2	1	0	2	1	2
3	1	2	0	1	2
4	2	1	1	0	1
5	3	2	2	1	0

d_{kl} = 'rectangular' distance between facility k and facility l

Table 3.7: Cost matrix and distance matrix for the 6-facility-problem

(a) Cost matrix

	1	2	3	4	5	6
1	0	5	2	4	1	0
2	5	0	3	0	2	2
3	2	3	0	0	0	0
4	4	0	0	0	5	2
5	1	2	0	5	0	10
6	0	2	0	2	10	0

(b) Distance matrix

	1	2	3	4	5	6
1	0	1	2	1	2	3
2	1	0	1	2	1	2
3	2	1	0	3	2	1
4	1	2	3	0	1	2
5	2	1	2	1	0	1
6	3	2	1	2	1	0

Table 3.8: Cost matrix and distance matrix for the 7-facility-problem

(a) Cost matrix

	1	2	3	4	5	6	7
1	0	5	2	4	1	0	0
2	5	0	3	0	2	2	2
3	2	3	0	1	0	2	5
4	4	0	1	0	5	2	2
5	1	2	0	5	0	10	0
6	0	2	2	2	10	0	5
7	0	2	5	2	0	5	0

(b) Distance matrix

	1	2	3	4	5	6	7
1	0	1	2	3	2	3	4
2	1	0	1	2	1	2	3
3	2	1	0	1	2	1	2
4	3	2	1	0	3	2	1
5	2	1	2	3	0	1	2
6	3	2	1	2	1	0	1
7	4	3	2	1	2	1	0

Table 3.9: Cost matrix and distance matrix for the 8-facility-problem

(a) Cost matrix

	1	2	3	4	5	6	7	8
1	0	5	2	4	1	0	0	6
2	5	0	3	0	2	2	2	0
3	2	3	0	0	0	0	0	5
4	4	0	0	0	5	2	2	10
5	1	2	0	5	0	10	0	0
6	0	2	0	2	10	0	5	1
7	0	2	0	2	0	5	0	10
8	6	0	5	10	0	1	10	0

(b) Distance matrix

	1	2	3	4	5	6	7	8
1	0	1	2	3	1	2	3	4
2	1	0	1	2	2	1	2	3
3	2	1	0	1	3	2	1	2
4	3	2	1	0	4	3	2	1
5	1	2	3	4	0	1	2	3
6	2	1	2	3	1	0	1	2
7	3	2	1	2	2	1	0	1
8	4	3	2	1	3	2	1	0

Table 3.10: Cost matrix and distance matrix for the 12-facility-problem

(a) Cost matrix

	1	2	3	4	5	6	7	8	9	10	11	12
1	0	5	2	4	1	0	0	6	2	1	1	1
2	5	0	3	0	2	2	2	0	4	5	0	0
3	2	3	0	0	0	0	0	5	5	2	2	2
4	4	0	0	0	5	2	2	10	0	0	5	5
5	1	2	0	5	0	10	0	0	0	5	1	1
6	0	2	0	2	10	0	5	1	1	5	4	0
7	0	2	0	2	0	5	0	10	5	2	3	3
8	6	0	5	10	0	1	10	0	0	0	5	0
9	2	4	5	0	0	1	5	0	0	0	10	10
10	1	5	2	0	5	5	2	0	0	0	5	0
11	1	0	2	5	1	4	3	5	10	5	0	2
12	1	0	2	5	1	0	3	0	10	0	2	0

(b) Distance matrix

	1	2	3	4	5	6	7	8	9	10	11	12
1	0	1	2	3	1	2	3	4	2	3	4	5
2	1	0	1	2	2	1	2	3	3	2	3	4
3	2	1	0	1	3	2	1	2	4	3	2	3
4	3	2	1	0	4	3	2	1	5	4	3	2
5	1	2	3	4	0	1	2	3	1	2	3	4
6	2	1	2	3	1	0	1	2	2	1	2	3
7	3	2	1	2	2	1	0	1	3	2	1	2
8	4	3	2	1	3	2	1	0	4	3	2	1
9	2	3	4	5	1	2	3	4	0	1	2	3
10	3	2	3	4	2	1	2	3	1	0	1	2
11	4	3	2	3	3	2	1	2	2	1	0	1
12	5	4	3	2	4	3	2	1	3	2	1	0

Table 3.11: Cost matrix and distance matrix for the 15-facility-problem

(a) Cost matrix

	1	2	3	4	5	6	7	8	9	10	11	12	13	14	15
1	0	10	0	5	1	0	1	2	2	2	2	0	4	0	0
2	10	0	1	3	2	2	2	3	2	0	2	0	10	5	0
3	0	1	0	10	2	0	2	5	4	5	2	2	5	5	5
4	5	3	10	0	1	1	5	0	0	2	1	0	2	5	0
5	1	2	2	1	0	3	5	5	5	1	0	3	0	5	5
6	0	2	0	1	3	0	2	2	1	5	0	0	2	5	10
7	1	2	2	5	5	2	0	6	0	1	5	5	5	1	0
8	2	3	5	0	5	2	6	0	5	2	10	0	5	0	0
9	2	2	4	0	5	1	0	5	0	0	10	5	10	0	2
10	2	0	5	2	1	5	1	2	0	0	0	4	0	0	5
11	2	2	2	1	0	0	5	10	10	0	0	5	0	5	0
12	0	0	2	0	3	0	5	0	5	4	5	0	3	3	0
13	4	10	5	2	0	2	5	5	10	0	0	3	0	10	2
14	0	5	5	5	5	5	1	0	0	0	5	3	10	0	4
15	0	0	5	0	5	10	0	0	2	5	0	0	2	4	0

(b) Distance matrix

	1	2	3	4	5	6	7	8	9	10	11	12	13	14	15
1	0	1	2	3	4	1	2	3	4	5	2	3	4	5	6
2	1	0	1	2	3	2	1	2	3	4	3	2	3	4	5
3	2	1	0	1	2	3	2	1	2	3	4	3	2	3	4
4	3	2	1	0	1	4	3	2	1	2	5	4	3	2	3
5	4	3	2	1	0	5	4	3	2	1	6	5	4	3	2
6	1	2	3	4	5	0	1	2	3	4	1	2	3	4	5
7	2	1	2	3	4	1	0	1	2	3	2	1	2	3	4
8	3	2	1	2	3	2	1	0	1	2	3	2	1	2	3
9	4	3	2	1	2	3	2	1	0	1	4	3	2	1	2
10	5	4	3	2	1	4	3	2	1	0	5	4	3	2	1
11	2	3	4	5	6	1	2	3	4	5	0	1	2	3	4
12	3	2	3	4	5	2	1	2	3	4	1	0	1	2	3
13	4	3	2	3	4	3	2	1	2	3	2	1	0	1	2
14	5	4	3	2	3	4	3	2	1	2	3	2	1	0	1
15	6	5	4	3	2	5	4	3	2	1	4	3	2	1	0

Table 3.12: Cost matrix and distance matrix for the 20-facility-problem

(a) Cost matrix

	1	2	3	4	5	6	7	8	9	10	11	12	13	14	15	16	17	18	19	20
1	0	0	5	0	5	2	10	3	1	5	5	5	0	0	5	4	4	0	0	1
2	0	0	3	10	5	1	5	1	2	4	2	5	0	10	10	3	0	5	10	5
3	5	3	0	2	0	5	2	4	4	5	0	0	0	5	1	0	0	5	0	0
4	0	10	2	0	1	0	5	2	1	0	10	2	2	0	2	1	5	2	5	5
5	5	5	0	1	0	5	6	5	2	5	2	0	5	1	1	1	5	2	5	1
6	2	1	5	0	5	0	5	2	1	6	0	0	10	0	2	0	1	0	1	5
7	10	5	2	5	6	5	0	0	0	0	5	10	2	2	5	1	2	1	0	10
8	3	1	4	2	5	2	0	0	1	1	10	10	2	0	10	2	5	2	2	10
9	1	2	4	1	2	1	0	1	0	2	0	3	5	5	0	5	0	0	0	2
10	5	4	5	0	5	6	0	1	2	0	5	5	0	5	1	0	0	5	5	2
11	5	2	0	10	2	0	5	10	0	5	0	5	2	5	1	10	0	2	2	5
12	5	5	0	2	0	0	10	10	3	5	5	0	2	10	5	0	1	1	2	5
13	0	0	0	2	5	10	2	2	5	0	2	2	0	2	2	1	0	0	0	5
14	0	10	5	0	1	0	2	0	5	5	5	10	2	0	5	5	1	5	5	0
15	5	10	1	2	1	2	5	10	0	1	1	5	2	5	0	3	0	5	10	10
16	4	3	0	1	1	0	1	2	5	0	10	0	1	5	3	0	0	0	2	0
17	4	0	0	5	5	1	2	5	0	0	0	1	0	1	0	0	0	5	2	0
18	0	5	5	2	2	0	1	2	0	5	2	1	0	5	5	0	5	0	1	1
19	0	10	0	5	5	1	0	2	0	5	2	2	0	5	10	2	2	1	0	6
20	1	5	0	5	1	5	10	10	2	2	5	5	5	0	10	0	0	1	6	0

(b) Distance matrix

	1	2	3	4	5	6	7	8	9	10	11	12	13	14	15	16	17	18	19	20
1	0	1	2	3	4	1	2	3	4	5	2	3	4	5	6	3	4	5	6	7
2	1	0	1	2	3	2	1	2	3	4	3	2	3	4	5	4	3	4	5	6
3	2	1	0	1	2	3	2	1	2	3	4	3	2	3	4	5	4	3	4	5
4	3	2	1	0	1	4	3	2	1	2	5	4	3	2	3	6	5	4	3	4
5	4	3	2	1	0	5	4	3	2	1	6	5	4	3	2	7	6	5	4	3
6	1	2	3	4	5	0	1	2	3	4	1	2	3	4	5	2	3	4	5	6
7	2	1	2	3	4	1	0	1	2	3	2	1	2	3	4	3	2	3	4	5
8	3	2	1	2	3	2	1	0	1	2	3	2	1	2	3	4	3	2	3	4
9	4	3	2	1	2	3	2	1	0	1	4	3	2	1	2	5	4	3	2	3
10	5	4	3	2	1	4	3	2	1	0	5	4	3	2	1	6	5	4	3	2
11	2	3	4	5	6	1	2	3	4	5	0	1	2	3	4	1	2	3	4	5
12	3	2	3	4	5	2	1	2	3	4	1	0	1	2	3	2	1	2	3	4
13	4	3	2	3	4	3	2	1	2	3	2	1	0	1	2	3	2	1	2	3
14	5	4	3	2	3	4	3	2	1	2	3	2	1	0	1	4	3	2	1	2
15	6	5	4	3	2	5	4	3	2	1	4	3	2	1	0	5	4	3	2	1
16	3	4	5	6	7	2	3	4	5	6	1	2	3	4	5	0	1	2	3	4
17	4	3	4	5	6	3	2	3	4	5	2	1	2	3	4	1	0	1	2	3
18	5	4	3	4	5	4	3	2	3	4	3	2	1	2	3	2	1	0	1	2
19	6	5	4	3	4	5	4	3	2	3	4	3	2	1	2	3	2	1	0	1
20	7	6	5	4	3	6	5	4	3	2	5	4	3	2	1	4	3	2	1	0

Table 3.13: Cost matrix and distance matrix for the 30-facility-problem

(a) Cost matrix

	1	2	3	4	5	6	7	8	9	10	11	12	13	14	15	16	17	18	19	20	21	22	23	24	25	26	27	28	29	30
1	0	3	2	0	0	2	10	5	0	5	2	5	0	0	2	0	5	6	3	0	1	10	0	10	2	1	1	1	0	1
2	3	0	4	0	10	4	0	0	2	2	1	0	5	0	0	0	0	2	0	1	6	1	0	1	2	2	5	1	10	5
3	2	4	0	3	4	0	5	5	5	1	4	1	0	4	0	4	0	6	3	2	5	5	2	1	0	0	3	1	0	2
4	0	0	3	0	0	0	0	2	2	0	6	0	2	5	2	5	1	1	1	1	2	2	4	0	2	0	2	2	5	5
5	0	10	4	0	0	5	2	0	0	0	0	2	0	0	0	0	2	1	0	0	2	0	5	1	0	2	1	0	2	1
6	2	4	0	0	5	0	1	2	2	1	4	10	10	2	5	5	0	5	0	0	0	10	0	0	0	4	0	10	1	1
7	10	0	5	0	2	1	0	10	10	5	10	10	6	0	0	10	2	1	10	1	5	5	2	3	5	0	2	0	1	3
8	5	0	5	2	0	2	10	0	1	3	5	0	0	0	2	4	5	2	10	6	0	5	5	2	5	0	5	5	0	2
9	0	2	5	2	0	2	10	1	0	10	2	1	5	2	0	3	0	2	0	0	4	0	5	2	0	5	2	2	5	2
10	5	2	1	0	0	1	5	3	10	0	5	5	6	0	1	5	5	0	5	2	3	5	0	5	2	10	10	1	5	2
11	2	1	4	6	0	4	10	5	2	5	0	0	0	1	2	1	0	2	0	0	0	6	6	0	4	5	3	2	2	10
12	5	0	1	0	2	10	10	0	1	5	0	0	5	5	2	0	0	0	0	2	0	4	5	10	1	0	0	0	0	1
13	0	5	0	2	0	10	6	0	5	6	0	5	0	2	0	4	2	2	1	0	6	2	1	5	5	0	0	1	5	5
14	0	0	4	5	0	2	0	0	2	0	1	5	2	0	2	1	0	5	3	10	0	0	4	2	0	0	4	2	5	5
15	2	0	0	2	0	5	0	2	0	1	2	2	0	2	0	4	5	1	0	1	0	5	0	2	0	0	5	1	1	0
16	0	0	4	5	0	5	10	4	3	5	1	0	4	1	4	0	0	3	0	2	2	0	2	0	5	0	5	2	5	10
17	5	0	0	1	2	0	2	5	0	5	0	0	2	0	5	0	0	2	2	0	0	0	6	5	3	5	0	0	5	1
18	6	2	6	1	1	5	1	2	2	0	2	0	2	5	1	3	2	0	5	1	2	10	10	4	0	0	5	0	0	0
19	3	0	3	1	0	0	10	10	0	5	0	0	1	3	0	0	2	5	0	0	5	5	1	0	5	2	1	2	10	10
20	0	1	2	1	0	0	1	6	0	2	0	2	0	10	1	2	0	1	0	0	5	2	1	3	1	5	6	5	5	3
21	1	6	5	2	2	0	5	0	4	3	0	0	6	0	0	2	0	2	5	5	0	4	0	1	0	0	0	5	0	0
22	10	1	5	2	0	10	5	5	0	5	6	4	2	0	5	0	0	10	5	2	4	0	5	0	4	4	5	0	2	5
23	0	0	2	4	5	0	2	5	5	0	6	5	1	4	0	2	6	10	1	1	0	5	0	0	4	4	1	0	2	2
24	10	1	1	0	1	0	3	2	2	5	0	10	5	2	2	0	5	4	0	3	1	0	0	0	5	5	0	1	0	0
25	2	2	0	2	0	0	5	5	0	2	4	1	5	0	0	5	3	0	5	1	0	4	4	5	0	1	0	10	1	0
26	1	2	0	0	2	4	0	0	5	10	5	0	0	0	0	0	5	0	2	5	0	4	4	5	1	0	0	0	0	0
27	1	5	3	2	1	0	2	5	2	10	3	0	0	4	5	5	0	5	1	6	0	5	1	0	0	0	0	0	0	10
28	1	1	1	2	0	10	0	5	2	1	2	0	1	2	1	2	0	0	2	5	5	0	0	1	10	0	0	0	2	2
29	0	10	0	5	2	1	1	0	5	5	2	0	5	5	1	5	5	0	10	5	0	2	2	0	1	0	0	2	0	2
30	1	5	2	5	1	1	3	2	2	2	10	1	5	5	0	10	1	0	10	3	0	5	2	0	0	0	10	2	2	0

(b) Distance matrix

	1	2	3	4	5	6	7	8	9	10	11	12	13	14	15	16	17	18	19	20	21	22	23	24	25	26	27	28	29	30
1	0	1	2	3	4	5	1	2	3	4	5	6	2	3	4	5	6	7	3	4	5	6	7	8	4	5	6	7	8	9
2	1	0	1	2	3	4	2	1	2	3	4	5	3	2	3	4	5	6	4	3	4	5	6	7	5	4	5	6	7	8
3	2	1	0	1	2	3	3	2	1	2	3	4	4	3	2	3	4	5	5	4	3	4	5	6	6	5	4	5	6	7
4	3	2	1	0	1	2	4	3	2	1	2	3	5	4	3	2	3	4	6	5	4	3	4	5	7	6	5	4	5	6
5	4	3	2	1	0	1	5	4	3	2	1	2	6	5	4	3	2	3	7	6	5	4	3	4	8	7	6	5	4	5
6	5	4	3	2	1	0	6	5	4	3	2	1	7	6	5	4	3	2	8	7	6	5	4	3	9	8	7	6	5	4
7	1	2	3	4	5	6	0	1	2	3	4	5	1	2	3	4	5	6	2	3	4	5	6	7	3	4	5	6	7	8
8	2	1	2	3	4	5	1	0	1	2	3	4	2	1	2	3	4	5	3	2	3	4	5	6	4	3	4	5	6	7
9	3	2	1	2	3	4	2	1	0	1	2	3	3	2	1	2	3	4	4	3	2	3	4	5	5	4	3	4	5	6
10	4	3	2	1	2	3	3	2	1	0	1	2	4	3	2	1	2	3	5	4	3	2	3	4	6	5	4	3	4	5
11	5	4	3	2	1	2	4	3	2	1	0	1	5	4	3	2	1	2	6	5	4	3	2	3	7	6	5	4	3	4
12	6	5	4	3	2	1	5	4	3	2	1	0	6	5	4	3	2	1	7	6	5	4	3	2	8	7	6	5	4	3
13	2	3	4	5	6	7	1	2	3	4	5	6	0	1	2	3	4	5	1	2	3	4	5	6	2	3	4	5	6	7
14	3	2	3	4	5	6	2	1	2	3	4	5	1	0	1	2	3	4	2	1	2	3	4	5	3	2	3	4	5	6
15	4	3	2	3	4	5	3	2	1	2	3	4	2	1	0	1	2	3	3	2	1	2	3	4	4	3	2	3	4	5
16	5	4	3	2	3	4	4	3	2	1	2	3	3	2	1	0	1	2	4	3	2	1	2	3	5	4	3	2	3	4
17	6	5	4	3	2	3	5	4	3	2	1	2	4	3	2	1	0	1	5	4	3	2	1	2	6	5	4	3	2	3
18	7	6	5	4	3	2	6	5	4	3	2	1	5	4	3	2	1	0	6	5	4	3	2	1	7	6	5	4	3	2
19	3	4	5	6	7	8	2	3	4	5	6	7	1	2	3	4	5	6	0	1	2	3	4	5	1	2	3	4	5	6
20	4	3	4	5	6	7	3	2	3	4	5	6	2	1	2	3	4	5	1	0	1	2	3	4	2	1	2	3	4	5
21	5	4	3	4	5	6	4	3	2	3	4	5	3	2	1	2	3	4	2	1	0	1	2	3	3	2	1	2	3	4
22	6	5	4	3	4	5	5	4	3	2	3	4	4	3	2	1	2	3	3	2	1	0	1	2	4	3	2	1	2	3
23	7	6	5	4	3	4	6	5	4	3	2	3	5	4	3	2	1	2	4	3	2	1	0	1	5	4	3	2	1	2
24	8	7	6	5	4	3	7	6	5	4	3	2	6	5	4	3	2	1	5	4	3	2	1	0	6	5	4	3	2	1
25	4	5	6	7	8	9	3	4	5	6	7	8	2	3	4	5	6	7	1	2	3	4	5	6	0	1	2	3	4	5
26	5	4	5	6	7	8	4	3	4	5	6	7	3	2	3	4	5	6	2	1	2	3	4	5	1	0	1	2	3	4
27	6	5	4	5	6	7	5	4	3	4	5	6	4	3	2	3	4	5	3	2	1	2	3	4	2	1	0	1	2	3
28	7	6	5	4	5	6	6	5	4	3	4	5	5	4	3	2	3	4	4	3	2	1	2	3	3	2	1	0	1	2
29	8	7	6	5	4	5	7	6	5	4	3	4	6	5	4	3	2	3	5	4	3	2	1	2	4	3	2	1	0	1
30	9	8	7	6	5	4	8	7	6	5	4	3	7	6	5	4	3	2	6	5	4	3	2	1	5	4	3	2	1	0

Chapter 4

Neural Networks in Conceptual Design

Sagar V. Kamarthi, Soundar R. T. Kumara
Intelligent Design and Diagnostics Research Laboratory
Industrial and Management Systems Engineering
The Pennsylvania State University
207 Hammond Building
University Park, PA 16802, USA

Abstract

Conceptual design is the most important and creative phase of the design process which demands the knowledge, intuition, and imagination of a designer. The success of a designer in this phase of design depends upon his or her ability to recall a set of previous design problems which are similar to the problem at hand and apply the previously discovered solution strategies to solve it. Presently, few computer systems have been developed to assist a human designer in the conceptual design to recall either the similar design problems or the plausible design solutions. This chapter describes the application of neural network *classification* and *associative memory* paradigms to develop computer systems that can assist a designer in the conceptual design.

4.1 Introduction

Recently, the competition for innovative products, the need for the automation of complex design processes, and the integration of design with manufacturing has motivated the research into the philosophy or theory underlying the design. Several design models have been proposed, and several implementations have been reported. The application of neural networks to implement design models has been a recent subject. This chapter discusses the application of neural networks to implement some of

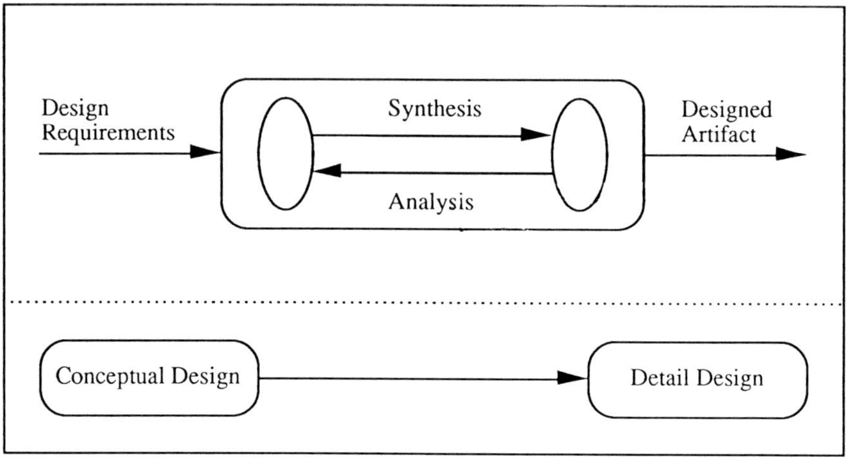

Figure 4.1: The design process simplified.

the useful design concepts.

4.2 General Idea of Design

Design is the process of devising artifacts to attain goals.[1] From common sense perspective, design is a process of putting together or relating ideas and/or objects in order to create a whole which hopefully will attain a certain purpose or function.[2] Though design has been an important process, and people have been involved in design for a long time, the nature of design has not been completely understood. A design process is not easy to define, nor is it easy to understand. Everyone has ones own ideas as to what design consists of. It is generally agreed that design consists of synthesis and analysis as shown in Figure 4.1. It is also commonly agreed that design broadly has two phases: *conceptual design* and *detail design*. The conceptual design is generally considered to require more creativity and synthesis than the detail design. It is clear, then, that when we study the design process, we should precisely state what design process we are studying. In this chapter we are mainly concerned with how neural networks can be used in the conceptual design.

4.3 Thinking Design Machine

Since the most critical decisions are made at this phase, conceptual design must be systematized for computer processing. Most of the conventional CAD systems, existing currently, deal with the detail design stage which often involves routine design processing such as geometric modelling and drawing. To capture the creativity involved in a design process, Suh and Sekimoto[3] proposed the "Thinking Design Machine (TDM)" based on the Axiomatic Design.[4] According to axiomatic design, design is the creation of the synthesized solutions that satisfy the perceived needs through the mapping between the *functional requirements* and the *design parameters* in the case of product design. In this chapter we use the term *design solutions* synonymous with design parameters for the sake of uniformity. The functional requirements are defined in the functional domain to satisfy the original needs given in the customer domain. The design solutions are created in the physical domain to satisfy the functional requirements. In accordance with the axiomatic design concept, the architecture of the TDM is divided into the following four steps:

Step 1: Definition of the functional requirements.

Step 2: Ideation or creation of the ideas. This step involves finding a set of plausible design solutions that satisfy the functional requirements defined in Step 1.

Step 3: Analysis of the proposed solutions to choose the best solution.

Step 4: Checking of the final solution.

This chapter primarily explains how neural networks can be used to build an *idea generation system* (IGS) in Step 2 of the TDM, to find a set of plausible design solutions corresponding to a given set of functional requirements of a design problem.

4.4 Idea Generation System (IGS)

In practice, an actual design solution depends on a designer's individual knowledge and creative process. Similarly, to generate creative designs, the IGS must have a broad range of knowledge and a right decision making ability. This is where the neural networks come into picture. Neural networks will enable the IGS to learn the relationship between functional requirements and the corresponding design solutions from the previously solved design problems, and based on this learning provide ideas to solve a new design problem.

Whatever a human learns through sensory experience is stored in long-term memory in the form of associations. Most of the real power of the advanced rational thought is developed through learning solution strategies to problems and learning to recognize similar problems. Finding a solution to a problem is essentially a process of recognizing important similarities in the different situations and to use this recognition to recall the previously learned solution strategies to solve the new problem.[5]

This is true in the case of a designer trying to solve a design problem also. A designer remembers all the design problems and the associated solutions that were encountered in his or her long-term memory. When faced with a design problem, a designer searches for the similar problems whose solutions have previously been discovered and uses those solutions to solve the present problem. If the designer is an experienced person, he or she has the knowledge of many design problems and the associated design solutions and hence can come up with a creative or innovative solution for a given design problem.[6] A close analogy can be given between an experienced designer and a chess master. The difference between a master and a novice is that the master has many more chess-patterns stored in his or her long-term memory. Such stored patterns allow the master to recognize whether the situation on the board is similar or identical to the one encountered in the earlier games and recall the best move.[1]

Since, human's rational thought primarily operates on associative memory, any IGS that assists a designer to come up with creative solutions in the conceptual design stage should have the following abilities:

1. To learn association between the design problems and design solutions.
2. To retrieve the design solutions of the design problems that are similar to the design problem at hand.

These requirements of the IGS can be addressed by neural network classification and associative memory paradigms. Before we discuss the application of neural networks for conceptual design, it is logical to decide upon the knowledge representation scheme for design problems and design solutions.

4.5 Knowledge Representation

A great deal of the superiority in the reasoning power that humans enjoy over animals is due to the enhanced cortical capability of symbolic representation. This is a valuable mechanism of a human brain because complex items can be reduced to simple expressions for the purpose of manipulation, for recording the discovered solutions and for solving the problems based on the known solutions.[5]

Similarly, to the IGS, proper representation of both design problems and design solutions is essential. In this case, any such representation should be suitable for the neural network application. If design problems and design solutions are treated as patterns they can be represented by vectors of their characteristic features. This vector representation is the most suitable form of representation for neural network applications. The following sections describe the details of this vector representation scheme.

Table 4.1: Functional requirements in the domain of cups, containers and bowls

FR1	Cleanability
FR2	Closability
FR3	Containability
FR4	Drinkability
FR5	Handlability
FR6	Sealability
FR7	Stability
FR8	Transferability

4.5.1 Representation of Design Problems

In the present chapter, we propose to represent a design problem by a binary vector. Each component in the binary vector corresponds to a functional requirement. The number of components in the vector is equal to the total number of functional requirements that will be encountered in a given problem domain, assuming that the total number of possible functional requirements in the problem domain are finite. For the purpose of illustration, let us consider the problem domain of cups, containers, and bowls. Table 4.1 gives the list of functional requirements of the devices in this example domain. Figure 4.2 gives some examples of design problems and their representations. Since, there are totally eight functional requirements in the problem domain, the size of the vector representing a design problem is chosen to be eight. If a component takes a value 1, the corresponding functional requirement needs to be satisfied by the design solution. Similarly, if a component takes a value 0, the corresponding functional requirement is not required by the design problem.

At the conceptual design stage the simplified binary representation of design problems, as explained above, should be good enough to characterize them. In conceptual design, only the concepts of the functional requirements and the associated structural descriptions of design problems are considered; the details such as dimensions, materials, and tolerance specifications are not important.

4.5.2 Representation of Known Design Solutions

Before deciding on the representation of design solutions, we propose two criteria for their representation:

1. The representation of each design solution should be unique. This condition ensures that no two design solutions have exactly the same representation.

2. The representations of a design problem and its design solution should be parallel in some way. This criterion ensures that the similar design problems have

FRS of Design Problems	Representation of Design Problems							
	FR1	FR2	FR3	FR4	FR5	FR6	FR7	FR8
Cleanability (FR1) Containability (FR3)	1	0	1	0	0	0	0	0
Closability (FR2) Containability (FR3) Drinkability (FR4) Handlabiliy (FR5)	0	1	1	1	1	0	0	0
Containability (FR3) Sealability (FR6) Transferability (FR8)	0	0	1	0	0	1	0	1

Figure 4.2: Representation of design problems.

the similar design solutions.

There can be many possible representations that can satisfy the above criteria. In this chapter we propose one such representation. Similar to the representation of a design problem, a design solution is also represented by a binary vector. This vector consists of two sub-vectors. Let us label them as left-sub-vector and right-sub-vector.

A left-sub-vector is similar to a design problem representation vector. Each component in the left-sub-vector corresponds to a functional requirement. The number of components in the vector is equal to the total number of functional requirements that can be encountered in a specific problem domain. As mentioned earlier, it is assumed that the total number of possible functional requirements in the problem domain are finite. Since there are totally eight functional requirements in the example design problem domain (see Table 4.1), the size of a left-sub-vector is chosen to be eight. If a component takes a value 1, it means that the corresponding functional requirement is being satisfied by the design solution and if a component takes a value 0, the corresponding functional requirement is not satisfied by the design solution.

A right-sub-vector is simply a binary number. It is added to its left-sub-vector to make the overall representation of a design solution unique. The size of this right-sub-vector is decided based on the expected maximum number of design solutions which will satisfy exactly the same set of functional requirements in a given design scenario. The design solutions, satisfying exactly the same set of functional requirements, will have exactly the same left-sub-vectors. Therefore, to differentiate such design solutions from one another, a binary serial number is added as the right-sub-vector to each left-sub-vector. Say, the expected maximum number of design solutions with exactly the same left-sub-vector is M. Then the size of the right-sub-vector n is chosen such that $M \leq 2^n$. In this chapter, n is arbitrarily chosen to be 3. Thus, in the present example, the total size of the design solution representation vector is 11. Figure 4.3 shows the representation of some cups, containers, and bowls as the examples of design solutions.

With this representation scheme of design problems and design solutions, we next move on to the application of neural networks for IGS.

4.6 Neural Networks for Idea Generation System

In IGS, neural networks play the role of learning design problems, design solutions and their association. For a new design problem, these neural networks will recall similar design problems and plausible design solutions. Let p_i be a new design problem whose best design solution s_i is to be found. Also, let p_j be a design problem with a known design solution s_j. Consider that a neural network has recalled p_j or s_j when

Design Solutions	Representation of Design Solutions										
	FR1	FR2	FR3	FR4	FR5	FR6	FR7	FR8	Binary Number		
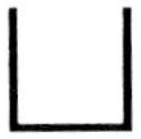	1	0	1	1	0	0	1	0	0	0	1
	1	0	0	1	1	0	1	0	0	0	1
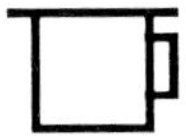	1	1	0	0	1	0	1	0	0	0	1
	0	1	0	1	1	0	1	0	0	0	1
	0	0	1	0	0	0	1	1	0	0	1
	0	1	0	0	1	0	1	0	0	0	1
	0	1	0	0	1	1	1	0	0	0	1
	1	0	0	1	0	0	0	0	0	0	1
	1	0	0	1	0	0	1	0	0	0	1
	1	1	0	0	0	0	1	0	0	0	1

Figure 4.3: Representation of design solutions of some cups, containers and bowls.

p_i is presented to the network. The correct design solution s_i can be found from the following steps.

1. The left-sub-vector of s_j describes the plausible design solution to p_i. From the analysis and evaluation of the plausible design solution, find the best solution to p_i. This step gives the left-sub-vector of s_i.

2. Once the best left-sub-vector of s_i is found, add an appropriate binary number to it as the right-sub-vector.

Neural networks can be used in two different schemes to build the IGS. In this chapter, we refer to the first scheme as the *classification scheme*, and the second one as the *mapping scheme*.

4.6.1 Classification Scheme

This scheme is based on the classification of design problems. The following are the essential steps involved in the classification scheme.

1. Classify known design problems into a set of families.

2. When a new design problem is encountered, classify it into one of the existing families based on some similarity measure.

3. If the new design problem does not belong to any of the existing families with the desired level of similarity, create a new family and place the new design problem as its first member.

4. If the new design problem is classified into one of the existing families, use the design solutions of the family members as the set of plausible design solutions to the new design problem. Here, it is assumed that the design solutions of the design problems in the existing families are known and accessible by some means.

5. If the new design problem is placed in the newly created family, the new design problem is quite different from the previously solved problems. Therefore, the design solution of the new design problem is found through relatively an exhaustive exploration.

The exploration of different design problems over a period of time will lead to the creation of the knowledge base of a wide class of design problems and their design solutions. This scheme provides both a one-to-one and a one-to-many relationship between a design problem and the plausible design solutions. When a design problem is classified into a family, the design solutions of the family members provide a set of plausible design solutions to the design problem.

In the classification scheme, as one can notice, the representation of a design solution is not much relevant. When a design problem is classified into an existing family of design problems, we have assumed that the design solutions of the family members are known and will somehow be accessible.

This scheme can be implemented using either a multilayer neural network or an adaptive resonance neural network. Sections 4.7 and 4.8 describe the classification scheme using a multilayer neural and an adaptive resonance neural network respectively.

4.6.2 Mapping Scheme

This scheme is based on the direct mapping between the design problems in the functional domain and the design solutions in the physical domain. For this reason, in the mapping scheme, unlike in the classification scheme, the representation of both design problems and design solutions is important. In the mapping scheme, the association between design problems and design solutions can be one-to-one, one-to-many, or many-to-one.

Similar to the classification scheme, the mapping scheme can also be implemented using either a multilayer neural network or an adaptive resonance neural network. The architectures of the multilayer neural networks used in these two schemes are almost the same. On the other hand, the architectures of the adaptive resonance networks used in these two schemes are not the same. The classification scheme can be implemented by an ART network, while the mapping scheme can be implemented by an ARTMAP network. Sections 4.9 and 4.10 describe the mapping scheme using a multilayer neural network and an ARTMAP network respectively.

4.7 Multilayer Neural Nets for IGS through Classification Scheme

The basic task underlying this scheme is the classification of design problems into families of similar design problems. Since design problems are represented by binary vectors, this task is similar to the pattern classification. The following steps present a general procedure for using a multilayer neural network for the classification of design problems. In this procedure, a neural network is trained by the backpropagation algorithm.[7] In this algorithm, training a neural network with a design problem means training the network in *auto-associative* mode with that design problem. In auto-associative mode, the input and the target patterns are the same in the backpropagation algorithm.

Step 1: Let the families of design problems be denoted by $P_1, P_2, \ldots, P_N$. Let $p_{K1}, p_{K2}, \ldots, p_{Km_K}$ be the members of the family P_K. Let the design solution of the design problem p_{Ki} be denoted by s_{Ki}. Let all design problems in all families put together be called the set of representative design problems $\{p_{Ki} \mid K = 1, 2, \ldots, N \text{ and } i = 1, 2, \ldots, m_K\}$. In Step 5, it will be clear that not every design problem classified into a family is included as its member and hence it cannot belong to the set of representative design problems. The design problem needs to meet a certain criterion to qualify as the member. Initially, let $N = 1$ and $m_1 = 1$. That means, initially, let there be a single family P_1 with a single member p_{11}. Also assume that the design solution s_{11} of the design problem p_{11} is known.

Train the neural network with the design problem p_{11} and go to Step 2.

Step 2: Pick a new design problem p_{*i} and use the trained neural network to classify it. If there are no new design problems to be classified, go to Step 7. When this new design problem p_{*i} is presented to the network, one of the following two things is possible:

1. The network responds with a stored exemplar p_{Kj} which is the closest match to the input design problem p_{*i}. In such a case, go to Step 3.
2. The network responds with a ghost image p_{**} which is different from any of the existing representative design problems. This happens if the input design problem p_{*i} is considerably different from any of the existing representative design problems. In such a case go to Step 6.

Step 3: At this point it is necessary to check if the input design problem p_{*i} and the retrieved design problem p_{Kj} are similar to the desired extent. One can use any suitable similarity or distance measure to check the similarity between p_{*i} and p_{Kj}. However, in our experiments not reported here, we used *Tanimoto's Coefficient*[8] as the similarity measure. If the similarity coefficient θ_{ij} computed on p_{*i} and p_{Kj} is greater than a desired threshold limit ρ_1, the input design problem p_{*i} is considered belonging to the family P_K. In such a case go to Step 4. Otherwise, go to Step 6.

Step 4: Since the input design problem p_{*i} is considerably close to the retrieved design problem p_{Kj}, the known design solution s_{Kj} can be used, with modifications if necessary, as the plausible design solution to determine the best design solution s_{*i}. Besides, the design solutions of the design problems in family P_K can be considered as the set of alternative plausible design solutions to the new design problem p_{*i}. Because of this reason, a multilayer neural network can provide a one-to-one as well as a one-to-many relationship between a new design problem and the plausible design solutions.

At this point it is necessary to decide whether the new design problem p_{*i} be added to family P_K and thus to the set of representative design problems. To make this decision go to Step 5.

Step 5: The decision regarding the inclusion of the new design problem p_{*i} as a representative design problem p_{Ki} can be based on the similarity coefficient θ_{ij} between p_{*i} and its closest family member p_{Kj}. This similarity coefficient θ_{ij} has already been computed in Step 3. If the new design problem p_{*i} and the already existing representative design problem p_{Kj} are very similar to each other, the new design problem p_{*i} need not be included as the representative member. Therefore if θ_{ij} is greater than a certain high threshold ρ_2, do not include p_{*i} to the set of representative design problems. In this case go to Step 2. Otherwise include the design problem p_{*i} in the family P_K and train the neural network with the whole set of representative design problems $\{p_{Ki} \mid K = 1, 2, \ldots, N,$ and $i = 1, 2, \ldots, m_K\}$ and then go to Step 2.

Alternatively, every incoming design problem p_{*i} can be included as the representative design problem and stored in the classification network. One severe problem with this alternative scheme is that, it may lead to the saturation of the network very fast. This scheme is suitable only when the number of design problems to be classified is relatively small.

Step 6: Since this new design problem p_{*i} is considerably different from all the existing representative design problems, create the $(N+1)$th family $P_{(N+1)}$ and include the new design problem p_{*i} as its first member $p_{(N+1)1}$. Update $N = (N+1)$ and train the neural network with the whole set of representative design problems $\{p_{Ki} \mid K = 1, 2, \ldots, N,$ and $i = 1, 2, \ldots, m_K\}$ and then go to Step 2.

Since the new design problem p_{*i} is quite different from the previously solved problems, there are no plausible design solutions to assist in determining its design solution. Therefore, the design solution to p_{*i} is to be found through a relatively exhaustive exploration.

Step 7: Classification of all new design problems is complete.

The above classification scheme using a multilayer feedforward neural network involves training the system again and again with the whole set of design problems because the system can only learn in batch mode. This type of batch training, each time a new design problem is to be learned, is not an efficient scheme. It takes an enormous amount of training time. In order to overcome this problem we need a neural network which learns design problems on-line. That means, the network should learn a new design problem without erasing the previously learned design problems. Fortunately, such a learning is possible through adaptive resonance networks (ART networks).

4.8 ART Networks for IGS through Classification Scheme

The problem currently investigated is one of classifying known design problems into a set of families in an adaptive manner so that any instance of a new design problem can be associated with the known design problems based on some similarity measure and the corresponding design solution can be retrieved.

Adaptive resonance networks are a class of neural networks governed by the designed principles of adaptive resonance theory introduced by Grossberg.[9,10,11] This class of networks is characterized by the capability of self-organization, self-stabilization, and self-scaling of the recognition codes in response to the arbitrary temporal sequences of many arbitrary input patterns of variable complexity. Self-organization is the capability of a network to organize itself based on a series or repeated presentation of inputs in the absences of an explicit teacher. Self-stabilization is the property of a network to dynamically buffer the learned codes against the relentless recording by irrelevant inputs. Self-scaling is the ability of a network to properly identify signal and noise embedded in a given input pattern. These are the important characteristics of any intelligent machine such as IGS that has to act autonomously to accomplish a desired task in an unknown environment.

ART1 is one of the adaptive resonance network models designed for the classification of binary patterns. This model is used in the present situation for the classification of design problems. In the further discussion, an ART1 network is simply referred as an ART network. Figure 4.4 gives an algorithm for the classification of design problems using an ART network. In this figure, the program Classify_Problems_by_Art_Classifier presents the design problems, one after the other, to the ART network in the same sequence as they naturally occur. The procedure Find_Problem_Membership performs the dynamics of the ART network which involves the classification and learning of the design problem presented to the network. The ART network offers the facility to adaptively classify patterns through the use of the pattern features. In a nut shell, the ART network can start with one design problem, remember its features, and when ever a new problem is encountered either it will classify it into an existing problem family or adaptively create a new problem family.

In the present context we are trying to build an intelligent system that can classify the design problems, with an arbitrary set of functional requirements, occurring in an arbitrary temporal sequence. Here one might ask the questions: How can the system remain stable by classifying only the familiar problems into their respective existing families and yet be plastic or adaptive enough to create new families when encountered with unfamiliar problems? How can the system retain its previously learned knowledge about the problems while continuing to learn new facts about them? In ART research, these questions are referred to by the design constraint stability-plasticity

```
program Classify_Problems_by_Art_Classifier (population_of_problems)
    initialize weight of all the bottom-up and top-down synapses
    do while (populations_of_problems is not nil)
            pick a problem prob_x from the population_of_problems
            call Find_Problem_Membership (prob_x, prob_x_membership)
            store problem prob_x and its membership prob_x_membership
            eliminate the problem prob_x from the population_of_problems
    end do
end

procedure Find_Problem_Membership (prob_x, prob_x_membership)
            compute bottom-up weighted input from F1 field to each node in F2 field
    do
            pick the available node j* which receives the maximum weighted input
            if (the similarity level between the top-down expectation of
            _winning node j* and the input problem is above vigilance limit) then
                    encode prob_x in bottom-up and top-down weights of node j*
                    assign prob_x_membership with problem family denoted by j*
            elseif (all committed nodes are inhibited in F2 field)
                    pick an uncommitted F2 node and make it the winning node j*
                    initialize bottom-up and top-down weights of node j* with prob_x
                    assign prob_x_membership with new problem family denoted by j*
            else
                    inhibit the node j* from being selected as winning node
            end if
    loop while (prob_x membership is not determined)
    return (prob_x_membership)
end
```

Figure 4.4: The ART algorithm for the classification of design problems.

dilemma faced by all intelligent systems capable of autonomously adapting in real time to unexpected changes in their world. Stability-plasticity dilemma is one of the major design constraints addressed by the ART networks.

As discussed before, design problems are considered as patterns and their functional requirements as the pattern features. adaptive resonance networks, basically, act as pattern classifiers and feature detectors based on sensory inputs. By virtue of these two basic characteristics, ART networks provide an excellent means for grouping of similar design problems into families and retrieval of representative features of the families.

In the previous section, the classification scheme using a multilayer neural network trained with backpropagation has been discussed. It can be noticed that, compared with a multilayer neural network, an ART network is superior in accomplishing the task of classification of design problems. The strength of the ART networks stems from their ability to solve stability-plasticity dilemma. Classification of design problems using a multilayer neural network is a batch process. On the other hand, it is a continuous process using an ART network. If one trains a multilayer neural network with a set of N design problems, it learns to recognize them. Later in time, if one wants the multilayer neural network to learn about a new design problem which is different from all the design problems in the set, one must retrain the multilayer neural network all over again with the set of $(N+1)$ design problems. The reason for this is simple. If the multilayer neural network is trained with only the new design problem instead of the set of $(N+1)$ design problems, it will disrupt the knowledge about the previously learned N design problems. Therefore, unlike in the case of ART networks, the learning process in the multilayer neural networks is not dynamic.

However, the multilayer neural networks, being associative memory models, are very efficient compared with the ART networks when they are put to the task of retrieval of the previously learned design problems. When a new design problem is presented as the stimulus to a multilayer neural network, it will generally retrieve one of the learned design problems that is closest to the new design problem. If the new design problem is drastically different from all the previously learned design problems, the multilayer neural network may come up with a ghost design problem that is synthesized out of an arbitrary set of features of the learned design problems. On the other hand, an ART network will never be able to retrieve one of the learned design problems that is closest to the stimulus design problem. Instead, when a new design problem is presented to it, an ART network will appropriately classify the new design problems into one of the existing design problem families followed by the retrieval of the representative features of that family. Further, if the new design problem does not belong to any of the existing families within the prescribed similarity limit, the ART network creates a new design problem family whose representative features are set equal to the features of the new design problem.

The adaptive creation of families of design problems, as described above, is not possible in conventional clustering algorithms. In some clustering procedures such as leader algorithm, one needs to specify the maximum distance limit among the design problems in each cluster. It is a difficult task to specify this limit because *a priori* one needs to know the statistical characteristics of the design problem population and these characteristics should not change with the addition of the new design problems to the existing ones. However, if one is able to specify the desired number of design problem families N, it is possible to arrive at this distance limit closely. In some other clustering procedures such as k-means algorithm, initially it is necessary to specify the number of design problem families N, and the seed for each family. The question is how to get these inputs to the clustering procedures. These problems are circumvented by the ART networks.[12]

4.9 Multilayer Neural Nets for IGS through Mapping Scheme

It has been shown that a two-layer network with an arbitrarily large number of nodes in the hidden layer can approximate any continuous function $f \in C(\Re^n, \Re^m)$ over a compact subset of $\Re^n$.[13] This property of a multilayer neural network can be used to directly associate design problems with their respective design solutions. This association will be learned by a multilayer neural network when it is trained with pairs of design problems and their respective known design solutions using the backpropagation algorithm.[7] In the training process the design problem used as the input patterns and the corresponding design solutions are used as the target patterns. The following are the essential steps involved in a multilayer neural network mapping scheme.

Step 1: Let p_i be a design problem and s_i be its design solution. Let R be the set of representative design problems with known design solutions. In Step 5, it will be clear that not every design problem presented to the neural network will be included in the representative design problem set; the design problem needs to meet a certain criterion to qualify as the representative design problem. Here, the concept of representative design problems is similar to the one explained in section 4.7 on the classification scheme using a multilayer neural network.

Let T be the set of training pairs to train the neural network. T is defined as $T = \{(p_i, s_i) \mid p_i \in R\}$. Initially, let there be only one representative design problem p_1 in R. Also assume that the design solution s_1 of the design problem p_1 is known.

Train the neural network with the training pairs in T.

Step 2: Pick a new design problem p_i and use the trained neural network to retrieve a most plausible design solution. If there are no new design problems to be classified, go to Step 6. When this new design problem p_i is presented to the network, one of the following two things is possible:

1. The network responds with a stored design solution s_j such that p_j is the closest representative design problem to the input design problem p_i, and $(p_j, s_j) \in T$. In such a case, go to Step 3.
2. The network responds with a ghost image s_* which is different from the design solution of any of the existing representative design problems. This situation happens if the input design problem p_i is considerably different from any of the existing representative design problems.

   Since the new design problem p_i is quite different from the previously solved problems, there are no plausible design solutions to assist in determining its design solution. Therefore, the best design solution to p_i is to be found through a relatively exhaustive exploration. Assume that the best design solution s_i to the new design problem p_i is found. In such a case go to Step 5.

Step 3: Since the input design problem p_i is similar to p_j, use s_j as the plausible design solution to determine the correct design solution s_i.

Since for every input design problem p_i there is only one plausible design solution s_j, in the mapping scheme, a multilayer neural network can provide only a one-to-one relationship between a new design problem and a plausible design solution. Recall that, in the classification scheme, a multilayer neural network is able to provide both a one-to-one and a one-to-many relationship.

At this point it is necessary to decide whether the new design problem p_i is to be added to the set of representative design problems R. To make this decision, go to Step 4.

Step 4: Compute a similarity coefficient θ_{ij} between the left-sub-vectors of s_i and s_j. As mentioned earlier, one could use a Tanimoto's Coefficient[8] as the similarity measure.

There are two possibilities at this point. If the similarity coefficient θ_{ij} is greater than a desired threshold limit ρ, the plausible solution s_j is considerably close to the correct design solution s_i. So, the neural network needs not learn the association between design problem p_i and its solution s_i. In this case go to Step 2. Otherwise, the plausible design solution s_j is not close enough to the correct design solution s_i and therefore the neural network needs to learn the association between design problem p_i and its solution s_i. In this case go to Step 5.

Step 5: Include the design problem p_i in set R and the training pair (p_i, s_i) in set T. Train the neural network with training pairs in T and go to Step 2.

Alternatively, each incoming design problems p_i, irrespective of the θ_{ij} value, can be included in R. This alternative scheme is good when the number of design problems to be classified is relatively small. If the number of design problems is too large, the network gets saturated.

Step 6: Classification of all new design problems is complete.

The application of a multilayer neural network in the mapping scheme has the same disadvantages that it has had in the classification scheme. Each time the map between a new design problem and its design solution is to be learned, the network must be trained with all the design problem and design solution pairs. This is so expensive in terms of training time. This scheme can provide only a one-to-one mapping between a design problem and its plausible design solution. That means, for a given design the network can only provide only one plausible design solution. A detailed discussion on the application of the multilayer neural networks in conceptual design can be found in Kumara *et al.*[14,15]

Therefore, in the mapping scheme a neural network is also needed which can map design problems with the design solutions adaptively instead of batch wise. Again adaptive resonance networks provide a useful solution to this problem. This time we need an ARTMAP network instead of an ART1 network used in the classification scheme.

4.10 ARTMAP Networks for IGS through Mapping Scheme

ARTMAP is another adaptive resonance network developed by Carpenter and Grossberg.[16] This network autonomously learns to classify arbitrarily many patterns occurring in an arbitrary sequence into a set of families based on predictive error.

This network is built up from a pair of ART modules: ART_a and ART_b. Each one of these modules is similar to the ART network discussed in section 4.8 of this chapter. These two modules are linked by an inter-ART module called Map Field. Both the ART_a and the ART_b modules exhibit all the properties discussed in connection with the ART networks in section 4.8. These properties are self-organization, self-stabilization, and self-scaling. They also address the stability-plasticity dilemma. In the present situation, the ART_a module learns about the design problems, and the ART_b module learns about the design solutions through self-organization. The ART_a module can learn by receiving an input stream of design problems, while the ART_b module can learn by receiving an input stream of design solutions. The ART_a and the ART_b modules can receive their input streams independently. In contrast, the Map Field module learns the association between the families created by the ART_a and the ART_b modules through supervised training. To train the Map Field module, a stream of design problems at the ART_a module and the respective known design solutions at the ART_b module are to be presented at the same time. Therefore, the ARTMAP network involves both the supervised and the unsupervised learning.

Let p_{*i} be a design problem and s_{*i} be its design solution. Let the families of the design problem be denoted by $P_1, P_2, \ldots, P_{N_a}$. Let $p_{J1}, p_{J2}, \ldots, p_{Jm_{aJ}}$ be the members of the family P_J. Let the families of design solutions be denoted by $S_1, S_2, \ldots, S_{N_b}$. Let $s_{K1}, s_{K2}, \ldots, s_{Km_{bK}}$ be the members of the family S_K.

By receiving the input stream of design problems, the ART_a module adaptively creates the families of design problems $P_1, P_2, \ldots, P_{N_a}$. Similarly, by receiving the input stream of design solutions, the ART_b adaptively creates the families of design solutions $S_1, S_2, \ldots, S_{N_b}$. The ART_a and the ART_b not only create the families adaptively but also maintain a most representative pattern of each family dynamically. Each time a new member is added to a family, the representative pattern of the family is updated. In a statistical sense, a representative pattern of a family can be considered as the mean of the family members. Let the representative patterns of $P_1, P_2, \ldots, P_{N_a}$ be denoted by $P_{m1}, P_{m2}, \ldots, P_{mN_a}$. Similarly, let the representative patterns of $S_1, S_2, \ldots, S_{N_a}$ be denoted by $S_{m1}, S_{m2}, \ldots, S_{mN_b}$.

While the ART_a and the ART_b module independently create families in design problem domain and design solution domain respectively, the Map Field builds the *map* between the families in these two domains. However, this map does not directly associate the design problems $\{p_{Ji} \mid J = 1, 2, \ldots N_a, \text{ and } i = 1, 2, \ldots, m_{aJ}\}$ to design solutions $\{s_{Ki} \mid K = 1, 2, \ldots N_b, \text{ and } i = 1, 2, \ldots, m_{bK}\}$. Instead the map is at the family level. The association is between a design problem family P_J and a design solution family S_K. If the ARTMAP is trained with a set of training pairs which covers the complete spectrum of design problems and design solutions, every family P_J in the design problem domain, possibly, should have learned a one-to-one association to a family S_K in the design solution domain. However, there is no guarantee that every family of design problems should have learned an association to a family of design solutions.

With this brief explanation of the dynamics of the ARTMAP, the following algorithm describes how to use the ARTMAP network in the conceptual design.

Step 1: Let R be the set of design problems with known design solutions. Let T be the set of training pairs to train the ARTMAP. T is defined as $T = \{(p_{*i}, s_{*i}) \mid p_{*i} \in R\}$. Initially, let there be only one design problem p_{*1} in R. Also assume that the design solution s_{*1} of the design problem p_{*1} is known.

Train the ARTMAP with the training pairs in T.

Step 2: Pick a new design problem p_{*i} and present it to the ART_a module. If there are no new design problems to be classified go to Step 6. When this new design problem p_{*i} is presented to the ART_a module, one of the following two things is possible:

1. The ART$_a$ module classifies the new design problem p_{*i} into one of the existing families P_J. If this is the case, go to Step 3.
2. If the new design problem p_{*i} is considerably different from the previously encountered design problems, the ART$_a$ module creates a new family $P_{(N_a+1)}$ and learns p_{*i} as its first member $p_{(N_a+1)1}$.

   Since the new design problem $p_{(N_a+1)1}$ is quite different from the previously solved problems, there are no plausible design solutions to assist in determining its design solution. Therefore, the best design solution to $p_{(N_a+1)1}$ is to be found through a relatively exhaustive exploration.

   If the best design solution s_{*i} to the new design problem $p_{(N_a+1)1}$ is found, use the design problem $p_{(N_a+1)i}$ and its know design solution s_{*i} to train the ARTMAP. This training will create the association between the family $P_{(N_a+1)}$ and S_K, considering that the ART$_b$ module has classified s_{*i} into S_K. Update $N_a = (N_a + 1)$. From here go to Step 2.

Step 3: Now that the new design problem p_{*i} is classified into the family P_J, there are again two possibilities.

1. The family P_J has previously learned the association to a family S_K. In such a case go to Step 4.
2. The family P_J has not learned an association to any existing family of design solutions. That means, there are no plausible design solutions to assist in determining the design solution to the design problem p_{Ji}. Therefore, the design solution to p_{Ji} is to be found through relatively an exhaustive exploration.

   If the best design solution s_{*i} to the new design problem p_{Ji} is found, use the design problem p_{Ji} and its know design solution s_{*i} to train the ARTMAP. This training will create the association between the family P_J and S_K, considering that the ART$_b$ module has classified s_{*i} into S_K. From here go to Step 2.

Step 4: At this point it is clear that p_{*i} is classified into P_J, and P_J has previously learned association to S_K. That means, the design solution s_{*i} of the new design problem p_{Ji} most likely belongs to S_K. Therefore, S_{mK} the representative pattern the family S_K can be used, with modifications if necessary, as the plausible design solution to the new design problem p_{Ji}. In addition to it, the members of the family S_K can be considered as the set of alternative plausible design solutions to the new design problem p_{Ji}. Because of this reason, the ARTMAP, can provide a one-to-one as well as a one-to-many relationship between a new design problem and the plausible design solutions.

If the best design solution s_{*i} to the new design problem p_{Ji} is found, use the design problem p_{Ji} and its know design solution s_{*i} to train the ARTMAP. This training will reinforce the existing association between the families P_J and S_K if the $\mathrm{ART_b}$ module has classified s_{*i} into S_K. Or, this training will create the association between the family P_J and S_Q if the $\mathrm{ART_b}$ module has classified s_{*i} into S_Q. From here go to Step 2.

Step 5: Classification of all new design problems is complete.

Of all the four neural network applications described above, the ARTMAP network provides the most useful application. The ARTMAP can classify both design problems and design solutions dynamically. It can also learn the design problems and design solutions independently. That means, even if the design solution is not known to a design problem, the ARTMAP can learn the design problem and vice versa. When presented with a new design problem, unlike the other three neural network applications, the ARTMAP can recall both similar design problems and plausible design solutions. Note that a multilayer neural network and an ART1 network in the classification scheme can recall only similar design problems; and a multilayer neural network in the mapping scheme can recall only a plausible design solution. Additionally, the ARTMAP can provide another advantage, though this is not included in the above algorithm. For a given arbitrary design solution, the ARTMAP can recall the plausible design problems that can be addressed by the design solution. This property of the ARTMAP can be very useful in a reverse approach in conceptual design.

4.11 Conclusions

This chapter initially discussed the nature of conceptual design and described the computer systems useful for the generation of creative solutions in this phase of design. It was proposed that the neural networks can be used for the classification and the associative recall of design problems and design solutions to assist a human designer in conceptual design. A representation scheme of design problems and design solutions for neural network applications were proposed. Following this, four important neural network schemes were described.

The usefulness of the four neural network schemes can further be improved by using the continuous valued vectors instead of the binary valued vectors for the representation of design problems and design solutions. Since the components of a vector can take continuous values between 0.0 and 1.0, they allow a more accurate representation of design problems and design solutions by assigning the varying weights to the functional requirements.[14]

4.12 References

1. H. A. Simon, *The Science of the Artificial*, (MIT Press, Cambridge, MA, 1981).

2. C. W. Churchman, *Proc. of the Congress on Planning and Design Theory, Plenary and Interdisciplinary Lecture*, (ASME, New York, 1987).

3. N. P. Suh, and S. Sekimoto, *Annals of the CIRP*, **39** (1) (1990) 145–148.

4. N. P. Suh, *The Principles of Design*, (Oxford University Press, New York, 1990).

5. E. W. Kent, *The Brains of Men and Machines*, (McGraw-Hill, Peterborough, NH, 1981).

6. Z. Zhang, and S. L. Rice, *Mechanical Engineering*, **111** (7) (1989) 58–60.

7. D. E. Rumelhart, G. E. Hinton, and R. J. Williams, *Parallel Distributed Processing: Explorations in the Microstructure of Cognition*, ed. D. E. Rumelhart and J. L. McClelland, **1**, (The MIT Press, Cambridge, MA, 1986).

8. S-T. Bow, *Pattern Recognition: Application to Large Data-Set Problems*, (Marcel Dekker Inc., New York, 1984).

9. G. A. Carpenter, and S. Grossberg, *Computer Vision, Graphics, and Image Processing*, **37** (1987) 54–115.

10. G. A. Carpenter, and S. Grossberg, *Applied Optics*, **26** (23) (1987) 4919–4930.

11. G. A. Carpenter, and S. Grossberg, *Computer*, **21** (3) (1988) 77–88.

12. S. R. T. Kumara, and S. V. Kamarthi, *Annals of the CIRP*, **41** (1) (1992) 213–216.

13. K. Hornik, M. Stincombe, and H. White, *Neural Networks*, **3** (1990) 551–560.

14. S. R. T. Kumara, and S. V. Kamarthi, *Journal of Intelligent Manufacturing*, **2** (1991) 281–292.

15. S. R. T. Kumara, and, I. Ham, *Annals of the CIRP*, **39** (1) (1990) 117–120.

16. G. A. Carpenter, and S. Grossberg, *Neural Networks* **4** (1991) 565–588.

Chapter 5

Knowledge Acquisition in Neural Networks and Expert Systems: The Case of Packer Selection in Oil Well Design

Rick L. Wilson and Ramesh Sharda
College of Business Administration
Oklahoma State University
Stillwater, OK 74078, USA

5.1 Introduction

Arguably, expert systems and neural networks have the common goals of simulating human intelligenceHuman intelligence, making knowledge available and providing training to novice personnel.[7,9] However, each approach uses different methods to achieve that goal. Expert systems try, as much as possible, to imitate the human reasoning process. They process knowledge sequentially, explicitly representing the knowledge (IF-THEN rules in a rule-based setting). Learning takes place external to the system, i.e., from the domain expert whose knowledge is extracted by the knowledge engineer. This tends to be the most time-consuming and critical portion of developing an expert system. Expert systems also use deductive reasoning in generating conclusions and recommendations, based upon the knowledge and facts presented to the system.

Conversely, neural networks offer a different approach than classical expert systems in simulating human intelligence. Neural networks simulate decision making by modeling the human brain (or how we believe the human brain to function). Information processing in neural networks is inherently parallel (though often times is simulated sequentially; thus, the term artificial neural networks). Learning in neural networks occurs internally or within the neural network. Most neural networks learn by example; the network is provided with training data showing characteristics of a particular case and the desired output. The network then 'learns' the relationships between the characteristics and desired responses as it sees a multiplicity of cases. The knowledge of neural networks is found in the internal weight structure of connecting neurons. While this process can also be time-consuming, this inductive approach to knowledge engineering does not require strict specification of IF-THEN rules or other knowledge representation schemes.

There have been very few attempts at comparing the predictive capability of rule-based expert systems as contrasted against artificial neural networks. Most studies of this nature[2] have simply compared the predictive capabilities of the two alternative approaches to that of the expert. However, this approach is subject to the interpretation errors of the human expert and the knowledge engineer. This paper directly assesses the performance of a feedforward artificial neural network to try to gain an understanding of how well a rule-based approach to decision making can be mimicked in a connectionist model. That is, the training and test cases are both generated using a rule-based system.

This exploratory study is undertaken within the domain of a design problem in the petroleum industry. The drilling and operation of an oil or gas well requires the use of a packer. Selecting an appropriate type of packer is dependent on key situation characteristics operationalized in the knowledge of a design expert. A prototype expert system had been previously developed to capture this expertise. In this study, examples used to train and test the neural network models are randomly generated from the rules of the prototype expert system. The performance of the neural network model is studied to see how well it learns the IF-THEN structure of the expert system.

The next section describes pertinent information about attributes of the problem under study. The specific design problem domain used for the study is identified and characterized. Following this, details of the development of back propagation artificial neural networks to compare to the expert system used in this problem domain are presented. Finally, we conclude with the analysis and discussion of our results.

5.2 Packer Selection Problem

The drilling and producing of an oil well usually requires the use of a *packer* during the life of the well, or at some point in the completion process. When a well is drilled, the casing (a steel pipe) is placed in the bore hole and cemented in place. Thus, the casing becomes a permanent part of the well. After this, a smaller pipe, the tubing, is placed inside the casing from the surface to the bottom of the well. A packer is then used to form a seal between the casing and the tubing at the bottom of the well.

The packer equipment has a multitude of potential uses in the construction and operation of a well. The packer can provide energy conservation, is a necessary safety feature, protects the casing of the well from corrosion and/or high pressure, and/or accounts for operation conditions which make it imperative for a packer to be part of the well design. For even the 'simplest' of well designs, packers can be extremely complex. The selection of the proper packer to suit the particular well conditions and requirements is a crucial design component for the safe completion of an oil or gas well.

Expertise is required for the proper selection of an appropriate packer. An employee new to the decision problem must learn through experience and observation of the more senior employees. In the company setting used in this study, it was estimated that the time period for this learning process can be several years before the employee can comfortably select the best packer for a given set of well conditions. Often times, the employee must verify his/her choice with the more experienced workers, the sales department and/or engineering.

Additionally, the timing of the need for this expertise is also unique. Packer orders are sometimes called in by oil companies at night or on weekends. Thus, there is a risk that the 'design experts' may not be readily available in an expedient manner. Another attribute for this company's particular situation is the geographic dispersion of service centers, where packer orders are taken. Thus, there is a need for the consistent application of design expertise across multiple service center sites.

As is seen, the characteristics of this design problem are quite conducive to the use of expert systems to help alleviate potential difficulties. First, it is obvious that expertise is required in the design process as far as determining the appropriate packer for a specific job. There are documented experts in the company that use their own set of heuristics and rules to determine appropriate packer use. As a corollary, an expert system for this problem can help beginners in packer selection become more knowledgeable in the area (i.e., the expert system can be used as a training tool).

Additionally, the geographical distribution problem and the expert accessibility problem can be assisted by capturing expertise in an expert system. The use of such captured knowledge can lead to better service provided to the oil company customers, improve the quality of decisions, and improve the consistency of such decisions throughout the company.

For this problem, a prototype, rule-based expert system was developed. A knowledgeable sales engineer at the company under study who performs the packer selection process on a regular basis was chosen as the expert. Since this was intended as a prototype expert system, the decision was kept to a manageable level. The problem domain may not be well bounded if one considers all different configurations and auxiliary equipment which is available. For this reason, the domain for this prototype expert system was limited to the selection of single string packers, which the expert felt was still a significant problem to be addressed. Basically, there were eight possible problem attributes that may be pertinent to the selection decision, and the expert system, on the basis of these attributes, provided recommendations from a set of six different single string packets. See Table 5.1 for the characteristics used in this selection decision.

Table 5.1: Packer selection problem characteristics

SETTING METHOD (1 of 3)
- Tubing
- Wireline
- Hydraulic
PACKER SETTING DEPTH (feet)
PACKER USE (at least 1 of 3)
- Treating
- Producing
- Injection
PRESSURE REQUIREMENTS (psi)

The original version of the prototype expert system provided a list of all possible packers which were appropriate for a given situation. An alternative version of the expert system could also be generated where a meta-rule can force the expert system to make only one packer recommendation (as the packer most closely matching the specifications of the design problem).

It is a common accepted perception that knowledge acquisition is the most difficult and time consuming process in the development of expert systems.[1] Neural networks may offer some advantages as contrasted to expert systems in the development of systems which simulate expert performance. Neural networks have been used previously in modeling expert performance.[3,4,5] Of interest is that neural networks do not require explicit rules to be developed and programmed. Thus, development time may be substantially reduced as contrasted with that of traditional symbolic approaches.[10] In our study, we will examine comparing the performance of neural networks to the previously developed expert system for packer selection.

5.3 Test Methodology

5.3.1 Data Set Generation

In order to develop neural networks to represent this design selection decision, paired problem characteristics - proper recommendations and observations are needed to be generated. Generation of an 'appropriate set' of input - desired output pairs is a nebulous task. Since this is an exploratory study, we did not vary the definition of what constitutes an appropriate input set. Our choice was to randomly generate an equal number of cases where one specific packer is recommended. Having equal representation of packer recommendations is based upon previous empirical findings in the neural network literature.[8] The cases were generated by randomly varying the problem characteristics, applying the rule-based expert system to determine the appropriate packer recommendation, and repeating the process until 40 instances where each packer was recommended were created. Similarly, the same process was repeated to generate 60 cases (10 for each packer type) to serve as the test set.

In order to investigate the possible effects of different size training sets, neural networks were trained on sets of 120 cases (20 cases per each packer), 180 cases (30 cases per each packer) and all 240 cases. In every set, order of presentation was random. Additionally, as previously mentioned, networks were trained to recommend only one packer (use of the 'closest match' meta-rule) as well as trained to recommend all packers who were qualified to be used in a particular situation. The same training (and testing) sets were used in each situation, with the appropriate changes to reflect the potential for multiple recommendations.

5.3.2 Neural Network Development

For this study, BRAINMAKER[6], a personal computer-based neural network software package which implements the backpropagation training algorithm, was used to construct and test trained neural network models. For each network trained in this study, a structure of 8 input neurons (one neuron for each problem characteristic), 10 hidden neurons and 6 output neurons (one neuron for each potential packer recommendation) were used. The number of hidden neurons used is always a design question in neural networks; ten hidden neurons was the default setting arrived at by BRAINMAKER and was used throughout the study.

As training cases are presented to the network, output neuron values are examined by the training procedure. For instance, consider a given training case, whose desired recommendation is the P_1 packer, that has output node values of P_1=0.87, P_2=0.01, P_3=0.12, $P_4 = P_5 = P_6$=0.0, where P_i represents the output neurons. Obviously, the desired output neuron values would have $P_1 = 1$ and the other neurons equal to zero. When training a neural network, a certain amount of variation away from the desired values is typically allowed at the output layer when determining whether the back propagation training procedure should adjust network weights to compensate. In this neural network implementation, this allowed variation is referred to as the training threshold. Thus, a training threshold of 0.1 would allow 0.1 variance at each output neuron away from the desired value without updating network weights. For the above example, such a training tolerance would cause network weights to be updated (i.e., P_1 and P_3 neurons exceed this allowed variation). Alternatively, if the training threshold was set at 0.2, no updates would be required. Note that real-time updating of the network occurred; network weights were updated when appropriate after each training case (as compared against each training epoch).

In training the networks in this study, a heuristic back propagation algorithm was used to ensure convergence (all cases in the training set were correctly classified). A stringent training threshold of 0.1 was initially used in the network and gradually relaxed until such a point when all training cases satisfied the training threshold criteria. The terminal threshold level was understandably higher for larger training

Table 5.2: Total test set correct recommendations

	RECOMMENDATIONS	
TRAINING SIZE	SINGLE	MULTIPLE
20	93.3%	93.3%
30	93.3%	93.3%
40	95.0%	93.3%

sets. The range of the terminal threshold level varied from 0.3 to a high of 0.45.

The learning rate of the network was gradually lowered through the network's evolution as the number of correct classifications increased. Initially, the rate was set at 0.8, lowered to 0.6 at 20% correct classifications, 0.4 at 40% correct classifications and 0.3 at 50% correct cases. Throughout, the smoothing rate (or momentum term) was kept constant at 0.6. Network convergence was achieved in all networks.

In evaluating the neural networks (testing the network predicted recommendations on the test set), a testing threshold, similar to the training threshold, was used. This testing threshold identified how stringent the allowable variation in output neurons can be when assessing whether the network is making a correct packer recommendation. In this study, a basic testing threshold of 0.499 was used. Thus, if an output neuron had a value that exceeded 0.5 and no other output neurons exceed that value, the network was said to recommend the corresponding packer associated with that output neuron. Cases where the network made more than one recommendation (more than one output neuron had values > 0.5) and where the network made no recommendation (no output neurons > 0.5) are further discussed in the results section.

5.4 Results

The measure used to determine how well neural networks can generalize about the packer selection problem is the performance of the network on packer use and design situations in the test set. Table 5.1 provides some raw performance data for the neural networks developed. As mentioned in the previous section, networks were trained on three different sized data sets (20, 30 and 40 cases each per packer) and were trained to make either a single recommendation or multiple recommendations based on the rule structure of the existing expert system. Table 5.2 indicates that the neural network was able to classify more than 93% of the cases correctly, and in one instance, made 95% correct recommendations.

Table 5.3 presents the information by packer type for each training set for the single recommendation approach. The percentages shown in Tables 5.2 and 5.3 include some exceptions to the 0.499 testing threshold limit previously identified. These exceptions are discussed below.

Table 5.3: Individual correct packer recommendations - test set

	PACKER TYPE					
TRAINING	P_1	P_2	P_3	P_4	P_5	P_6
20	100%	90%	100%	100%	90%	80%
30	100%	90%	90%	100%	90%	90%
40	100%	90%	100%	100%	90%	90%

Tables 5.4 and 5.5 provide a more detailed description of the specific testing cases that are somewhat problematic. Table 5.4 presents test case information when the network provides a single recommendation, while Table 5.5 illustrates similar data about the neural network test cases when in the multiple recommendation mode. Note that the case number is included only to help differentiate among the individual cases. As will be discussed, in almost all cases where a neural network could not recommend the proper packer, there existed a 'borderline' condition. Such a condition can be characterized as approaching a demarcation point, based on the design problem's specifications, where one packer's 'range of recommendability' is ending and another packer's 'range' is just beginning. This occurs as a function of the numerical rules in the expert system.

As mentioned above, there were some cases (notably, cases 23, 44, 51 and 53) where more than one packer was recommended by the neural network. In all of these cases, there was a packer whose corresponding output neuron was unquestionably activated much higher than the other. Thus, the neural network clearly distinguished which packer was recommended for the specific problem conditions. If the highest activated neuron did correspond to the expert systems recommendation, it was treated as a correct decision (cases 23, 44, 51 and 53). If this was not true (case 58), the recommendation of the neural network was treated as erroneous.

There was also one test case (case 25) where no output neurons met the testing threshold. However, the P_3 output neuron was the highest activated neuron, significantly larger than all others. Since P_3 was the recommended packer provided of the expert system, this case was counted as a correct decision by the neural network.

The other test cases identify where the neural network did not make the correct recommendation (as defined by the expert system). There appeared to be an underlying, dominant theme in these occurrences. The numeric characteristics of the depth and pressure characteristics of the problem domain closely matched cut-off points where the rule-based system would change its recommendation from one packer type to another. In essence, most of the misclassifications occurred when one of either the depth or pressure characteristic met the specifications of both the correct and incorrectly recommended packer, while the other numeric characteristic narrowly exceeded (or was narrowly below) the specification of the packer incorrectly recommended by the neural network. For instance, consider case 47, where the expert system recommends P_5 and the neural network recommends P_4. Both packer types met the desired

Table 5.4: Test case analysis - single recommendation networks

CASE #	ES	NN	TRAINING	CASE CHARACTERISTICS
20	P_2	P_1	all	Pressure matched/depth conflict
23[a]	P_3	P_3	20	Two recommendations - P_4 also
25[a]	P_3	P_3	20	No recommendations - $P_3 = 0.436$
26	P_3	P_2	30	Pressure matched/depth conflict
44[a]	P_5	P_5	20	Two recommendations - P_1 also
47	P_5	P_4	all	Depth matched/pressure conflict
53[a]	P_6	P_6	30	Two recommendations - P_3 also
	P_6	P_3	40	Depth matched/pressure conflict
55	P_6	P_3	20,40	Pressure matched/depth conflict
58	P_6	P_5	20	Two recommended - P_5 highest, P_6
			30	Depth matched/pressure conflict

KEY:

ES - expert system recommendation for appropriate packer type
NN - neural network recommendation for appropriate packer type
TRAINING - per packer training set size applicable for the case
CASE CHARACTERISTICS - specific identification of why case was problematic

[a] case counted as correct recommendation

setting method and packer use characteristics of the problem. Both types can also be used in design situations at the depth of this particular problem instance. However, the pressure requirements of this situation narrowly exceed the upper limit for P_4. Thus, it appears that the neural network has not learned the exact upper bound on the pressure variables found in the rule-based expert system.

As shown in Table 5.4 under the heading Case Characteristics, the other cases where the neural network recommends packers incorrectly, had similar characteristics. For instance, case 55, where P_6 is the correct packer (according to the expert system) and P_3 is the choice of the neural network, the two packers both are applicable for the pressure requirements of the particular design case, whereas the depth requirements barely exceed the stated limits of P_3's applicability.

Table 5.5 is a similar identification of troublesome cases when the network was trained to make multiple recommendations. There was some difficulty in recommending P_2 as one of a group of applicable packers (cases 8, 9, 11 and 14). P_2 possesses very similar characteristics to P_1, and this probably led to the network's difficulties. Also note that in case 8 (trained with the 20 cases per packer set), case 14 and case 37, one of the desired recommended packers had an output neuron activation level less than 0.5, but still significantly different from others and greater than 0.45. These cases were counted as a correct packer choice by the neural network. Case 24 was another instance of where the neural network recommends two packers when only one was appropriate. The neural network did correctly choose P_3 (its activation level considerably higher than P_6); of interest is that the problem characteristics had depth requirements of exactly the upper limit on the third packer's applicability in design.

In summary, the neural network performed at an overall rate of better than 93% correct recommendations. The recommendation successes differed for the various packer types. Developing neural networks from enhanced training sets with additional training instances did not seem to aid in their ability to capture more expertise in the packer selection process. In analyzing the incorrect neural network recommendations, there appeared to be a recurrent theme. The continuous problem characteristic variables, pressure and depth, seemed to be the 'cause' of the incorrect choices. Specifically, the neural network did not universally learn the exact upper or lower bounds found in some of the rules of the expert system.

5.5 Discussion and Conclusions

In general, the neural network models appeared to mimic the rule-based expert system used in packer selection fairly well. Obviously, a performance level of 100% accuracy would be desired for a high level of confidence when considering the use of neural networks in place of a rule-based approach for this specific design problem. However, we believe the results are promising and would like to discuss a couple of issues raised by this study.

First, the random generation of cases used in the training and testing sets may

Table 5.5: Test case analysis - multiple recommendation networks

CASE #	ES	NN	TRAIN	CASE CHARACTERISTICS
4	P_1P_3	P_1	40	$P_3 = 0.37$ (close)
8	$P_1P_2P_3P_6$	$P_1P_3P_6$	30,40	$P_2 < 0.25$
[a]		$P_1P_2P_3P_6$	20	$P_2 = 0.45$
9	$P_1P_2P_3P_6$	$P_1P_3P_6$	20,30	$P_2 < 0.23$
[a]		$P_1P_2P_3P_6$	40	$P_2 = 0.44$
11	$P_1P_2P_3P_6$	$P_1P_2P_3P_6$	20,30	$P_2 = 0.25$
14[a]	$P_2P_3P_6$	$P_2P_3P_6$	40	$P_2 = 0.46$
20	$P_2P_3P_6$	P_2P_6	20	low pressure
24[a]	P_3	P_3P_6	30,40	two recommended. P_2 also
37[a]	$P_4P_5P_6$	P_5P_6	20	$P_4 = 0.48$ (at cutoff pressure for P_4)
47	P_5P_6	$P_4P_5P_6$	all	depth matched/pressure conflict
58	P_6	P_5P_6	20,40	depth matched/pressure conflict

KEY: NN - neural network recommendation for appropriate packer type

TRAIN - per packer training set size applicable for the case

CASE CHARACTERISTICS - specific identification of why case was problematic

[a]case counted as correct recommendation

impact the assessment of the neural networks' recommendation ability. However, the random generation procedure was necessary in order to achieve any kind of meaningful results in this experiment. As it turns out, it appeared that the number of training cases that presented packer recommendation 'cut-off points' between two different packers were under represented. The neural network learned to make proper recommendations in many situations, but did not do quite as well where hard limits or constraints were placed on packer applicability. For instance, consider this hypothetical rule sequence in the packer selection expert system:

$$R(1)\ \text{If depth} \leq 3000, \quad \text{recommend} \quad P_1$$

$$R(2)\ \text{If depth} > 3000, \quad \text{recommend} \quad P_2$$

The neural network models often had a difficult time making the proper recommendation if the depth was 2900, exactly 3000 or 3100. As was seen in the Results section, may of the incorrect packer selections occurred at such hard boundary points.

The implication of using neural networks as a system providing expertise from this seems straightforward. Exemplar cases in the training set must appropriately represent these hard, continuous variable numeric boundary points. Care must be undertaken to include cases in the training set to allow the neural network to learn and generalize from both sides of such constraints. In this packer selection problem, the neural network dealt well with the categorical situational variables (how the packer was used, the desired setting method), but not as well with numerical constraints on packer applicability. Initial evidence would suggest that more emphasis in the neural network learning process should be placed on adequately representing such constraints and that these concepts may be more difficult to learn than other relationships.

Second, it is unlikely in this problem domain that there would be an equal probability of each packer being recommended the same number of times over a given finite time frame. Likewise, the random generation of case characteristics probably does not mirror the actual case characteristics distributions. While past empirical studies have indicated that neural network developers should use an equal distribution across categories in the training set,[8] testing accuracy may be negatively impacted by such an approach in constructing the test sets in this domain. In this study, the ability of the neural network to properly recommend the selections of P_4 and P_1 appeared flawless. If most actual design problem characteristics match situations similar to those cases, then accuracy figures reported here may be understated. Both of the points mentioned above simply identify the limitations of the pure random approach in generating the data used in developing and evaluating the neural networks from the expert system.

The flexibility employed in interpreting correct recommendations should not be viewed as a negative comment on neural network performance. The hard and fast rules of the expert system are simply heuristic guidelines used by the expert. Having the neural network recommend two different packers when the expert system recommends one is just an indication that there is not a clear cut decision on which packer is most appropriate. These situations only indicate that the neural network is recognizing the existence of a boundary point or a hard constraint limit falling near the given set of design circumstances.

While the increased training set size appeared to have no impact, these results only show that the first set of 120 cases adequately allows the neural network to learn the basic packer characteristics. As previously mentioned, specific cases intended to delineate the number of quantitative rule constraints in the expert system would have to be added in order to improve the neural network recommendation accuracy. As a potential factor affecting network performance, it appears that 'quality' of training cases may outweigh quantity, but this assertion is only speculative.

As with any experiment involving neural networks, the choice of network structure, the network training approach and other pertinent factors may impact the results of the study. Since the intent of this study was introductory in nature, there was no investigation into the impact of neural network specifications on packer selection performance. Obviously, this would potentially be an area for future study.

The results of this study of neural networks as a comparative intelligent advisory system to rule-based expert systems were relatively encouraging. Achieving at least 93.3% accuracy in recommendations appears to be a good performance. By further investigating how neural networks can better emulate rule based systems in this and other domains, the entire field of encapsulating human intelligence can be advanced.

Neural networks offer distinct advantages in the area of systems which capture expertise. One such advantage is that there may not explicitly be a domain expert involved in the capture of knowledge in the neural network approach. Past cases can be used in training the neural network. In practice, it is also not reasonable to expect the expert to think of every potential problem, especially as circumstances may change. Therefore, expert systems do have some limitations in terms of their ability to generalize or to adapt to a changing environment. Neural networks, on the other hand, specifically can adapt to changing information (retraining) and by their nature are designed to be able to generalize above and beyond just from the training cases presented in their construction phase. There have been a number of documented studies which have shown the potential generalization capabilities of neural networks.[8]

However, as compared to expert systems, neural networks do possess some potential shortcomings. The lack of explicitly stated rules and, additionally, the inability to generate a reasoning path due to the unique knowledge representation scheme, may make neural networks less acceptable to the user of such a system. These items may arise since the internal weights of the neural network, where 'knowledge' is stored, are difficult to interpret.

Ultimately, as neural network technology matures and more evidence is presented regarding the potential of neural networks, one can expect that expert systems and neural networks will be used together in a synergistic fashion for modelling human intelligence and decision making.[7] Of interest in this study is how well neural networks can learn rules from an existing expert system. If one is to take advantage of the generalizability and adaptability of neural networks as compared to the capability of expert systems, we must have confidence that the representations of knowledge prevalently used today can be adequately handled in the neural network approach to knowledge processing. If neural networks can adequately mimic such representations, existing expert systems can be dynamically adapted via the connectionist approach in the future. Similarly, future knowledge-based systems can be generated by neural network learning rather than through the sometimes painful knowledge engineering process.

5.6 References

1. T. Byrd, K. Cossick, and R. Zmud, "A synthesis of research on requirements analysis and knowledge acquisition techniques," *MIS Quarterly* (March, 1992) 117-138.

2. R. Fozzard,G. Bradshaw, and L. Ceci, "A connectionist expert system that actually works," in *Advances in Neural Information Processing Systems*, I, D. Touretsky, ed., (Morgan Kauffman, San Mateo, CA, 1989) 248-255.

3. S. Gallant, "Connectionist expert systems," *Communications of the ACM,* **31** (2) (February, 1988) 152-169.

4. C. Gingrich, D. Keuspert, and T. McAvoy, "Modeling human operators using neural networks," *ISA Transactions*, **31** (3) (1992) 81-90.

5. K. Saito, and R. Nakano, "Medical diagnostic expert system based on pdp model," *Proceedings of the IEEE International Conference on Neural Networks*, San Diego, CA (1988).

6. J. Stanley, and E. Bak, *Introduction to Neural Networks.* (California Scientific Software, Sierra Madre, CA, 1989).

7. W. VerDuin, "The role of integrated ai technologies in product formulation," *ISA Transactions*, **31** (2) (1992) 151-157.

8. R. Wilson, and R. Sharda, "Bankruptcy prediction using neural networks," *Decision Support System*, in press (1993).

9. F. Zahedi, "An introduction to neural networks and a comparison with artificial intelligence and expert systems," *Interfaces*, **21** (2) (Mar-Apr 1991), 25-38.

10. M. Zeidenberg, *Neural Network Models in Artificial Intelligence*, (Ellis Horwood, New York, 1991).

Chapter 6

Setup Generation and Feature Sequencing Using an Unsupervised Learning Algorithm

C. L. Philip Chen
Department of Computer Science and Engineering
Wright State University
Dayton, OH 45435 USA

Abstract

An unsupervised learning algorithm is presented which categorizes the design features in a setup for machining process. Setup generation is a major task in automated process planning. Based on generated setups, fixture configuration can then be realized. A setup is formed based on approach direction of features and tool types for making the features. The proposed algorithm and architecture incorporate multiple objective functions into setup generation. Intersected and non-intersected features within a setup are identified. Associative memory approach along with a geometric approach is used to identify intersected features and the sequences of making them. After the feature sequence is determined, several algorithms are proposed to obtain the best tool sequence of making the features in a setup.

6.1 Introduction

This paper presents setup generation and feature sequencing in process planning using neural networks unsupervised learning method. To machine a single part, the geometric description of the part model is needed to be specified first. Recently, using feature-based design environment (FBDE),[1,2] the geometric model of the desired part can be generated. The FBDE allows the users to create a part by specifying the feature types, attachment faces and dimensions of predefined features interactively.

Feature translation stage translates the design feature to the manufacturing feature for the machining process. The machining operation of a feature includes cutting tool specification, depth of cuts, feed rates, number of paths, total machining time, etc. Currently, the Rapid Design Systems[3] is an example that is developed successfully to generate these data.

Setup sequencing is a method to collect groups of features to be made and to determine sequence necessary to make these features in certain fixturing configurations build-up. A setup is a fixturing configuration to process features using tool(s) and fixturing element(s). To machine a single part with several features, a number of different setups may be required. Features within a setup may be intersected or interacted. The sequence of making features within one setup is an important issue. Within a setup, one feature may require several tools to make. The sequence of making features within one setup using the minimum number of tool changes is an important job for reducing part formation time. Setup planning is a planning process to generate setup sequencing and fixture generation. It includes how to decide the configuration of the fixture components as well as the location of the components to be clamped to the workpiece. Based on approach direction and tool commonality, similar features are collected for a setup. Several related works in this area are discussed in the following paragraphs.

Hayes[4] proposed a squaring graph that outlines all methods for getting the raw material into a square shape with minimal material waste. The graph indicates sequences for processing the raw material. Hayes also defined interaction graph that discovers possible features interaction and sequence to process these features from the pre-defined rules acquired from machinists. By finding the commonality between squaring and interaction graph, setup sequence and feature sequence can be roughly determined. The system did not discuss the important issue concerning how the features are collected together in one particular setup. Determining how features are collected in one setup can reduce the tool changes and solve the sequence of features.

Chang[5] grouped feature clusters based on tool approach direction. He then defined precedence among different features and machining processing. He defined approach and feed directions used for setup generation. "The approach direction of a feature is an unobstructed path that a tool can take to access the feature in the workpiece. The feed direction of a feature is the direction of tool motion necessary to cut the feature." Two levels of sequencing can be determined. The global level determines the final cluster and its sequence. The setup level determines the feasibility of the features to be made in the particular setup. The first level finds the feature clusters based on tool approach direction. A feature can appear in one cluster only. Based on the pre-defined precedence constraint, a cluster can be refined. The second level refines the clusters again based on commonality of the tools. Clusters are reordered if there is any conflict on pre-defined precedence.

In most current systems, a setup is formed by grouping features that have the same approach direction. A setup is redundant and needs to be eliminated if all its features belong to other setups. In order to keep one feature stay in one and only one cluster, most current systems need to detect whether a feature is in other clusters. This process needs to compare all the features in every cluster. The clusters are refined based on commonality of the tools to minimize the number of tool changes.

The Rapid Design System (RDS)[3] is a Wright Laboratory in-house research project to integrate product and process design using an advanced Computer-Aided Design/Manufacturing/Inspection System for machined parts. The RDS provides both generative and variant (or retrieval) planning approaches. One of the goals of the RDS is to dramatically reduce the time it takes to go from design (sketches, engineering drawings, or CAD models) to the manufacture (and inspection) of a part. It is anticipated that the RDS will enable the same or next day production of machined parts.

The RDS has been developed using interactive Feature-Based Design Environment (FBDE) graphical environment for creating, manipulating, and editing a feature-based part model. The designer designs by adding feature instance to the starting feature. The set of currently available features is shown in Figure 6.1.

The RDS is designed to achieve this objective by giving immediate manufacturing feedback to the designer, thereby giving the designer the ability to assess the manufacturability of a given design as he/she creates it. The designer will no longer "just" design a part and let the manufacturing engineer figure out how to make it. The RDS will also capture the knowledge of the shop floor personnel, so that all the manufacturing expertise of the shop may be applied to every job, instead of the few jobs that the shop expert(s) sees. This paper addresses setup generation and feature sequencing in the RDS.

The proposed approach uses a self-organized, unsupervised learning scheme to group similar features based on not only approach direction but also tool commonality. Different with previous work[5] the proposed research determines the setups with consideration of tool approach direction and commonality of tools in one step. Algorithms for sequencing features and sequencing tools among features are also determined.

6.2 Setup Generation

Let us define *approach direction of a feature* to be an unobstructed path that a tool can take to access the feature in the workpiece. Some features may have more than one approach direction. Because of this multiple approach directions, one feature may be grouped to more than one cluster. The proposed method will eliminate this ambiguity. The approach directions of features are listed in Table 6.1. A set of feasible operations are needed to process a feature. Each operation may need more than one tool. Tool selection rules for making a particular feature are stored in database.

Suppose a feature, F_i, needs a set of tools, T_i, to process, where $T_i \subseteq \mathbf{T}$, $\mathbf{T}$ is the tool set. We can represent a set of tools, T_i, by an *n-ordered-tuple*,

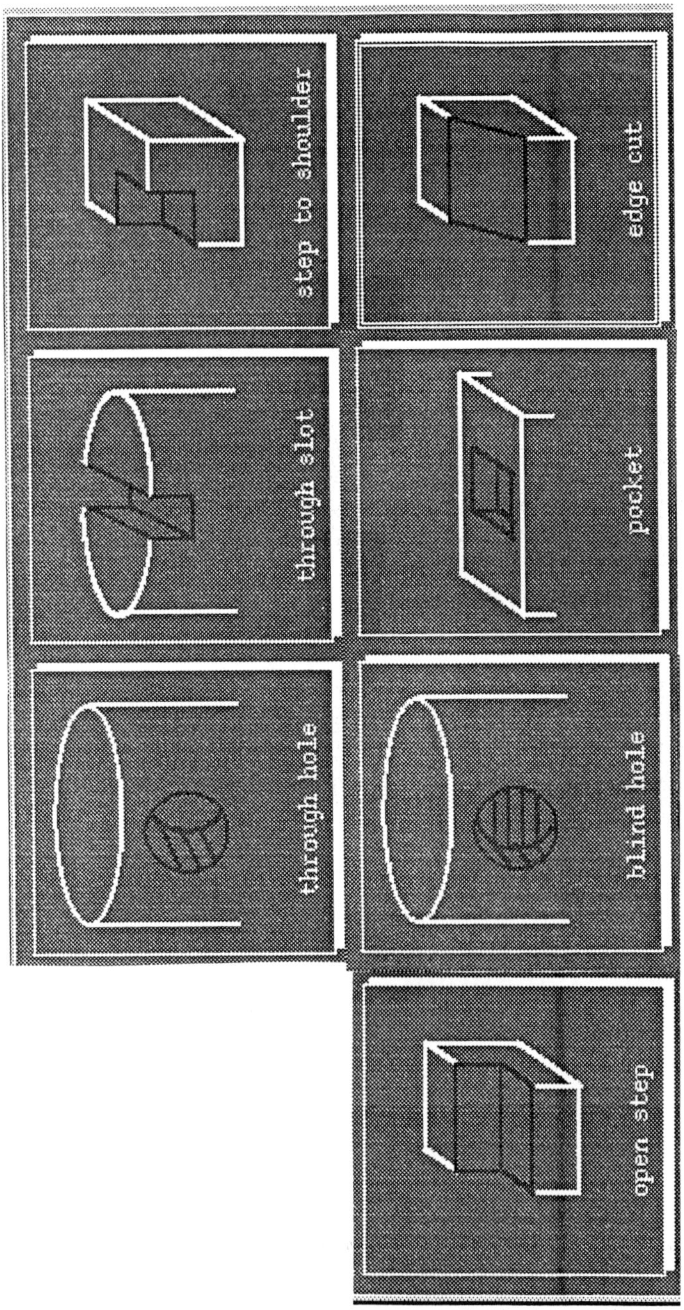

Figure 6.1: The supported features

Table 6.1: Approach directions of features

Features	Number of Approach Direction
Blind-hole	1
Through-hole	2
Blind-pocket	1
Open-step	2
Through-slot	1
Edge-cut	2
Step-to-Shoulder	3

$< {}^it_1, {}^it_2, {}^it_3, \ldots, {}^it_n >$. Each element in the n-tuple represents the tool needed for processing the feature F_i. We can define binary values, 0 or 1, to the value of each element. If the value of the element is 1, the corresponding tool is needed for processing the feature F_i; otherwise the corresponding tool bit is set to 0. Therefore, a set of tools needed to process a feature is represented by a binary pattern.

Approach direction can be determined similarly. If we fix the workpiece in a fixed orientation, we can define approach direction of a feature by a six-digit of ordered binary pattern, $< +x, +y, +z, -x, -y, -z >$. If a digit is 1, the feature can be made using the corresponding approach direction to process. The feed direction of a feature (i.e., the direction of tool motion necessary to cut the feature) can be determined based on the geometry of features and workpiece material. Based on the above definition, the setup can be generated automatically using the unsupervised learning algorithm. The concept of general unsupervised learning algorithm is given next.

6.2.1 General Unsupervised Learning

In this research, the role of unsupervised learning is to cluster patterns based on their feature-values. The feature-values for the setup generation are binary patterns defined above. Cluster size is controlled by some distance function. Refer to the learning network structure shown in Figure 6.2, The network has bottom-up weight (b_{ij}), the N-digit input patterns (x_i, $1 \leq i \leq N$), and the output clusters. The initial bottom-up weight (i.e., b_{i1}) is $x_i^{(1)}$; that is the bottom-up weight of the first cluster, b_{i1}, is equal to the first pattern, i.e., $x_i^{(1)}$, $1 \leq i \leq N$. When every new cluster is self-organized, the initial bottom-up weight of this new cluster will be the input pattern that forms this cluster. Based on the defined distance measure and cluster size, clusters are self-organized. The unsupervised learning algorithm is listed in the following.

General Unsupervised Learning Algorithm

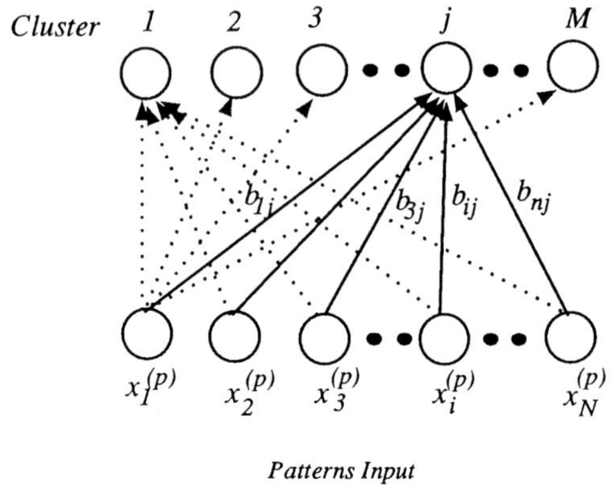

Figure 6.2: General architecture for unsupervised leanrning

Step 1: [*Initialize and form the first cluster.*] Let $b_{i1}(0) = x_i^{(1)}$, $1 \leq i \leq N$, $p \leftarrow 2$, and set a threshold value, Γ.

Step 2: [*Apply a new input,* $\mathbf{x}^{(p)}$.]

Step 3: [*Compute distance and threshold test.*] Find a cluster j for which the distance measure, ξ, satisfies the threshold value limit, continue; otherwise, go to Step 5.

Step 4: [*Update connective weight for cluster* j.] $b_{ij}(s+1) = g(x_i^{(p)}, b_{ij}(s))$, where $g(\cdot)$ is the weight update function. Record this pattern to this cluster. If all input patterns have been applied, stop; otherwise, set $p \leftarrow p+1$ and go to Step 2.

Step 5: [*Create a new cluster,* k.] Let $b_{ik}(0) = x_i^{(p)}$. If all input patterns have been applied, stop; otherwise, set $p \leftarrow p+1$ and go to Step 2.

End of General Unsupervised Learning Algorithm

Usually, the distance measure is the hypersphere radius or the Euclidean distance between the pattern p and the center of the cluster. Use the network shown in Figure 6.2. If the Euclidean distance measure is used, the Euclidean distance between a pattern, $\mathbf{x}^{(p)}$, and cluster j is defined as $\xi = \sum_{i=1}^{N}(b_{ij} - x_i^{(p)})^2$, where b_{ij} is the weight of the links between ith element of pattern p and cluster j, and $x_i^{(p)}$ is the ith element of the input pattern p, $1 \leq i \leq N$. A new cluster will be formed if the distance measure of a given pattern and existing clusters are within the limit of the threshold value.

The updated weight for the bottom-up weight of cluster j in $(s+1)$th iteration when pattern p is given is based on the following equation.

$$b_{ij}(s+1) = g(x_i^{(p)}, b_{ij}(s)),$$

where $g(\cdot)$ is the weight updated function. One example for the update function is $b_{ij}(s+1) = A_i x_i^{(p)} + B_j b_{ij}(s)$, where $A_j = 1/(n_j+1)$ is to average out the input pattern, p, to all existing patterns in the clusters; and $B_i = n_j/(n_j+1)$ is to average out the existing weights, where n_j is the number of the patterns that fall into the same cluster (i.e., cluster j).

Using the unsupervised learning algorithm a cluster can be formed automatically based on similarity of the features. The algorithm updates the weight based on the similarity function. Using this algorithm, groups of features can be generated. Each group represents a setup. Next section discusses weight updated criteria for function $g(\cdot)$ for setup generation.

6.2.2 Weight Update: AND update and OR update Rules

In order to determine clusters of features that have the same approach direction and common tools, we represent a feature by a $6+n$ binary ordered pattern. That is a pattern, F_p, is represented by the feature-value of <*Approach Direction, Tool Type*>, or specifically, the value of $< +x, +y, +z, -x, -y, -z,\ {}^pt_1,\ {}^pt_2, \ldots,\ {}^pt_n >$, where the superscript denotes the feature p. We then divide the neural networks into two subnets approach direction subnet and tools subnet. Each subnet has its own weight updating rule. For the approach direction the logic AND operation is used, while for the tools subnet we use the logic OR operation. The update criteria are explained below.

As shown in Table 6.1, some features may have more than one approach direction. As we discussed above, these multiple approach directions may cause ambiguity of assigning features to clusters a feature is assigned to more than one cluster. The logic AND operation is to eliminate this ambiguity. The AND operation applies to the bit level; that is if the corresponding approach direction digit is 1, then $b_{ij}(s+1)$ is updated correspondingly. For example, if we have an approach direction sub-pattern, ${}^ax_i, < 1,0,1,0,0,0 >$, which corresponds to approach from $+x$ and $+z$ directions, and it forms a cluster. If another sub-pattern with approach direction $< 1,1,0,0,0,0 >$ enters to the network, the updated $b_{ij}(s+1)$ weight is $< 1,0,0,0,0,0 >$, which means this cluster has common approach direction on $+x$ direction. If other patterns whose sub-patterns share this information, we can assign these patterns into the same cluster based on the similarity measure ξ and threshold value Γ. According to the AND updating rule, the update weight for cluster j is thus ${}^ab_{ij}(s+1) = {}^ax_i^{(p)}$ AND ${}^ab_{ij}(s) = {}^ax_i^{(p)}\ {}^ab_{ij}(s)$, where ${}^ax_i^{(p)}$ is the approach direction sub-pattern, $< +x, +y, +z, -x, -y, -z >$, of pattern p.

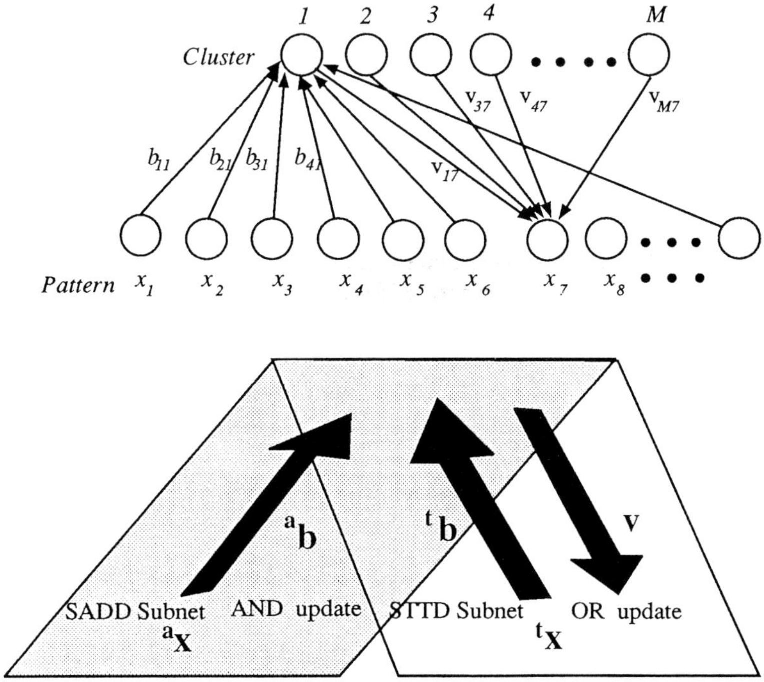

Figure 6.3: The proposed architecture for setup generation

The approach direction information dominates the cluster forming. Two features cannot be clustered together if two features have common tools but no common approach directions. Since for grouping the clusters the approach direction information is more important than tools commonality, we can refine clusters after approach direction information is found. That is, we don't assign a feature to a cluster before we discover tools commonality information. Based on this, we can design a subnet that discovers features that have similar (exactly or partially the same) approach directions. As shown in Figure 6.3, the subnet SADD (Similar Approach Direction Discovery) takes the approach direction sub-pattern as input and assign the feature to clusters that have similar approach direction temporarily. The subnet STTD (Similar Tool Type Direction Discovery) takes the tool type sub-pattern as input and assigns the feature to a cluster that shares the information of both similar approach direction and maximum tool type overlap. The STTD subnet that discovers cluster information based on tool commonality is discussed in the following.

The STTD subnet takes tools information that makes a feature. A feature may need several tools to machine. Features in a cluster may share some common tools (but not always all the same tools). If we can assign features that have most common tools in a cluster, then the number of tool changes in a setup may be reduced. To increase this possibility, according to the tool sub-pattern of a feature, we can design an OR update rule to update the weight in a particular cluster. The logic OR operation is to increase probability of common tools. Similar to the AND operation, the OR operation also applies to the bit level; that is, if the corresponding tool digit is 1, then $b_{ij}(s+1)$ is updated correspondingly. For example, if we have a tool sub-pattern, $< 1,0,1,0,0,1 >$, which means to make this feature, tools t_1, t_3, and t_6 are needed. And suppose that this tool set forms a cluster. If another sub-pattern with tool sub-pattern, ${}^t x_i$, $< 0,1,1,0,0,0 >$ enters to the network and is assigned to this cluster, the updated $b_{ij}(s+1)$ weight is $< 1,1,1,0,0,1 >$, which means this cluster needs tools t_1, t_2, t_3, and t_6. If other patterns whose sub-patterns share this information, we can assign these patterns into the same cluster based on the similarity measure ξ and threshold value Γ. According to the OR updating rule, the weight is thus ${}^t b_{ij}(s+1) = {}^t x_i^{(p)}$ OR ${}^t b_{ij}(s) = f({}^t x_i^{(p)} + {}^t b_{ij}(s))$, where ${}^t x_i^{(p)}$ is the tool sub-pattern $< {}^p t_1, {}^p t_2, {}^p t_3, \ldots, {}^p t_n >$, and $f(\eta) = 1$ if $\eta \geq 1$, or $f(\eta) = 0$ otherwise.

In STTD subnet, in addition to bottom-up weight ${}^t b_{ij}$, there are top-down weights v_{ij}. The top-down weight is to feedback the selected similar approach direction clusters to the tool sub-pattern. Using this feedback weight combining with the tool sub-pattern, we can assign a feature to a cluster that has both similar approach direction and maximum tool type overlap. The Self-Organized Setup Generation (SOSG) algorithm that discovers setup clusters is given below.

Self-Organized Setup Generation (SOSG) Algorithm

Input Feature-names, feature-values, approach direction sub-patterns, ${}^a x_i$, $1 \leq i \leq N_a$, and tool sub-patterns, ${}^t x_i, 1 \leq i \leq N_t$.

Output Setups that consist of features and the number of setups, M.

Step S1: [*Initialize and form the first cluster.*] Let ${}^a\mathbf{b}_1 \triangleq {}^a b_{i1}(0) = {}^a x_i^{(1)}, {}^t\mathbf{b}_1 \triangleq {}^t b_{i1}(0) = {}^t x_i^{(1)}, p \leftarrow 2$, and set the similarity measure, $\Gamma = 1$, where ${}^a b_{ij}$ is the connective weight between the input ${}^a x_i$ (i.e., approach direction) and the cluster j; and ${}^t b_{ij}$ is the connective weight between the input ${}^t x_i$ (i.e., tool type) and the cluster j.

Step S2: [*Apply a new input,* $, \mathbf{x}^{(p)}$.] Apply a new input, $\mathbf{x}^{(p)} \triangleq ({}^a\mathbf{x}^{(p)}, {}^t\mathbf{x}^{(p)})$, and set the top-down weight $\mathbf{v}_m \triangleq v_{im} = 0$, $m = 1, 2, \ldots M$.

Step S3: [*Compute similarity and threshold test.*] Select all possible clusters for which $\sum_{i=1}^{N_a} {}^a x_i^{(p)}\, {}^a b_{im} \geq \Gamma$, for $m = 1, 2, \ldots M$, where M is the number of clusters that have been discovered. Let J be the number of the selected clusters and set $v_{im}(t) = {}^t b_{im}$, $m = 1, 2, \ldots J$. Store this pattern to these clusters temporarily and continue to next step; otherwise, no such clusters can be found, go to Step S6.

In this step, the approach direction of all the clusters that match with the given input, even with only one digit, are selected. The top-down weight of the selected clusters, v_{im}, $m = 1, 2, \ldots, J$, are set to ${}^t b_{im}$.

Step S4: [*Discover cluster based on tool commonality*] The decision for assigning the input to a cluster is performed as follows:

$$y_m = \sum_{i=1}^{N_t} v_{im} {}^t x_i^{(p)}, \quad m = 1, 2, \ldots, M. \tag{6.1}$$

In this step, selection of the best matching existing cluster, j, is performed according to the maximum criteria as follows:

$$y_j = \max_{m=1,2,\ldots,J} y_m. \tag{6.2}$$

Step S5: [*Update connective weight.*] Record this pattern to this cluster (i.e., j) and update

$${}^a b_{ij}(s+1) = {}^a x_i^{(p)} {}^a b_{ij}(s), \tag{6.3}$$

$${}^t b_{ij}(s+1) = f({}^t x_i^{(p)} + {}^t b_{ij}(s)), \tag{6.4}$$

where $f(\eta) = 1$ if $\eta \geq 1$, or $f(\eta) = 0$ otherwise. In this step only the weight of the cluster j with the maximum matching tools is updated.

If all input patterns have been applied, stop; otherwise, set $p \leftarrow p + 1$ and go to Step S2.

Step S6: [*Create a new cluster, k.*] Let ${}^a b_{ik}(0) = {}^a x_i^{(p)}$, ${}^t b_{ik}(0) = {}^t x_i^{(p)}$. If all input patterns have been applied, stop; otherwise, set $p \leftarrow p + 1$, $k \leftarrow k + 1$ and go to Step S2.

End of Self-Organized Setup Generation Algorithm.

An example is given to illustrate stages of learning of the SOSG algorithm and designed network. A design with 12 features shown in Figure 6.4 is given. Features 1 to 4 are open pockets, feature 5 is a shoulder, features 6 and 7 are blind holes, features 8 to 11 are through holes, and feature 12 is a shoulder. The approach directions and the tool types for each feature are listed in Table 6.2, where a feature is represented by a row pattern. The stages of operation are enumerated as follows.

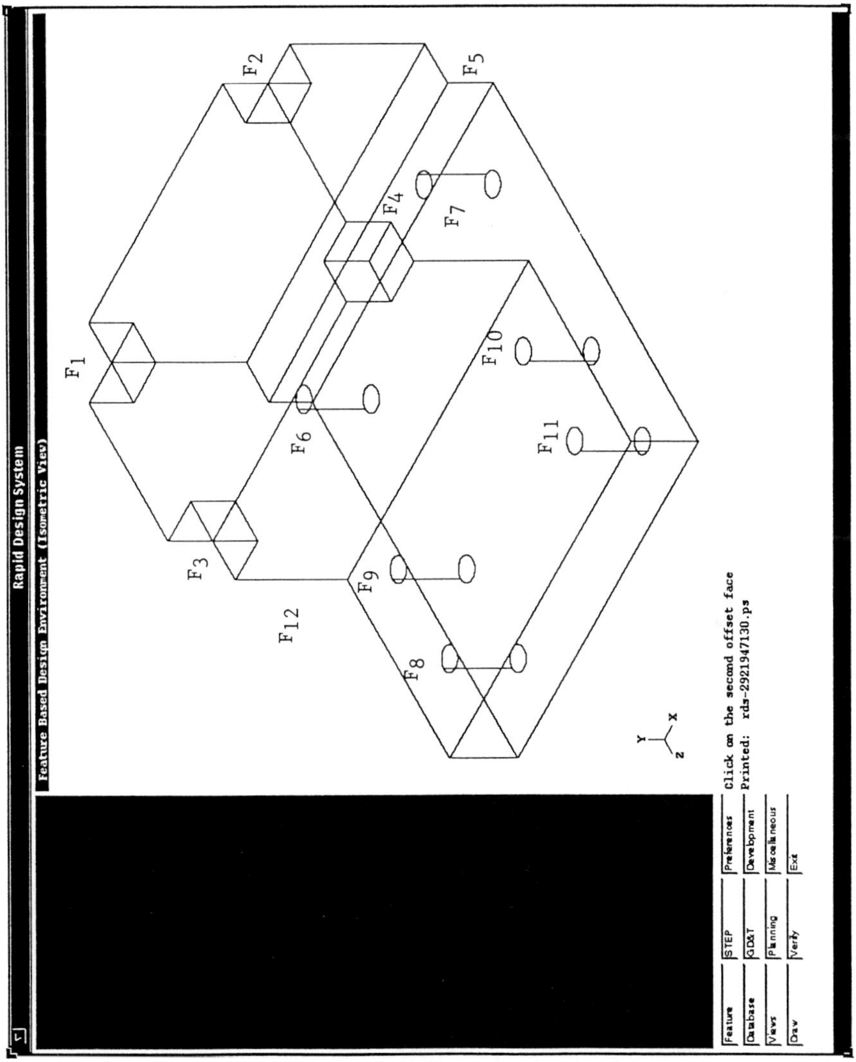

Figure 6.4: A sample part

Table 6.2: Features and approach directions of a sample part

Features	$+x$	$+y$	$+z$	$-x$	$-y$	$-z$	t_1	t_2	t_3	t_4	t_5	t_6	t_7	t_8
F_1	1	0	1	0	1	0	1	1	0	1	0	0	0	1
F_2	0	0	1	1	1	0	1	1	0	1	0	0	0	1
F_3	1	0	0	0	1	0	1	1	0	1	0	0	0	1
F_4	0	0	0	1	1	0	1	1	0	1	0	0	0	1
F_5	1	1	1	1	0	0	1	1	0	1	0	1	0	0
F_6	0	1	0	0	0	0	1	0	1	1	0	0	0	0
F_7	0	1	0	0	0	0	1	0	1	1	0	0	0	0
F_8	0	1	0	0	1	0	1	0	1	1	0	1	0	0
F_9	0	1	0	0	1	0	1	0	1	1	0	1	0	0
F_{10}	0	1	0	0	1	0	1	0	1	1	0	1	0	0
F_{11}	0	1	0	0	1	0	1	0	1	1	0	1	0	0
F_{12}	1	0	0	1	1	1	0	1	0	0	1	1	1	1

Step S1: The pattern F_1 is presented, the first cluster is formed. The bottom-up weight $^{\mathbf{a}}\mathbf{b}_1$ = [1 0 1 0 1 0], and $^{\mathbf{t}}\mathbf{b}_1$ =[1 1 0 1 0 0 0 1].

Step S2: Present the pattern F_2 and set $\mathbf{v}_1$ = [0 0 0 0 0 0 0 0].

Step S3: Compute $\sum_{i=1}^{N_a} {}^a x_i^{(2)}\, {}^a b_{i1} = 2$. Find $J = 1$ and set $\mathbf{v}_1 = {}^t\mathbf{b}_1$ = [1 1 0 1 0 0 0 1].

Step S4: Apply Eq. 6.1, find $y_1 = 4$, and the best existing cluster is cluster 1.

Step S5: Assign feature F_2 to cluster 1 and update weights according to Eqs. 6.3 and 6.4. The new bottom-up weight becomes ${}^a\mathbf{b}_1 =^a \mathbf{x}^{(2)}\, {}^a\mathbf{b}_1$ = [0 0 1 0 1 0], and ${}^t\mathbf{b}_1 = f({}^t\mathbf{x}^{(2)} +^t \mathbf{b}_1)$ = [1 1 0 1 0 0 0 1].

If we continue, features F_3 and F_4 are also assigned to cluster 1. The new bottom-up weights that after F_3 and F_4 are assigned to cluster 1 are ${}^a\mathbf{b}_1$ = [0 0 0 0 1 0], and ${}^t\mathbf{b}_1$ = [1 1 0 1 0 0 0 1].

If the feature F_5 is presented, Step S3 gives $\sum_{i=1}^{N_a} {}^a x_i^{(5)}\, {}^a b_{i1} = 0$, thus, a new cluster is created. Similarly, features F_6 and F_7 fall to the 2nd cluster. The new bottom-up weights are ${}^a\mathbf{b}_2$ = [0 1 0 0 0 0], and ${}^t\mathbf{b}_2$ = [1 1 1 1 0 1 0 0].

When feature F_8 enters to the network, from Step S3, two clusters are found (i.e., $J = 2$). From Step S4, cluster number 2 is selected to have the maximum number of tool overlap. Thus, feature F_8 is assigned to cluster 2 and the new bottom-up weights are ${}^a\mathbf{b}_2$ = [0 1 0 0 0 0], and ${}^t\mathbf{b}_1$ = [1 1 1 1 0 1 0 0]. Continue the procedures, finally we have features F_1, F_2, F_3, F_4, and F_{12} assigned to cluster 1 or setup 1, and features F_5, F_6,F_7,F_8, F_9,F_{10}, and F_{11} in cluster 2 or setup 2.

6.3 Feature Sequencing

After we determine the setups, we need to determine the sequence of making features in each setup and the sequence of finishing each setup. To determine feature sequence in each setup, we need to discover intersected features and non-intersected features. Intersected features are the features nested together. The sequence of making intersected features depends on tools, material, geometric constraint, and manufacturing practice. Several works[4,6] have uncovered this problem. Because of these constraints, intersected features have fixed sequence, while sequence of non-intersected features is independent. We can use tooling information to combine these two groups. Furthermore, the overall sequence of making features in a setup is the sequence of making intersected features and non-intersected ones.

To solve sequencing intersected features, we use Episodal Associative Memory (EAM) approach.[1] The EAM is an approach to build a memory that can efficiently and accurately connect a given problem or idea to relevant information. The EAM has been built to self-organize designs on the basis of qualitative geometry and topology. In the EAM, designs are self-organized using regularities on the basis of qualitative geometry and topology. This means that there are cluster memories which remember parts are similar on the basis of overall dimensions, or on the basis of top surface features, etc. The purpose of the EAM is to aid the human designer so that actions can be based not only on the conceptual structures embedded in the system but also experience acquired from prior episodes.

6.3.1 Feature Interactions in Process Planning

The term *feature interactions* have several different interpretations in process planning research. The common idea across all usage is that the geometric relationships between features have an impact on the process plan. At a very low level this is quite obvious, such as the case when generating NC code. The distances and directions between features are used explicitly in generating a cutter path. Most researchers have used the idea of feature interactions to express the complications introduced into the process planning task when certain features are arranged in particular geometric orientations relative to one another.

The MACHINIST program[4] looks for feature interactions when generating the fixturing, and feature sequencing portions of the process plan. MACHINIST uses special rules aimed at particular interactions, and avoids those interactions by reordering a sequence of features, or putting features into different setups. For example, consider the hole drilled into the edge cut or bevel on the edge of the block (See Figure 6.5). The hole must be drilled after the edge cut because the drill will slide off or "walk" down the slope of the edge cut. Hayes points out that these feature interactions are an instance of subgoal interactions found in many planning domains by many researchers.

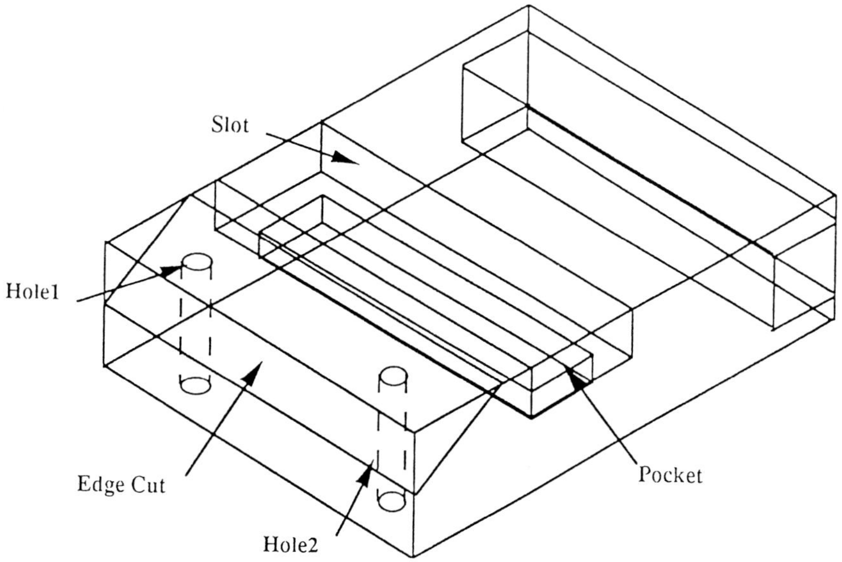

Figure 6.5: A sample part with interacted features

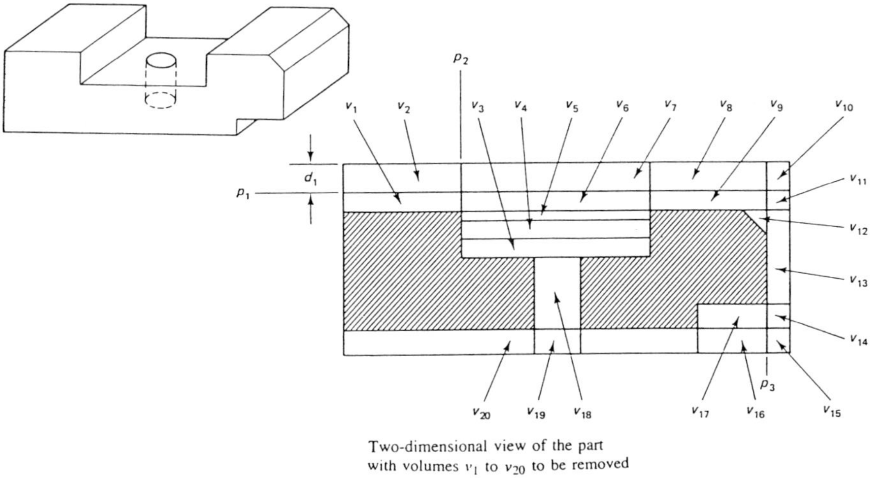

Figure 6.6: A sample part with interacted features a slot and a hole (adopted from[6])

Kusiak[6] took a slightly different approach to feature interactions. He defined machinable volumes. Each representation of machinable volume has corresponding geometric features. Based on the selection of machines, tools, and fixtures, the alternative set of features is then evaluated as to its manufacturability, and the set of features that has the least cost is chosen as the representation. The final plan is the best removal sequence to remove machinable volumes. Consider the geometry of Figure 6.6.[6] Geometric interactions among the two pockets and the hole result in several possible interpretations. Given these interpretations, it is up to the planner to decide which set of features would be least costly to manufacture.

By defining cost of each removal volume, Chvatal[7] uses integer programming technique to choose the most optimal set of feature representations given several possible alternatives for several sets of features. Although this is a very general approach, it appears to generate alternatives that an experienced machinist would not consider. The approach is so general that it wastes time generating many alternatives and then evaluating them rather than generating the most probable alternative first.

In the QTC,[5] feature interactions are again used to reason about geometric relations between features. There are two main interactions dealt with in the QTC: the nested type and the intersection type. In the QTC the actual boundary representations of the features are used in an intersection operation to determine the type of feature interaction. Besides the results of the geometric operations, the feature types are also used to identify the type of interaction, and thus the applicable rules that govern their removal.

The common idea across all usage is that the geometric relationship between features has an impact on the process plan. For example, consider the hole drilled into the edge cut or bevel on the edge of the block (See Figure 6.5). The hole must be drilled after the edge cut because the drill will slide off or "walk" down the slope of the edge cut. Our approach to sequencing interacting features involves an associative memory that can retrieve previous designs on the basis of qualitative geometry.[1] By creating an associative memory that the process planners can "teach," we can transfer the burden of knowledge capture to the machine which is much more patient, attentive, and remembers more details than a human. This paper describes the implementation of such a memory. The term *feature interactions* has several different interpretations in process planning research.

6.3.2 The EAM Scheme for Feature Interaction

As stated earlier, geometric relationships between features are one of the causes of feature interactions. Throughout the feature sequencing literature, certain geometric relationships between features are cited as causing problems in process planning nesting and intersection. These are exactly the types of relationships we want to recognize. By using approach faces and the self-organizing aspects of the EAM, these relationships can be organized by the EAM into "regular" groups or categories of information with which a rule-of-thumb can be associated.[1]

A method will be presented in the next section which captures very qualitative information about the geometric relationships between features in the form of a binary pattern. By self-organizing (through the use of an unsupervised learning neural network) these patterns into groups, we have formed a regular collection of information. Looking at this regular collection as an entity, there are several ideas that can be associated with that entity. In particular an order of removal can be associated with that group, or cluster.

6.3.3 Approach Faces and Classify-geom Function

Let an approach face be part of a manufacturing feature that, when projected, would intersect the exterior surface of the part and would constitute the plane through which a cutting tool must pass in order to create that feature.

A *classify-geoms* function has been implemented to operate certain geometric operations such as union ($\cup$), intersection ($\cap$), and difference (-). By using the classify-geoms function on approach faces, and examining the results, the geometric relationships between the approach faces can be determined.

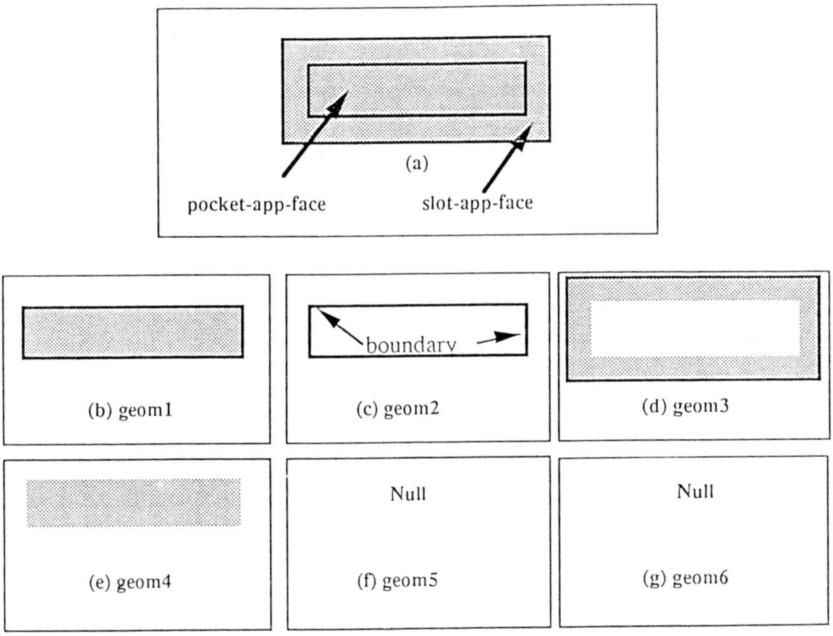

Figure 6.7: Classify-geom for slot and pocket

The approach faces for slot and pocket in Figure 6.5 are shown in Figure 6.7(a). Six geoms that are generated from classify-geoms are explained in the following.

geom1: The part of *slot-app-face* that is inside *pocket-app-face*, see Figure 6.7(b).

geom2: The part of *slot-app-face* that is on the boundary of *pocket-app-face* , see Figure 6.7(c).

geom3: The part of *slot-app-face* that is outside *pocket-app-face*, see Figure 6.7(d).

geom4: The part of *pocket-app-face* that is inside *slot-app-face*, see Figure 6.7(e).

geom5: The part of *pocket-app-face* that is on the boundary of *slot-app-face*, see Figure 6.7(f).

geom6: The part of *pocket-app-face* that is outside *slot-app-face* , see Figure 6.7(g).

6.3.4 Patterns for the Results of Classify-geoms

Each geom returned from the classify-geoms function can either be a piece of geometry or a null geom. A null geom represents no geometry. Geom6 in the above example (Figure 6.7(g)) is a null geom. Geom6 represents the part of *pocket-app-face* that is outside the area of *slot-app-face*. Since there is no part of *pocket-app-face* that is outside the area of *slot-app-face*, the geom returned is null.

The results of the classify-geom function must be coded into numeric values in order to be used as input to the EAM. If we interpret a null geom as "0" and any other geom as "1," then the results of the classify-geom function could be viewed as a list of six binary values. Each bit in this list would signify the absence or presence of geometry by a 0 or a 1 respectively. The results of the classify-geom function shown in Figure 6.7(b) through 6.7(g) would be coded as: $geom1 \rightarrow 1$, $geom2 \rightarrow 1$, $geom3 \rightarrow 1$, $geom4 \rightarrow 1$, $geom5 \rightarrow 0$, $geom6 \rightarrow 0$.

Thus the results would be the list: (1 1 1 1 0 0). Notice that geom1 through geom3 are the slot approach face **in**, **on the boundary of**, and **on** the pocket approach face respectively (see the definition of the classify geom function given earlier). Conversely, geom4 through geom6 are the pocket approach face **in**, **on the boundary** of, and **on** the slot approach face respectively.

The pattern generated by coding the results of the classify-geom function characterizes the geometric relationship between the two approach faces, and therefore the geometric relationship between the two features. As seen in Figure 6.7(a), one approach face is totally inside another. The pocket approach face is "nested" inside the slot approach face. When one approach face is nested inside another, it means that one feature is "nested" inside the other. The pocket in Figure 6.7(a) nested at the bottom of the slot. With this geometric information (that one feature is nested inside another), it is possible to make some manufacturing decisions regarding the two features.

Given that the results of the classify-geom function are coded into a binary pattern, some geometric relationships can be deduced from that pattern. As seen in the example above, the pattern (1 1 1 1 0 0) was generated from the slot and the pocket, and the pocket was found to be nested inside the slot. Thus that pattern (1 1 1 1 0 0) indicated those features are nested. In fact, any two features that are nested will generate that pattern. There are three geometric relationships that can be distinguished using the coded results of the classify-geom function. See Table 6.3.

"Nested Large" means that the first feature is larger than the second feature. "Nested Small" means the first feature is smaller than the second. The pattern (1 1 1 1 0 0) is "Nested Large." This is because the classify-geom function was called with the slot as the first argument. If the pocket was passed as the first argument, then the results would have been (1 0 0 1 1 1) "Nested Small."

Table 6.3: Geometric relationships using classify-geom results.

	Relationship		
Geom	Nested Large	Nested Small	Tangent
geom1	1	1	0
geom2	1	0	1
geom3	1	0	1
geom4	1	1	0
geom5	0	1	1
geom6	0	1	1

Table 6.4: Interactions table

Approach Face of	hole1	hole2	slot	pocket	edge cut
hole1	-	(0 0 1 0 0 1)	(0 0 1 0 0 1)	(0 0 1 0 0 1)	(0 0 1 1 1 1)
hole2	(0 0 1 0 0 1)	-	(0 0 1 0 0 1)	(0 0 1 0 0 1)	(0 0 1 1 1 1)
slot	(0 0 1 0 0 1)	(0 0 1 0 0 1)	-	(1 1 1 1 0 0)	(0 0 1 0 0 1)
pocket	(0 0 1 0 0 1)	(0 0 1 0 0 1)	(0 0 1 1 1 1)	-	(0 0 1 0 0 1)
edge cut	(1 1 1 1 0 0)	(1 1 1 1 0 0)	(0 0 1 0 0 1)	(0 0 1 0 0 1)	-

6.3.5 Table of Interactions Between Features

The classify-geom function is applied to every pair-wise combination of features, and the results are collected to create a table. Every entry in the table is the result of a classify-geom function call. For the part shown in Figure 6.5, Table 6.4 is generated.

The results of the classify-geom call on the approach face of the slot and the approach face of the pocket are shown in the (3, 4) entry of Table 6.4. This table represents some degree the geometric relationships of all the intersected features in a particular setup.

6.3.6 Sequencing Interaction Features using the EAM

The input pattern to the neural network is essentially an interactions table like that in Table 6.4 except that the table contains only the features that have an interaction. The pattern is then the concatenation of all the rows of the table from row 1 to row N. We can concatenate the value from interactive table to form a vector of binary values.

Features that have interactions require special consideration when determining a processing sequence. The name of interacting features can be found, as is the results of the classify-geom function. Using the list of interacting features and the interactions table a pattern can be constructed for input to the general unsupervised learning neural network mentioned before. The unsupervised learning neural network groups these patterns into clusters based on similarity. Features with similar interactions will produce patterns that are similar, and will therefore fall into the same cluster. The unsupervised learning neural network returns a cluster identifier, indicating into which cluster the pattern fell. Using standard symbolic processing techniques, a database can be built using the cluster identifier as a key into the database. In this manner various data can be associated with that cluster, and retrieved using that cluster identifier. Thus given a set of interacting features, a pattern is built, it is clustered, and a cluster identifier is returned.

6.3.7 Training the Initial EAM

Before the EAM can be exercised, it must be "taught" some initial interacting features. The clusters that were formed were identified in the data files that the unsupervised learning system automatically creates. A portion of the clustered patterns details which patterns were clustered together as shown in Figure 6.8.

Cluster 0 (ID number 0 and 4) contains interacting feature groups that partially overlap each other. For holes with this type of interaction, the general rule is to machine the smaller hole first. Also a problem to anticipate is in drilling the second hole, the walls of the first hole might be deformed, so reducing the feed rate would be appropriate. Cluster 1 (ID number 1, 2, and 8) contains interacting feature groups that are "through" features (they extend the length of the part) that are inside one another. In general the feature with the largest approach face is machined first. An exception to this rule would be group 8. Although not shown, the edge cut is a "contoured milled surface." This is an operation using a ball-end mill. Using a ball-end mill is a time consuming process if a reasonable surface finish is desired because the ball-end mill is stepped over a very small fraction between every pass. By milling the through-slot first, some of the edge cuts do not have to be machined, because it would have been removed by the previous operation. Cluster 2 (ID number 3, 5, 7, 9, and 11) contains interacting feature groups in which one feature is nested inside another feature. Again the general rule of thumb is to machine the feature with the largest approach face first. An exception to this is group 9, a hole on an edge cut. The hole should be drilled first, machining the edge cut first destroys the flat surface on which the hole must be drilled. Cluster 3 (ID number 6) contains one interacting feature group. These are three pockets nested inside one another. The general rule is to machine from the top to the bottom, i.e., machine from the largest approach face to the smallest. Cluster 4 (ID number 10 and 12) contains two interacting feature groups. Again, machining the feature with the largest approach face first is the rule.

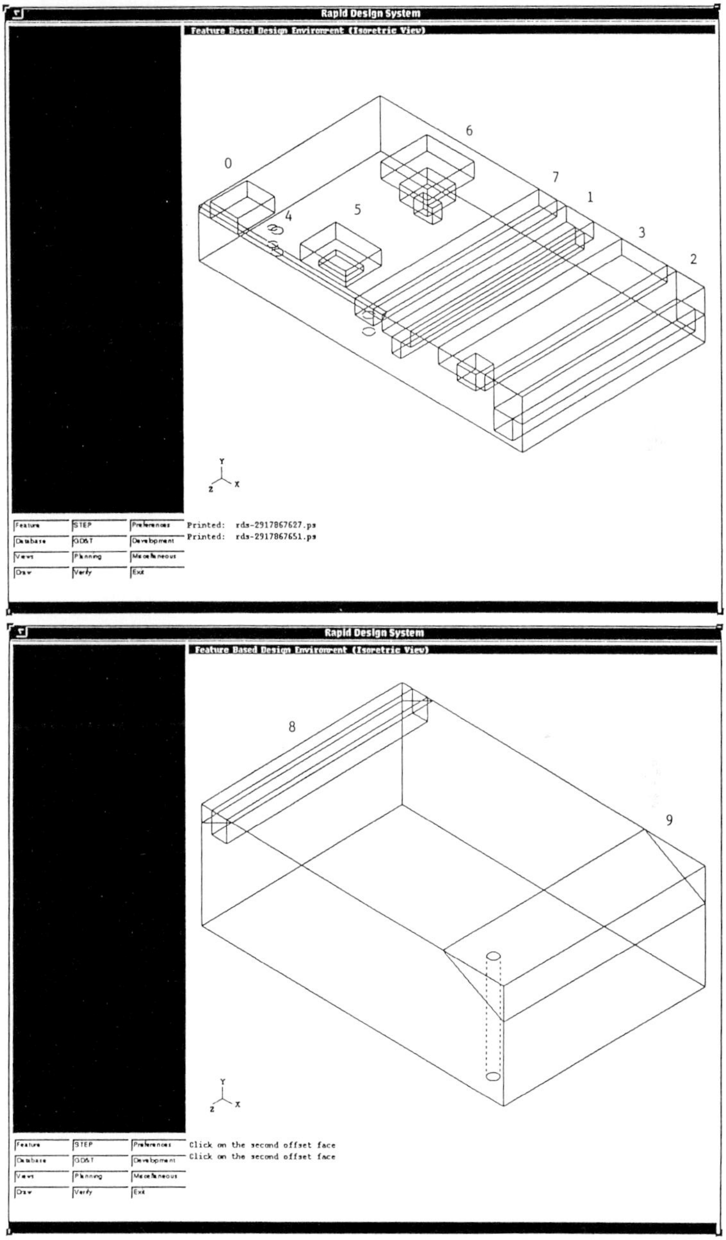

Figure 6.8: Intersected features design for EAM.

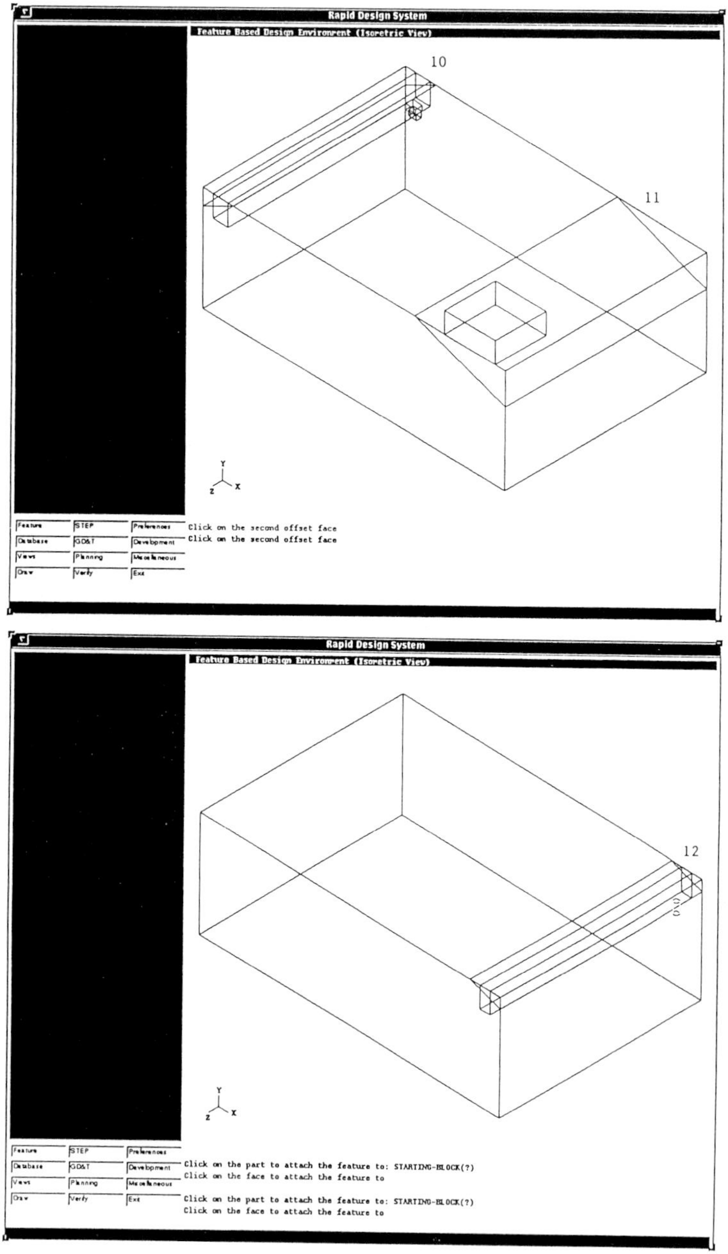

Figure 6.8: Intersected features design for EAM.

6.3.8 Recall Feature Sequence

Using the interaction features clusters stored in the memory, as long as new features have approach faces defined, the EAM can classify the relationships using approach faces. The classified approach faces are then used to recall the appropriate plan, and other pertinent information.

6.3.9 Tool Graph

After intersected feature sequences have been decided, we need to determine the overall sequence of a setup. A setup may consist of two kinds of features intersected and non-intersected. As we mentioned above, we may have several clusters of intersected features. Each cluster or setup has its own feature sequence. In each setup, we may also have independently non-intersected features. In general, we can represent the tool sequence to make a feature in a setup by a Directed Acyclic Graph (DAG). Each node in the DAG is the tool name. The edges in the DAG are the precedence constraints that the nodes must follow. An example of the DAG is shown in Figure 6.9(a). Next, we shall combine the tools' DAGs of all features into a single tool graph indicating the sequence of producing all the features in a setup. Since we have determined the sequence of making intersected features, we can combine tool DAGs of intersected features into another tool DAG. This can be done by adding tool precedence constraint from feature F_i to feature F_j, where F_i must execute before F_j. As shown in Figure 6.9(b), two tool DAGs have been combined by adding an edge from the terminal node of the tool DAG of F_i to the initial node of the tool DAG of F_j.

6.3.10 Merging Tool Graphs

After combining tool DAGs of intersected features, we now only have several independent tool DAGs. Each DAG represents either the tool sequence of every non-intersected feature or tool sequence of combined intersected features. To determine tool sequence of making features in a setup, we try to minimize the number of tool changes. The following properties are given to support the minimization algorithm.

Property 1: The number of tool changes to make a feature is $k-1$ if there exists k distinct tool nodes in the tool DAG.

Here we suppose that the machine has the first tool attached. The number of tool changes equals to the number of tools required minus one.

Property 2: The number of tool changes to make m features in a setup is $\sum_{i=1}^{m} k_i - 1$, if each feature requires k_i distinct tools and $T_i \cap T_j = \emptyset$ for all i and $i \neq j$.

Similarly, using the required tools, the machine processes all features in a setup. Suppose we can collect common tools from different tool DAGs into the same group and combine these common tool nodes into a group-node in the new DAG.

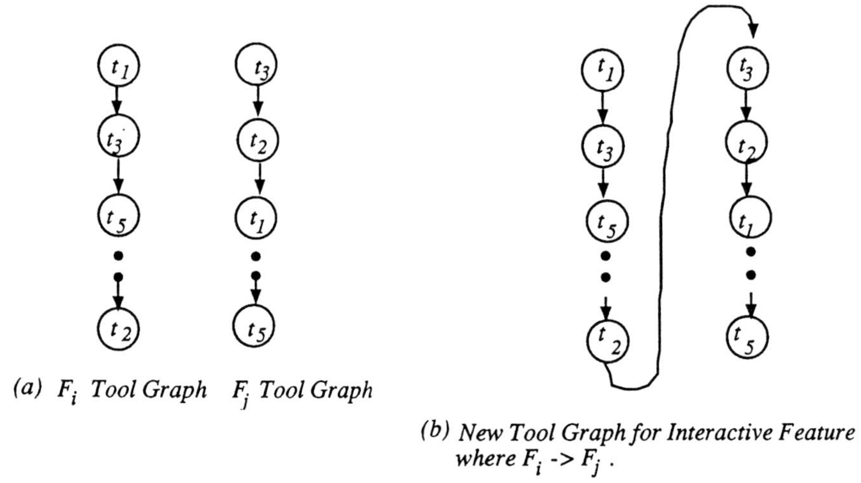

Figure 6.9: (a) Tool DAGs for two intersected features, $F_i \rightarrow F_j$ and (b) the combined tool DAGs

Each group-node represents the same tool to process different features in tool DAGs. Some group-nodes in the new DAG may consist of only one node from the old DAGs, meaning that this feature is made by this tool, while others may have several, meaning that several features can be made by using the same tool. The number of tool changes for processing this new tool DAG is the number of group-nodes minus 1. To find the tool sequence with the minimum number of tool changes, we should find the possible minimum number of group-nodes. Thus, we have the following property.

Property 3: The number of tool changes in a precedent tool DAG is $k - 1$ if there exists k tool group-nodes in the tool DAG and the immediate precedent pair of nodes do not have the same tool name.

Although the same tool name may exist in different group-nodes in the new DAG, because there exists precedence constraint in the new tool DAG, we still need to change the tool. In other words, without violating precedence constraint, given a set of tool DAGs we should try to construct a new tool DAG by combining the same tool node together, and to increase the number of the same tools in a group-node as possible.

The following Discover-And-Merge (DAM) algorithm groups the same tool into a group-node and merges them into a new DAG.

Algorithm DAM (Discover-And-Merge)

Input: A set of tool DAGs, tool sequence for each DAG.

Output: A new tool DAG with the minimum number of group-nodes and each group-node has the maximum number of tool nodes from the original tool DAGs.

Step 1: [*Initialization*] Select a tool DAG, DAG_i.

Step 2: [*Select another tool DAG*] Select another tool DAG, DAG_j.

Step 3: [*Find a path and Compare*] Select a path, p_j, from DAG_j. Follow the precedence constraint, a path is the collection of tool nodes starting from any node to a terminal node (a node without any successor). Compare all the tool nodes in this path with the nodes in DAG_i. By satisfying precedence constraint, record total number of the nodes, N_{p_j}, that have the same tool names.

Step 4: [*Loop*] Repeat Step 3 until all the paths have been checked. Let $N_{\max} = \max_{p_j} N_{p_j}$. Let the corresponding path that has the number $N_{\max}$ be $p_{\max}$

Step 5: [*Merge to DAG*] Merge DAG_j into DAG_i by combining nodes in path $p_{\max}$ to the corresponding nodes in DAG_i.

Step 6: [*Stopping Criteria*] Go to Step 2 until all the tool DAGs have been checked.

End of Algorithm DAM

In this algorithm, Steps 3 and 4 form an iterative loop that finds the maximum number of the same tools to overlap between two DAGs. Step 5 merges two DAGs together. These steps try to compare all the tools as possible, thus the maximum number of similarities can be found. The more nodes that can be merged, the less tool changes become. Using this algorithm, Figure 6.10 shows the combined tool DAG from several tool DAGs.

6.3.11 Sequencing Tools in Each Setup

Given the new generated tool DAG amongst features, an optimal tool sequence of making features can be generated by the following algorithm.

Algorithm OTS (Optimal Tool Sequence)

Input: The new tool DAG for the setup.

Output: Optimal tool sequence for this setup.

Step 1: [*Loop*] For the nodes in the tool DAG, do the following. If all the nodes in the tool DAG have been selected, stop; otherwise, continue.

Step 2: [*Select a node*] Select a node, t_i that has no predecessors.

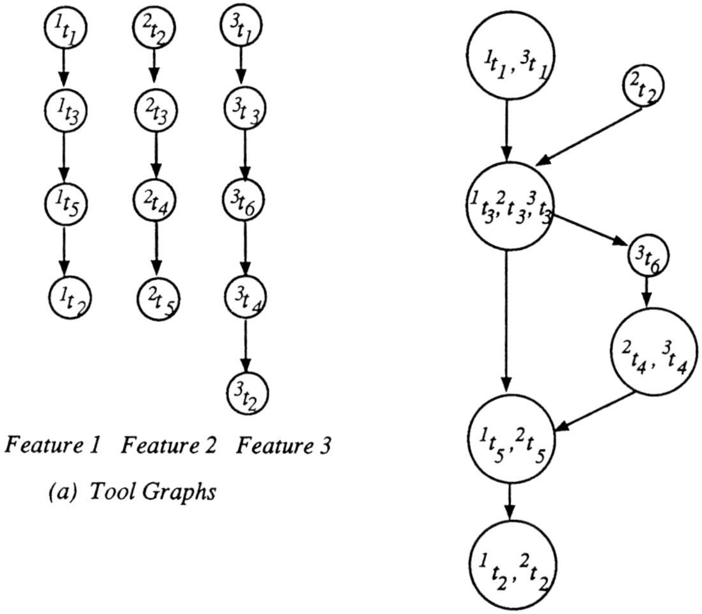

(b) Combined Tool Graph

Figure 6.10: Three tool DAGs and the new combined tool DAG

Step 3: [*Generate Node*] Output the node t_i.

Step 4: [*Update the tool DAG*] Delete the node t_i and all edges leading out of t_i from the tool DAG. Go to Step 1.

End of Algorithm OTS

As an example, given the tool DAG for the setup in Figure 6.10, beginning with the tool t_1, the algorithm OTS produces the final tool sequence $\{t_1, t_2, t_3, t_6, t_4, t_5, t_2\}$. Based on the tool sequence above and the new tool DAG shown in Figure 6.9, tool t_1 visits feature F_1 and F_3, tool t_2 visits feature F_2, tool t_3 visits feature F_1, F_2, and F_3, etc.

6.4 Conclusion and Future Work

Integration of design and manufacturing is a crucial issue in automated process planning. The FBDE along with the EAM draws a designer's intention through CAD model effectively. The proposed unsupervised learning approach using AND and OR updates rules to cluster features based on the approach direction and tool type. A memory associative approach discovers the feature sequences within a setup. A discover-and-merge algorithm merges tool graph of features into a new tool graph. An optimal tool sequence algorithm is introduced to find the best sequence across the features in a setup. Future work includes

1. generate setups not only based on tool type and approach direction, but also tolerance information, material, and machining operation, etc.,
2. generate fixturing configuration for a setup, and
3. generate setup sequence based on fixturing information.

Acknowledgements

The support from the National Science Foundation Research Grant number DDM-9005755 and the United States Air Force Contract No. F33615-87-C-5250 to the RDS project is gratefully acknowledged. The author also would like to thank supports of other members in the RDS project, especially, Dr. Yoh-Han Pao and Dr. G. M. Radack of Case Western Reserve University. The author also gratefully thanks software supports from AIWare Inc., and Wisdom Inc.

6.5 References

1. Y. H. Pao, K. Komeyli, D. Shei, S. LeClair, A. Winn, "The Episodal Associative Memory: Managing Manufacturing Information on the Basis of Similarity and Associativity," *Journal of Intelligent Manufacturing,* **4** (2) (1993) in press.

2. A. A. G. Requicha and J. H. Vandenbrande, "Form Features for Mechanical Design and Manufacturing," *Proc. of ASME International Computers in Engineering Conference* Anaheim, CA (1989) 47-52.

3. S. R. LeClair, "The Rapid Design System: Memory-Driven Feature-Based Design," Technical Report, Wright Lab., *Wright-Patterson Air Force Base*, (Dayton, Ohio, 1993).

4. C. Hayes, "Machining Planning: A Model of an Expert Level Planning Process," Ph.D. Dissertation, Carnegie Mellon University, (December, 1990).

5. T. C. Chang, *Expert Process Planning for Manufacturing,* (Addison-Wesley, Reading, MA 1990), 94-97.

6. A. Kusiak, *Intelligent Manufacturing Systems*, (Prentice Hall, Englewood Cliff, NJ, 1990) 159-165.

7. V. Chvatal, "A Greedy Heuristic for the Set-Covering Problem," *Mathematics of Operations Research,* **4** (3) (1979) 233-235.

Chapter 7

Scheduling Computation Tasks onto a Multiprocessor System by Mean Field Annealing of a Hopfield Neural Network

Nirwan Ansari, Zeeman Z. Zhang, and Edwin S. H. Hou
Center for Communications and Signal Processing
Department of Electrical and Computer Engineering
New Jersey Institute of Technology
University Heights
Newark, New Jersey 07102 USA

7.1 Introduction

The Hopfield neural network is a recurrent network that has been successfully applied to many optimization problems.[1] The framework of using the Hopfield neural network to solve an optimization problem involves two major tasks:

1. Constructing the Hopfield energy function that is appropriate for the problem.
2. Adopting and designing a recursive mechanism in minimizing the energy function. The Hopfield energy function can be effectively minimized by simulated annealing (SA).

Recently, Mean Field Annealing (MFA) has been proposed for the minimization of the Hopfield energy function.[2,3,4] Such an approach has been demonstrated to be robust and efficient.

In this chapter, the Multiprocessor Scheduling Problem (MSP) will be described. The principles of the Hopfield neural network, the simulated annealing, and the mean field theory (MFT) will be reviewed; the numerical implementation in solving the

MSP problem by mean field annealing will be discussed. Though the major goal of this chapter is to map the MSP problem onto a framework that can be solved by MFT, the general procedure discussed can be applied to solving other optimization problems.

The chapter is organized as follows. The multiprocessor scheduling problem along with its constraints will be defined in Section 2. In Section 3, the Hopfield energy function is discussed. Derivation of the Hopfield energy function for the Graph Bisection problem and the MSP problem are described in detail. In Section 4, a review on the mean field theory is presented and a set of mean field equations are also derived for the MSP problem. Numerical calculations and experimental results are presented in Section 5. Section 6 is concluded with a summary and discussion.

7.2 The Multiprocessor Scheduling Problem

7.2.1 Problem Statement

The Multiprocessor Scheduling Problem has been a challenge to researchers in various areas such as computer engineering, operation research, robotics and manufacturing.[5–7] The MSP problem can be stated as scheduling a set of partially ordered computation tasks onto a multiprocessor system so that an objective function will be optimized.

The Multiprocessor Scheduling Problem deals with distributing the load of the processors efficiently over time for the tasks to be executed. This kind of problems arise whenever a common set of resources, such as tasks and processors, must be used to make a variety of different assignments in the shortest period of time. The objective of the MSP is to assign and sequence the use of those shared resources such that the tasks can be processed in the shortest period of time. In other words, when the system is optimized, the processing constraints are satisfied and the processing costs are minimized.

The general multiprocessor scheduling is extremely difficult to solve and is known to be *NP*-hard.[8] The difficulty of the problem depends heavily on the topology of the precedence relations among the computation tasks, the number of parallel processors, the topology of the multiprocessor system, the uniformity of the task processing time, and the performance criteria chosen to be optimized. Hu[9] developed an $O(n)$ algorithm for the case with tree-like task graph and equal processing time. Coffman and Graham[10] developed an $O(n^2)$ algorithm for arbitrary task graph and equal processing time, but the number of processors is restricted to two. However, if any of the restrictions are generalized, the multiprocessor scheduling problem immediately becomes *NP*-hard.

Due to the intractability of the multiprocessor scheduling problem, various heuristic approaches have been developped to solve it[5–7,11–13] Kasahara and Narita[12,13] proposed a heuristic algorithm (critical path/most immediate successors first) and an optimization/approximation algorithm (depth first/implicit heuristic search). These algorithms combine the branch-and-bound method and the critical path method to obtain an approximate solution. Chen *et al.*[6] developed a state-space search algorithm (A^*) coupled with a heuristic derived from the Fernandez and Bussell bound to obtain an approximate solution very close to the optimal solution. However, the computation process is slow. *Hou et al.*[7] developed a genetic algorithm approach to obtain fast approximate solutions of the multiprocessor scheduling problem.

In the following discussion, the usual assumption of an MSP that a set of identical processors capable of independent operation on independent tasks is made. A compound task submitted to the multiprocessor system consists of a set of M tasks, denoted as $\{T_1, T_2, \ldots, T_M\}$, and a partial ordering of these tasks. This partial ordering can be represented by a directed acyclic task graph, *TG*, which consists of a finite nonempty set of vertices, $\mathbf{V}$, such that, if there is a directed path from node i to node j, it implies that task T_i precedes task T_j. To describe the task graph, which gives the precedence relationships indicated by the partial ordering, the collection of vertices $\mathbf{V} = \{T_1, T_2, \ldots, T_M\}$ and directed connection pairs, are defined as c_{ij}, which implies that, if c_{ij} exists, then task T_i must be completed before T_j can be initiated. Given a task graph and a multiprocessor system with P processors, a task scheduling problem must be developed, such that, under the shortest time period, it gives a description of the tasks to be executed by each processor as a function of time. The schedule must not violate any of the precedence relationships or the requirement that no more than one processor can be assigned to a task at any time, and no more than one task can be executed in a processor at the same time.

Note that, in this chapter, the following assumption is made: the execution time for each task is known *a priori*; once a processor is assigned a task, it must keep working on this task until it is completed. As an example, a simple task graph with 10 tasks is illustrated in Figure 7.1. The description of the relationship of the tasks can be indicated by an $M \times M$ matrix $\mathbf{C}$, whose elements are c_{ij}, for $i, j = 1, 2, \ldots, M$ and M is the number of tasks.

From Figure 7.1, one can think that, the problem of finding an optimal schedule for a multiprocessor system with P processors can be considered as to assign the computation tasks to the processors in such a way that the precedence relations are maintained and that all the tasks are completed in the shortest possible time. That is, the finish time, when the last task is completed, is as short as possible.

7.2.2 Constraints of the MSP

The MSP, as shown in Figure 7.1, can be mapped onto the processor - time slot space with the following constraints:

1. Each task occupies one processor-time slot space (p, t) only.

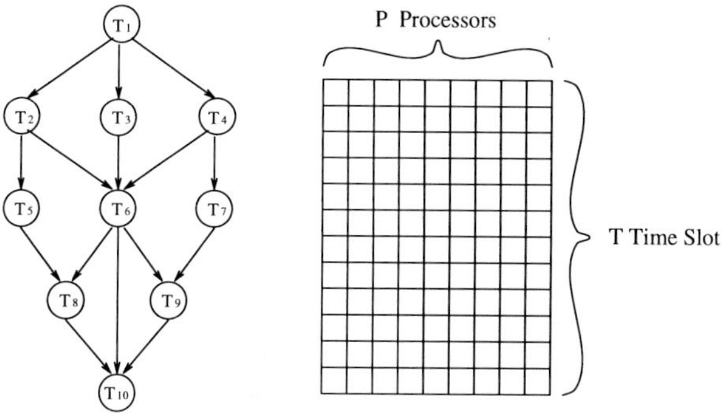

Figure 7.1: Mapping of tasks T_i onto the processor - time slot (p, t).

2. At most P tasks can be executed in each unit-time, where P is the number of processors.

3. If task i and task j are connected in the task graph, there is a precedence relationship between task i and task j. That is, If k preceding tasks are connected to task i, the time slot at which task i is executed must be preceded by the k tasks in the preceding time slots.

7.3 The Hopfield Energy Function

Neural networks have recently been considered as a good alternative for solving difficult optimization problems.[14] One of the most important contributions in Hopfield's pioneering work[1,15,16] is the concept of an energy function. Hopfield and Tank[1] formulated the Traveling Salesman Problem (TSP) onto a highly interconnected neural network, and made exploratory numerical studies on modest-size problems by minimizing the Hopfield energy associated with the network.

The term energy function comes from a physical analogy to a magnetic system originally.[17] The concept of the energy function is of much wider applicability. The most important property of an energy function is that it should decrease as the system evolves in the dynamic evolution, and must be minimized once a stable or optimum state is reached.

7.3.1 The Hopfield Neural Network

A simple Hopfield neural network can be depicted by a block diagram shown in Figure 7.2. The output of each neuron is one if the weighted sum of the inputs is greater than a threshold w_{j0}; otherwise, it is zero. This procedure can be described mathematically as follows:

$$E_j = \sum_{i \neq j} w_{ij} S_i + w_{j0}, \tag{7.1}$$

where

$$S_j = \begin{cases} 1, & \text{if } E_j > 0, \\ -1 & \text{otherwise.} \end{cases} \tag{7.2}$$

Here E_j is defined as the j th component of the energy function; w_{ij} is the weight connection between neuron i and neuron j; S_j is the state of neuron j. It can be shown[18] that, the network is stable if the weight matrix W is symmetric with all zeros on the main diagonal; that is $w_{ij} = w_{ji}$, for all i and j, and $w_{ii} = 0$, for all i. An example of using the Hopfield neural network in solving the Graph Bisection problem will be discussed next.

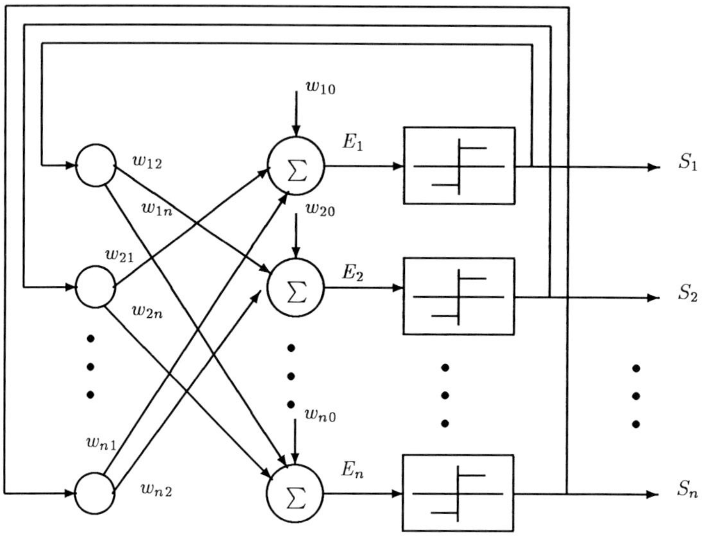

Figure 7.2: The Hopfield neural network model.

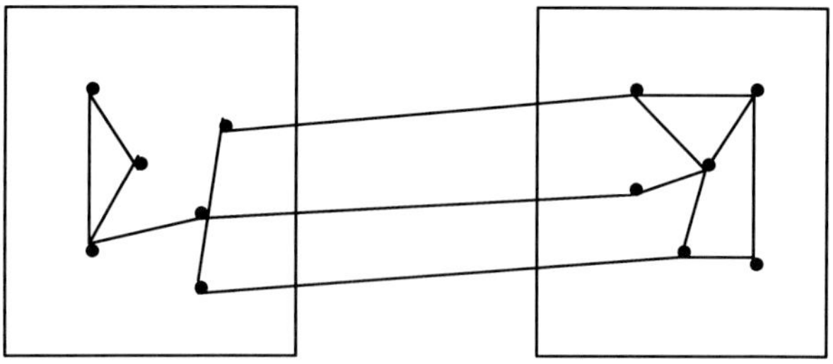

Figure 7.3: The graph bisection problem.

7.3.2 The Hopfield Energy Function for the Graph Bisection Problem

The Hopfield neural network shown in Figure 7.2 can be operated in two modes. In the first mode, the state of the neurons is assumed known, and the corresponding weights are to be determined. In the second mode, the connections among the neurons are given, the corresponding states of the neurons such that some specific constraints or requirements are met are to be determined. As an example of operating the Hopfield neural network in the second mode, discussion on how to solve the Graph Bisection problem (GB)[4,19,20] by the Hopfield network, is provided below.

The GB problem can be defined as follows: Given a set of N nodes with a given connectivity, partition them into two halves such that the net connectivity (cutsize) is minimized between the two halves as shown in Figure 7.3. This problem is mapped onto a neural network by denoting each node as a neuron. Each neuron, denoted by S_i, is turned "on" or "off" respectively, depending on which of the two halves node i belongs to. Thus, S_i is mathematically defined by:

$$S_i = \begin{cases} 1, & \text{if node } i \text{ in the right side set,} \\ -1, & \text{otherwise.} \end{cases} \tag{7.3}$$

The connectivity between two nodes is defined by:

$$c_{ij} = \begin{cases} 1, & \text{if node } i \text{ and } j \text{ are connected, and } i \neq j, \\ 0, & \text{otherwise.} \end{cases} \tag{7.4}$$

Note that the product $c_{ij}S_iS_j$ is zero whenever nodes i and j are not connected. The product is positive when nodes i and j are connected in the same partition, and is negative if they are in separate partitions. An energy function can be defined below such that when the energy is minimized, the net connectivity is also minimized.

$$E_1 = -\frac{1}{2}\sum_{ij} c_{ij}S_iS_j. \tag{7.5}$$

On the other hand, $\sum_i S_i = 0$ when the partition is well balanced. Hence, another energy function which satisfies the balance requirement can be defined by

$$E_2 = \frac{1}{2}(\sum_i S_i)^2. \tag{7.6}$$

Thus, the total energy function of the Hopfield neural network for the graph bisection problem takes the form:[4]

$$\begin{aligned} E &= E_1 + E_2 \\ &= -\frac{1}{2}\sum_{ij} c_{ij}S_iS_j + \frac{\alpha}{2}(\sum_i S_i)^2 \end{aligned} \tag{7.7}$$

where the imbalance parameter α sets the relative strength between the cutsize and the balancing term.

The Graph Bisection problem serves as a good example demonstrating how a constrained optimization problem is mapped onto an unconstrained problem by incorporating the constraints into the energy function. In this example, E_1 can be considered as the cost term, and E_2 the constraint. In general, to solve an optimization problem by the Hopfield network, the energy function must be chosen such that the cost function and the constraints are appropriately represented.

7.3.3 The Hopfield Energy Function for the MSP

The Hopfield energy for the task scheduling problem will be similarly derived to reflect the cost and constraints of the problem. Let the task precedence in a task graph be represented in such a way that if task j precedes task i, $j < i$ (meaning task j precedes task i). The case in which each task has the same execution time is considered first and then the case where different tasks have different execution times are considered later.

The constraints for the first case were presented in Section 2.1, and are rewritten as follows for convenience:

1. Each task occupies one time slot only.
2. There are P processors, and thus at most P tasks can be accomplished in each unit-time.
3. If k preceding tasks are connected to task i, task i executed at the current time slot must be preceded by the k tasks in the preceding time slots.

Denote $S_{ia} = 1$ or 0 according to whether task i is executed in time slot a, or not, respectively. Note that for the MSP problem, the neuron variable takes on 1 or 0 rather than 1 or -1. Define c_{ij}, the connectivity between task i and task j, as in Eq. (7.4). The above constraints are thus represented by the following respective energy functions:

$$E_1 = \sum_{ij}\sum_{ab}\delta_{ij}(1-\delta_{ab})S_{ia}S_{jb} = \sum_{i}\sum_{a}\sum_{b\neq a} S_{ia}S_{ib} \tag{7.8}$$

$$E_2 = \sum_{a}[(\sum_{i} S_{ia} - P)^2(\sum_{j} S_{ja})] \tag{7.9}$$

$$E_3 = \sum_{i}\sum_{a} S_{ia}\sum_{j=1}^{i-1} c_{ji}(1-\sum_{b=1}^{a-1} S_{jb})^2 \tag{7.10}$$

Note that, when the solution is optimized under the constraints, the following condition must be satisfied automatically,

$$\sum_a S_{ia} = 1, \text{for all } i, \tag{7.11}$$

and the values of S_{ia}, for all i and a, are either 1 or 0. We can speed up the convergence of the algorithm by adding the following two auxiliary energy components:[21]

$$E_4 = \sum_i (1 - \sum_a S_{ia})^2, \tag{7.12}$$

and

$$E_5 = \sum_i \sum_a S_{ia}(1 - S_{ia}). \tag{7.13}$$

The total energy for the Task Graph, E_T, becomes

$$E_T = \alpha E_1 + \beta E_2 + \gamma E_3 + \xi E_4 + \lambda E_5 \tag{7.14}$$

where α, β, γ, ξ and λ are the Lagrange parameters[22] used to weigh the significance of E_1, E_2, E_3, E_4, and E_5, respectively. Eq. (7.8) reflects Constraint (1). When E_1 is minimized (theoretically min. $\{E_1\} = 0$), then the condition that $S_{ia} = S_{ib} = 1$, for $a \neq b$, cannot exist. That is, each task should not be executed more than once. E_2 in Eq. (7.9) is used to enforce Constraint (2). Thus, once minimum E_2 is achieved, the schedule should correspond to the most efficient one because this constraint tries to keep as many processors occupied as possible in a unit time or to let all processors idle in that unit time. Note that, a unit time not occupied by any processors is not considered as part of the total execution time. Clearly, E_3 in Eq. (7.10) is always positive, and if Constraint (3) is satisfied, minimum E_3 can be obtained. A schedule that violates the precedence relationship less will have a larger value of E_3.

For the later case in which each task might have a different execution time, the task graph can be decomposed into a different task graph. Each task in the new task graph may be a subtask of a task in the original task graph. It is assumed that each task in the original task graph can be decomposed into several subtasks such that each subtask requires the same common execution time. In this case the new task graph falls into the former category, and thus, it is sufficient to consider only the former case.

7.4 Mean Field Theory and Simulated Annealing

7.4.1 Mean Field Theory

The mean field theory approximation is a well known technique in physics. It was first introduced for neural networks application by Peterson.[23] A brief description of the mean field theory approximation is given below. For more detailed treatment, readers are referred to.[2,4,20,23-25]

The statistical mechanism of simulated annealing or mean field annealing is maneuvered according to the Boltzmann distribution

$$B(\mathbf{S}') = \frac{\exp[\frac{-E(\mathbf{S}')}{T}]}{Z}, \tag{7.15}$$

where $\mathbf{S}'$ is any one of the possible configurations specified by the corresponding neuron set;

$E(\mathbf{S}')$ is the energy of the corresponding configuration;

T is the parameter called temperature;

Z is the partition function given by

$$Z = \sum_{\mathbf{S}'} \exp[\frac{-E(\mathbf{S}')}{T}], \tag{7.16}$$

and the $\sum$ is the sum of all possible neuron state configurations.

In the mean field theory, instead of concerning the neuron variables directly, their means are adopted, and they are defined by

$$\begin{aligned} F_i &= < S_i > \\ &= 1 \cdot P_T(S_i = 1) - 1 \cdot P_T(S_i = -1) \\ &= P_T(S_i = 1) - P_T(S_i = -1), \end{aligned} \tag{7.17}$$

and

$$\mathbf{F}' = < \mathbf{S}' >, \tag{7.18}$$

where S_i is a neuron;

F_i is the mean of neuron S_i;

$P_T(S_i = 1)$ and $P_T(S_i = -1)$ are the probabilities for $S_i = 1$ and $S_i = -1$, respectively;

$\mathbf{S}'$ is any one of possible configurations;

$\mathbf{F}'$ is the mean configuration corresponding to $\mathbf{S}'$.

Thus, in the mean field, Eq. (7.15) becomes

$$B(\mathbf{F}') = \frac{\exp[\frac{-E(\mathbf{F}')}{T}]}{Z}, \tag{7.19}$$

and the method to find global saddle point of the energy function, using continuous variables, can be derived through the following deductions.[20,23]

Consider a simple case of one single neuron state S first:

$$\sum_S \exp[\frac{-E(S)}{T}] = \sum_S f(S), \tag{7.20}$$

where S is the state value of a single neuron, and $f(S)$ is defined by

$$f(S) = \exp[\frac{-E(S)}{T}]. \tag{7.21}$$

Note that $f(S)$ can be replaced by an expression of integral over continuous variables F as follows

$$f(S) = \int_{-\infty}^{\infty} f(F)\delta(S-F)dF. \tag{7.22}$$

Thus, Eq. (7.20) can be written as

$$\sum_S f(S) = \sum_S \int_{-\infty}^{\infty} f(F)\delta(S-F)dF. \tag{7.23}$$

Since δ - function can be represented by

$$\delta(t) = \frac{1}{2\pi j}\int_{-j\infty}^{j\infty} \exp(xt)dx, \tag{7.24}$$

Eq. (7.23) can be written as follows

$$\begin{aligned}\sum_S f(S) &= \frac{1}{2\pi j}\sum_S \int_{-\infty}^{\infty}\int_{-j\infty}^{j\infty} f(F)\exp[H(S-F)]dHdF \\ &= \frac{1}{\pi j}\int_{-\infty}^{\infty}\int_{-j\infty}^{j\infty} f(F)\exp\{-HF + \log\frac{1}{2}[\sum_S \exp(HS)]\}dHdF. \end{aligned} \tag{7.25}$$

Generalizing to the case of N neurons, and define

$$\begin{aligned} Z &= \sum_{\mathbf{S}'} \exp[\frac{-E(\mathbf{S}')}{T}] \\ &= \sum_{S_1'}\sum_{S_2'}\cdots\sum_{S_N'} \exp[\frac{-E(\mathbf{S}')}{T}] \\ &= C\prod_i \int_{-\infty}^{\infty}\int_{-j\infty}^{j\infty} \exp[-\tilde{E}(\mathbf{F}',\mathbf{H}',T)]dH_i dF_i, \end{aligned} \tag{7.26}$$

where, C is a complex constant coefficient, F_i and H_i are the ith components of vectors $\mathbf{F}$ and $\mathbf{H}$, respectively. Comparing Eq. (7.20) and Eq. (7.25) to Eq. (7.26), $\tilde{E}(\mathbf{F}',\mathbf{H}',T)$ called the effective energy function is given by

$$\tilde{E}(\mathbf{F}',\mathbf{H}',T) = E(\mathbf{F}')\frac{1}{T} + \sum_i \{H_i F_i - \log\frac{1}{2}[\sum_{S_i} e^{H_i S_i}]\}. \tag{7.27}$$

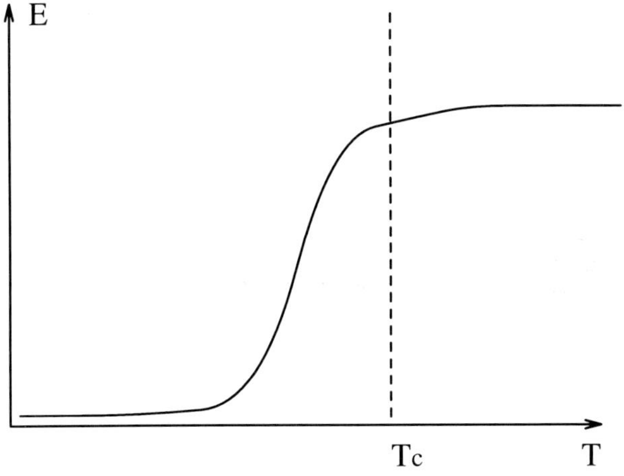

Figure 7.4: The energy $E(F_i)$ as a function of the temperature T.

As has been indicated by Peterson,[20,23] by using a saddle point expansion of **F**, one can see that the partition function Z is actually dominated by the saddle point, i.e.,

$$Z \simeq K \exp[- \tilde{E} (\mathbf{F_0'}, \mathbf{H_0'}, T)], \tag{7.28}$$

where K is a constant, and (F_0, H_0) is the saddle point of Eq. (7.27).

Thus, the statistical mechanism of the MFT governed by Eq. (7.19) is likewise determined by the mechanism of the saddle points. The statistical mechanism of the neural network can be, therefore, determined by the saddle points which are defined by

$$\frac{\partial \tilde{E}}{\partial H_i} = 0, \tag{7.29}$$

and

$$\frac{\partial \tilde{E}}{\partial F_i} = 0. \tag{7.30}$$

An important property of the effective energy function $\tilde{E} (\mathbf{F}, \mathbf{H}, T)$ is that it is a smooth function of the temperature T. The energy values, resulted from the solutions of Eq. (7.29) and Eq. (7.30), can be decreased to the global minimum which is illustrated in Figure 7.4. Eq. (7.29) and Eq. (7.30) can be solved iteratively by either asynchronous or synchronous method.

7.4.2 The Mean Field Approximation for the Graph Bisection Problem

Let us consider the mean field approximation of the Graph Bisection problem which was presented in the previous section, where $S_i = -1$or 1, for all $i = 1, 2, \ldots, N$. The energy function was defined by Eq. (7.7), and is rewritten below for convenience,

$$E = -\frac{1}{2}\sum_i \sum_j c_{ij} S_i S_j + \frac{\alpha}{2}(\sum_i S_i)^2, \tag{7.31}$$

where

$$S_i = \begin{cases} 1, & \text{if node } i \text{ in the right side set,} \\ -1, & \text{otherwise,} \end{cases} \tag{7.32}$$

and

$$c_{ij} = \begin{cases} 1, & \text{if node } i \text{ and } j \text{ are connected and } i \neq j, \\ 0, & \text{otherwise.} \end{cases} \tag{7.33}$$

Replacing S_i by the mean field variable F_i in Eq. (7.31), the following effective energy function,[23] $\tilde{E}\,(\mathbf{F}, \mathbf{H}, T)$, is obtained:

$$\tilde{E}\,(\mathbf{F}, \mathbf{H}, T) = E(\mathbf{F})\frac{1}{T} + \sum_i [H_i F_i - \log(\cosh H_i)]. \tag{7.34}$$

According to Eq. (7.29) and Eq. (7.30) (i.e., $\frac{\partial \tilde{E}}{\partial H_i} = 0$ and $\frac{\partial \tilde{E}}{\partial F_i} = 0$),

$$H_i = -\frac{1}{T}\frac{\partial E(\mathbf{F})}{\partial F_i}, \tag{7.35}$$

and

$$F_i = \tanh H_i = \tanh[-\frac{1}{T}\frac{\partial E(\mathbf{F})}{\partial F_i}], \tag{7.36}$$

such that, for the GB problem, the solution of F_i under each temperature T can be solved iteratively:

1.
$$F_i^{(new)} = \tanh[\sum_j c_{ij} F_j^{(old)}/T]. \tag{7.37}$$

2. After convergence in Step 1, reduce the temperature T gradually, and repeat step 1 until $\mathbf{F}$ converges.

7.4.3 The Mean Field Approximation for the MSP

For the case, $S_i = 1$ or 0, the effective energy function can be obtained as follows

$$\tilde{E}\,(\mathbf{F},\mathbf{H},T) = E(\mathbf{F})\frac{1}{T} + \sum_i [H_i F_i - \log\frac{1}{2}(1+e^{H_i})]. \tag{7.38}$$

The corresponding equations to find the solutions of F_i can be derived below using the saddle point concepts,

$$\frac{\partial\,\tilde{E}}{\partial H_i} = F_i - [\frac{1+e^{H_i}}{e^{H_i}}]^{-1} = 0, \tag{7.39}$$

$$\frac{\partial\,\tilde{E}}{\partial F_i} = \frac{\partial E}{\partial F_i}\frac{1}{T} + H_i = 0. \tag{7.40}$$

Thus,

$$H_i = -\frac{\partial E}{\partial F_i}\frac{1}{T}, \tag{7.41}$$

and

$$\begin{aligned} F_i &= [1+e^{-H_i}]^{-1} \\ &= \{1+\exp[\frac{\partial E}{\partial F_i}\frac{1}{T}]\}^{-1} \\ &= \frac{1}{2}[1+\tanh(-\frac{1}{2T}\frac{\partial E}{\partial F_i})]. \end{aligned} \tag{7.42}$$

7.4.4 The Mean Field Equations for the MSP

According to Eq. (7.8) - Eq. (7.14), and Eq. (7.42), the following mean field equations for the MSP problem are obtained:

$$\frac{\partial E_1}{\partial F_{ia}} = \sum_{b\neq a} 2F_{ib}, \tag{7.43}$$

$$\frac{\partial E_2}{\partial F_{ia}} = 2(\sum_j F_{ja} - P)\sum_j F_{ja} + (\sum_j F_{ja} - P)^2, \tag{7.44}$$

$$\frac{\partial E_3}{\partial F_{ia}} = \sum_j^{i-1} c_{ji}(1 - \sum_b^{a-1} F_{jb})^2, \tag{7.45}$$

$$\frac{\partial E_4}{\partial F_{ia}} = 2(\sum_b F_{ib} - 1), \tag{7.46}$$

$$\frac{\partial E_5}{\partial F_{ia}} = 1 - 2\sum_j\sum_b F_{jb}. \tag{7.47}$$

Substitute Eq. (7.43) to Eq. (7.47) into Eq. (7.42), the iterative update equation becomes:

$$F_{ia} = \frac{1}{2}\{1 + \tanh[-\frac{1}{2T}(\alpha\frac{\partial E_1}{\partial F_{ia}} + \beta\frac{\partial E_2}{\partial F_{ia}} + \gamma\frac{\partial E_3}{\partial F_{ia}} + \xi\frac{\partial E_4}{\partial F_{ia}} + \lambda\frac{\partial E_5}{\partial F_{ia}})]\}, \qquad (7.48)$$

for all i and a.

7.5 Numerical Implementation and Simulations

7.5.1 Numerical Calculations

After having formulated the Hopfield energy function and the MFT updating rule, the system is annealed by lowering the temperature gradually, with the expectation that undesired local minima can be avoided through the stochastic mechanism.

According to Eq. (7.41) and Eq. (7.42), the spinsystems onto which the optimization problems are mapped typically have two phases; at a high enough temperature, the system relaxes into the trivial fixed point, initial value $F_{ia}(0)$, which is a completely symmetrical state, where all $F_{ia}(0)$ are equal.[25]

As the temperature is lowered, a phase transition is passed at $T = T_c$ and as $T \longrightarrow 0$ fixed points $F_{ia}^{(*)}$ emerge, representing the specific decision made as to the solution to the optimization problem. These fixed points are characterized by

$$\prod \triangleq \frac{1}{N}\sum_{ia}(F_{ia}^{(*)})^2 = 1, \qquad (7.49)$$

where N is the number of neurons (tasks).

For the simulations at least two alternatives are available. One is to use a fixed temperature approach with T chosen below T_c. The other option is annealing where one chooses a temperature slightly above T_c and then anneals down to some value until the saturation $\prod$ is reached.

As far as the number of sweeps per temperature goes, a dynamical approach is taken here. At each temperature T_n, the MFT equations are iterated until the convergence criteria ($N_{sweep}(T)$)

$$N_{sweep}(T) \triangleq \frac{1}{N}\sum |F_{ia}(t+1) - F_{ia}(t)| < \epsilon, \qquad (7.50)$$

where ϵ is the convergence factor, is met. In summary, the algorithm is implemented in the following manner:

1. For a given task graph, determine c_{ij} described by Eq. (7.4).

2. Set the Lagrange parameters of the respective energy function which was discussed in Section 3.

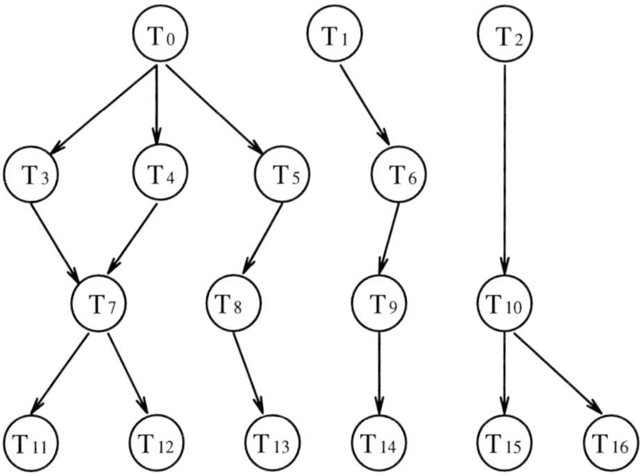

Figure 7.5: A 17 - task graph.

3. Determine the initial temperature T_0, such that $T_0 \geq T_c$.

4. Initialize with $F_{ia} = \frac{1}{K} + 0.001 * rand[-1, 1]$, where K is the product of the number of processors and the approximate execution time.

5. Anneal with a linear cooling schedule; i.e., $T_n = 0.9T_{n-1}$ until $\prod \geq 0.9$.

6. At each temperature, iterate Eq. (7.48) until $N_{sweep}(T)$ is met according to Eq. (7.50).

7.5.2 Simulation Results

For presentation, an arbitrary task graph shown in Figure 7.5 is used for simulation. When implementing the MFT annealing algorithm numerically, the straightforward iteration method of Eq. (7.48) which is rewritten below for convenience, is used at each temperature to obtain the steady state neuron values,

$$F_{ia} = \frac{1}{2}\{1 + \tanh[-\frac{1}{2T}(\alpha\frac{\partial E_1}{\partial F_{ia}} + \beta\frac{\partial E_2}{\partial F_{ia}} + \gamma\frac{\partial E_3}{\partial F_{ia}} + \xi\frac{\partial E_4}{\partial F_{ia}} + \lambda\frac{\partial E_5}{\partial F_{ia}})]\}. \tag{7.51}$$

The schedules obtained for the 17 task graph shown in Figure 7.5. are illustrated in Figure 7.6.(a), (b), (c), for cases with 2, 3, and 4 processors, respectively. Note that optimal solutions are obtained in these cases.

A more complicated task graph with 40 tasks is shown in Figure 7.7. The schedules for the task graph shown in Figure 7.7 for cases with 3, 5, 7 processors are

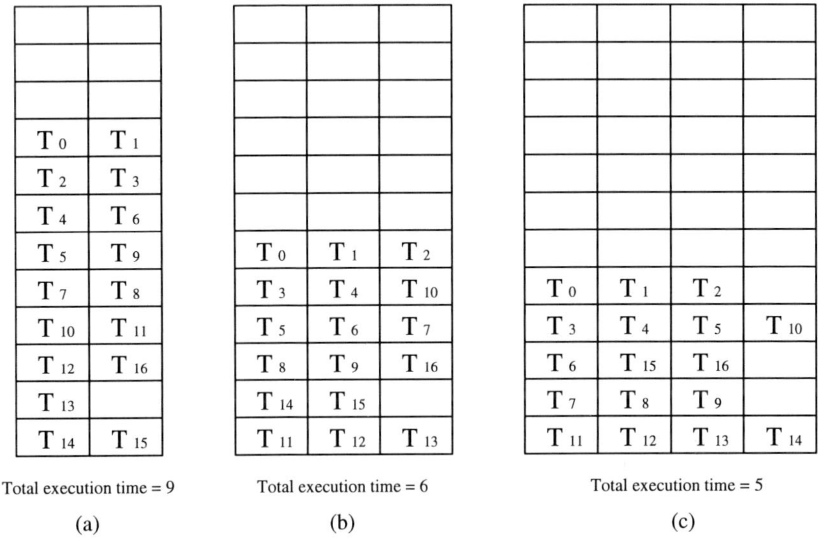

Figure 7.6: The schedules obtained for the 17 - task graph shown in Figure 7.5 by MFA with (a) two processors, (b) three processors, and four processors, respectively.

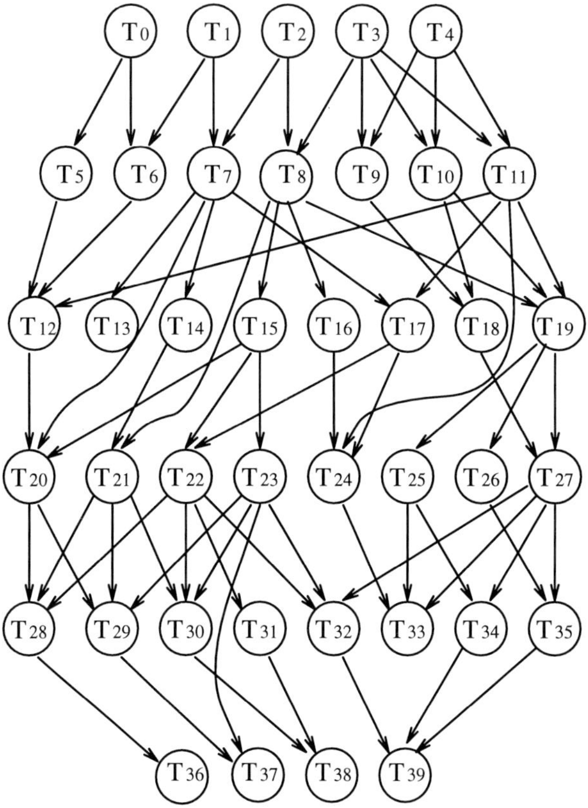

Figure 7.7: A 40 - task graph.

T_0	T_1	
T_3	T_4	T_6
T_2	T_5	T_9
T_{10}	T_{11}	
T_8	T_{12}	T_{18}
T_7	T_{15}	T_{16}
T_{13}	T_{17}	T_{23}
T_{14}	T_{19}	T_{24}
T_{25}	T_{26}	T_{27}
T_{20}	T_{21}	T_{34}
T_{22}	T_{35}	
T_{30}	T_{31}	T_{32}
T_{29}	T_{38}	
T_{28}	T_{33}	
T_{36}	T_{37}	T_{39}

(a) Total execution time = 15

T_0	T_1	T_2	T_3	
T_4	T_5	T_6	T_7	
T_{10}	T_{11}	T_{13}	T_{14}	
T_8	T_9	T_{12}	T_{17}	
T_{15}	T_{16}	T_{18}	T_{21}	
T_{19}	T_{20}	T_{22}	T_{23}	T_{24}
T_{25}	T_{26}	T_{27}	T_{28}	T_{29}
T_{30}	T_{31}	T_{32}	T_{34}	T_{35}
T_{33}	T_{36}	T_{37}	T_{38}	T_{39}

(b) Total execution time = 9

T_0	T_1	T_2	T_3	T_4		
T_5	T_6	T_7	T_8	T_9	T_{10}	T_{11}
T_{13}	T_{14}	T_{15}	T_{16}			
T_{12}	T_{17}	T_{18}	T_{19}	T_{21}	T_{23}	
T_{20}	T_{22}	T_{24}	T_{25}	T_{26}	T_{27}	
T_{28}	T_{29}	T_{30}	T_{31}			
T_{32}	T_{33}	T_{34}	T_{35}			
T_{36}	T_{37}	T_{38}	T_{39}			

(c) Total execution time = 8

Figure 7.8: The schedules obtained for the 40 - task graph shown in Figure 7.7 by MFA with (a) three processors, (b) five processors, and seven processors, respectively.

illustrated in Figure 7.8(a), (b), (c), respectively. The solutions obtained for this problem are 15, 9, and 8, respectively, as compared to the optimal solutions of 14, 9, and 7, respectively.

7.6 Conclusions

The framework of using mean field annealing in solving the Multiprocessor Scheduling Problem has been developed, simulated and evaluated. It has been demonstrated through experimental results that mean field theory is an effective optimization technique for solving the MSP problem. The difficulty generally lies on mapping a problem onto a framework that is solvable by mean field annealing. In summary, the construction of the framework for any problem consists of:

1. Defining an appropriate neuron variable,
2. constructing the Hopfield energy function which appropriately reflects the constraints and costs of the problem,
3. deriving the mean field equations from the Hopfield energy function,
4. selecting the Lagrange parameters in accordance with the significance of each component of the energy function, and
5. updating the mean field variables by annealing according to a cooling schedule.

In conclusion, optimal or near optimal solutions to the MSP problem can be achieved by using mean field annealing.

7.7 References

1. J. J. Hopfield and D. W. Tank, "Neural computation of decisions in optimization problems," *Biological Cybernetics,* **52** (4) (1985) 141-156.
2. C. Peterson and E. Hartman, "Explorations of the Mean Field Theory learning algorithm," *Neural Networks,* **2** (1989) 475-494.
3. Z. Z. Zhang, N. Ansari, E. Hou, and P. Yi, "Multiprocessor scheduling by mean field theory," *Proceedings of the International Joint Conference on Neural Networks,* **IV** Baltimore, MD (June, 1992) 582-587.
4. C. Peterson and B. Soderberg, "A new method for mapping optimization problems onto neural network," *International Journal of Neural Systems,* **1** (1) (1989) 3-22.

5. C. V. Ramamoorthy, K. M. Chandy, and M. J. Gonzalez, "Optimal scheduling strategies in a multiprocessor system," *IEEE Transactions on Computers,* **C-21** (2) (1972) 137-146.

6. C. L. Chen, C. S. G. Lee, and E. S. H. Hou, "Efficient scheduling algorithms for robot inverse dynamics computation on a multiprocessor systems," *IEEE Transactions on Systems, Man, and Cybernetics,* **18** (5) (1988) 729-743.

7. E. S. H. Hou, H. Rong, and N. Ansari, "Efficient multiprocessor scheduling based on genetic algorithms," *IECON 90, 16th conference of the IEEE Industrial Electronics Society,* Nov. 27-30, 1990, Pacific Grove, CA, 1239-1243.

8. M. R. Garey and D. S. Johnson, *Computers and Intractability: A Guide to the Theory of NP-Completeness,* (Freemen, San Francisco, CA, 1979).

9. T. C. Hu, "Parallel sequencing and assembly line problem," *Operations Research,* **9** (1961) 841-848.

10. E. G. Coffman and R. L. Graham, "Optimal scheduling for two-processor systems," *Acta. Informatica,* **1** (1972) 200-213.

11. T. L. Adams *et al.*, "A Comparison of list schedules for parallel processing systems," *CACM,* **17** (1974) 685-690.

12. H. Kasahara and S. Narita, "Practical multiprocessing scheduling algorithms for efficient parallel processing," *IEEE Transactions on Computers,* **C-33** (11) (1984) 1023-1029.

13. H. Kasahara and S. Narita, "Parallel processing of robot-arm control computation on a multimicroprocessor system," *IEEE Journal of Robotics and Automation,* **RA-1** (2) (1985) 104-113.

14. J. A. Anderson and E. Rosenfeld, *Neurocomputing, Foundations of Research,* (MIT Press, Cambridge, MA, 1988).

15. J. J. Hopfield, "Neural networks and physical systems with emergent collective computational abilities," *Proceedings of the National Academy of Science,* **79** (1982) 2541-2554.

16. J. J. Hopfield, "Neurons with graded response have collective computationed properties like those of two - state neurons," *Proceedings of the National Academy of Science,* **81** (1984) 3088-3092.

17. R. Hecht-Nidson, *Neurocomputing,* (Addison-Wesley, Reading, MA, 1989).

18. M. Cohen and S. Grossberg, "Absolute stability of global pattern works," *IEEE Transactions on System, Man, and Cybernetics,* **SMC - 13** (1983) 815-926.

19. D. E. Van den Bout and T. K. Miller, "Graph partitioning using annealed networks," *IEEE Transactions on Neural Networks,* **1** (2) (1990) 192-203.

20. C. Peterson and J. Anderson, "Neural networks and NP - complete optimization problems: a performance study on the graph bisection problem," *Complex Systems,* **2** (1988) 59-71.

21. F. Kamoun and M. K. Mehmet Ali, "A neural network shortest path algorithm for optimum routing in packet-switched communications networks," *Proceedings of IEEE Global Telecommunications Conference,* Phoenix, Arizon, (December 2-5, 1991) 120-124.

22. D. G. Luenberger, *Linear and Nonlinear Programming,* (Addison-Wesley, Reading, MA, 1984).

23. C. Peterson, "A mean field theory learning algorithm for neural networks," *Complex System,* **1** (1987) 995-1019.

24. C. C. Galland and G. E. Hinton, "Experiments on discovering high order features with mean field Modules," *Technical report CS-115 dept. of Computer Science,* University of Toronto (May, 1989).

25. C. Peterson, "Applications of Mean Field Theory neural networks," *Dept. of Theoretical Physics, Technical Report CS-1153,* University of Lund, (August, 1989).

Chapter 8

Multi-Functional Neural Networks for System Identification

Tep Sastri
Department of Industrial Engineering
Texas A&M University
College Station, TX 77843-3131 USA

Abstract

System identification of dynamical stochastic systems, based on input-output time series data, can be conveniently accomplished by means of multilayer neural networks, using derivative-based learning paradigms. Most existing research works, however, utilize the black-box approach to neuro-identification. They are consequently limited to non-linear interpolation or just one-step-ahead prediction, due to the lack of generalization capability. A closely related problem to the multiple-step prediction is sequential process monitoring and change detection. The present study proposes two novel neural network designs using multiple subnetworks and a hierarchical architecture, which is built from feedforward layers with lateral connections and correlations of process measurements. The first neural network can detect certain real-time changes in a non-stationary, non-linear stochastic process; the second neural network is able to perform accurate multiple-step prediction for on-line applications. Two methods for training connection weights of the proposed neural network architectures, called the direct and the indirect mapping, are discussed. Several examples on the design and implementation of the proposed ideas are given.

Knowledge to be gained from this study will enable production engineers to design an appropriate neural net detection/prediction scheme for on-line process/quality control applications in manufacturing. There are several practical applications suitable for the proposed designs: for example, sensor failures detection and process monitoring of parameter drifting and adaptive predictions of nonstationary time series for system's planning and control.

8.1 Introduction

Most studies of multilayer feedforward neural networks to date have been uni-functional; e.g., pattern recognition,[28] non-linear input-output mapping,[25] signal processing,[18] and vector association by associative memory. In some applications where more than one function is required; e.g., for system identification and control, uni-functional neural networks are connected to achieve the overall required performance,[4,33]. To deal with signal feedback function, cascaded architectures similar to series-parallel connections in electrical circuits have been proposed.[31] Typically, all of the existing works are based on the assumption that the input and output time series associated with a dynamical system are stationary. As a consequence, once the training is over, the neural network is assumed to adequately represent the system input-output relationship, which will hold for future data as well.

In many real dynamical systems, the underlying stochastic processes are only locally stationary and are subject to change at some unknown points in time. In the system theory literature such non-stationary systems have been modeled as semi-Markov processes with jump parameters.[50] The idea is to allow the control system to randomly switch, among a finite number of possible models, to the one that best describes its behavior at a given time. This concept of model switching is also useful for some neural network applications in system identification and change detection.[43,46]

A neural network for recursive identification of model-switching dynamical systems must be multi-functional. The main tasks of the neural network should include on-line monitoring of the system output to detect a process change, systematic switching to the best model in the pre-determined set, and periodical recursive updating of the connection weights in order to continue to produce an unbiased estimate of the system output. To design such a change-detection neural network system is the first objective of this paper. This design is particularly useful for solving some recursive estimation problems for which analytical formulation is not always mathematical tractable and, sometimes, does not even yield a practical solution.[9,30]

Closely related to the detection-estimation problem is the multiple-step prediction of a dynamical system output; such a problem arises in the field of system planning and control. A neuro-identification system that can detect a process change, and track the output at the same time, may not predict accurately beyond one step ahead. Multiple-step prediction performance critically depends on the neural network generalization capability, which in turn depends on the network structure.

The second objective of this paper is to present a hierarchical neural network architecture that can produce a good multiple-step prediction accuracy, without much increasing computational and memory requirement of the processing elements. The hierarchical architecture can be integrated to the sequential model-change detection (MCD) neural network to perform on-line adaptive prediction of a non-linear, non-stationary discrete-time system. The underlying stochastic process is assumed to be in the NARMAX (non-linear autoregressive moving-average with external inputs) class of models.

The remaining subsections give a brief introduction to the key concepts of the paper. These definitions are fundamental to the discussions to follow.

8.1.1 System Identification of Dynamical Stochastic Systems

In a dynamical system, current output measurements depend not only on input signals, but also on their earlier values. System identification has the objective of inferring a model of relationship among the observed input-output signals through data analysis that is guided by some practical criteria. Thus, a pragmatic view is often adopted by the system engineer toward the application in mind for selecting among hypothesized candidate models rather than from a precise mathematical description.[26] According to Ljung, two simple rules by which the candidate models are evaluated are as follows: (1) A good model is one whose prediction errors are independent of the past data; (2) the best model structure is an optimum tradeoff between flexibility, indicated by a greater number of parameters in the model, and parsimony or a minimum model order. These rules are also useful for identification of the most suitable neural network architecture for a given dynamical system.

A practical solution to some difficult system identification problems might be best achieved by an automatic input-output mapping. The need for an automatic identification tool is justifiable, especially when the problem is difficult and the conventional methods of statistical model identification and parameter estimation are tedious and time consuming. The only requirement is that such mapping does not need an explicit system model specification. This assumption is logical, considering that the main purpose of practical system identification is to capture relevant relationships between the input and the output time series. Therefore, as long as the mapping of input data to the output captures such relationship, it would yield an adequate representation of the underlying process.

Existing automatic techniques of system identification are based on using a reduced-order parametric model to approximate an unknown system. Durbin-Levinson identification algorithm[2] is such an example in which the approximate representation of a time series is an autoregressive model of finite order. The Group Method of Data Handling of Ivaknenko is another automatic identification procedure, which employs polynomial regression models for the approximation purpose. However, to be least dependent on a specific model structure information, a practical automatic system identification tool must be non-parametric and free from restrictive model specifications. Neural networks with non-linear activation functions possess this property.

8.1.2 Non-stationary and Non-linear System Dynamics

Let Y_t denote a real-valued random variable representing the output observation of a dynamical system at time t. A collection $\{Y_t\}$ is defined as the stochastic process generating the observed time series, $\{y_t\}, t \in T$, where T denotes a set of integers. In a broad sense, ensemble-averaged statistical properties of a non-stationary time series change with time. In order to model non-stationarity in a time series, it may be reasonable to assume that such a series can be approximated by a number of local stationary (equivalently, piece-wise stationary) time series, each having different mean and covariance values, and the underlying process of the dynamical system switches among the stationary models associated with the local stationary segments. The idea of using "piece-wise stationary" models to approximate a complex non-homogeneous process is to simplify the system identification task. The price one pays is in increased complexity of a software design for implementing the multiple system models.

Some nonlinear time series models are linear in the model parameters; a well-known example is the bilinear model,

$$y(t) + \sum_{j=1}^{p} a_j y(t-j) = \sum_{j=0}^{r} c_j e(t-j) + \sum_{i=1}^{m} \sum_{j=1}^{k} b_{ij} y(t-i) e(t-j) \tag{8.1}$$

where $c_0 = 1$ and $\{e(t)\}$ is a zero-mean white noise sequence. Other non-linear models are the quadratic Volterra model, the threshold autoregressive models and the state-dependent models.[34,39] These models are respectively given by:

$$y(t) + a_1 y(t-1) + \ldots + a_n y(t-n) + \sum_{r=0}^{p} \sum_{s=0}^{q} c_{rs} y(t-r) y(t-s) = v(t) \tag{8.2}$$

where $\{c_{rs}\}$ are constant or time varying parameters of the Volterra model,

$$y(t) = a_0^{(j)} + \sum_{i=j}^{k_j} a_i^{(j)} y(t-i) + e^{(i)}(t) \text{ iff } y(t-d) \in \Re^{(i)}, j = 1, 2, \ldots, l \tag{8.3}$$

where $k_1, k_2, \ldots, k_i$ denote the orders of the autoregression in the l threshold regions, and

$$y(t) + \sum_{i=1}^{k} a_i y(t-1) y(t-i) = \mu y(t-1) + \sum_{j=1}^{l} c_j y(t-1) e(t-j) \tag{8.4}$$

where the autoregressive coefficients are $\{a_i\}$ and the moving average coefficients are $\{c_j\}$, respectively. The process has a nonzero mean μ and all the model parameters are functions of the process level at time $t-1$. It can be shown that the bilinear and the threshold autoregressive models are special cases of the state dependent model. Multivariate extensions are obvious.

Non-linear phenomena such as jumps or abrupt changes may be caused by a variation in frequencies of external inputs.[49] For a state-dependent process, local abrupt changes have been successfully modeled by piece-wise ARMA models with jump parameters. Note that the relationship between piece-wise linear models and non-linearity (e.g., caused by external excitations) implies a duality between non-linearity and non-stationarity of a stochastic process.

Due to the model-change behavior of an underlying process, such as the threshold autoregressive process, ensemble-averaged statistical properties of the output series are time varying; i.e., the output time series becomes non-stationary as the consequence. Now, since process non-linearity can be approximated by a number of piece-wise linear models, the ensemble of piece-wise linear stationary models must yield a resultant model whose moments are time varying. Therefore, piece-wise linear models can be used to represent both process non-linearity and non-stationarity.

8.1.3 Multiple-step Prediction of Time Series

A general non-linear prediction problem, which is not dependent on a specific time series model, may be stated as follows: given a stationary time series up to the current time, $y^t(t) = \{y(t), y(t-1), \ldots, y(t-n)\}$ a predictor $\hat{y}(t+m) = f(y^t)$ is to be found such that a specified error criterion; e.g., the mean-square error $E\{[y(t+m) - \hat{y}(t+m)]^2\}$, is minimized. It is well known that the min-MSE m-step-ahead predictor is the conditional expectation $E[y(t+m)|y(t), y(t-1), \ldots, y(t-n)]$. Further if the process $\{Y_t\}$ is Gaussian, then the conditional expectation is linear in $\{y(t), y(t-1), \ldots, y(t-n)\}$. The prediction problem now reduces to finding a set of parameters $a_0, a_1, \ldots, a_n$ such that $\hat{y}(t+m) = \sum_{j=0}^{n} a_j y(t-j)$ minimizes the MSE function. This conditional expectation is also known as the least-squares predictor.

Even for the case that the conditional probability density function of $y(t+m)$ given y^t exists, analytic solution of the conditional expectation is usually not possible. The method recommended in the literature[49] is recursive numerical integration of the Chapman-Kolmogorov equation. However, the multiple-step least-squares predictions are known to give misleading results with increasing m (e.g., all predictions may tend to zero). According to Tong, a working alternative method of obtaining non-linear least-squares prediction is to compute the conditional expectation directly from the time series (without postulating any model). Non-parametric techniques have also been recommended. Tong's suggestion indicates that practical multiple-step non-linear prediction by an automatic mapping function is preferable to a model-based approach.

The optimal m-step-ahead linear predictor, on the other hand, can be obtained by bootstrapping one-step at a time, from the optimal-MSE one-step-ahead predictor.[19] The bootstrapping procedure simply replaces unknown future data values by the predictions; the conditional expectations of future errors are replaced by zero. However, it is not true that bootstrapping a one-step-ahead non-linear prediction to m steps will yield an optimal m-step prediction; there has not yet been an established theory for multiple-step non-linear prediction at the present time. It seems that neural networks may offer a working solution for the non-linear prediction problem while there are no better alternatives around.

8.2 Neuro-Identification of Time Series

In the systems theory literature the term structural identification means the determination of the form of a system model which best fits the given data set. For linear systems, model structure is completely specified by the model order (dimensions of the input and output variables) and time delay (or time lags). Non-linearity, if present, may be detected by making use of higher-order correlation functions of the system input-output time series. For example, a non-zero correlation function like $E[y(t+k)y^2(t)]$ has been used to indicate existence of a non-linear distortion.[6] Knowledge gained from correlation analysis of this type can assist the system engineer in hypothesizing a number of tentative model structures which will be further validated by model residuals analysis. This conventional method is tedious and may yield nonunique representations.

Following the model structure identification phase, appropriate parameter estimation algorithms can be applied for residuals computation and model adequacy testing purposes. The extended least squares and the recursive maximum-likelihood algorithms[26] have been used to produce unbiased estimates of system parameters in the presence of non-linear noise terms.

Non-linear stochastic system identification is a very difficult problem; as Billings[5] stated, no one technique could be recommended as providing an acceptable solution. The present state of the art has not changed, even after a decade has passed. Exact identification of non-linear functions for sampled-data stochastic systems has not yet been possible and a means for approximating a non-linear mapping function for such a system is thus necessary.[11]

Linear and non-linear model identification through time series are discussed next. Following this, neuro-identification and neural network designs for mapping input and output of discrete-time dynamical systems are introduced.

8.2.1 Time Series Model Identification

A time series model is a function that transforms a white noise sequence into time series. The simplest model is the linear filter of a stationary time series.[8] The linear filter is expressed as an infinite-order moving average of a white-noise input. A parsimonious representation of the linear filter is known as the finite-order ARMA model,

$$y(t) = \frac{C(q^{-1})}{A(q^{-1})}\, e(t), \tag{8.5}$$

where $\{e(t)\}$ is a zero-mean white noise process, q^{-1} is the back-shift operator; i.e.,

$$\begin{aligned} q^{-j}e(t) &= e(t-j), \quad j = 1, 2, \ldots, \\ C(q^{-1}) &= 1 - c_1 q^{-1} - \cdots - c_{nc} q^{-n_c}, \text{and} \\ A(q^{-1}) &= 1 - a_1 q^{-1} - \cdots - a_{n_a} q^{-n_a}. \end{aligned}$$

The degrees of the polynomials A and C, are determined during the iterative model identification phase by some tools of time series analysis; e.g., the sample autocorrelation and the sample partial autocorrelation functions (SACFs and SPACFs). This idea is based on the fact that the statistical properties of a stationary time series do not change over time. Therefore a sequence of, say k observations (i.e., a window of length k) at time t, $\{y(t+1), \ldots, y(t+k)\}$, is assumed statistically identical to any other windows of k consecutive observations. In other words, theoretical ACFs and PACFs of the ARMA models can be used as templates for model identification of a given time series. The conventional practice of statistical ARMA model identification is to first guess the degrees n_a, and n_c, which will provide a closest match between the SACF and SPACF of the data at hand and the corresponding theoretical functions. Following this structural identification phase, the parameters are estimated and diagnostic tests are performed as necessary, until an adequate model is obtained.

Time series sequences of input and output variables are valuable for the identification of an underlying system model[8,26] In manufacturing process monitoring and control applications, the most general class of the discrete-time models is the nonlinear auto regressive-moving average with external inputs (NARMAX). Essentially, it is a direct generalization of the linear ARMAX models, which have been widely used in speech recognition, machine vision, chemical process control and other manufacturing applications. The NARMAX representation is given by:

$$y(t) = F[y(t-1), \ldots, y(t-n_y), u(t-1), \ldots, u(t-n_u), e(t), \ldots, e(t-n_e)] \quad (8.6)$$

where $y(t)$ and $u(t)$ denote real-valued random variables representing respectively the output and input observations of a discrete-time system at time t, $F(\cdot)$ denotes a general nonlinear function (e.g., a polynomial function of finite degree), n_y, n_u and n_e are the time lags of the NARMAX model, and e(t) is a white-noise process. In the case for which no lagged error terms are present the deterministic NARX model is given by:

$$y(t) = F[y(t-1), \ldots, y(t-n_y), u(t-1), \ldots, u(t-n_u)]. \quad (8.7)$$

The NARMAX model form is so-far the most general representation of non-linear stochastic systems that includes several existing non-linear models as special cases. Due to the general form of F, it is easy to see that even the state-dependent model (4) is a special case of the NARMAX. Further there is a clear relationship to the well-known class of the linear ARMA and the ARMAX models.

By and large, estimation of parameters in a stochastic time series model, either by an off-line or an on-line procedure, has been mainly based on the maximum likelihood approach or the method of least squares. Among the existing on-line (or recursive) identification approaches, the most useful class of system identification tools agree sequential prediction error algorithm.[19] By this approach, model parameters are chosen so that the sum of squares of the errors between the true system output (the observed time series) and the predicted output is minimized. Sequential updating of the parameter estimate, after a new data point $\{u(t), y(t)\}$ is obtained, can be done recursively by the algorithm, provided that appropriate starting values are available.

The prediction error algorithm is closely related to the Kalman filters and the Robbins-Monro stochastic approximation. Fundamentally, sequential estimation techniques which are based on the derivatives of a quadratic error criterion function, or by linearization of a non-linear model, are similar to the derivative-based neural network learning methods. However, many system identification techniques are not directly useful for training neural networks that possess many connections, because they would require a long computation time and a good deal of data storage at each processing step.

8.2.2 Nonlinear System Identification

The major practical problem associated with the general NARMAX models is that there has been no general methodology for the identification of a specific function F for a given non-linear system. To simplify the identification problem the response surface has been assumed to be a polynomial function of finite degrees in all variables. This class of non-linear functions is powerful, according to Chen and Billings, since it can approximate many types of non-linearities. In addition, polynomials are also linear in the model parameters which simplifies the estimation problem. For stable dynamical systems with control inputs, the polynomial model prediction has shown to be more accurate than the linear counterparts.

The traditional non-linear identification procedure is quite similar to the Box-Jenkins iterative time-series identification method: Given a finite sample of input-output time series $\{u(t), y(t)\}$, the structure of a tentative model is first determined through data analysis, based on correlation functions, and the tentative model parameters are estimated so that an error criterion function is minimized. This iterative approach is tedious and requires a great deal of time and skill of a well-trained statistician. Yet the resulting model is no more than a representation (out of several possibilities) of the real stochastic process, subject to the individual's opinion. Such difficulties, which are inherent to most non-linear identification problems, stem from the fact that the construction of a model requires a priori knowledge of the underlying process, which is generally not available in practical situations.

There are numerous techniques for non-linear structural identification and model parameter estimation. However, of all the parametric and non-parametric estimation approaches, only the pattern recognition and block-oriented systems methods[14,17,20] are most closely related to the neuro-identification methodology. The idea behind the block-oriented systems approach is that black-box identification may be avoided by decomposing the dynamical system into components which preserve the system structure and yet provide relevant informaton needed for a control application. The system structure is modeled by blocks of linear and non-linear elements in cascade. A disadvantage of this approach has been that it requires time consuming experimentation very much the same as that needed for the determination of a multilayer neural network architecture; i.e., finding the numbers of neurons and hidden layers for an application.

The pattern recognition method, on the other hand, is more promising than the block approach because it can directly capture deterministic patterns and correlations in the data. Although data correlations do not contribute to a unique model structure identification, this method is less time consuming than any other identification methods. The only assumption about the input-output series is that they are ergodic so that the correlation estimators can be made arbitrarily accurate (in principle), given a sufficiently long record of observations.

8.2.3 Neuro-Identifiction and Generalization

System identification by multilayer neural networks, or neuro-identification[45], consists of (1) the determination of time-lag information of the system input and output for the determination of a neural network input vector and topology and (2) iterative training of the synaptic strengths or connection weights which minimize an error criterion. The network training, an emulation of the data generator's transfer function, is analogous to model parameter estimation in conventional system identification. Selection of a parameter estimation method with good convergence properties, such as the prediction error algorithm for multilayer neural network training, is only one aspect of the overall network design problem. Even though the state of neural networks research is advancing rapidly, there are still some important issues remaining to be addressed: (1) to design a general NARMAX neuro-identifier which yields unbiased output estimation and good generalization capability; (2) to reduce the computational load and memory requirement of training algorithms for on-line learning of multilayer neural networks for multiple-step prediction; and (3) to extend the design to non-stationary time series change detection. This present study is primarily concerned with all these issues.

Historically, multilayer neural networks, trained by the back-propagation procedure as non-linear maps have been extremely successful in static pattern recognition applications.[28] Recently, they have also been applied as universal approximators to a large class of non-linear functions. For example, Billings *et al.*[7] shows that the multilayer perceptron (MLP) with sigmoidal transformation is a nonlinear map, which is equivalent to a high-degree polynomial function of the inputs to the network. The major advantage of such neural network mapping is in its ability to approximate any nonlinear input-output relationships to any desired degree of accuracy, provided that there are enough processing elements in the network and that appropriate training data is used in a sufficiently large number of iterations. Adding extra artificial neurons would correspond to having additional terms in the polynomial approximating function.

To some extent, model structure information is needed for the design of a neuro-identifier. Similar modeling problems which are typical in system identification, such as model misspecification, may also result if insufficient lagged terms of $u(t)$, and $y(t)$ are assigned as the network input.[7] In practice complete information is never available in real system identification and therefore several sources of model errors and uncertainties may result in an inadequate mapping. One way to alleviate some of the modeling problems is to incorporate information about alternative models and model-validation hypothesis testing into the network structure to facilitate the model structure determination. Such a multi-functional neural network should be able to select the best model from a pre-determined set after a certain amount of input-output data are processed by the neuro-computing system. Existing multilayer neural networks do not yet have this capability.

The majority of existing neuro-identifiers are universal approximators of non-linear input-output maps. The multiple-step out-of-sample predictions of non-linear time series as reported in the literature have not yet been satisfactory. Most authors demonstrate their results using either non-linear models with low orders and uncorrelated inputs, see for example,[12] or employ some chaotic time series which are essentially white noise.[29]

Multiple-step prediction outside the training sample, known as extrapolation in the literature of dynamical systems, is defined in this study as "out-of-sample generalization". The present state of the neural network research in non-linear time series is mainly in interpolation; the term generalization is synonymous with interpolation along the best fit surface which generates the input-output map.[29] In other words, most research results are concerned with in-sample generalization. Categorically, longer than one-step-ahead predictions are seldom used, because the traditional purpose of dynamical system identification has been in iterated maps, which may then be used for synthesizing data with the characteristics of true data. Extrapolations are poor and tend to become unstable. Non-linear prediction methods, according to Lowe and Webb,[29] are "not likely to be significantly better than simple linear methods", unless the data generator is static (i.e., stationary and deterministic).

Good generalization performance would be hard to get, if the goal of neural network training were to obtain a universal approximator. Therefore, the need for a new approach to non-linear system identification is clear; a neural network for out-of-sample generalization must be designed to capture the process dynamic in order to do more than high-dimensional curve fitting. One way to achieve this goal might be through multi-functional neural nets, which are also capable to learn serial correlations in the stochastic observations and be able to directly represent adequate process knowledge in the connections.

8.3 Neural Network Architectures

Two types of neural network architectures for input-output mapping of a dynamical system are presented in the following two sections: (1) direct mapping and (2) indirect mapping. Both architectures are extendable to non-linear, non-stationary stochastic systems as well. Out-of-sample neural network generalization, based upon these two architectures, is introduced next.

8.3.1 Direct-Mapping Neural Networks

In direct mapping, also called direct learning (DLN) in,[44] the idea is to directly transfer predetermined knowledge of process models into a neural network structure and the connection weights, thus bypassing the time consuming weight training and iterative computer experimentation. Through direct learning, information about the model structure is used to specify the number of nodes in a single-layer neural network and the model parameter values (or their estimates) are used directly as the connection strengths. As a consequence, the output of the network is exactly equal to the conditional expectation of the target, provided that the input-output model is linear in the parameters. Justifications for the direct learning neural network are given in.[44]

There are several useful non-linear models that can be represented by the DLN approach; the polynomial nonlinear autoregressive-moving average with external inputs (NARMAX), the threshold autoregressive (TAR), the bilinear and the quadratic Volterra models[34] are all linear in the parameters. Figure 8.1 illustrates a bivariate threshold autoregressive DLN with m members in the model set. The process may switch from one model in the set to another according to the following description:

$$y(t) = a_0^{(i)} + a_1^{(i)}y(t-1) + a_2^{(i)}y(t-2) + \ldots + a_k^{(i)}y(t-k) + e^{(i)}(t) \qquad (8.8)$$

if $\{y(t-1), \ldots, y(t-k)\} \in \Re^{(i)} =$ i-th region in the k-dimensional space $\Re^k, \{e^{(i)}(t)\}$ is a white noise process, $a_0(i)$ is a vector of constant coefficients and $a_j^{(i)}, j = 1, 4 \ldots, k$ are $n \times n$ matrices of the AR parameters, y(t) is an n-vector of observations ($n = 2$ in Figure 8.1), and $i = 1, 2, \ldots, m$. The switching time is assumed random, because at a given time (e.g., a process sampling instant) it is not known in advance which model in the set is the best description of the process. Given that on-line data windows are submitted sequentially, the neural net can be used as a process monitor in the following manner: at each sampling time it computes one-step-ahead prediction errors (innovations) and performs parallel multiple statistical

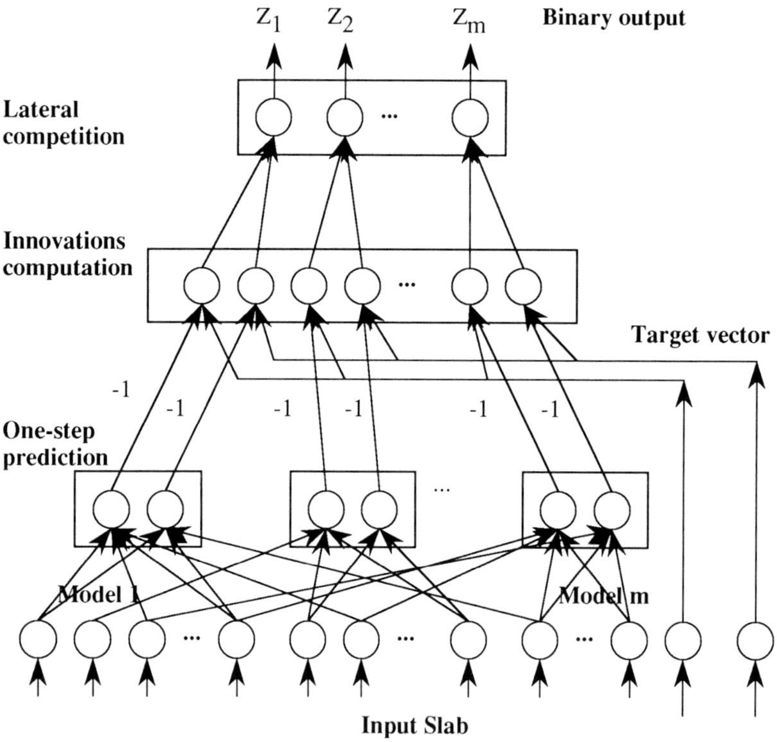

Figure 8.1: Multimodel identification by DLN

hypothesis tests on the innovation sequences. The output node that produces uncorrelated errors (white-noise innovations) with a minimum variance will identify the best model for the most recently submitted input vector. For a bivariate time series, a two-dimensional moving data window of an appropriate number of observations must be specified.

Each submodel in Figure 8.1 is a bivariate AR representation, and the network output from a typical subnetwork is the conditional expectation on the input data up to time $t-1$. For example, a typical subnet output for a bivariate AR(2) is given as follows:

$$\hat{y}(t) = \begin{pmatrix} \hat{y}_1(t) \\ \hat{y}_2(t) \end{pmatrix} = \begin{pmatrix} a_1^{(1)} & a_2^{(1)} \\ a_1^{(2)} & a_2^{(2)} \end{pmatrix} \begin{pmatrix} y_1(t-1) \\ y_2(t-1) \end{pmatrix}. \tag{8.9}$$

It is clear that the direct-mapping neural network yields the exact conditional expectation, given knowledge of the underlying process models and parameters. Extensions to the general multivariate polynomial NARMAX and other models that are linear in the parameters is straightforward.[44]

8.3.2 Indirect-mapping Neural Networks

In the situation where only a partial system knowledge is available, but plenty of process measurements are at hand, a "gray box" mapping neural network is a viable alternative to tedious multivariate time series analysis. Such an indirect input-output map provides a universal approximation function, depending on the non-linear activation function used at each processing element. For example, when the transformation function is sigmoidal the resulting map yields a non-linear polynomial function of all inputs to the neural network.

Under fairly weak conditions on the functions $f(\cdot)$ and $g(\cdot)$ in Eq. (8.10) below, a multilayer neural network can be constructed to approximate the mapping over a training set,

$$y(t+1) = f[y(t), y(t-1), \ldots, y(t-n_y)] + g[u(t), u(t-1), \ldots, u(t-n_u)] \tag{8.10}$$

where $n_u \leq n_y$ and $(u(t), y(t))$ is an observed input-output pair of the single-input single-output (SISO) deterministic system at time t.[31] The gray-box mapping may also be defined by a single function like Eq. (8.7). The neural network then becomes a universal approximator of the dynamical system similar to a polynomial multiple regression model fitting, based on the least squares principle, to a given data set. This type of modeling exercise is normally performed during a preliminary system analysis, when knowledge about the underlying process is incomplete. The task of weight estimation is delegated to the neural network training procedure (e.g., the error back-propagation). The learning performance criterion is in minimizing the mean-square error of the one-step-ahead prediction. As discussed earlier, the resulting indirect map cannot perform adequately as a multiple-step-ahead predictor beyond the training set.

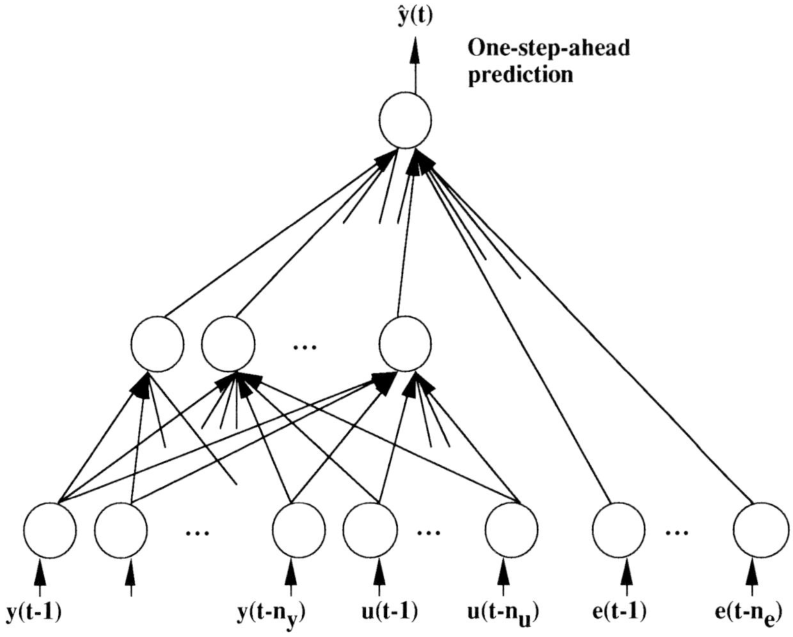

Figure 8.2: An ARMAX neural network with linear errors.[7]

8.3.3 Two Architectures for Indirect Mapping

A neural network map of a single-input single-output NARX process with a linear (additive) noise model is proposed[7] and shown in Figure 8.2. The partial knowledge required is the parameters n_u, n_y, and n_e corresponding to the time-lags of the input, the output and the error terms, respectively. The authors neither explain how the error inputs for training the network might be obtained, nor how the network might be extended to include non-linear noise terms.

It is easy, on one hand, to extend the Billings et al. architecture to polynomial NARMAX simply by connecting the error inputs, based on the innovations, to all hidden nodes where sigmoidal transformation is performed. On the other hand, computation of the time-lagged error inputs will be more involved than that of the direct learning network. An iterative procedure for calculating the innovations and storing their time-lagged values is deemed necessary for both cases. But, unlike the direct mapping approach, the indirect map may not produce a stable error sequence during the training since the indirect estimates of the connection weights, contaminated by ill-behaved feedback errors, may not meet a stability criterion for parameter convergence.[19]

Werbos *et al.*[52] propose a time-lagged recurrent network (TLRN) architecture which is also capable of encompassing the NARMAX models. By time-lagged recurrence, it means that a PE at time t is allowed to receive the output from any other PEs at time $t-1$. The vector of inputs to the network at time $t, x(t)$ of dimension $n+N$, is made up of time-lagged feedbacks from the hidden and output PE and an exogenous m-dimensional input vector, $X(t) = x_1(t), \ldots, x_m(t)$. The network structure is a special multilayer perceptron (MLP) with the total number of inputs equal to $N+n+1$. The original TLRN is described by the following equations:

$$\begin{aligned} x_i(t) &= X_i(t), \quad 1 \leq i \leq m \\ v_i(t) &= \sum_{j=0}^{i-1} W_{ij} x_j(t) + \sum_{j=i}^{N+n} W'_{ij} x_j(t-1), \quad m+1 \leq i \leq N+n \\ x_i(t) &= f[v_i(t)], \quad m+1 \leq i \leq N+n \\ \hat{y}_i(t) &= x_{i+N}(t), \quad 1 \leq i \leq n \end{aligned} \tag{8.11}$$

where f denotes the sigmoid function, and x_0 represents the constant 1.0. W_{ij} and W'_{ij} are the connection strengths between nodes i-th and j-th, corresponding to the outputs at time t and $t-1$ respectively. The authors suggest that the weight adaptation may be done by minimizing the squared error exactly as in the error back-propagation scheme. The network architecture is depicted in Figure 8.3. $X(t)$ is the same as $u(t)$ that is used in the NARMAX equation. Here n and m are the dimension of the input and output vectors, respectively. The time lag value is one in Eq. (8.11).

It may be noted that the parameter N is left to the user to specify, which means that the network topology is dependent on the predetermined numbers of inputs and hidden nodes for a given problem. The $N+n+1$ input nodes (including the bias) are fully connected to each of the $N-m$ PEs in the hidden slab and also to each of the n PEs in the output slab. The input slab (or buffer) is composed of m external inputs at time t and $N+n-m$ time-lagged internal inputs (from the hidden and output layers). In addition to the time-lagged feedbacks to the input slab, there are also weighted time-lagged connections to all hidden and output PEs. The total number of nodes is equal to $2(N+n)-m+1$. It is necessary that the number of the hidden PEs be specified by the designer, given known values of n_y and n_u.

The TLRN architecture may be extended to include output measurements with general time lags longer than one period by simply adding the following nodes and connections:

$$\sum_{k=2}^{n_y} \sum_{j=i}^{N+n} W_{ij}^{(k)} x_j(t-k), \quad m+1 \leq i \leq n+N$$

where n_y is the largest lag value for y. Similarly, time-lagged inputs $x_i(t-k)$ ($i = 1, \ldots, m$ and $k = 1, 2, \ldots, n_u$) can be included in the original TLRN formulation,

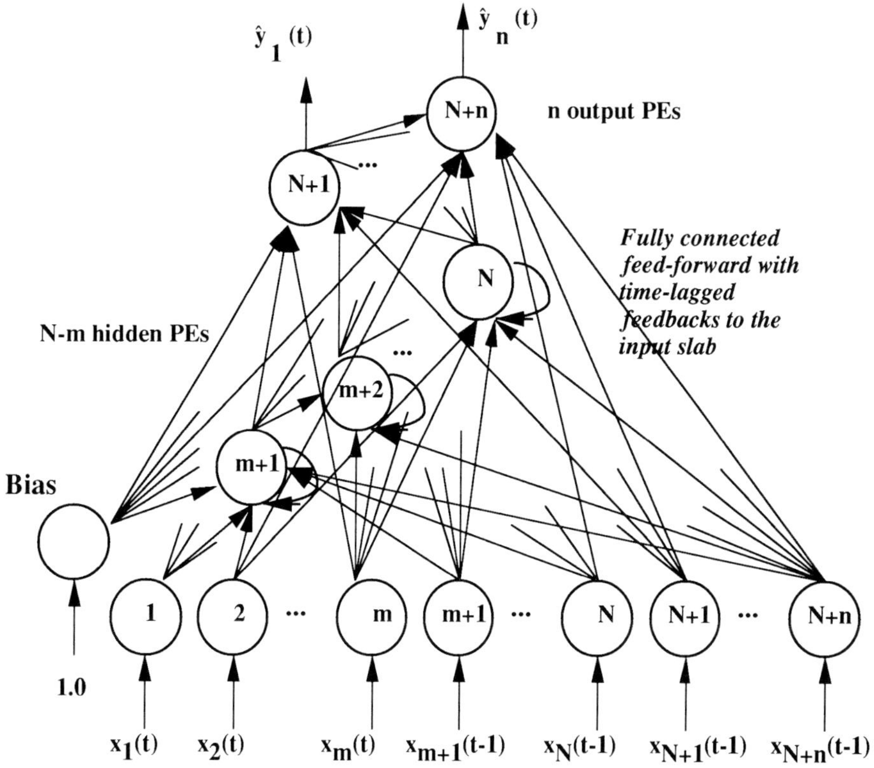

Figure 8.3: The time lagged recurrent neural network (TLRN)

Eq. (8.11). Since time-lagged error inputs may be interpreted as a special case of external inputs to the dynamical system, it then follows that the TLRN network can be made general to subsume any NARMAX models of arbitrary structure. Note that the extra lags correspond to additional nodes in the network. The total number of an m-input, n-output NARX, for example, is equal to $m(n_u+1)+2(N-m)+nn_y+n+1$, or $2N+m(n_u-1)+n(n_y+1)+1$. The number of the hidden PEs is fixed at $N-m$. Thus, for given n and m values, the number of the hidden PEs depends on N and vice versa.

The following examples are intended to explain how the network architecture may be determined for a given problem.

Example 3.1

Consider a general single-input single-output NARX model $y(t) = F[y(t-1), y(t-2), u(t-1), u(t-2)]$ for which a TLRN is to be developed to perform one-step-ahead prediction to time t, given observed data up to time $t-1$. F is an unknown non-linear function. The partial knowledge about this input-output map is $n = m = 1$, and $n_u = n_y = 2$. The total number of input nodes, including the bias, is $2N+5$. If the number of the hidden PEs is chosen to be one, then $N = 2$ and the total # of nodes is 8. This network is shown in Figure 8.4a. Outputs from nodes 6 and 7 are delayed, before being sent to the input slab. Note that the total number of nodes is not 9 since there is no external input at time t.

Example 3.2

Suppose that we are dealing with a multivariate NARX system having $n = 2$ and $m = 3$. It is desired to construct a TLRN for the one-step-ahead prediction, 2.

$$\hat{y}(t) = \begin{pmatrix} \hat{y}_1(t) \\ \hat{y}_2(t) \end{pmatrix} = f[\mathbf{y}(t-1), \mathbf{u}(t), \ \mathbf{u}(t-1)]'$$

The input vector for this network consists of 6 components $u_1(t), u_2(t), u_3(t), u_1(t-1), u_2(t-1)$, and $u_3(t-1)$, an unknown number of time-lagged signals from the hidden slab, and 2 time-lagged output values $y_1(t-1)$ and $y_2(t-1)$; $n_y = n_y = 1$. The total number of nodes is $2N+5$. Choosing a single hidden node, we have $N-m = 1$ and $N = 4$. Hence the total number of nodes is 13. This TLRN structure is given in Figure 8.4b.

There is an important advantage that TLRN can offer over the alternative architecture by Billings et al.; the feedforward signals present in any layer of a TLRN essentially comes from all the layers below. In other words, any one layer is fully connected to all layers above it, not just to the layer immediately above as in ordinary MLP networks. Such special connections provide multiple nesting of the sigmoidal transformation; this is equivalent to having many extra cross-product terms for all

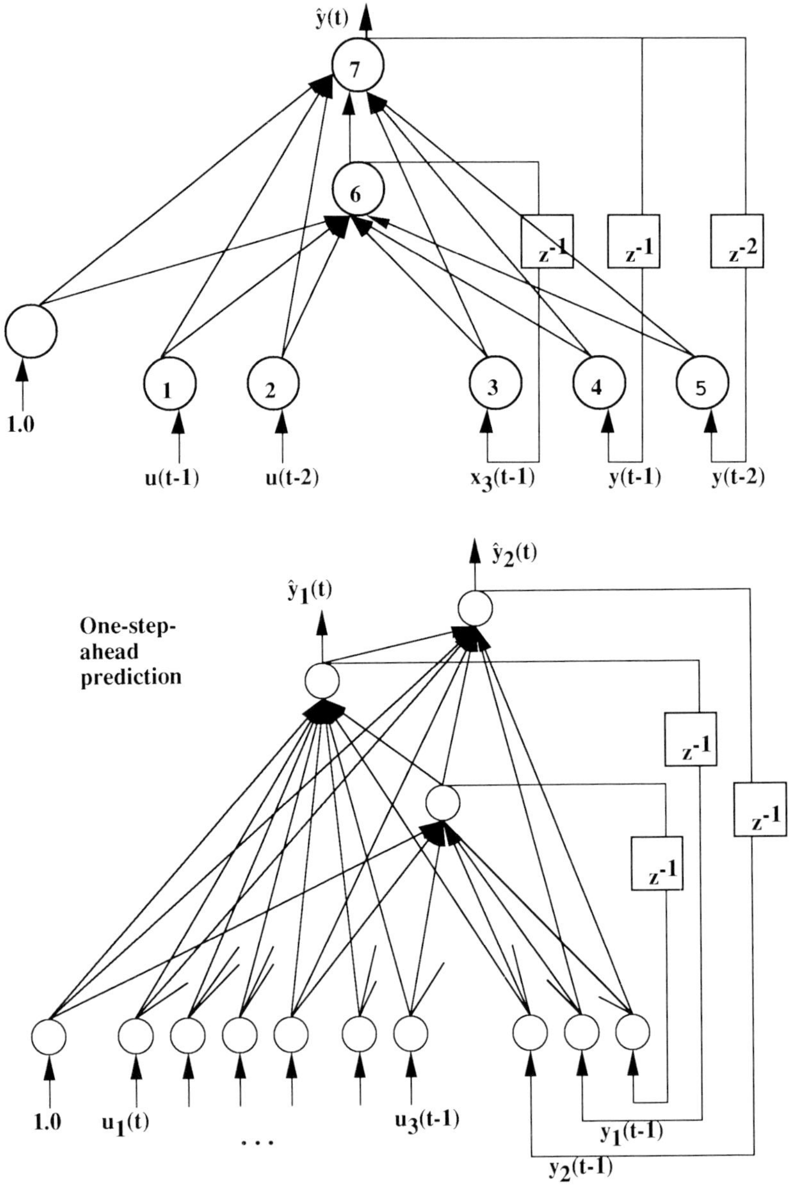

Figure 8.4: a) A TLRN for a univariate NARX, b) A TLRN for a multivariate NARX

signals within the neural network. For some highly non-linear problems, these extra connections should increase the interpolation accuracy.

In the following presentation only TLRN will be used instead of the Billings et al.architecture because of its greater design flexibility. However, the neural networks of the present study have not yet implemented the feed-back connections from the hidden PEs; the commercial software package used in this study does not support the TLRN special feedback connections.

8.3.4 A Modified TLRN Structure

A useful modification has been made to the original TLRN in this study; the purpose is to make it easy to determine the number of the hidden units directly from the NARMAX model order (n and m) and time-lag information (n_u and n_y). This is done by a redefinition of the input dimension. Let m represent the total number of all input and output measurements, including their time-lagged values. The definition of n is the same as before. Next replace the lag-1 recurrent inputs form the output slab and hidden PEs by the lag-1 values from the m input signals.

As a consequence the total number of input nodes, including the bias, would be $2m + 1$. Equating the original number of inputs, $N + n$, to $2m$ and solve for N, it follows that $N = 2m - n$. Now the number of the hidden PEs is $(2m-n)-m = m-n$, and the maximum total number of nodes in the modified TLRN becomes $3m + 1$.

The modified TLRN has some advantages over the original design; the complicated feedback associated with time lagged signals to the input slab are simplified, and the new design gives a unique architecture without having to guess for the number of the hidden units. The lag-1 inputs created from the m input signals may not be necessary for some non-linear maps. However, in multiple-step prediction of a dynamical stochastic system, the time-lagged inputs can help improve generalization accuracy.

Consider for example the following non-linear ARMA (NARMA) model

$$y(t) = a_1 y(t-1) + a_2 y(t-1)e(t-1) + a_3 y(t-1)y(t-2) + e(t) \tag{8.12}$$

where $\{e(t)\}$ is a white noise process with mean m and variance s^2. The one-step-ahead least-squares predictor is given by

$$\hat{y}(t+1) = \mu + a_1 y(t) + a_2 y(t)e(t) + a_3 y(t)y(t-1) = f_1[y(t), y(t-1), e(t)]. \tag{8.13}$$

Thus, the time-lagged input signals are $y(t), y(t-1)$, and $e(t)$. In practice, the time-lag information is determined from statistical correlation analysis. The modified TLRN for one-step-ahead prediction of this NARMA time series would have $m = 3, n = 1$, two hidden PEs and the total number of nodes would be 10. The 3 lag-1 delayed input nodes would correspond to $[y(t-1), y(t-2), e(t-1)]$, but the redundant $y(t-1)$ input node may be deleted to simplify the network structure.

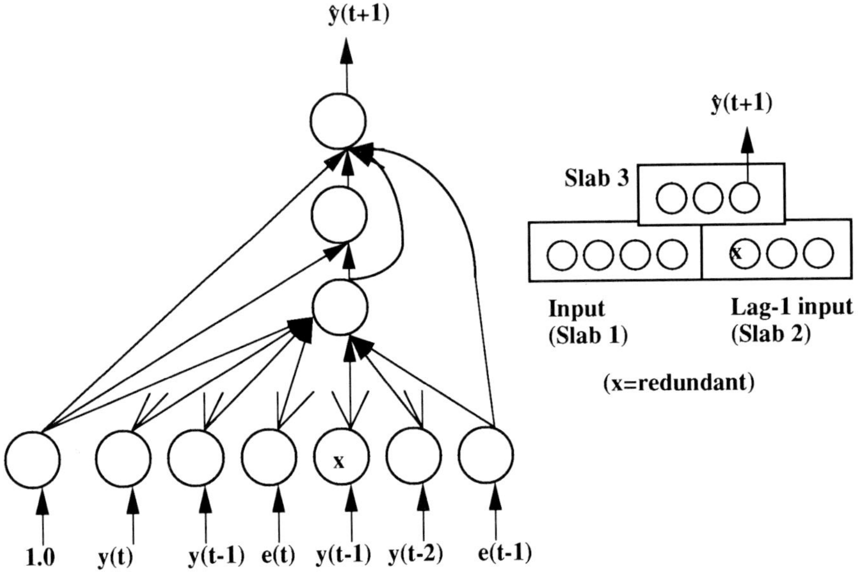

Figure 8.5: A modified TLRN for a NARMA process

An apparent difficulty in neuro-identification of NARMA time series is due to the unobservable (noise) inputs to the neural network. One way to go around this problem is to create $\{e(t)\}$ by a random number generator. As long as the computer-generated white noise sequence is bounded and belongs to the same compact set as the unobservable noise process, the network stability and convergence properties will not be affected.[44]

8.4 Hierarchical Neural Networks

One way to improve upon the multiple-step prediction accuracy is to design an appropriate network structure which captures the time evolution of the stochastic process that generated the time series data. This section presents a novel hierarchical neural network design based on the time-lagged recurrent architecture proposed by Werbos, which encompasses the NARMAX stochastic difference equation, for performing multiple-step prediction beyond the training set.

Following a brief introduction on the forward chaining concept, a novel hierarchical neural network architecture for multiple-step-ahead prediction is introduced. Numerical examples of an application of the proposed idea are also presented: two simulation results and one report on multiple-step-ahead prediction of a real time series are given.

8.4.1 Forward Chaining of Neural Network Output

The present state of research in neuro-identification has been concerned with non-linear deterministic functions with additive white noise (for example,[31,35,52]). The goal of such a neuro-identification approach is to infer an unknown functional relationship from given input-output training samples. In other words, the neural net attempts to reconstruct the time series generator from the training samples such that the input-output functional relationship is close to the true function in the mean-square error sense.

The majority of the existing research uses multilayer perceptron networks trained by the back-propagation learning rule[36] to do one-step-ahead prediction with good accuracy. Recently, Werbos *et al.*[52] have advanced the state-of-the-art by proposing a neural network training procedure, called forward chaining for multiple-step in-sample prediction of single-input single-output (SISO) time series. The network learning rule used by them is the ordered-derivative algorithm for time-lagged recurrent network, which is also called the "back-propagation through time" (BTT) method. The forward chaining can be straightforwardly applied for on-line prediction of future observations following the training phase. Results by Werbos et al. show that the method worked very well for ARMA time series.

Basically, in order to predict a value $y(t+k)$ of an output time series by forward chaining, the one-step prediction of $y(t+1)$, conditional on the observed data up to time t would be made first. Then this predicted value would be treated as if it were the true observation to compute another one-step prediction from $t+1$ to $t+2$. The procedure is bootstrapped in this manner to the target time $t+k$ (see Figure 8.6). The forward chaining procedure may be repeated, either sequentially or randomly, at each point $t = 1, 2, \ldots, T-k$, within the training sample of T observations. The k-step prediction error is then computed and back propagated to adjust the weights of the network. After the training is completed, the neural network may only be used to forecast $y(t+k)$; intermediate prediction at leadtimes less than k cannot be learned since the supervised learning procedure is based on a single target $y(t+k)$. It may be noted that the bootstrapping operation introduces a time delay (wait time) to every iterative learning step and might greatly increase the data storage and the total training time in real operations where multiple-step predictions at various leadtimes are required.

8.4.2 A Hierarchical Neural Network

The use of time series data at time t and $t-1$ for training the one-step-ahead prediction is necessary to provide the TLRN network with correlation information inherent in

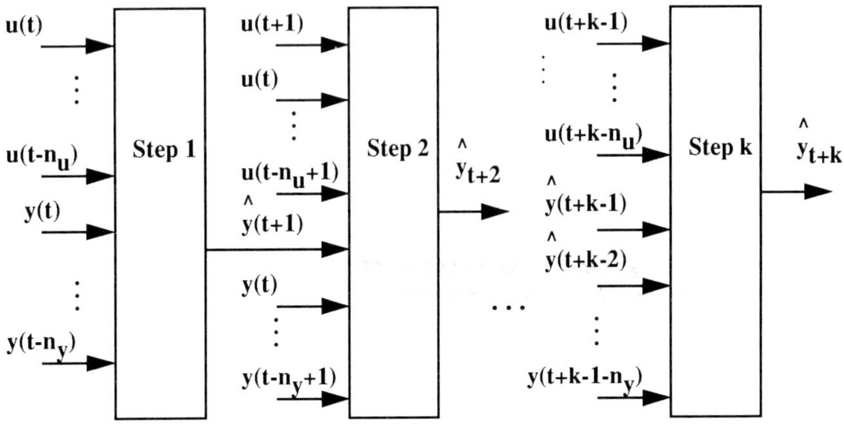

Figure 8.6: Forward chaining concept

the measurements of a dynamical system. This requirement is even more critical for multivariate input vectors as described in the Werbos' original design. In order to predict accurately over a prediction lead time, the neural network must be able to capture time-dependent causal relations in the time series. Thus, time lags greater than one will have to be included in the input Slab 1. Rather than completely rely on a bootstrapped training procedure (e.g., the method of Werbos *et al.*[51]) to accomplish this purpose, we choose to introduce the forward chaining directly into the hierarchical network architecture as illustrated in Figure 8.7 for a NARMA process. Here Slab1 and Slab2 of each level in the hierarchy provide the necessary inputs to the hidden and the output PEs in Slab3. The connections for the indirect map are the same as discussed previously (see Figure 8.5).

The architecture of the hierarchical network in Figure 8.7 is completely extendable to a general k-step-ahead prediction ($k > 3$) of any SISO model. For the NARMA(2,1) prediction problem the input signals $\{y(t-j), j > 2\}$ and $\{e(t-i), i > 1\}$ are not needed. A more compact design with 2 nodes in Slab 2 also works equally well. The extra input nodes, however, may be used to expand the model to NARMA(3,2) if such a need arises.

The hierarchical architecture can be extended further to a general NARMAX (n_y, n_u, n_e). The idea is applicable to both direct and indirect maps. However, it is much easier to do multiple-step prediction using indirect mapping of an unknown NARMAX process;one only needs to know the model dimension and time-lag orders n_y, n_u, and n_e for a stochastic dynamical system of interest. Techniques for model structure identification[6] may be used for determining the time lags.

The hierarchical neural network architecture for the general NARMAX model is

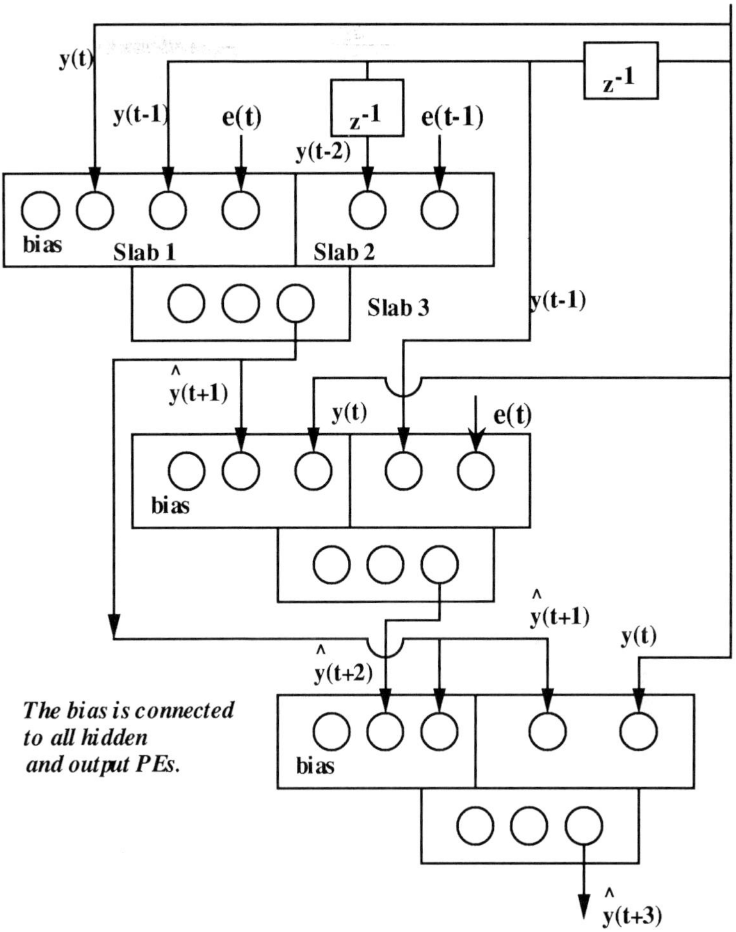

Figure 8.7: A hierarchical TLRN: three step prediction of NARMA (2,1)

a straightforward extension of the NARMA network in Figure 8.7. The number of levels in the hierarchy would correspond to the maximum prediction leadtime (i.e., number of steps or time periods) to be made from a given time t. The inputs to the first slab of any level would be the current and previous measurements from a process monitoring system plus the time-lagged predictions and other data from the level direcly below. The local memory of a processing element can be used to store the most current lagged data and innovations computed on-line.

Numerical Example 4.1

A NARMAX model in Chen and Billings[11], shown in Eq. (8.14), is used to generate an output and an input time series of 700 observations (*Data Set A*). The underlying non-linear polynomial model is linear in the parameters:

$$\begin{aligned} y(t) &= 0.7578y(t-1) + 0.389u(t-1) - 0.03723y^2(t-1) + 0.3794y(t-1)u(t-1) \\ &+ 0.0684u^2(t-1) + 0.1216y(t-1)u^2(t-1) + 0.0633u^3(t-1) - 0.739e(t-1) \\ &- 0.368u(t-1)e(t-1) + e(t) \end{aligned} \tag{8.14}$$

where $\{u(t)\}$ is a uniformly distributed random sequence, the distribution function being a Uniform (-0.8,1.2). The white-noise error sequence, $\{e(t)\}$, is an $N(0, 0.01)$ Gaussian process. The NARMAX model is stable, but it has a very low order and small noise variance. A statistical test indicates that the time series $\{y(t)\}$ is a white noise series. Such characteristics are typical of most published results in the nonlinear system identification literature.

The hierarchical TLRN for this map is almost identical to Figure 8.7, with an exception that the inputs to the network are based on the following mapping functions:

$$\begin{aligned} \hat{y}(t+1) &= f_1[y(t),\ u(t),\ e(t)], \\ \hat{y}(t+2) &= f_2[\hat{y}(t+1),\ u(t+1)], \\ \hat{y}(t+3) &= f_3[\hat{y}(t+2),\ u(t+3)]. \end{aligned} \tag{8.15}$$

The number of the input signals to the three levels are respectively, 6, 4, and 4.The number of the hidden PEs for all levels is the same as the first level; i.e., $m - n = 3 - 1 = 2$. The prediction capability of the hierarchical neural network is very well demonstrated in Figure 8.8 and Figure 8.9. The out-of-sample generalization to three steps ahead is extremely accurate, even though the output series is not statistically different from a white noise sequence. This excellent predictive capability is also due to the persistently exciting inputs $u(t), u(t+1)$, and $u(t+3)$ employed by the neural network.

Numerical Example 4.2

An hourly water consumption record from the city of Arlington, Texas, provides the real time series used in this example. The water use record is for the month of April,

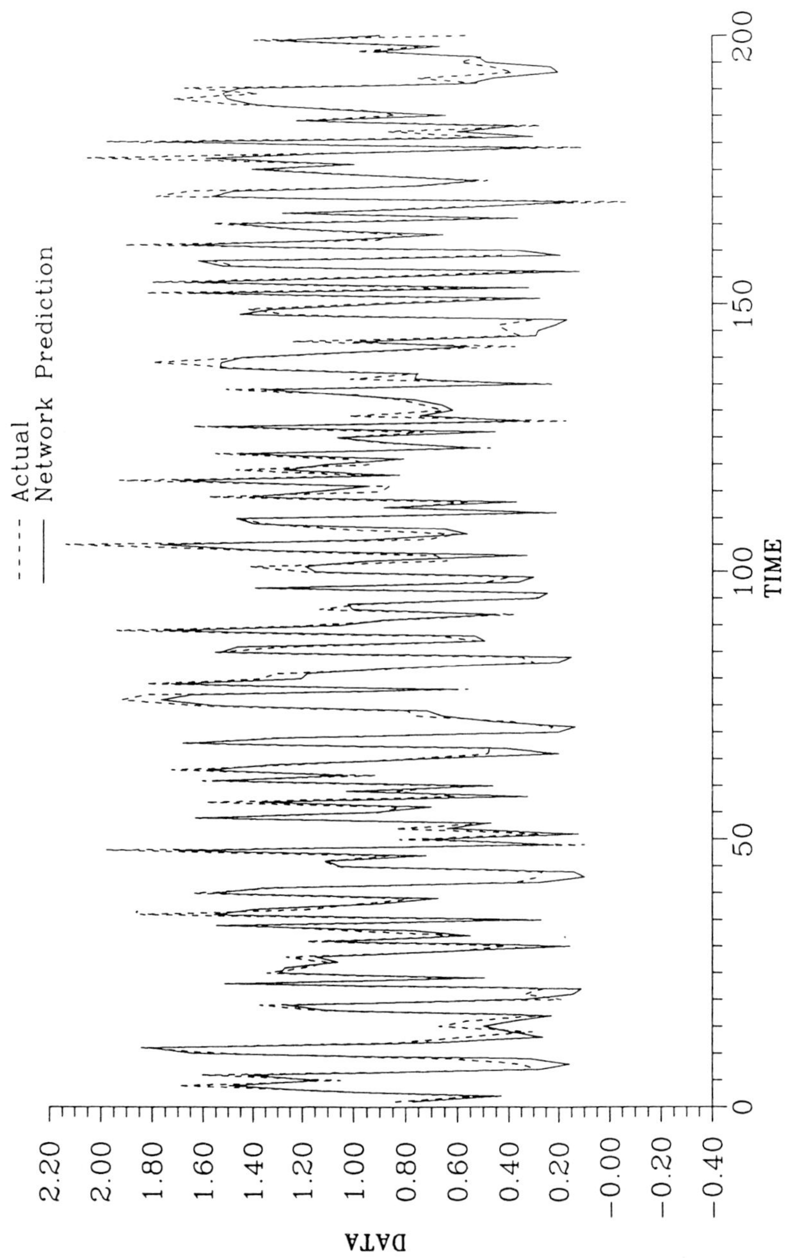

Figure 8.8: Hierarchical TLRN's one-step, out-of-sample prediction (data set A)

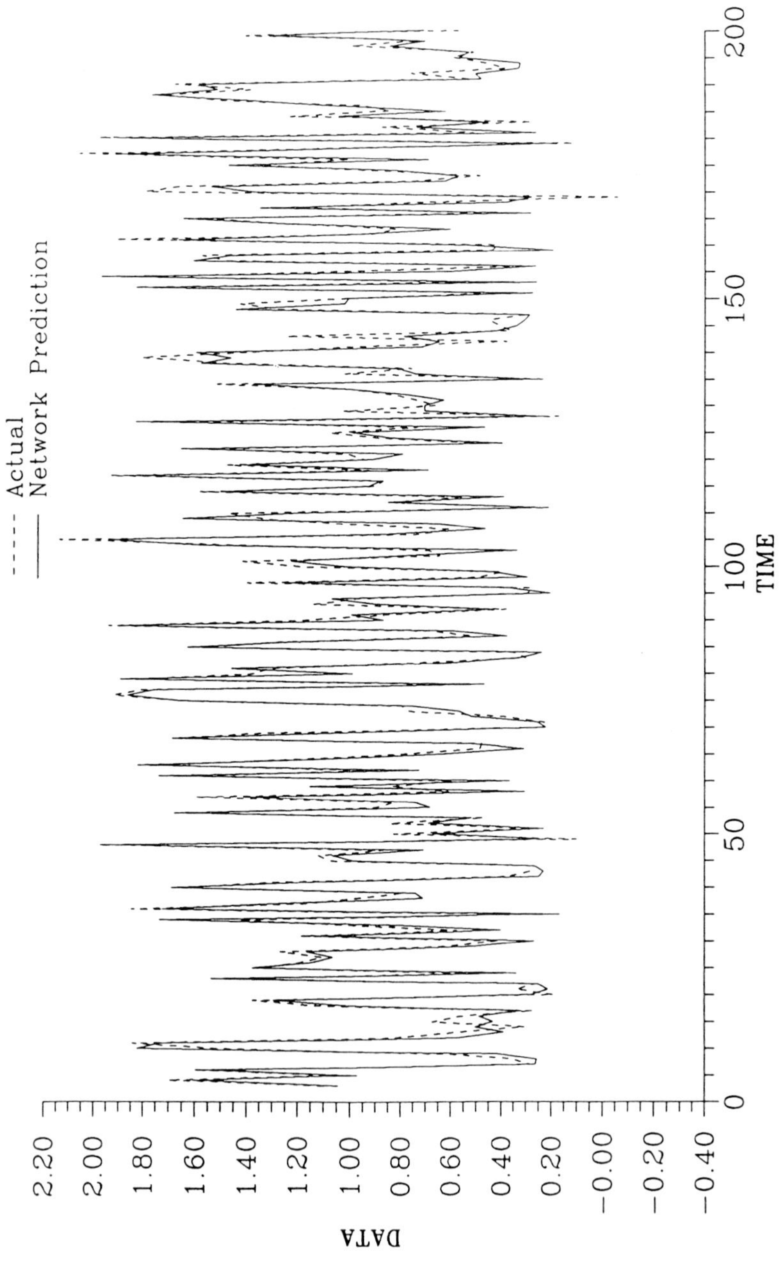

Figure 8.9: Hierarchical TLRN's three-step, out-of-sample prediction (data set A)

1989, and consists of 720 observations (Data Set B). The time series is characterized by irregular periods of hot and cold days mixed with sporadic rainfalls. A preliminary analysis of the water use data over the whole year of 1989 shows that the underlying process is seasonal, stochastic and non-stationary. The non-linear and non-stationary effects of rainfalls, cold weather fronts and summer heating are difficult to formulate mathematically. In this situation one cannot use the direct learning approach.

The hourly observations exhibit a daily cycle of 24 hours, and one annual seasonal cycle with a peak during the Summer. Nonhomogeneous behaviors like time-varying noise variance, randomly fluctuating amplitudes, and outlier observations are seen throughout the year. The sample autocorrelation functions of the data show largest correlations between the hourly consumptions 24 hours apart and 1 hour apart. Having available only the historical water use record as a priori information about the stochastic process, the objective of this experiment is to test the validity of the hierarchical neural network concept.

The correlation analysis suggests that the following NARMA mapping function might be appropriate

$$y(t) = F[y(t-1), y(t-23), y(t-24), y(t-25), e(t), e(t-1), e(t-23), e(t-24), e(t-25)]. \tag{8.16}$$

The time lags of one and twenty-four periods correspond to the two largest sample autocorrelations; the interaction between the memories of one and twenty-four hours apart implies that the observations $y(t-23)$ and $y(t-25)$ should accompany $y(t-24)$. The innovation inputs are needed to account for residuals autocorrelation, which would be present if only the time-lagged data values are used.

A hierarchical TLRN for this NARMA map for forecasting one to twelve-hours ahead, consisting of twelve hierarchical levels, has been constructed from (17) above. The $2m$ inputs to the first level for one-step-ahead prediction of $y(t+1)$ are $[y(t), y(t-1), y(t-22), y(t-23), y(t-24), y(t-25), e(t), e(t-1), e(t-22), e(t-23), e(t-24), e(t-25)]$, after all redundant input nodes have been eliminated. The modified TLRN architecture has $m = 6$ and $n = 1$; thus there are $m - 1 = 5$ hidden PEs for each level of the hierarchy. The modified TLRN architecture for this process can be constructed similar to the NARMA network in Figure 8.7. The total of all nodes is 19 in the first level.

The inputs to the second level are simply the one-step forward chaining of the first level, $\hat{y}[(t+1), y(t), y(t-21), y(t-22), y(t-23), y(t-24), e(t), e(t-21), e(t-22), e(t-23), e(t-24)]$. This simple forward-chaining scheme is repeated for the level 2 to the last level of the hierarchy.

Randomly generated error inputs and their lagged values, having the same statistical characteristics as the innovations associated with the same month of the previous year, have been used as pseudo error inputs for training the network and for the out-of-sample generalization test. The training samples are from the first two weeks of the data and the test data set is based on the last two weeks of the time series. The in-sample and out-of-sample predictions for the leadtime of 12 hours ahead are depicted in Figures 8.10 and 8.11, respectively.

The multiple-step forecast performance beyond the training set is quite good; the hierarchical neural network is able to accurately predict the new cyclical patterns with respect to the times of the peaks and the troughs in the last two weeks of the time series. It does not completely map the random fluctuations in the training data, a desirable characteristic of a good filter; these extreme values are either outliers or transient responses to extreme weather conditions.

The neural network does not very well predict the last two 24-hour cycles of the data. A closer examination reveals that the hourly water use measurements during the last two days of the month, which correspond to a weekend, behave uniquely different from the weekday patterns. The last weekend water use pattern happened to increase significantly from the level of the water consumption during the first two weeks, in which the network was trained. Obviously, the neural network cannot respond to this "untrained" water use behavior.

Discussions

Two different neural network modeling approaches to system identification from input-output time series are presented in this section. In the first situation a complete knowledge of the underlying model and parameter values are required; the resulting neural network map is called direct mapping, or direct learning, neural net. The second case uses only a partial knowledge of the input-output system in terms of the time-lag and order of the variables involved; the necessary time-lag relationship can be discovered by means of simple correlation analysis of a given time series. Both neural network maps aim at one-step-ahead prediction of the output variable of a discrete-time dynamical system.

Out-of-sample generalization for multiple-step forecasting beyond the training data can be achieved by a simple forward time-shifting operation on the neural-net map of an NARMAX process. The modified time-lagged recurrent network (TLRN) is used as the building block for contructing a multi-level hierarchical neural-net architecture. The hierarchical architecture has been shown to be valid, through empirical analyses, given that the inherent time-lag of the given time series is longer than one period.

8.5 Neural Networks for Process Change Detection

In computer-controlled manufacturing systems, process monitoring and data collection are performed by on-line computers. On-line measurements are necessary since an optimal control law depends on the state feedback to provide stability, optimality, and desired timely response to external disturbances. The effects of uncontrollable

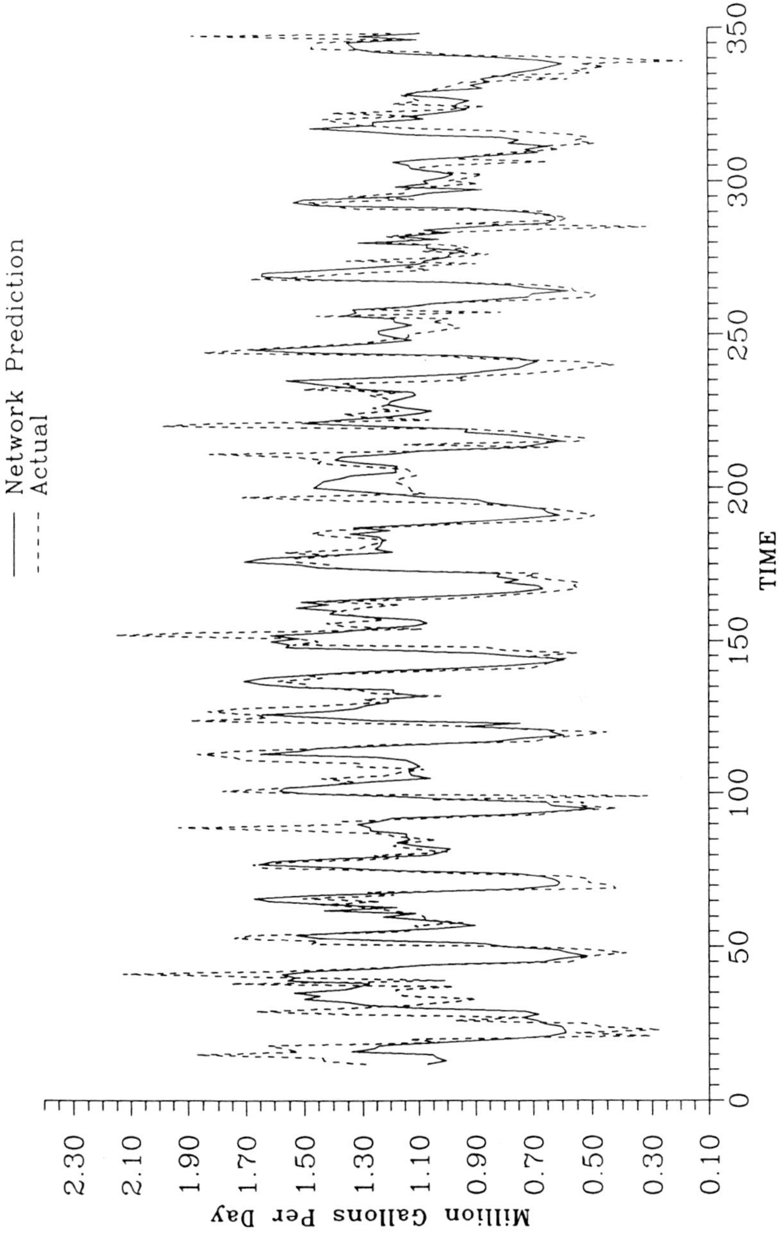

Figure 8.10: Hierarchical TLRN's 12-step-ahead in sample prediction (data set B)

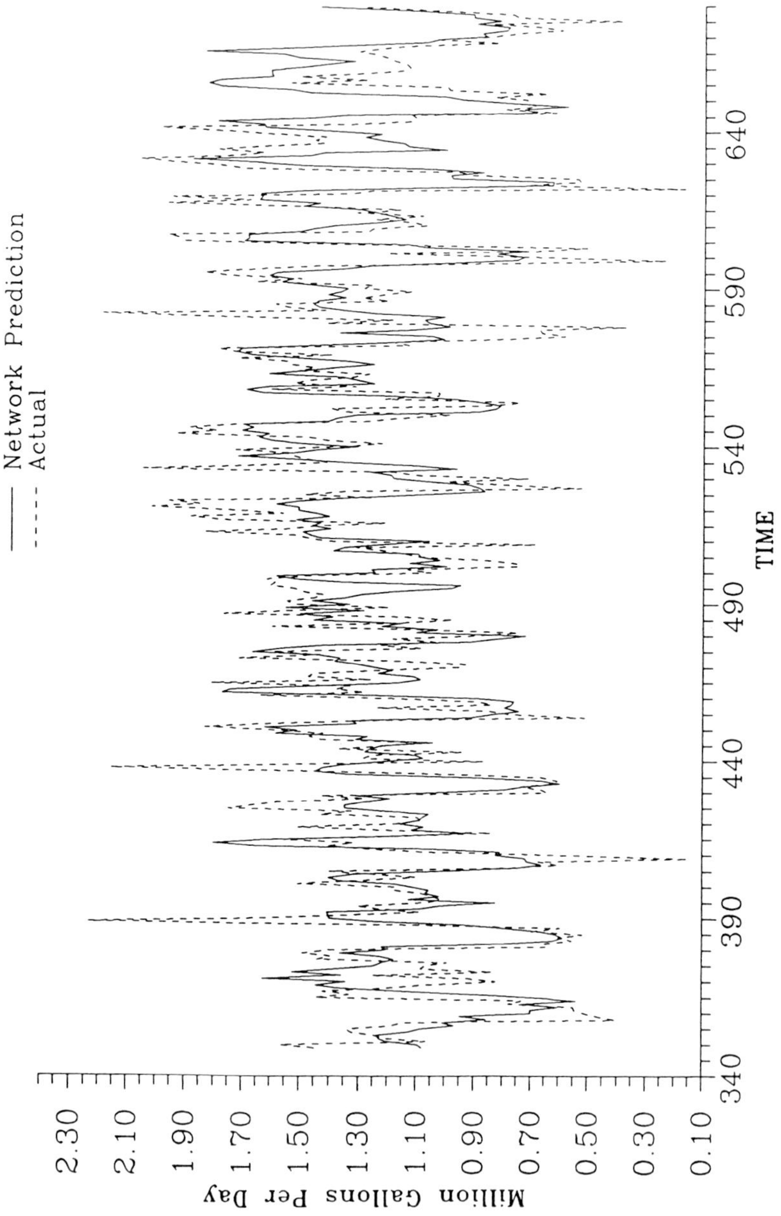

Figure 8.11: Hierarchical TLRN's 12-step-out of sample prediction (data set B)

disturbances may cause the process level or model parameters to change abruptly. Thus it may be necessary that some sequential detection mechanism for recursive identification of abrupt changes is considered in the design of an adaptive control system.

There are numerous reasons why a model of a stochastic process may become inadequate following its successful on-line implementation. One reason is that it is a natural tendency of any dynamical system to change over time due to a change in control inputs or time-varying disturbances.

This adaptive control problem is analytically difficult. However, in some situations the problem can be simplified by assuming that when a change occurs, the process model may abruptly switch from one to another within a set of known models. Process change detection in this environment is equivalent to on-line monitoring and identification of a "template" which best describes an incoming sequence of the process measurements during a specified sampling period. This pattern-recognition approach to the detection of a process model switching is the focus of this section.

The model change detection approach to be presented is based on the use of artificial neural networks for pattern recognition, which have demonstrated several advantages over the traditional statistical classification methods. One interesting property of the neural networks as reported in the literature is their robustness even when input distributions are non-Gaussian and the underlying processes non-linear.[28] This advantage is highly desirable in process manufacturing applications, since off-line data analysis and statistical model identification are time consuming and costly. Although off-line techniques give better accuracy in general, but in long run operations the difference may not be significant.

In this section two prototypes of the neural network approach for on-line model change detection, in the dynamic model-switching environment, are introduced. The process model is assumed to follow the NARMAX models; this class of models includes the bilinear, the quadratic Volterra models, and ARMAX models as special cases. The connection strengths of the first neural-network design (a DLN) are a priori parameter estimates of the underlying models (limited to the linear-in-parameter type), which have been predetermined from the historical data of a given process. These initial estimates can be sequentially updated by a recursive parameter adaptation algorithm, for instance, the recursive least squares technique.[26,41] The second change-detection method to be presented is based on a supervised learning neural network known as the learning vector quantization.[23] Finally, on-line model change detection performance of the two networks will be demonstrated by computer simulation experiments.

8.5.1 Multiple Model Approaches

The conventional multiple-model approach to system identification problem is described as follows: Given a number of possible values of system parameters and measurement noise statistics, multiple input-output models of the uncertain system can be hypothesized and a separate filter (i.e., a recursive state estimation algorithm) is formulated for each hypothesis. Each hypothesis defines specific values of the system matrices, disturbance-input matrix, measurement noise matrix, and initial conditions on the state measurement.[48] The traditional Bayes' rule is used to estimate the likelihood that a specified hypothesis (and the associated model) is correct, given an observed sequence of input-output signals. The model with the highest likelihood value is then selected as the winner. This approach is thus based on the statistical classification theory. Some shortcomings of this approach are that the required probability density functions are generally unknown and if there are several models and several parameter choices, a large number of parallel filters would be involved. As a consequence, this approach demands a great deal of on-line computation.

The success of the multiple-model identification approach is dependent not only on the initial choice of the likely models, but also on the criterion chosen for the hypothesis testing. The greatest advantage of the multiple-model approach is realized when a number of candidate models can be developed on theoretical as well as on empirical grounds; thus a knowledge base that contains physical understanding as well as empirical knowledge, or experience, about the dynamic system can be used for a priori model identification. Because of their richer use of system information, multiple-model identification algorithms have demonstrated better performance than adaptive filtering techniques based on single models.[3,24] The multiple model techniques, however, require extensive software development and maintenance.

With the advent of parallel processors and neuro-computing technology, the multiple-model approach to recursive system identification can now be utilized more practically to yield powerful results. It is the author's belief that a promising modern application of the multiple-model concept of system theory is in the design of multi-functional neural networks for recursive system identification.

8.5.2 Other Change Detection Techniques

The problem of detecting abrupt changes in dynamical systems is important because of its relation to many applications in system design, process monitoring, control, and prediction. In this section existing successful change detection methods and their associated criteria for efficient detection and change compensation are briefly discussed. The knowledge to be gained is useful for the design of a neural network change-detection system.

An abrupt process change may be interpreted as system malfunctioning; e.g., a process sensor failure. The study of such a problem has led to the design of successful failure detection techniques.[53] A more recent advancement is in the design of a stable adaptive control system[32] that can maintain its integrity following an uncertain change. In some situations, an abrupt change in a system output may be caused by a real disturbance effect that has not been modeled by the data processor; in this case, timely detection of a change in the process and the subsequent recursive parameters updating can result in better system prediction accuracies.[38,39]

As noted by Willsky,[53] failures of sensors (or measurement systems) may cause abrupt changes in the functional relationship between the input and the output variables or some increase in the measurement errors; a bias in the state estimate may result. Changes may also manifest themselves as an increase in the process noise level. Recursive identification techniques can be useful in such situations, since a continuing decision must be made, while a fault is being isolated and a control action taken, to restore the drifted system state. These problems are also common in manufacturing process monitoring and control.

The design of a failure detection system involves several issues, namely: 1) rapid failure detection (sensitivity), (2) low rate of false alarms, (3) reasonable computer storage and computation time requirements, and (4) parallel processing implementations. The last issue indicates a need for a parallel computing algorithm, since sequential change detection algorithms are too slow to perform multiple hypothesis tests.

Divergence of state estimates caused by uncertainties in a dynamical system, parameters, inputs, or measurement-error statistics can be prevented by simultaneously estimating the uncertain parameters and noise statistics and by using this on-line information to adapt the filter gains so that the filter is adaptable to (or "learning") the time-varying effects. In view of a connectionist, the process model parameters may be thought of as "connection strengths", or as weights between the input and output processing elements (nodes) in a neural network model.

8.5.3 Distance Metrics for Change Detection

Measures of similarity, such as the distance between two vectors in a vector space, have been used in the application of neural networks for pattern recognition; a stored pattern ("template") is recalled if it has a high degree of similarity to the input pattern. Some of the well known measures of similarity and distance metrics are the correlation coefficient, the Euclidean distance, the Hamming distance, the Mahalanobis distance, and the maximum posterior probability distance.[22] These metrics possess great flexibility since they can be selected to deal with real-valued vectors, sets of non-numerical values, binary codes, or text strings. In pattern recognition, both distance measures and discriminant functions are used to classify input patterns.

The correlation of two sequences of continuous-valued samples $\mathbf{X} = (x_1, x_2, \ldots, x_n)$ and $\mathbf{Y} = (y_1, y_2, \ldots, y_n)$ is given by

$$c = \sum_{i=0}^{n} x_i y_i \tag{8.17}$$

This measure has the same interpretation as the inner product of the two vectors constructed from the two sequences. In case X is a lag-k observation vector of the process $\mathbf{Y} = \{y_i\}$; i.e., $X = \{y_{i-k}\}$, then the lag-k sample autocovariance measure is computed by

$$c_k = \frac{1}{n-k} \sum_{i=1}^{n-k} (y_i - \bar{y})(y_{i+k} - \bar{y}), \quad k = 0,\ 1,\ 2,\ \dots\ ,\ K \tag{8.18}$$

where $\bar{y}$ is the mean of the sequence of observations. The lag-k sample autocorrelation is the normalized value where $r_k = c_k/c_0$ where c_0 is the variance estimate of the time series. Related to the sample autocorrelation measure is the sample partial autocorrelation coefficient at a given lag k, Φ'_{kk} which can be determined from the Yule-Walker equation, using the Durbin's formulation.[15]

The Euclidean distance is a useful pair-wise similarity measure of two vectors

$$d(X,Y) = \|X - Y\| = \sqrt{\sum_{i=j}^{n} (\chi_i - y_i)^2} \tag{8.19}$$

This similarity measure has been used in pattern recognition where the smallest distance of an unknown pattern from a standard pattern (within a set of standard templates) is an indication that it is the closest match to that template. The class label of the matched template is taken as the identification of the unknown pattern.

Related to the Euclidean distance is the Mahalanobis distance

$$d_{w(X,Y)} = \sqrt{(X - Y)^T\, W(X - Y)} \tag{8.20}$$

in which the weighting matrix W is the inverse of the covaraince matrix of the two vectors and T denotes the transpose. The Mahalanobis distance reduces to the Euclidean distance if the vectors are first transformed by multiplying them with the square root of the weighting matrix.

To detect a change in the underlying model of a process, fixed-length moving sequences of observations ("moving windows") can be used as sequential inputs to the model-change detection neural network. However, sequences of one-step prediction errors (equivalently, the innovations) from a filter using, say, an i-th model in a set of S standard models of a stochastic process are more useful input. This is because when a filter is operating optimally with respect to the mean-square error criterion, its innovations sequence will be a white noise. Thus, traditional statistical tests can be conveniently used for on-line diagnosis of the process model over time.

The innovation is defined as follows: $e_i(t) = y(t) - \hat{Y}_i(t|t-1)$ where $\hat{Y}_i(t|t-1)$ is the conditional expectation of output series for the next sampling instant, using the i-th model, $i = 1, 2, \dots, S$, and given all the available measurements to time $t-1$. A useful distance measure which is a function of the innovations is

$$d_i(t) = \frac{1}{\sqrt{N-1}} d(Y_N(t), \hat{Y}_{i,N}(t)) = \sqrt{\sum_{j=t-N+1}^{t} \frac{e_i^2(j)}{N-1}} \tag{8.21}$$

where $\{y(t), y(t-1), \ldots, y(t-N+1)\}, \hat{Y}_{i,N}(t) = \{\hat{Y}_i(t|t-1), \ldots, \hat{Y}_i(t-N+1|t-N)\}$, and N is the width of the moving window.

The distance in Eq. (8.21) is an estimate of the innovations standard deviation. A criterion for model identification may be based on the minimum distance, min $\{d_i(t)\}$. If the model producing this minimum value is different from the current model, then we may conclude that a model switching has occurred. The identified model will have the minimum prediction variance of all the candidate models with respect to the most recent moving window.

The portmanteau statistic[26] for testing model adequacy is a sum of squared residual autocorrelations,

$$Q_i(t) \;=\; N(N+2)\sum_{k=1}^{K}\frac{r_k^2\,[e_i(t)]}{N-k}. \tag{8.22}$$

When the innovations are used instead of the conventional model residuals, the lag-k sample autocorrelation from the i-th filter is given by,

$$r_k[e_i(t)] \;=\; \frac{N}{N-k}\cdot\frac{\sum_{j=1}^{N-k} e_i(t-j)e_i(t-j-k)}{\sum_{j=1}^{N} e_i^2(t-j)}. \tag{8.23}$$

The statistic is minimum for the best model for which the innovations are white or near-white noise. Together with the standard deviation metric, they provide the most reliable diagnosis on model change/switch from the optimal one. Sequential tests based on the two detection statistics are straightforward; inferences on the approximate time when a model switching occurred may be obtained, given that information about the average response delay of the change-detection statistic is available.

Finally, the mean absolute deviation, $m_i(t) = |\mu_i(t)|$ is a statistical measure of biasedness in an innovations sequence computed from

$$m_i(t) \;=\; |\mu_i(t)|$$

$$\mu_i(t) \;=\; \frac{1}{N}\sum_{j=0}^{N-1}\left(e_i(t-j)-\bar{e}_i(t-j)\right) \tag{8.24}$$

where $\bar{e}_i$ is the moving average of the i-th sequence of N innovations at time t. This mean-absolute-deviation measure is useful in detecting a change of a non-zero process mean.

8.5.4 Two Neural Networks for Model Change Detection

The architecture of a successful neural network detection system for a given application depends on available process information and input-output requirements of the neural network to be designed. Two cases are considered here:

1. It is assumed that a set of S time series models that completely describes a process' model-switching behavior is available to the analyst. Thus, the analyst has knowledge of the variables and time-lag values; e.g., n_a and n_c Eq. (8.5), including some a priori parameter estimates of the individual models. However, the time when a model switching event may occur, or which model the process may switch to, are unknown.

2. It is assumed that the sample autocorrelation functions (SACFs) and the sample partial autocorrelation functions (SPACFs) of the S typical process output signals are available. In this case, knowledge of the exact underlying model for each of the S signal categories is not important; the detection objective is simply to identify which of the typical patterns is most statistically similar to the current output signal vector collected from the process. This scenario is not uncommon in process monitoring and quality control in manufacturing systems. Systematic changes in process output measurements are normally manifested as differing patterns of the SACFs and SPACFs, although they are not always uniquely different.

A design prototype of the first neural network architecture (based on DLN) is given in Figure 8.12 for a model-switching environment in which the process model transition is within a class of TAR models. This prototype can be easily extended to deal with ARMAX and polynomial NARMAX processes, for example, by adding more input nodes to the first layer of the network so that $\{u(t), u(t-1), \ldots\}, \{e(t-1), e(t-2), \ldots\}$, and lagged cross product terms can be input to the network. The connection weights are the available initial estimates of the model parameters and the lagged errors are the process innovations available at the current time.

The TAR representations for the model-change detection (to be named MCD) net in Figure 8.12 for $i = 2, 3, 4, 5$ and 6, are given in Eq. (8.8) and where $a_0^{(i)}$ are related to the non-zero process means by the equation,

$$a_0^{(i)} = \mu_i \left(1 - \sum_{j=1}^{i} a_j^{(i)}\right). \tag{8.25}$$

The third layer of the network calculates a specified function of the innovations coming from each processing element in the second layer; for example, $f_i(i) = |e_i(t)|$. In this case the minimum of $f_i(t)$ identifies the model which yields the minimum absolute prediction error at the sampling time t. The MINNET layer picks this minimum and outputs the binary vector $Z(t)$ (i.e., only one element, corresponding to the model with min f, has the value of 1.0; all the remaining elements are zero). Detail of the MINNET algorithm can be found in Lippmann.[28]

There are several possible ways to choose $f_i(t)$; for example, by using at least one of the three detection metrics above. Reliable statistical performance of a change detector can be assured by choosing a proper window width which is best (yielding

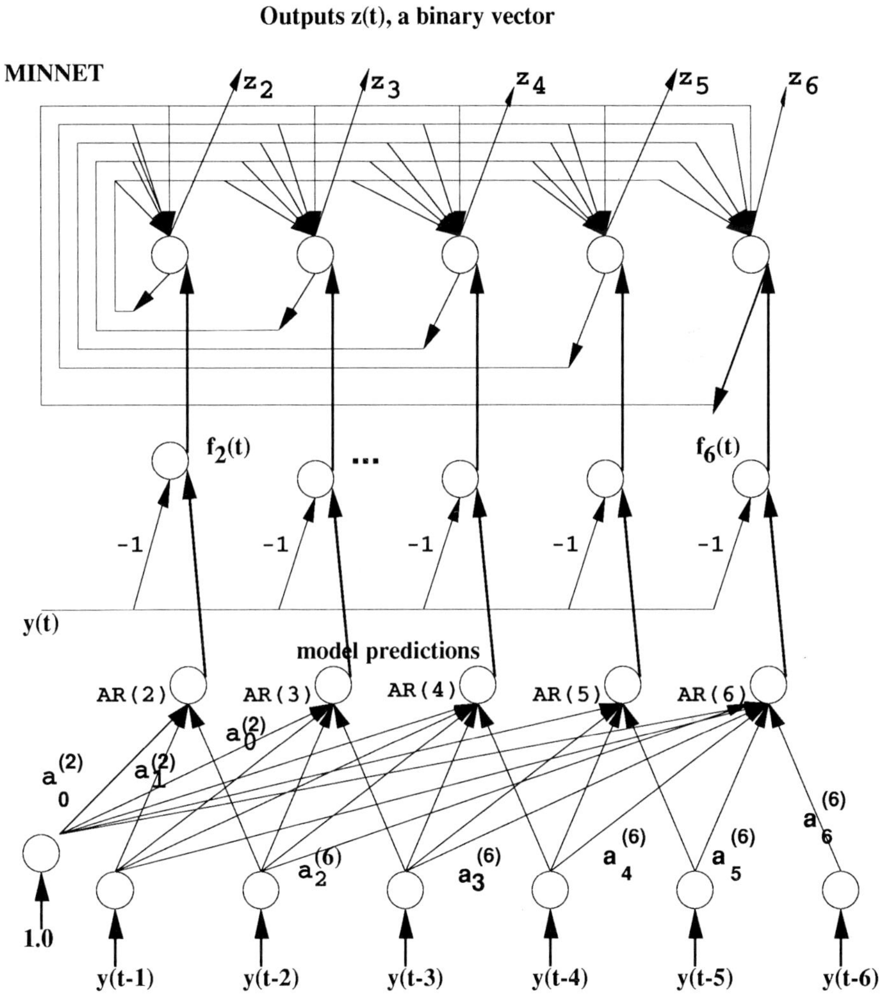

Figure 8.12: A TAR model change detection neural network

a minimum average run length with an acceptable detection accuracy level) for the particular process to be monitored. Another design problem is about how uncertainty in the available initial estimates of the model parameters may be reduced. To solve this problem, the initial parameter estimates (equivalently, the neural network weights) can be revised sequentially, as new process signals (input-output measurements) are being received through time. This requirement makes it necessary that the neural network weights must be adaptive so that it is responsive to incoming data. The on-line network training and implementation issue will be discussed in the next Section.

Two neural network models that can deal with the Case B detection problem are the multilayer perceptron trained by the backpropagation procedure[36] and the learning vector quantization (LVQ) network. The LVQ network is the focus of the present study; an application of the backpropagation network to the time series identification problem is presented elsewhere.[47]

An excellent introduction to the background of vector quantization techniques is in Ahalt *et al.*[1] The vector quantization procedure is concerned with quantizing an input space into a number of regions or classes, each of which is represented by a reproduction vector. The total set of reproduction vectors is called "codebook", which is constructed by a competitive training procedure or by the Kohonen's rule.[23] The codebook in this paper is based on theoretical ACFs and PACFs of the models in the given set.

The codebook is constructed by a training procedure as follows. Starting from initial vectors (i.e., weight vectors) that are representative of the data set (or the process generating the data), the training algorithm iterates through the training sample (consisting of a number of training vectors) and recursively adjusts the weight vectors each time until a convergence condition is satisfied.

Let S be the number of classes in the input vector space. Further let the weights between all the input nodes and an i-th node in the layer of S distance-calculation nodes of the LVQ network be denoted by $\mathbf{W}_i(n)$, where n is the learning iteration number. The updated weight vector at the iteration $n+1$ is given by

$$\mathbf{W}_i(n+1) = \mathbf{W}_i(n) + \alpha(n)[\mathbf{X} - \mathbf{W}_i(n)]\eta_i \tag{8.26}$$

where $\alpha(n)$ is the learning rate at iteration n. In this study $\alpha(n) = \alpha(n-1)/n$, $\alpha(0) = 0.01$; to ensure convergence the learning rate is made to decrease monotonically toward zero. The output η_i of the i-th node is determined as follows:

$$\eta_i = \begin{cases} 1 & \text{if } d(\mathbf{X}, \mathbf{W}_i(n)) \leq d(\mathbf{X}, \mathbf{W}_j(n)) \\ & \text{and } \mathbf{X} \text{ is in the } i\text{th class} \\ -1 & \text{if } d(\mathbf{X}, \mathbf{W}_i(n)) \leq d(\mathbf{X}, \mathbf{W}_j(n)) \\ & \text{but } \mathbf{X} \text{ is not in the } i\text{-th class} \end{cases} \qquad i, j = 1, 2, \ldots, S. \tag{8.27}$$

Otherwise, the weight vector is not adjusted.

8.5.5 On-line Implementation Consideration

Once the connection weights have been determined, the MCD and the LVQ networks can be implemented in a process control computer. The MCD net does not require preprocessing of the time series since it works directly on the process input-output signals. The LVQ net, on the other hand, requires on-line recursive calculation of the sample autocorrelations and the sample partial autocorrelations of the process output signals. However, the LVQ procedure is based on the Euclidean distance which requires a smaller number of computational steps than that required by the MCD network for the same on-line application.

After additional on-line process information has become available, recursive weight adaptation may be started in order to calibrate ("tune") the *a priori* estimates. Another need for on-line weight adaptation arises whenever the detection performance of the network has degraded. For the MCD network, on-line adaptation may be done by a recursive identification technique, e.g., the recursive least-squares (RCLS) algorithm or the prediction-error algorithms. The RCLS weight adaptation equation is similar to the stochastic approximation algorithm; i.e.,

$$\hat{\Theta}(t) = \hat{\Theta}(t-1) + \frac{P(t)H^T(t-1)}{1+H(t-1)P(t)H^T(t-1)}\, e(t) \qquad (8.28)$$

where $e(t)$ is the innovations, $P(t)$ is known as the estimation-error covariance matrix, $H(t) = [y(t-1), \ldots, y(t-n_y), u(t), u(t-1), \ldots, u(t-n_u)]$, $e(t)$ denotes the innovations, and $\hat{\Theta}$ is an estimate of the parameter vector Θ in an ARX model. Extensions to any other linear-in-parameter models are straightforward.

In case of the LVQ network, on-line revision of the codebook is needed to reduce any problem due to poor distribution of the trained weight vectors. A method called conscience mechanism[16] has been suggested as a means to achieve equi-probability distribution of weight vectors within the input pattern space. Equiprobable weights are important, since the LVQ procedure sometimes causes underutilized nodes after a training. The conscience method simply forces the network to undergo an additional competition among the nodes. It introduces another distance measure, which is biased by relative frequency. A node has been assigned to a class, such that the nodes that are chosen ("win" the competition) too often will have greater biased distances (that will result in their losing the next competition). On the other hand, those nodes that have low win frequencies will have smaller biased distances; therefore, no nodes will be either under- or over-utilized after an adequate number of training iterations.

8.5.6 Simulation Experiments

Two computer simulation experiments, one for each network, are presented in this section. The primary purpose of the experiments is to validate the ideas behind the design of sequential model-change detection neural networks. The second purpose is in testing the author's hypothesis on neural network training sample design:

"To generalize beyond the training stage to the on-line model change detection, the training procedure should make use of theoretical information as well as empirical information of the process to be monitored."

The hypothesis is implicitly underlying the architectural design of the first network (the MCD net in Figure 8.12) since the number of nodes and the numerical values of the connection strengths are determined from knowledge of the model and parameter values and historical data of the process of interest. For the LVQ network, this hypothesis may be used to guide the training sample design and adaptation of a codebook.

Experiment 1

This first experiment is designed to simulate on-line operation of the MCD net for the model-switching TAR process described earlier. Three synthetic sequences of 3300 observations each, are created from the parameter values shown in Table 8.1. The noise variances of the time series are respectively 0.01, 0.10, and 1.00. The three time series are governed by the same model-switching events which are assumed to take place at regular intervals and the time between model changes equals to 300 periods (Figures 8.13-8.15). The 300 warm-up data points are deleted from all series and the remaining 3000 observations are saved in a data file prior to the start of the simulation experiment. This simulation experiment is an improved version of the one presented in.[42]

The logical flow chart of the simulation exercise is given in Figure 8.14. The experiment is repeated three times for each time series, using three different window widths of $N = 50$, 100 and 300 respectively. At each sampling instant t, an input vector, $[y(t)y(t-1)\dots y(t-6)]$, is read from the data file and submitted to the MCD network. The innovations (one-step prediction errors) are computed and saved for each model at every sampling instant. The procedure continues in a loop until the next model evaluation time when the three change-detection measures (Eqs. (8.21-8.23) are computed. In this experiment, the evaluation points are taken at $N, 2N, 3N, \dots$. Actually, the time between evaluations may be made smaller in order to reduce detection delays following real model changes. The evaluation interval determination depends on the individual process to be monitored and, therefore, is a user's choice.

Two plots showing time-varying behavior of the moving-window Q statistic are shown in Figure 8.17 and Figure 8.18, respectively. Observe that the trajectory of $Q_3(t)$, for example, stays at its low level during the two intervals when AR(3) is the underlying model of the process, regardless of the window width N. Thus this detection measure is performing as expected, although it is very sensitive to transients following a model switching event. The innovation variance metric, $d_i(t)^2$ has smaller variability for a larger N. For $N = 300$ the evaluation point exactly coincides with the last observation in the change interval, and there is no interference from the innovations of the preceding model prior to the switching event. Thus the innovations are from the same model and the variance distance value will drop to a minimum if

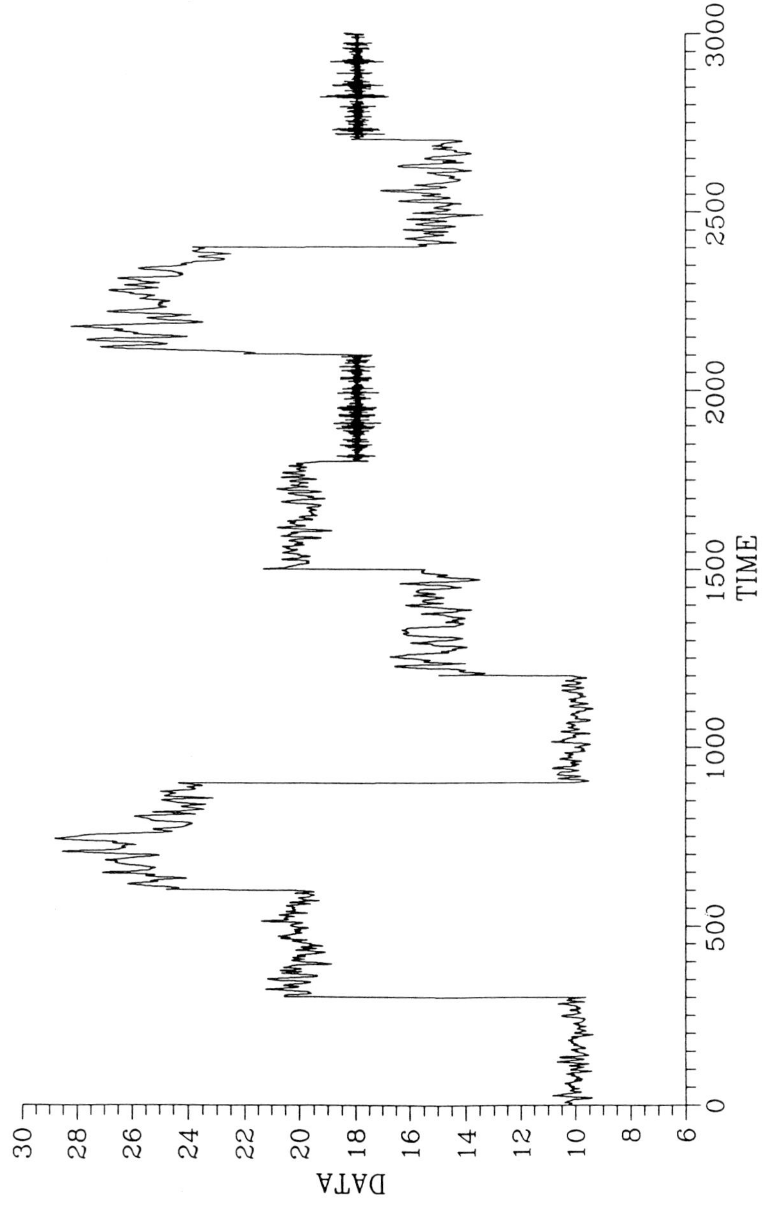

Figure 8.13: The first time series (variance = 0.01)

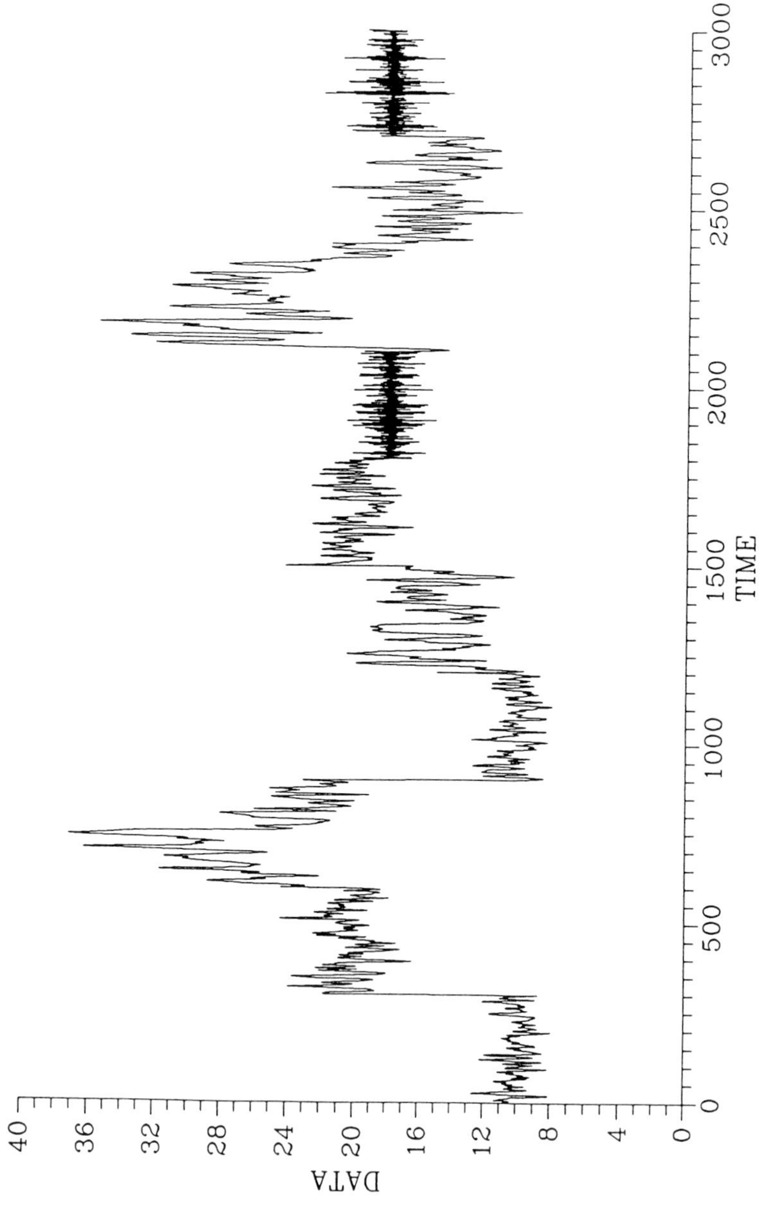

Figure 8.14: The second time series (variance = 0.1)

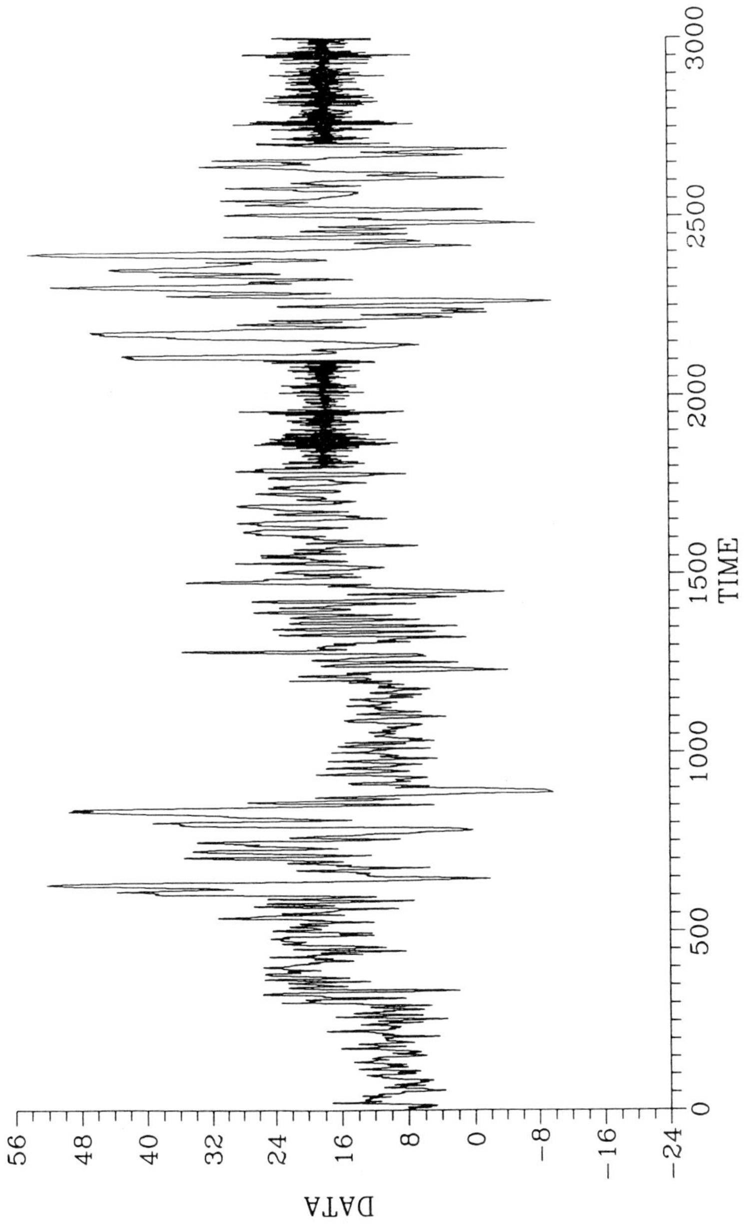

Figure 8.15: The third time series (variance = 1)

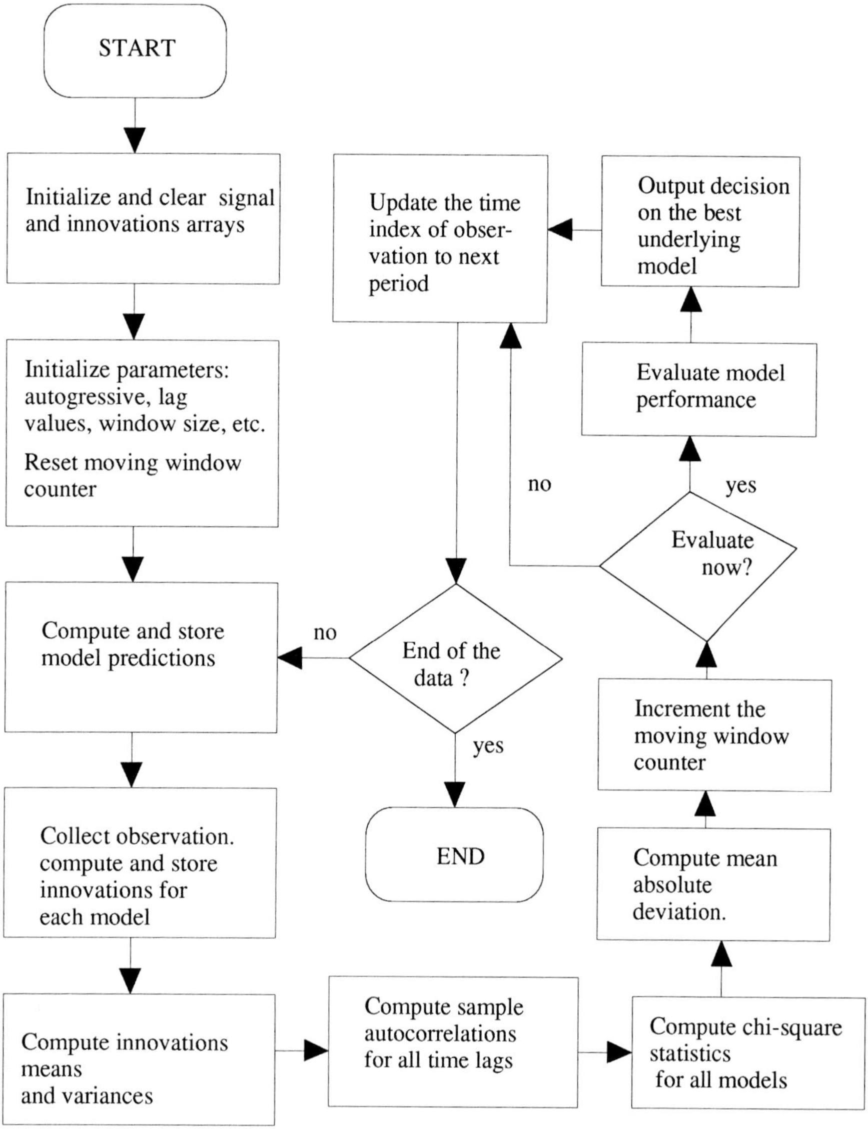

Figure 8.16: Flow chart of simulation experiment A

the underlying time series model matches with that of a given subnetwork.

The mean absolute deviation statistic, $m_i(t)$ also exhibits a better detection accuracy for a larger window size; as before, the last evaluation of each model-interval gives the best performance. However, depending on the magnitude of relative difference in the mean value of the two consecutive models associated with the recent change, this statistic may undergo a large jump and transient fluctuations. Therefore, this distance metric is not reliable unless the transients die out soon enough before the start of the next evaluation point.

A summary of the overall detection performance of the MCD neural network is presented in Table 8.2. The entries in the table are computed from the win frequencies of the AR nodes, based on each of the three individual measures. The win frequency for any AR node is the number of instants it is picked by the MINNET out of the total number of evaluation instants for a given simulation run. The % model-change detection accuracy for each measure is the total number of times it correctly detects a model switching out of 100 occurrences. It may be noted that there are six simulation runs (3 sequences x 2 window widths) in this experiment.

A few conclusions can be drawn from this experiment as follows: (1) The moving-2window absolute mean deviation, $m(t)$, and the innovations variance, $d^2(t)$ are more accurate than the Q statistic; (2) The change-detection accuracy for each measure is affected by N as well as by the noise level of the process; (3) There seems to be some interaction between the process noise variance and the chosen window width. Although this small-scale simulation experiment is far from being conclusive, nevertheless the network design and the change detection procedure are clearly valid. The MCD net is certainly capable as an on-line model-change detector, given that an appropriate choice for a detection measure and a window width is made, taking the process noise level into consideration.

Experiment 2

This second experiment is designed to test both the performance of the LVQ network as a time series pattern classifier and the training sample design hypothesis stated above. There are three tests conducted during the experiment; they are based upon some learning/testing scenarios similar to traditional classroom teaching.

Test #1: The procedure for this test is described as follows: "Create a theoretical codebook from the mathematical models of the model-switching process of interest. Expand this set of reproduction vectors by adding uniformly distributed noises in order to create as many training and testing pattern vectors as desired. Train the theoretical codebook by iterating through the training samples till the learning rate becomes practically zero. Then test the model identification accuracy of the network, using a set of test patterns not used before in the training."

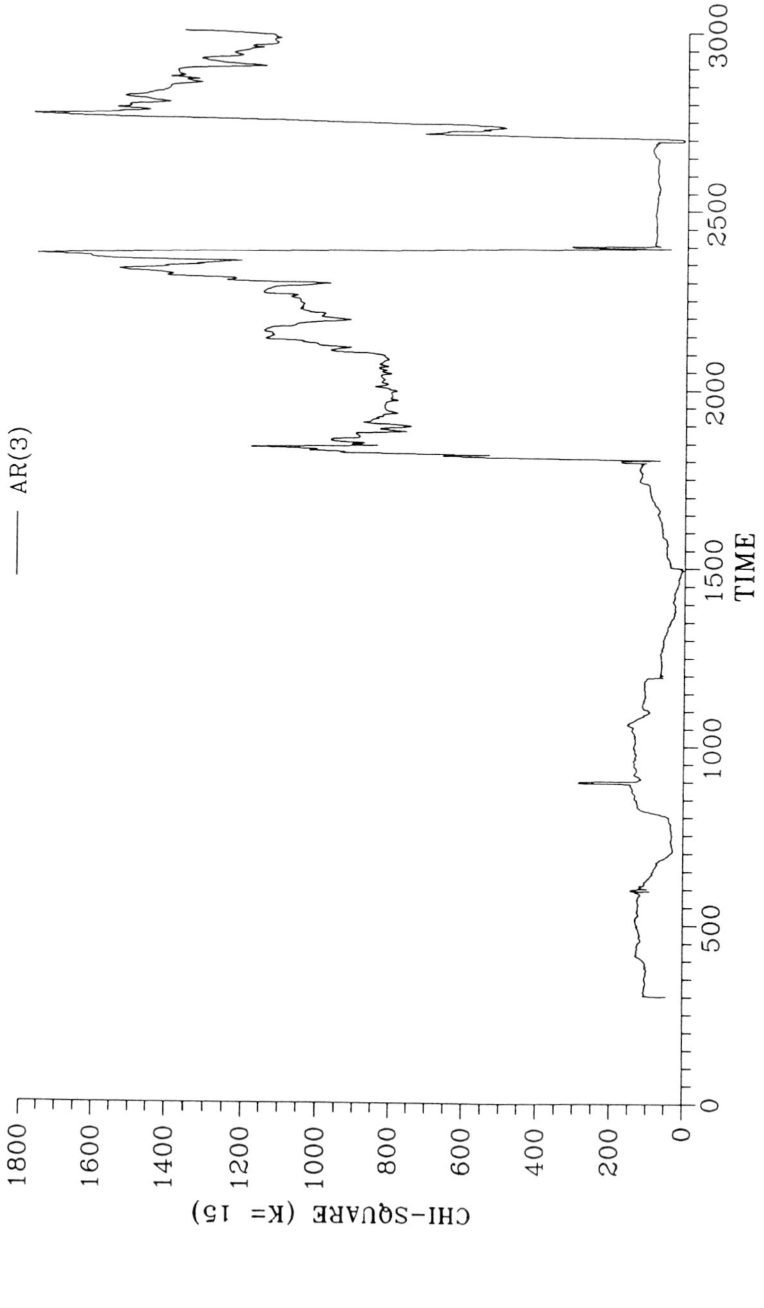

Figure 8.17: Time trajectory of the Q statistic variance = 1, window = 300

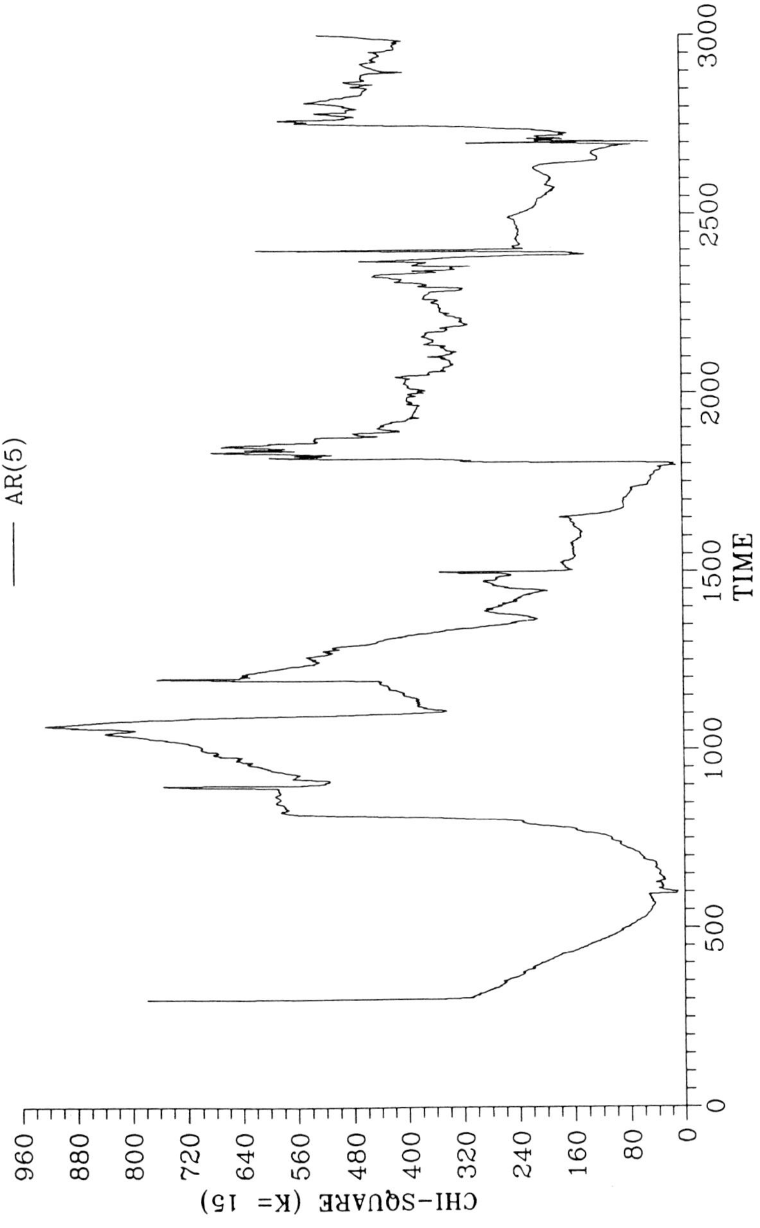

Figure 8.18: Time trajectory of the Q statistic variance = 1, window = 300

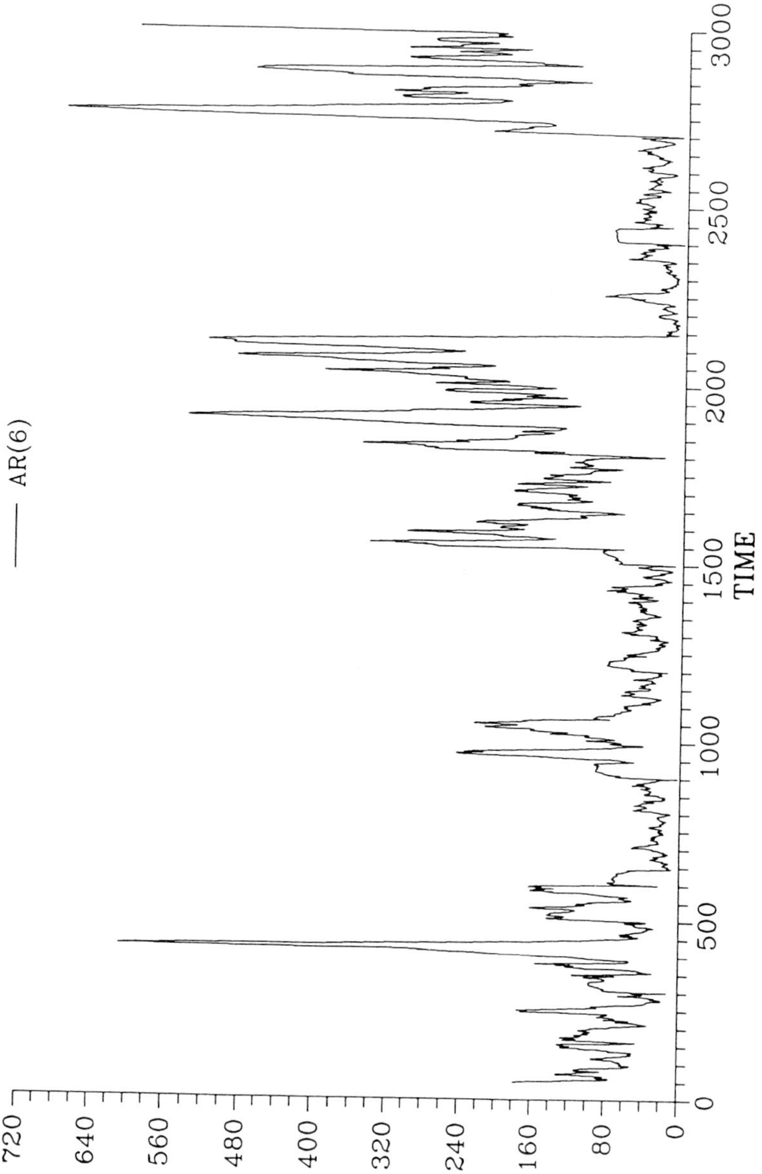

Figure 8.19: Time trajectory of the Q statistic variance = 1, window = 50

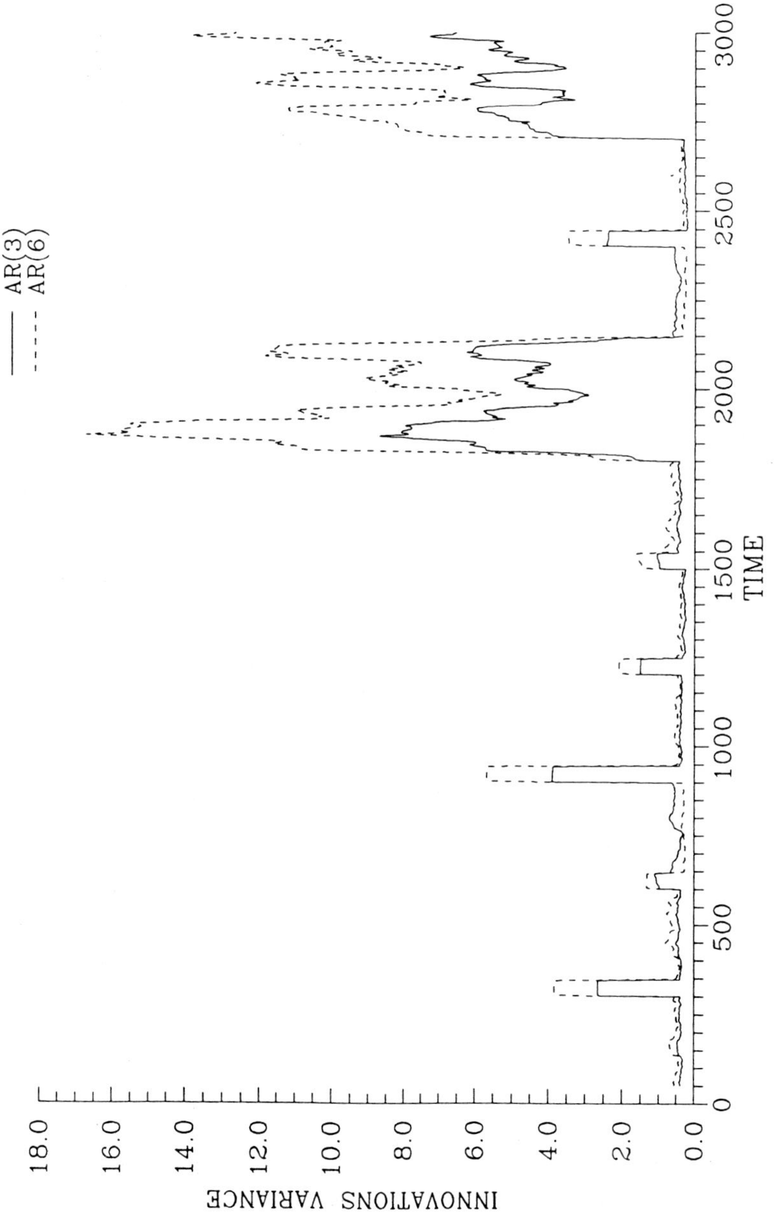

Figure 8.20: Time tracking of the innovations variance, variance = 1, window = 300

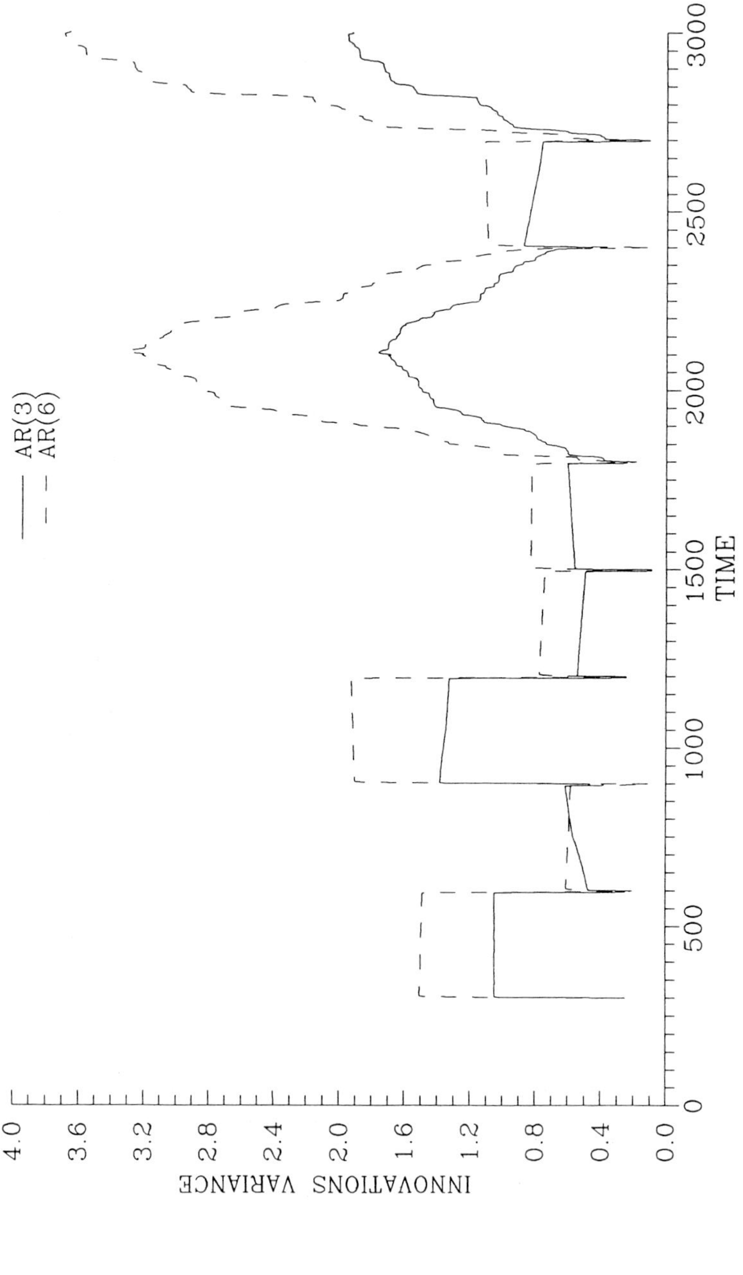

Figure 8.21: Time tracking of the innovations variance, variance = 0.01, window = 300

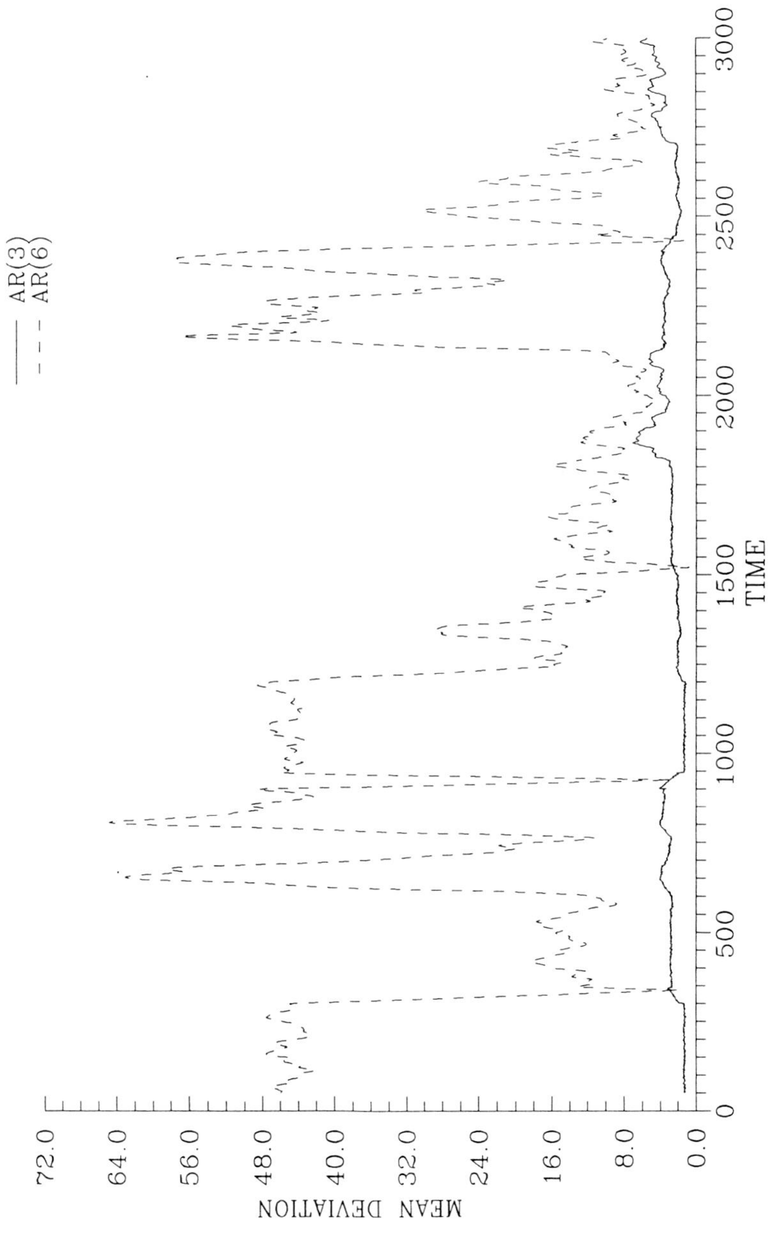

Figure 8.22: Time tracking of the mean absolute deviation, variance = 0.1, window = 50

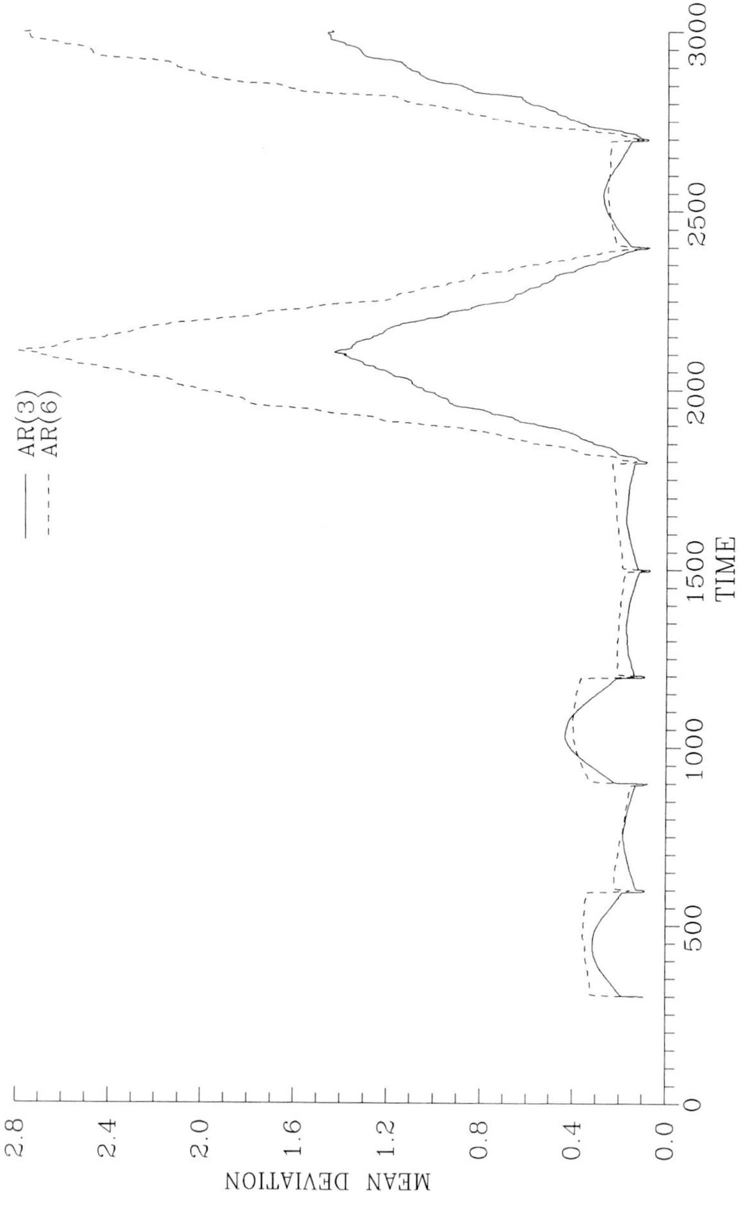

Figure 8.23: Time tracking of the mean absolute deviation, variance = 0.1, window = 300

This procedure is analogous to teaching a theory in a class, followed by a practice session using text-book problems, then the students are tested by a different, but similar, set of theoretical problems. Sixteen theoretical reproduction vectors (each of which is a 48×1 vector of lag-1 to lag-24 autocorrelation coefficients and lag-1 to lag-24 partial autocorrelation coefficients) are computed from the parameters of the 16 ARMA models described in Table 8.3. The computation method for ACFs and PACFs can be found in a time series analysis text book. Ten replications of each theoretical vector are then created by adding uniformly distributed random errors which are in the range $[-0.1, 0.1]$. The total of 160 noisy pattern vectors so created is divided into 80 training and 80 testing vectors. The test results of the LVQ network, after being trained and tested this way, are presented in Table 8.4. The network is seen to be 100% correct with respect to the noisy variations of the theoretical codebook.

Test #2: The procedure for this test may be described as follows: "Create a theoretical codebook for use as initial weight vectors of the LVQ net and train it by the same noisy theoretical patterns as in Test #1. But rather than test the trained network by other noise-added theoretical patterns, use a test set generated from a completely different source."

This procedure is analogous to giving a student, who has been taught and trained by theoretical problems, a set of practical problems to solve. The underlying theory of the test problems is still the same as the one which the student has learned. The sixteen models in Table 8.3 are based on one parameter set per model; in other words, each of the 16 classes has only one member. Next, ten synthetic time series sequences of 400 observations are generated for each of the 16 models, resulting in 160 time series sequences. SACFs and SPACFs of the 160 time series are computed by a statistical software package [SAS/ETS, Version 5, 1987]. The test sample for the Test #2 experiment consists of 80 patterns of these SACFs/SPACFs. The trained LVQ net of Test #1 is then tested by this test set and the results are summarized in Table 8.4.

As the consequence of the more complex test, the overall model identification accuracy now drops from 100% to 84.5%, with the lowest performance in the ARMA group being only 66.7%. This drop in the accuracy is not surprising, since the training knowledge is limited to only the theoretical information. It is expected that the overall accuracy will improve when additional empirical information is used in training.

Test #3: The purpose of this test is to validate the stated hypothesis that the network model identification accuracy would improve, if the initial theoretical codebook were trained by some empirical data prior to a difficult test. This test procedure is similar to the classroom teaching method where students learn both the theory and practical problems before attempting to solve other practical problems.

The test results presented in Table 8.4 show clearly that the hypothesis of this paper is valid; the network which has acquired both theoretical and empirical knowledge through training actually improves the overall model identification accuracy from 84.5% to 90.6%. The accuracy would be higher if it was not because of the failure of the network to recognize the MA(4) patterns.

Discussions

The two neural nets in this study provide different alternative approaches to the on-line change detection problem in which a process only makes random transition within a set of known models. The MCD network is a hybrid design which combines the MINNET with recursive system identification and sequential statistical test. The second neural net approach is a straightforward application of the learning vector quantization technique to an on-line time series pattern recognition problem. Unlike the MCD neural network, the LVQ network does not need detailed knowledge of process models. Therefore, it does not have the capability to perform diagnostic statistical test on each model. The selection of the best model (or pattern) is based on similarity between an unknown SACFs/SPACFs pattern and a template. On the other hand, the MCD can pick a statistically optimal model after a model switch in the monitored process.

The capability of the LVQ network can be extended to on-line model-change detection if the codebook is associated with detailed model descriptions. The fundamental difference between the two approaches is that explicit process model information is distributed in the connections of the MCD net, but the trained codebook vectors only store indirect knowledge on the process output signals via the SACFs/SPACFs.

The detection accuracy of the MCD network depends on the model adequacy metric, the moving-window width, and the process noise variance magnitude. Among the three measures, the innovation variance is the best model-change detection statistic that yields 99.4-100% average accuracy over all six simulation runs. This is not conclusive yet, since the process means are uniquely different, so it is relatively simple to detect a shift. A more comprehensive simulation that includes other types of parameter change is one of our future research tasks to be carried out.

8.6 Conclusions

The hierarchical neural network architecture succeeds in capturing time dependence behaviors in training data for multiple-step prediction. Its validity is demonstrated through the unbiased seasonal forecasting of new measurements of municipal water consumption rates, despite the various kinds of unmodeled non-stationarity and unexplained variabilitiy. For instance, external meteorological inputs have not been used in the design of the training samples, but their influences are significant. Further the hierarchical architecture is not yet multi-functional; multiple subnetworks and model switching functions could be incorporated to enhance the precision of the neural network and result in a lower forecast error variance. These extensions are by no means

Table 8.1: Parameters and description of Experiment 1

Model: AR(i) $i = 2, \ldots, 6$	Time of switch[a]	$E(y)^b$ and $a_0^{(i)}$	$a_1^{(i)}$ to $a_i^{(i)}$
2	1, 901	10, 1.630	1.490 -0.653
3	1201, 2401	15, 0.645	2.146 -1.598 0.409
4	1801, 2701	18, 112.2	-1.876 -1.781 -1.201 -0.373
5	301, 1501	20, 1.940	1.840 -0.893 -0.613 0.879 -0.310
6	601, 2101	25, 0.450	2.400 -2.414 1.889 -1.586 0.900 -0.207

[a]The process switches each model randomly.
[b]Non-zero mean of the process.

Table 8.2: MCD network detection

Noise Variance	Q N=50	d N=50	m N=50	Q N=100	d N=100	m N=100	Q N=300	d N=300	m N=300
0.01	86.7	100	93.3	100	100	100	100	100	100
0.10	88.3	100	90.0	96.7	100	100	100	100	100
1.00	95	98.3	98.3	100	100	100	100	100	100
Avg	90	99.4	93.9	98.9	100	100	100	100	100

Ljung-Box statistic Q for white-noise innovations test.

Table 8.3: Model parameters of the theoretical codebook

Model ARMA(p, q)	AR Parameters	MA Parameters
1,0	0.843	
2,0	-1.017 0.660	
3,0	-1.359 1.132 -0.453	
4,0	1.891 1.795 1.215 0.379	
5,0	1.482 0.552 -0.431 -0.723 -0.305	
6,0	-1.348 1.199 -1.313 0.681 -0.302 0.167	
0,1		-0.716
0,2		-1.345 0.659
0,3		0.679 -0.462 -0.361
0,4		1.534 1.123 0.943 0.411
2,1	-1.909 0.918	-0.454
2,2	-1.465 0.666	-0.537 0.625
3,1	-1.072 0.912 -0.334	-0.432
3,2	0.827 -0.315 -0.409	0.680 -0.257
4,1	1.647 0.419 -0.586 -0.300	0.400
4,2	1.352 0.467 -0.358 -0.314	-0.420 0.316

Table 8.4: ARMA model identification tests of the LVQ net (Experiment #2)

Model:	Number of Correct Identification (5 rep./model)		
ARMA(p,q)	Test #1	Test #2	Test #3
1,0	5	5	5
2,0	5	5	5
3,0	5	5	5
4,0	5	3	5
5,0	5	5	5
6,0	5	3	4
%Accuracy	100	86.7	96.7
0,1	5	5	5
0,2	5	5	5
0,3	5	5	5
0,4	5	5	0
%Accuracy	100	100	75
2,1	5	5	5
2,2	5	5	5
3,1	5	0	5
3,2	5	5	5
4,1	5	5	5
4,2	5	0	5
%Accuracy	100	66.7	100
Overall %	100	84.5	90.6

One parameter set for each model.

easy and require more research before the conceptual designs presented in this study become useful as practical adaptive prediction tools for manufacturing applications.

The modified TLRN architecture, which is the basis for the indirect learning neural networks is easy to build and can be implemented by a commercial software. If there are effects on generalization accuracy caused by the elimination of the time-recurrent feedback connections from the hidden PEs, it is not clear at the present time. However, one disadvantage of having too many hidden elements and connections is in increasing the prediction error variance. It is believed that the modified architecture should be preferable for applications in which generalization is more important than unbiased mapping.

The lag-1 input slab proves to be advantageous for a prediction problem such as the multiple-step forecasting of hourly water consumption; it adds extra time-lag inputs to the network and helps in protecting the long-term prediction quality from decaying too rapidly. In addition, the use of computer-generated white-noise inputs seems to alleviate instability usually caused by ill-behaved time-lagged innovations.

The random error inputs also induce realistic variabilities to the multiple-step-ahead prediction, which otherwise would look too smooth.

The direct-learning is useful when specific information about alternative models, which are linear in parameters, is available. The neural network architecture based on the DLN concept is fundamental to the model-change detection approach of this paper. However, this proposed system is not restricted to only DLN; stationary segments of a non-stationary time series may be used to train TLRNs which can then be used as the subnetworks in the change-detection system. If each subnetwork is designed as a hierarchical network (based on the 3-slab structure), then multiple-step predictions can be achieved following a confirmed model-change detection. Statistical performance evaluation of each subnetwork is now based on multiple-step prediction errors.

Acknowledgements

This material is based upon work supported by the National Science Foundation under Grant No. ECS-9014109. The government has certain rights in this material references. Partial support is obtained from the Engineering Research in Applications Program, Texas Higher Education Coordinating Board, 1989-1992.

8.7 References

1. S. C. Ahalt, A. K. Krishnamurthy, P. Chen, and D. E. Melton, "Competitive learning algorithms for vector quantization," *Neural Networks*, **3** (1990) 277-290.

2. S. T. Alexander, *Adaptive Signal Processing Theory and Applications*, (Springer-Verlag, New York, 1986).

3. M. Athans and D. Willner, "A practical scheme for adaptive aircraft flight control systems," *Symp. on Parameter Estimation Techniques and Applications in Aircraft Flight Testing*, NASA Flt. Res. Ctr., Edwards AFB, April 1973.

4. N. Bhat and T. J. McAvoy, "Use of neural nets for dynamic modeling and control of chemical systems," *Computers Chemical Engineering*, **14** (4/5) (1990) 573-583.

5. S. A. Billings, "Identification of non-linear systems - a survey," *IEE Proceedings*, **D 127** (6) (1980) 272-285.

6. B. A. Billings and W. S. F. Voon, "Structure detection and model validity tests in the identification of non-linear systems," *IEE Proceedings*, **D130** (4) (1986).

7. S. A. Billings, H. B. Jamaluddin, and S. Chen, "Properties of neural networks with applications to modelling non-linear dynamical systems," *International Journal of Control*, **5** (1) (1992) 193-224.

8. G. E. P. Box, and G. M. Jenkins, *Time Series Analysis: Forecasting and Control*, (Holden-Day, San Francisco, CA, 1976).

9. L. Campo, P. Mookerjee, and Y. Bar-Shalom, "State estimation for systems with sojourn-time-dependent Markov model switching," *IEEE Transactions on Automatic Control*, **36** (2) 238-243.

10. M. Asdagli, "Nonlinear prediction of chaotic time series," *Physica*, **D35** (1989) 335-356.

11. S. Chen and S. A. Billing, "Representations of non linear systems: the NARMAX model," *International Journal of Control,* **49** (3) (1989) 1013-1032.

12. S. Chen and C. F. N. Cowan S. A. billings, and P. M. Grant, "Paralle recursive prediction error algorithm for training layered neural networks," *International Journal of Control,* **51** (6) (1990) 1215-1228.

13. E.De Boer, "Polynomial correlation," *Proceedings of IEEE*, **67** (1979) 317-318.

14. J. Durbin, "The approximate distribution of partial serial correlation coefficients from residuals from regression on Fourier series," *Biometrika*, **67** (1980) 335-349.

15. D. DeSieno, "Adding a conscience to competitive learning," *Proc. of the Second Annual IEE International Conference on Neural Networks*, **1** (1988).

16. S. Goldburg and A. Durling "A computational algorithm for the identification of non-linear systems," *Journal of Franklin Institute*, **291** (1971) 427-447.

17. R. P. Gorman and T. J. Sejnowski, "Learned classification of sonar targets using a massively parallel network," *IEEE Transactions on Acoustics, Speech, and signal Processing*, **36** (7) (1988).

18. R. R. Goodwin and K. S. Sin, *Adaptive Filtering Prediction and Control*, (Prentice-Hall, Englewood Cliffs, NJ, 1984).

19. R. Hofstadter and G. N. Saridis "Feature selection for non-linear stochastic system classification," *IEEE Transactions on Automatic Control*, **AC-21** (1976) 375-379.

20. R. L. Kashyap and A. R. Rao, *Dynamic Stochastic Models from Empirical Data*, (Academic Press, New York, 1976).

21. T. Kohonen, *Self-Organization and Associative Memory* (Second Edition), (Spinger-Verlag, New York, 1988).

22. T. Kohonen, "The self-organizing map," *Proc. of the IEEE*, **78** (9) (1990) 1464-1480.

23. I. D. Landau,"Elimination of the real positivity condition in the design of parallel MRAS," *IEEE Transactions on Automatic Control*, **23** (1978) 1015-1020.

24. A. Lapedes and R. Farber,. "How neural nets work," in Anderson, D. Z. (Ed.], Neural Information Processing Systems *Proc. of the IEEE Nips Conference*, Denver, CO (1987) (American Institute of Physics, New York), pp. 442-456.

25. L. Ljung, *System Identification Theory for the User*, (Prentice-Hall, Englewood-Cliff, NJ, 1987).

26. G. M. Ljung and G. E. P. Box, "On a measure of lack of fit in time series models," *Biometrica,* **65** (2) (1978) 297-303.

27. R. P. Lippmann, "An introduction to computing with neural nets," *IEEE ASSP Magazine*, (April 1987), 4-22.

28. D. Lowe and A. R. Webb, "Time series prediction by adaptive networks: a dynamical systems perspective," *IEE Proceedings* **F138** (1) (1991) 17-24.

29. V. J. Mathews and J. K. Tugnait, "Detection and estimation with fixed lag for abruptly changing systems," *IEEE Transactions on Aerospace and Electronic Systems*, **AES-19** (5) (1983) 730-739.

30. K. S. Narendra and K. Parthasarathy, "Identification and control of dynamical systems using neural networks," *IEEE Transactions on Neural Networks*, **1** (1) (1990) 4-26.

31. K. Narendra and A. M. Anaswamy, *Stable Adaptive Systems, Prentice Hall*, (Englewood Cliffs, NJ, 1989).

32. D. Nguyen and B. Widrow, "The truck backer-upper: an example of self-learning in neural networks," in Miller, Sutton and Werbos (Eds.), *Neural Networks for Robotics and Control* (MIT Press, Cambridge, Mass., 1990).

33. M. B. Priestley, *Non-linear and Non-stationary Time Series Analysis*, (Academic Press, New York, 1988).

34. H. Reininger and D. Wolf. "Nonlinear prediction of stochastic processes using neural networks" in L. Torres, E. Masgrau, and M. A. Lagunas (eds.), *Signal Processing V: Theory and Applications*, (Elsevier Science Publisher B.V., 1990)

35. D. E. Rumelhart and J. L. McClelland, *Parallel Distributed Processing: Explorations in Microstructure of Cognition*, (MIT Press, Cambridge, MA, 1986).

36. D. E. Rumelhart, G. E. Hinton, and R. J. Williams. "Learning representations by back-propagating errors," *Nature,* **323** (1986) 533.

37. T. Sastri, "A state-space modeling approach to time series forecasting," *Management Science*, **31** (11) (1985) 1451-1470.

38. T. Sastri, "A Recursive Algorithm for Adaptive Estimation and Parameter Change Detection of Time Series Models," *Journal of Operational Research Society*, **37** (10) (1986) 987-999.

39. T. Sastri, "Rainfall intervention analysis for on-line applications", *Journal of Water Resources Planning and Management*, **115** (4) (July 1989) 397-415.

40. T. Sastri, "Sequential method of change detection and adaptive prediction of municipal water demand", *International Journal of Systems Science*, **18** (6) (1987) 1029-1049.

41. T. Sastri, "Multipass Seasonal Adjustment Filter," *Management Science*, **35** (1) (1989) 100-123.

42. T. Sastri, "Neural networks for detection of process change in manufacturing systems," *Proceedings of the Joint US/German Conference on New Directions for Operations Research in Manufacturing, National Institute of Standards and Technology*, Gaithersburg, MD, (July 30-31, 1991).

43. T. Sastri and C. O. Malave, "Direct learning and knowledge updating in neural nets," *Proceedings of the Artificial Neural Networks in Engineering*, (Nov. 15-18, 1992), St. Louis, MO.

44. T. Sastri and G. N. Wang, "Neuro-identification of time series for on-line prediction," to appear in *Identification and Control of Dynamical systems, a special issue of Modelling and Scientific Computing*, (Dec. 1992).

45. T. Sastri, "Multiple-step-ahead Prediction by Hierarchical Neural Networks", *Proceedings of DGOR/ORSA Conference on Recent Developments and New Perspectives in Operations Research*, Hagen, Germany (June 25-26, 1992).

46. T. Sastri, J. R. English, and G. N. Wang, "Neural networks for time series model identification and change detection," Working Paper INEN/QC/WP/03/07-90, Industrial Engineering Dept., Texas A&M University (1990). Also in *Advances in Artificial Intelligence in Economics, Finance, and Management*, a special issue (1993) (forthcoming).

47. R. F. Stengel, *Stochastic Optimal Control Theory and Application*, (Wiley, New York, 1986).

48. H. Tong, *Nonlinear Time Series. A Dynamical System Approach*, (Oxford University Press, New York, 1990).

49. J. K. Tugnait, "Detection and estimation for abruptly changing systems," *Automatica*, **18** (5) (1982) 607-615.

50. P. J. Werbos, "Neurocontrol and related techniques," in Maren, A. J. , C. T. Harston, and R. M. Pap (Eds.), *Handbook of Neural Computing Application*, (Academic Press, New York, 1990).

51. P. J. Werbos, T. McAvoy, and T. Su "Neural networks, system identification and control in the chemical process industries," in White, D. , and D. Sofge (Eds.), *Handbook of Intelligent Control* (Van Nostrand, New York, 1992).

52. A. S. Willsky, "A survey of design methods for failure detection in dynamic systems," *Automatica*, **12** (1976) 601-611.

Chapter 9

Neural Network Applications in On-line Monitoring of a Turning Process

Guangming Zhang and Raju G. Khanchustambham
Department of Mechanical Engineering and Institute for Systems Research
University of Maryland
College Park, Maryland 20742 USA

Abstract

The need to improve quality and reduce scrap rate while increasing the production rate is motivating industry to consider untended machining as a viable alternative. On-line monitoring of a machining process is the key component to success for an untended machining operation. In this chapter, a framework for sensor-based intelligent decision-making systems to perform on-line monitoring is proposed. Such a monitoring system interprets the detected signals from the sensors, extracts the relevant information, and decides on the appropriate control action. Emphasis is laid on applying neural networks to perform information processing, and to recognize the process abnormalities in a machining operation. A prototype monitoring system is implemented to demonstrate the working mechanism. For successful implementation of the developed intelligent monitor, an instrumented force transducer is designed for signal detection and is used in a real time turning operation. A neural network monitor based on a feedforward back-propagation algorithm is developed and tested under the machining of advanced ceramic materials and steel. The monitor is trained by the detected cutting force signal, the measured surface finish , and the observed tool wear. The superior learning and noise suppression abilities of the developed monitor enable high success rates for monitoring the machining process.

9.1 Introduction

In recent years, manufacturing engineers have been faced with the difficult task of improving productivity without compromising on quality. The complexity of modern day components makes this task difficult. Computer Integrated Manufacturing (CIM) systems have emerged in response to the demands for greater flexibility, productivity, precision and quality. The manufacturing industry is now considering untended machining as a viable alternative to meet these demands. In an untended machining process various tasks, such as sensing the effect of process variables and adjusting the conditions accordingly, have to be done by appropriate sensors and associated monitors. Consequently, the development of an effective on-line monitoring system is the key to the successful implementation of an untended machining process.

Substantial research has been done in the area of on-line monitoring of machining processes.[1-6] Recognizing the need of an intelligent human operator out of the manufacturing loop, powerful sensors, either built-in or attached to machine tools, have been designed and fabricated with great success. Examples of typical sensors are force dynamometers and vibration detectors. When they are used in a machining system, information related to the machining process can be abstracted from the measured signals and interpreted through signal processing. Based on the interpretation, an inference is usually made whether the machining process should continue on, or a control action should be taken to make correction. It has been well accepted that a general on-line monitoring system consists of, at least, sensing elements, signal processing devices, signal processing algorithms, information interpretors, and a decision-making mechanism. A literature survey of the developed on-line monitoring system indicates that the major concern of an automated machining system is the identification of the tool wear status as the machining process is going on.[1-6] This concern would be more evident in precision machining since the tool wear has a direct influence on part dimensions and the finish of the machined surfaces. Furthermore, prompt identification of a severe tool wear assures a safe cutting operation. Consequently, on-line tool wear information is indispensable in order to achieve a fully automated machining operation.

The main objective of this research is to develop an intelligent on-line monitoring system through a neural network approach. The monitoring system detects the cutting force produced during machining, estimates the tool wear status, and finish quality from dynamic variation of the detected cutting force signals, and makes the decision for taking corrective action when it is needed. This research work consists of the design of a force transducer and its application to signal detection in a real-time machining process, and the development of a neural network monitor. The monitor is built on feedforward back-propagation algorithm. Under an application circumstance, the monitor is first trained for information processing, and later applied for the cutting force and surface finish monitoring during the machining of advanced ceramic materials.

9.2 On-line Monitoring Methodology

The productivity of the factory of the future and the quality of the products it produces will, in part, depend on the intelligent utilization of computers to monitor and control the machines involved in production. This demands that the supervising personnel and the computer systems provide accurate and reliable information about the status of the machines and the quality of the operations they perform. This requires, therefore, a much better understanding of the machining processes and the functions they perform, so that sensors and the associated decision-making systems can be designed. According to Balakrishnan, one can achieve a fully untended machining if one can monitor the following tasks successfully.[9]

1. Workpiece monitoring (e.g., surface finish, automatic setup, gauging measurement)

2. Process monitoring (e.g., adaptive control, chip congestion detection)

3. Machine monitoring (e.g., vibrations of gearbox, spindle and machine tool table)

Figure 9.1 presents a general picture of an on-line monitoring system. The three major parts of the implemented monitoring system are: a force transducer, a neural network monitor, and a decision-making advisor. The basic working principle of this monitoring system is in-process verification through indirect measurement. It means that the detected cutting force signal may not directly reflect the tool wear status or surface finish quality. However, a mathematical model is built to establish the inherent relationships between the detected force signal and the monitoring targets, such as tool wear and surface finish quality. Interpretation of the detected signals retraces the actual machining operation. Neural networks are of particular help in such an application.

9.2.1 Force Transducer

The designed force transducer shown in Figure 9.1 consists of a tool holder, four strain gages, two bridge amplifiers, and a data acquisition device. The strain gages are attached to the tool holder. During machining, the generated cutting force produces strains on the tool holder. The strain gages convert the strains to measurable voltage signals through the bridge amplifiers. The data acquisition device digitizes and stores the voltage signals. A quantitative relation between the cutting force and the measured voltages, established from a calibration process, helps in determining the magnitude of the cutting force from the measured voltage signals.

The strain gage-base sensor system was calibrated prior to the tests to establish the transformation matrix relating the voltage signals and the cutting force generated during the machining process. The relationship between the applied forces and the

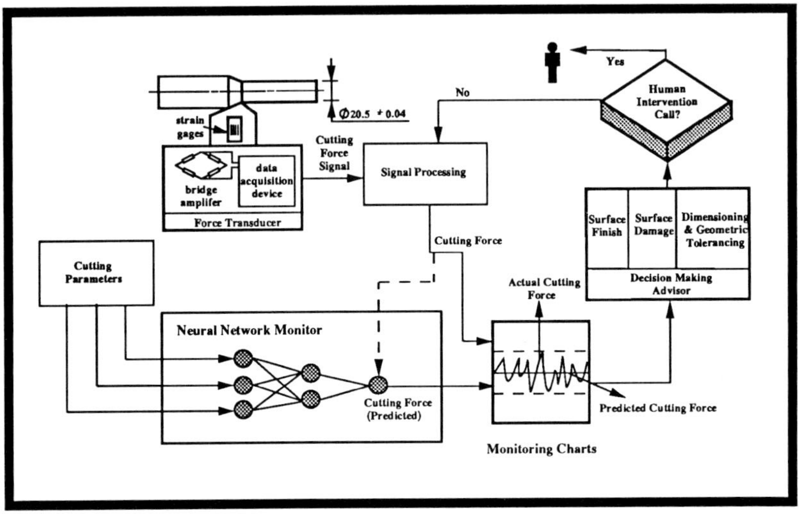

Figure 9.1: Basic structure of the implemented on-line monitoring system

voltage outputs of the strain gage are shown in Figures 9.2 and 9.3. The transformation matrix, T_r, is defined as the relation between the forces and voltages:

$$[T_r] = \frac{Input}{Output} = \frac{V_{out}}{F}$$

The above relation can be written in matrix form as:

$$[T_r] = \begin{bmatrix} \frac{\Delta V_z}{\Delta F_z} & \frac{\Delta V_z}{\Delta F_x} \\ \frac{\Delta V_x}{\Delta F_z} & \frac{\Delta V_x}{\Delta F_x} \end{bmatrix}$$

From the values of tables in Figures 9.2 and 9.3, we have:

$$[T_r] = \begin{bmatrix} T_{11} & T_{12} \\ T_{13} & T_{14} \end{bmatrix} = \begin{bmatrix} 0.0283 & 0.0000 \\ -0.0003 & 0.0253 \end{bmatrix}$$

Each element of $[T_r]$ is the transformation relation of the ith voltage output and the jth cutting force component. The values of elements of $[T_r]$ were obtained by finding the slopes of the graphs of Figures 9.2 and 9.3. The force matrix is calculated as:

$$[F] = (inv([T_r]))\,[V]$$

The above reaction can be written as:

$$\begin{bmatrix} F_z \\ F_x \end{bmatrix} = \begin{bmatrix} 35.3357 & 0.0000 \\ 0.4190 & 39.5257 \end{bmatrix} \begin{bmatrix} V_z \\ V_x \end{bmatrix}$$

Load (lbs)	Voltage Tangential (volts)	Voltage Feed (volts)
10.0	0.1186	0.4204
20.0	0.1227	0.7054
30.0	0.1192	0.9452
40.0	0.1119	1.2148
50.0	0.1097	1.4136
60.0	0.1036	1.7138
70.0	0.1038	1.9307
80.0	0.0976	2.2067
90.0	0.1039	2.4667

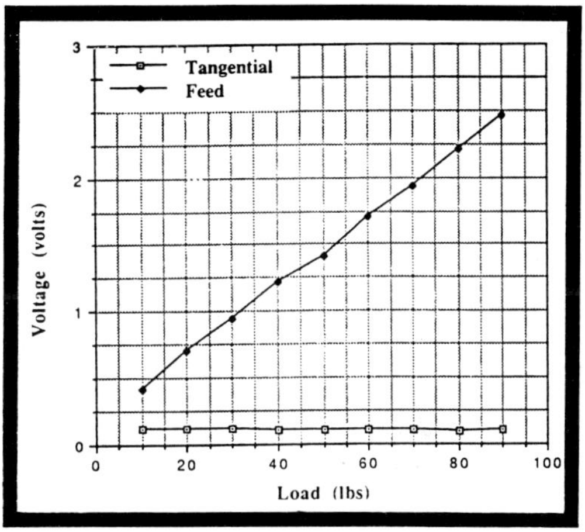

Figure 9.2: Calibration in feed direction

Load (lbs)	Voltage Tangential (volts)	Voltage Feed (volts)
10.0	0.4137	0.2173
20.0	0.7137	0.2199
30.0	0.9815	0.2209
40.0	1.2855	0.2193
50.0	1.5800	0.2206
60.0	1.8426	0.2199
70.0	2.1349	0.2189
80.0	2.4064	0.2198
90.0	2.4064	0.2198

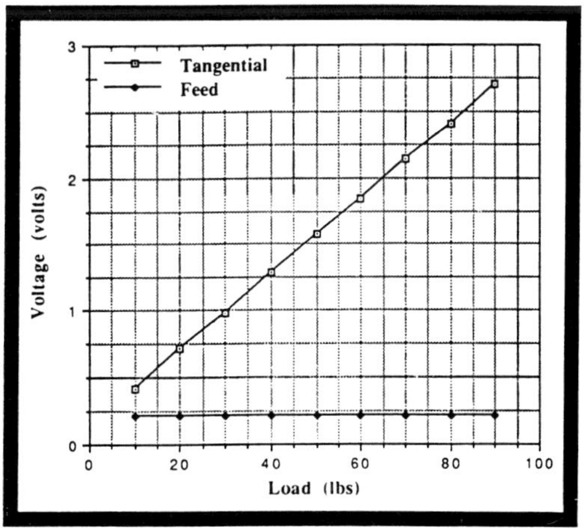

Figure 9.3: Calibration in tangential direction

where F_z and F_x are components of cutting force in tangential and feed directions, respectively.

It is evident that the higher the measured voltage, the larger the cutting force produced during machining. Since the cutting force increases with tool wear, detection of the dynamic variation of the cutting force produced during machining may provide useful information on tool wear status and the finish quality of the surface being machined.

9.2.2 Neural Network Monitor

In order to perform information processing from the detected signals, a neural network monitor based on a feedforward back-propagation algorithm has been developed and implemented in an on-line monitoring system.[7–8] The main characteristics of the on-line monitor are: 1) layered architectures; 2) strictly feedforward connections between the neurons; and 3) no lateral, self, or back-connections. Based on the principle of back-propagation network (BPN), all the information flow is feedforward. The important characteristic of the back-propagation network is that it forms a mapping from a set of input stimuli to a set of output nodes using features (hidden layer) extracted from the input patterns. By features, we mean the correlation of the activity among different input nodes. The ability to make the complex distinctions, even when the presented pattern is different from those on which the network was previously trained, is due to the feature detection and generalization abilities which the network was trained into the middle or hidden layer nodes. These networks undergo supervised learning, i.e., they are taught to classify input into one of the several *a priori* categories.

The neural network monitor developed to monitor a machining process is divided into two stages. The first stage is the process of obtaining a set of weight connections between individual nodes and a set of threshold values of nodes in hidden layer and output layer. The second stage is to implement the trained network in a real time machining operation, as shown in Figures 9.1 and 9.12.

In this work, variable thresholds on the hidden nodes and the output nodes, and variable weight connections between individual nodes are used. As the activity of a neuron is closely modeled by a sigmoid function, for each node a sigmoid shape (S-shape) transfer function is used. Therefore, each node represents a non-linear function of the form,

$$Y_j = \frac{1}{1 + \exp(-(X_j + \theta_j))}$$

where $X_j = \sum_i Y_i W_{ij}$, Y_j = output of node in layer j, Y_i = output of node in preceding layer i, and W_{ij} = weights of interconnections.

The three main stages in training the monitor (i.e., finding a useful set of values for the interconnection weights and threshold values of nodes) are listed as follows.

1. The forward pass: where the output of each node is calculated.

2. The backward pass: where weight and threshold changes of each node takes place.
   Weights are adjusted by:

$$\begin{aligned} w_{ij}(t+1) &= w_{ij}(t) + \eta\delta_j Y_i + \alpha(W_{ij}(t) - W_{ij}(t-1)) \\ \theta_j(t+1) &= \theta_j(t) + ch\_thre \end{aligned}$$

   In this equation $w_{ij}(t)$ is the weight from the hidden node i or from an input node j at time t; Y_i is either the output of node i, or is an input; η is a gain term; α is a momentum term; δ_j is an error from node j; and ch_thre is change in the threshold value of each node. If node j is an output node, then

$$\begin{aligned} \delta_j &= Y_j(1-Y_j)(d_j - Y_j) \\ ch\_thre(t+1) &= \eta\delta_j + \alpha(\theta_j(t) - \theta_j(t-1)) \end{aligned}$$

   where d_j is the desired output of node j, and Y_j is the actual output. If node j is an internal hidden node then

$$\begin{aligned} \delta_j &= Y_j(1-Y_j)\sum_0^k \delta_k W_{jk} \\ ch\_thre(t+1) &= \eta\delta_j + \alpha(\theta_j(t) - \theta_j(t-1)) \end{aligned}$$

   where k is over all nodes in the layers above node j.

3. Termination: where the network stops training when the network's output is close to the desired output.

   The error for the network is calculated as follows:

$$E = \frac{1}{2}\sum_{i=1}^{k}(d_j - Y_j)^2$$

Ceramics Monitor

It has been known that the cutting force is related to the cutting parameters such as feed, depth of cut, and the spindle speed. For the purpose of monitoring a machining process through the cutting force and surface finish detection, a mapping function between the two detected signals and the three cutting parameters should be established. Figure 9.4 illustrates the basic structure of the implemented on-line monitor in this work. The monitor has two independent models, namely the cutting force model and the surface roughness model. Each of the two models consists of an input layer, a hidden layer, and an output layer. In the cutting force model, the three nodes in the input layer represent feed, depth of cut, and the cutting speed. In the hidden layer, two nodes are chosen for maximizing the effect to generalize the input information into the correlation of the activity among the three input nodes, rather than to simply memorize the input patterns.[5]

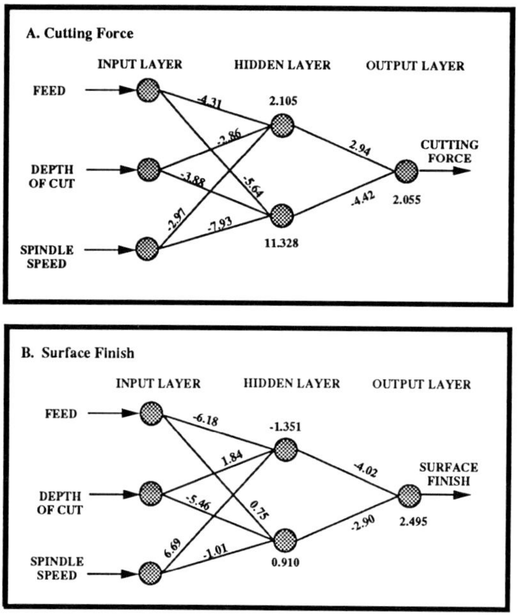

Figure 9.4: Basic structure of the network used for ceramics

Steel Monitor

It is well known that a tool will produce relatively higher loads as it begins to wear during the cutting operation. For effective process monitoring it is important that the signal used varys progressively as the tool wears, and not just at the point when it breaks. Force measurement is currently the most reliable and accurate sensing method in metal cutting operations, as the cutting force increases with flank wear due to an increase in the contact area of the wear land with the workpiece. It is generally assumed that the components of cutting force are related to flank and crater wear.[10–12] According to Wright, however, cutting force information by itself is inadequate for tool wear detection because its magnitude also depends on the cutting velocity.[13] Another problem is that although flank wear tends to increase the cutting force, the accompanying crater wear tends to reduce it, so that the magnitude of the cutting force may not show any sensitivity to tool wear.[13] But Ramalingam[6] proposed a model in which the ratio of the feed force to the cutting force (tangential force) is used as the measure of flank wear of a cutting tool during turning. According to Ramalingam[6], for the same cutting conditions, both cutting force and feed force increases with the flank wear. But feed force is more sensitive to the flank wear compared to the tangential cutting force. So, the resulting cutting force direction in the feed-tangential plane will change with increasing flank wear, as the feed force increases more rapidly than the tangential cutting force. By using cutting force ratio as an indicator of wear regime, one can take into account of the change in the magnitude as well as the direction of the cutting force with the flank wear. Furthermore, this eliminates the problem of using the force magnitude to the sensitivity of tool wear. At high temperatures, the magnitude of the cutting force may decrease due to the decrease of work hardening at the tool-workpiece interface. Due to this fact, the magnitude of the cutting force may decrease, but the ratio of the feed force to the cutting force will not be effected (i.e., it will increase with flank wear) as both components are affected by work hardening. Apart from force ratio, other machining parameters, like feed, speed, nose radius of the cutting insert or tool etc., also affect the machining process. When a high cutting speed is chosen, the insert may deform plastically as a result of the high tangential force. This is usually caused by several interrelated factors. For example, high cutting speed causes the temperature of the tool to increase locally, a factor which is further exacerbated when a small nose radius is used. This local increase in temperature, coupled with the high speed causes the tool geometry to change. So the chip flow pattern is modified accordingly, leading to tool wear. By using a larger nose radius on the insert, the heat can be more easily dissipated. It is possible to increase the cutting tool life substantially by a proper variation of the cutting feed rate throughout the cutting process.[14]

Figure 9.5 illustrates the basic structure of the network used to monitor the machining of the steel work piece. The model has six input nodes, four hidden nodes, and two output nodes. The six nodes in the input layer represent cutting speed, feed, depth of cut, time, nose radius, and force ratio. Each of the output nodes represent

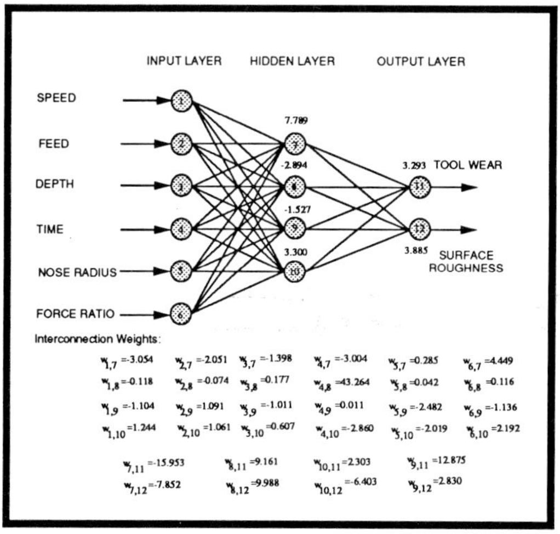

Figure 9.5: Basic structure of the network used for steel

tool wear and surface roughness. The four hidden nodes are chosen to minimize the memorization of input data rather than to generalize it by the trained network.

9.2.3 Experimentation and Training Process

Experimentation

Experimental tests on machining of a specific ceramic material were conducted to provide training examples for adjusting the weights connecting the nodes distributed in the input, hidden and output layers. The experiments were conducted in the Advanced Design and Manufacturing Lab of the Mechanical Engineering Department at the University of Maryland, College Park campus. The experimental setup used to perform the tests is illustrated in Figure 9.6. A CNC milling machine was used to conduct the machining tests. A tool holder with Polycrystalline Diamond Compact (PDC) tool insert and a designed force transducer were fixed on the machine tool table with the help of a fixture. The workpiece, aluminium oxide ceramic, was mounted to the spindle of the machine, which could be rotated at any desired speed. The setup for measuring the cutting forces is shown in Figure 9.6.

Ceramic bars of length 10 cm and diameter 2 cm were used for machining tests. To ensure that the train examples are information rich, a method called *factorial design at two levels* was used to set the values of the three cutting parameters. Specifically, 0.2 mm/rev and 0.40 mm/rev for feed, 0.1 mm and 0.2 mm for depth of cut, and 400 rpm and 600 rpm for spindle speed were used. For a combination of these cut-

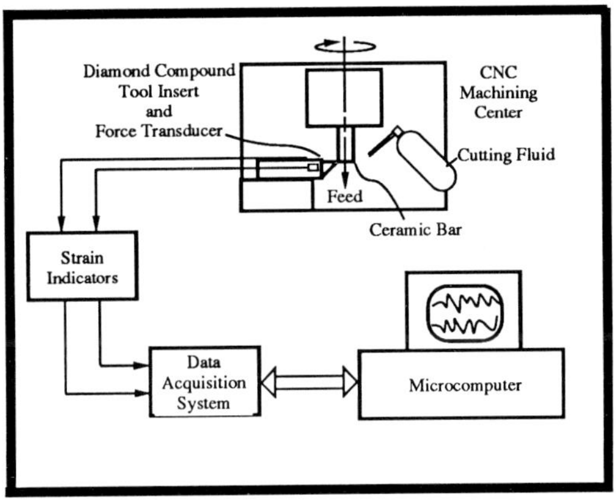

Figure 9.6: Experimental setup for machining of ceramic bars

ting parameter settings, several machining tests were carried out for obtaining the measurements of the cutting force and surface finish. Different cutting fluids were used during machining to determine their effect on cutting force and surface finish. Figures 9.7a and 9.7b present the recorded cutting force and surface finish measurements. Note that the mean value of the cutting force data and the mean value of the surface profile heights served as their representatives in the training process. Figures 9.8a and 9.8b graphically represent the mean values of the measured cutting force and surface finish for one of the cutting fluid used. The quality of the training examples, with regard to the information carried, can be evidenced by examining four pair measurements, for example, under two-level feed settings. The average of these four pair measurements is a good estimate of the main effect of feed on the cutting force, or the surface finish.

Training Process

Once the architecture of the network is determined, the network has to be trained on the examples. All the values of training examples are normalized between 0 and 1. This is because each node represents a nonlinear sigmoid function and gives an output which lies between the same limits; i.e., 0 and 1. This also eliminates the saturation of the sigmoid function. The values of training examples are normalized using the relation:

$$V_{nor} = \frac{(0.9 - 0.1)(V_{cur} - V_{min})}{V_{max} - V_{min}} + 0.1$$

where

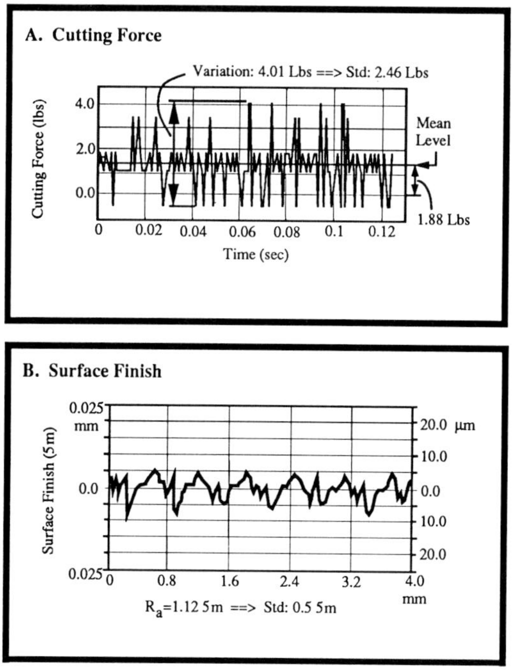

Figure 9.7: Recorded cutting force and surface finish measurements

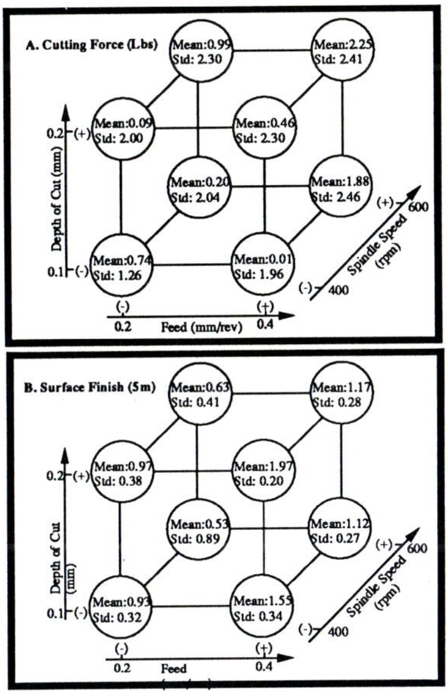

Figure 9.8: Measured mean values of cutting force and surface finish

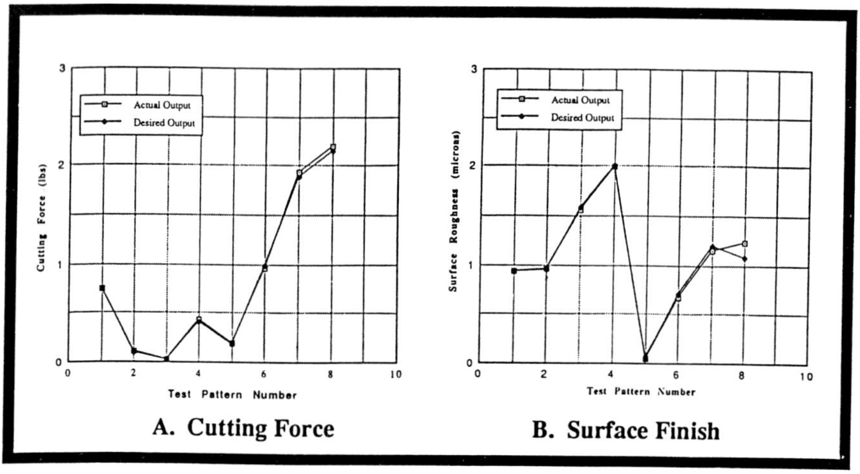

Figure 9.9: Plots of correlation between the predicted and actual values for Ceramic Bars

V_{max} = maximum value of the parameter
V_{min} = minimum value of the parameter
V_{cur} = current value of the parameter
V_{nor} = normalized value of the parameter.

The weights and threshold values derived from the training of the networks used for monitoring the machining of ceramics, using the training examples, are illustrated in Figures 9.4a and 9.4b. By feeding the values of cutting parameters to the input nodes of the trained network, cutting force and surface roughness can be predicted. Comparisons between the predicted and measured cutting forces and surface roughness, as shown in Figures 9.9a and 9.9b, can be made to show the closeness between them, indicating the superior learning and noise suppression abilities of the developed neural network monitor in information processing. The success rate of monitoring the cutting force and the surface roughness was above 90% ((desired output - actual output)/ desired output), from the trained network.

To further verify the applicability of the feedforward backpropagation network is also trained with the experimental data, taken from.[4] The derived weights and threshold values are illustrated in Figure 9.5. Tool wear and surface finish were predicted using testing examples and Figures 9.10a and 9.10b illustrate the correlation between the predicted and the actual values. Three types of network architectures

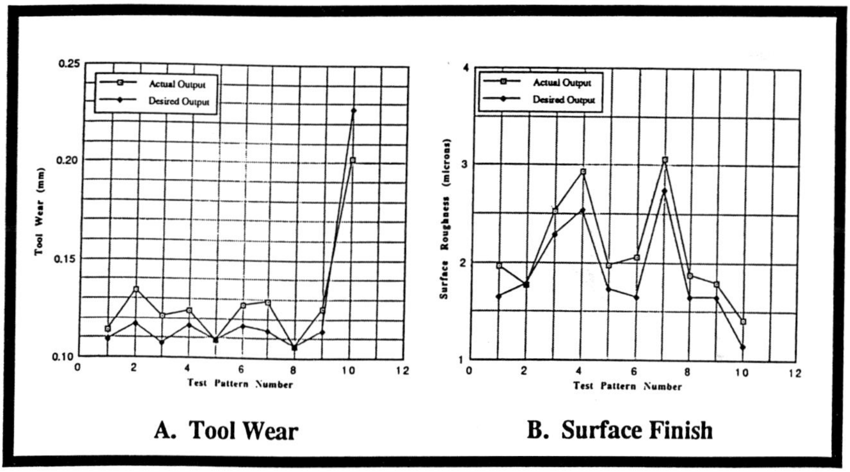

Figure 9.10: Plots of correlation between the predicted and actual values for steel bars

were used to train the monitor—tool wear alone was predicted in the first type, surface finish alone was predicted in the second type and both were predicted in the third type. Prediction of surface finish was found closer to actual value in the third type of network compared to the second type, where only surface finish was predicted. This is because the tool wear effect on surface roughness was taken into consideration for terminating the training process; i.e., for obtaining the weights and threshold values. The third type of network was thus chosen to minimize the false alarms for both tool wear and surface roughness.

9.3 Applications

9.3.1 Effect of Cutting Parameters on Cutting Force and Surface Roughness

For a ceramic material, the developed monitor is used to find the relationship between the cutting parameters, and the cutting force and surface roughness. Machining of ceramics is more difficult than machining of metals. Unlike metal machining, the feed force is more than the tangential force. This is mainly because of the hardness

Table 9.1: Effect of cutting parameters on cutting force

PARAMETER VALUE	CHANGED PARAMETER	ACTUAL OUTPUT	CHANGED OUTPUT	PERCENTAGE CHANGE
0.40 mm/rev	0.36 mm/rev	1.88 lbs	1.523 lbs	-18.99%
0.10 mm	0.09 mm	1.88 lbs	1.836 lbs	-2.3%
600 rpm	540 rpm	1.88 lbs	1.0156 lbs	-45.98%

Table 9.2: Effect of cutting parameters on surface roughness

PARAMETER VALUE	CHANGED PARAMETER	ACTUAL OUTPUT	CHANGED OUTPUT	PERCENTAGE CHANGE
0.40 mm/rev	0.36 mm/rev	1.12 μm	0.8015 μm	-28.44%
0.10 mm	0.09 mm	1.12 μm	1.086 μm	-3.1%
600 rpm	540 rpm	1.12 μm	1.503 μm	+34.19%

of ceramics and due to the change in the cutting mechanism; i.e., the material is removed by fracture mechanism. The machining of steel is primarily by plastic deformation. One way of knowing the effect of cutting parameters on cutting force and surface roughness is by decreasing the original value of the cutting parameter under consideration by 10% and finding its effect on the output from the trained neural network by keeping other cutting parameters unchanged.

Table 9.1 shows the results for one particular set of cutting parameters on cutting force. It can be seen from Table 9.1 that, the depth of cut has the least effect on the cutting force and speed has the greatest positive influence on cutting force. Feed has a medium effect. Other factors, such as tool wear etc., affect the process minimally. After considering all other sets of cutting parameters, it was found that the most efficient way of machining; i.e., low cutting force, can be obtained by having a low feed (0.2 mm/rev) and a low cutting speed (78.5 ft/min), which was confirmed with the experimental results.

Table 9.2 shows the results on surface roughness. It can be seen from the Table 9.2 that, as speed is decreased, surface roughness increases. Again the depth of cut has the least effect on surface roughness. Feed has a medium effect. After considering all other parameter settings, it was found the best surface quality can be obtained by having a low feed (0.2 mm/rev) and a high cutting speed (118 ft/min), which was confirmed with the experimental results.

9.3.2 On-Line Monitoring of a Turning Process

It should be pointed out that the implementation of the developed monitor in a real time machining operation requires an additional piece of information, i.e., the estimate of the dynamic variation of the monitoring target(s), such as the cutting force and/or surface finish. This additional information enables the monitor to distinguish the external noise related to the machining process abnormalities from the natural, or inherent process variations, evidences of which are shown in Figures 9.7a and 9.7b. In this work, estimates of the dynamic variations of the two monitoring targets were obtained by two steps. The first step was to obtain the two estimates at each of the turning tests. These estimates are presented in Figures 9.8a and 9.8b. In the second step, two pooled estimates, representing the natural variation of the cutting force and surface finish during machining were calculated from the measured estimates. These two pooled estimates were the standard deviations of the cutting force (2.12 Lbs.) and the surface finish (0.52 μm), respectively.

To demonstrate applicability of the proposed on-line monitoring system, a prototype monitoring system using the developed neural network monitor has been implemented on a CNC milling machine to monitor the machining of advanced ceramic materials, as shown in Figure 9.1. The objective of such a monitoring system is to control the appearance of micro-cracks on the machined surface, the dimensional accuracy, and the finish quality of the machined surface. It is assumed that a large cutting force leads to severe surface damage. Therefore, the two monitoring targets are the cutting force and the surface finish. Figures 9.11a and 9.11b are the two monitoring charts obtained during the turning process. The center lines of these two charts respectively represent the predicted cutting force and surface finish through training. The upper and lower limits on the two charts are the warning lines of the monitoring system. The limits are constructed based on the 3-σ principle, which indicates that the turning process is in its normal status as long as the detected cutting force signal, or the measured surface finish, is within the upper and lower limits. Whenever a detected signal is out of the two limits, the machining process goes on to an abnormal status. It is evident from the two monitoring charts shown in Figures 9.11a and 9.11b, the turning process under monitoring is in a normal status because all the detected and measured signals are within the limits. At the initial stages of the turning process, the neural network function, i.e., the trained weights and thresholds, is static in nature. As neural networks allow incremental improvement as new data is made available, the neural network function can be made dynamic. To make the neural network function dynamic, the current monitoring data (either cutting force or surface roughness) is fed back to the monitor. The monitor compares this new data with the previously stored data in the knowledge base and retrains its weights and thresholds if the data is different. Therefore, the network constantly keeps the new information stored and the database will be updated, which is not possible with any other statistical methods, like, linear regression. As the reliable information is accumulated, more aspects of the true nature of the turning process will be revealed. By this process a trained neural network learns from experience and updates its knowledge and stores it in the interconnection weights.

The prototype system has been tested with satisfaction on the turning operation. Under many circumstances, the detected cutting force signal hit the upper warning

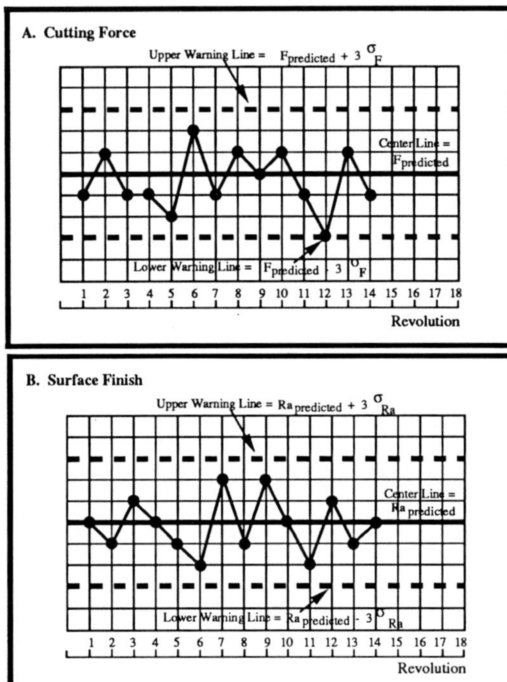

Figure 9.11: On-line monitoring charts recorded during machining

line. The machining operation was stopped immediately and severe surface damage was observed. The worn tool was replaced by a new tool and the turning process was resumed to its normal status. When the detected cutting force signal hit the lower warning line, a severe tool breakage was observed. The breakage caused the depth of cut during machining to drop to a level where there was almost no contact between the workpiece and the tool. However, false alarm sometimes occurs (especially during the cutting force monitoring) due to the complexity of cutting mechanism, such as effects of built-up edges and non-homogeneous distributions of workpiece material properties. As a result, the decision-making advisor built in the monitoring system will call on human intervention only under circumstances when the two monitoring targets are hitting their warning lines. There is, however, an associated side-effect, i.e., the decrease of the sensitivity of the monitoring system for an effective detection of the process abnormalities. Further improvements are being made to balance the need between the false alarm elimination and the detection sensitivity.

The proposed on-line monitoring system has been tested with satisfaction to predict the monitoring targets, such as tool wear and surface finish, directly. Figure 9.12 illustrates the implementation of an on-line monitoring system for machining of steel, where tool wear and surface roughness are monitored directly. The force signals from sensors are low pass filtered and force ratio (feed to tangential force) is determined. This ratio, along with the other machining parameters, is fed into the trained neural network and tool wear and surface finish are predicted. By monitoring the predicted values, the human operator (or control system) can act accordingly to optimize the turning process.

9.4 Conclusions

A prototype system to perform an untended machining operation has been developed. Through an on-line detection of the cutting force and the control of surface finishmeasurements, the monitoring system has been successfully used to assure satisfactory performance during the machining of advanced ceramic materials. The success rate of monitoring was above 90%. A neural network monitor can serve as one of the most efficient tools in finding an optimum set of machining parameters to a quality engineer as well as to a machining operator by predicting the effect of machining parameters on the machining process beforehand. Serving as the brain of the untended machining system, the neural network monitor processes the machining-related information from the detected signals, compares the extracted information with the pre-determined warning limits, and passes the results to the built-in decision-making advisor. The advantages of artificial neural networks are explored in this work. It has been shown that through appropriate selection of architecture of the network, noise can be minimized and the process variables can be predicted accurately, indicating that neural networks can become a promising modeling tool for use in on-line monitoring of machining processes.

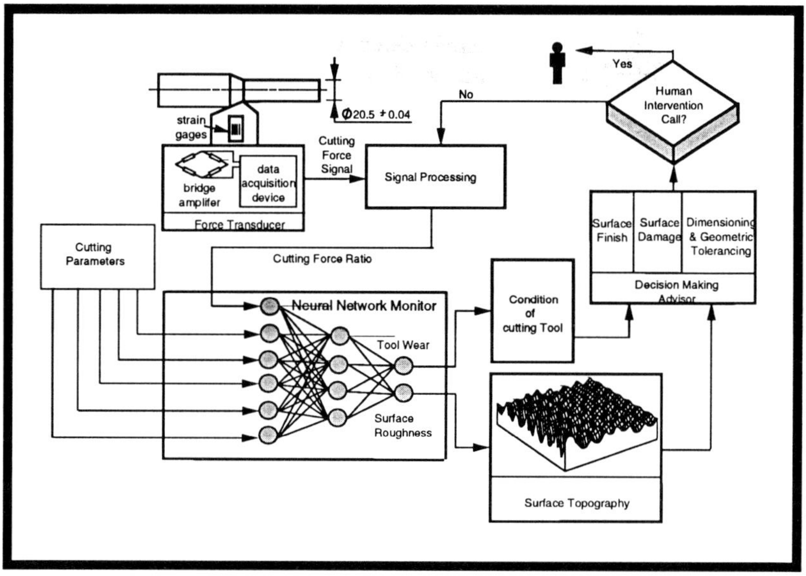

Figure 9.12: Basic structure of the implemented on-line monitoring system for machining of steel

Acknowledgements

The authors acknowledge the support of the Systems Research Center at the University of Maryland at College Park under Engineering Research Centers Program: NSFD CDR 8803012, and the University of Maryland General Research Board. The assistance of Mr. K. F. Arnold and S. Yerramareddy by giving their experimental results is greatly appreciated. Special thanks are due Mr. Tsuwei Hwang for his help in experimentation assistance and preparation of graphics.

9.5 References

1. S. M. Arsovski, "Wear sensors in the adaptive control systems of machine tools," *International Journal of Production Research*, **21** (3) (1983).

2. S. Jetly, " Measuring tool wear on-line: some practical considerations," *Manufacturing Engineering*, (July 1984).

3. H. Suzuki, and K. J. Weinmann, " An on-line tool wear sensor for straight turning operations," *Journal of Engineering for Industry, Transactions of ASME*, **107** (Nov. 1985).

4. K. F. Arnold, "Measurement of cutting forces as they relate to flank wear," M. S. Thesis, Dept. of Mechanical Engineering, University of Missouri-Columbia, MO (1989).

5. Raju G. Khanchustambham, "A neural network approach to on-line monitoring of machining processes," M. S. Thesis, Department of Mechanical Engineering, University of Maryland, (May 1992).

6. T. Shi and S. Ramalingam, "Real-time flank wear sensing," *Fundamental Issues in Machining*, PED **43** (1990).

7. R. Lippmann, "An introduction to computing with Neural Nets," *IEEE ASSP Magazine*, (April 1987) 4-22.

8. J. L. McClelland, D. Rumelhart, *et al.* , *Parallel Distributed Processing*, (The MIT Press, Cambridge, MA, 1986).

9. P. Balakrishnan, and J. C. Macbain, "Monitoring Systems For Unmanned Machining," *SME technical paper*, **MR** (1985) 85-479.

10. K. Danai, and A. G. Ulsoy, *An Adaptive Observer for On-Line Tool Wear Estimation in Turning*, Part 1-theory, Part 2-Results (1987).

11. A. De Filippi, and R. Ippolito, "Adaptive Control in Turning: Cutting Forces and Tool Wear Relationships for P10, P20, p30 Carbides," *CIRP Annals*, **17** (1969) 377-379.

12. G. F. Micheletti, De Filippi, and R. Ippolito, *Proceedings of the CIRP International Conference on Manufacturing Technology,* (Ann Harbor, Michigan, Sep. 1967), 513-524.

13. D. W. Yen, and P. K. Wright, "Adaptive Control in Machining - A new approach based on the physical constraints of Tool Wear Mechanisms," *ASME Journal of Engineering for Industry,* **105** (1) (Feb. 1983) 31-38.

14. Clement Fortin and Marek Balazinski *et. al,* "Study of the influence of Feed Variation on Tool Wear, Fundamental Issues In Machining," PED **43** (1990).

15. R. G. Khanchustambham and G. M. Zhang, "A Neural Network Approach to On-line Monitoring of a Turning Process," *Proceedings of International Joint Conference on Neural Networks,* Baltimore, Maryland, **2** (1992) 889-894.

Chapter 10

Neural Adaptive Systems for Machining Errors Modeling

Hung-Kang Jan
Machine Design and Engineering Division
Mechanical Industry Research Laboratories, MIRL-C100
Industrial Technology Research Institute
Chutung, Hsinchu, Taiwan 310

C Richard Liu
School of Industrial Engineering
Purdue University
West Lafayette, IN 47907 USA

Abstract

This chapter presents a neural network based methodology for tracking time-varying machine tool volumetric errors. This methodology serves as a practical approach to achieve real-time machining quality control on CNC machine tools. To solve the inherent 3D time-varying problem, analytical as well as neural network approaches are employed in parallel to coup with nonlinearity. A multiple-sensor system is incorporated with the model for real-time CNC machine tool system monitoring and data acquisition. The data acquired by the sensor array will be processed by a trained neural network and the corresponding machining quality (workpiece dimensional accuracy) will be jointly predicted by the analytical and neural net models. The results demonstrate that neural network based methodology is capable of predicting the errors of any entire workpiece, or, if needed, the same information can serve as fast and excellent reference for on-line error compensation.

10.1 Introduction

Due to global market competition, deciding on a cost-justifiable method to practice "manufacturing for quality" has been a challenge for both industry and academia. A practical approach which is capable of performing real-time machining quality control on CNC machine tools is urgently needed in metal-removal industry. At the same time, there has been an increasing interest in the use of sensors in an automated manufacturing system (e.g., CNC machine tool) for in-process measurements, real-time process monitoring and error compensation to secure product quality. With cheaper but more powerful microcomputer-based multiple sensors systems, real-time error compensation (adaptive control) or quality monitoring becomes more promising and economical. Some previous works[10,11,17] present good examples of such an approach. However, for a manufacturing environment in which the workpiece configurations are diverse, such an approach is usually restricted by the unavailability of sensors, inaccessible measurements of position, hostile operating environment and the lack of effective analysis methodology for large amount of sensory data. All of these together, result in a very low signal-to-noise ratio and slow response to the changing environment.

Thus, in order to achieve "manufacturing for quality" in a real factory environment, developing a feasible approach has been a very attractive challenge for both industry and academia. In response to the situation, this research presents a methodology for monitoring machining quality (dimensional accuracy) in real time for the CNC machine systems using artificial neural network approach. This methodology provides a feasible and robust model to predict the dimensional errors of workpiece under any normal operating condition. The very same information generated by the model can also be used for feedback control systems to perform active dimensional error compensation for prismatic workpieces.

10.2 Artificial Neural Networks

Artificial neural networks (ANN) are mathematical models which tend to simulate the way the human brain functions. They are also referred to as parallel distribution processors, connectionisms, adaptive systems, adaptive networks or neurocomputers. Neural networks have been -proven effective in solving various domains of problems such as pattern or speech recognition,[1,19] image processing,[9] signal processing,[3] control,[8,14] etc.

According to Hecht-Nielsen,[4] a neural network is formally defined as a parallel, distributed information processing structure consisting of processing elements interconnected via unidirectional signal channels called connections. Each processing element has a single output connection that branches into as many collateral connections as desired. The processing element output signal can be of any mathematical type desired. Neural networks possess several unique characteristics to outperform the classical methods or knowledge based systems:[12]

1. the ability to exploit a vast amount of sensory information,
2. the ability to respond with high speed to sensory inputs,
3. a great degree of robustness and fault/noise tolerance due to their distributed representation,
4. have general nonlinear mapping capabilities despite the complexity of underlying systems, whereas traditional fault detection techniques involve detailed modeling,
5. ability to generalize (or discover) the underlying rules of systems by learning rather than by a given algorithm. This property makes neural networks particularly suitable for solving nonlinear complex systems.

There are many types of neural networks for solving various problems. The structures of a neural network are generally characterized by the following three elements:[16]

1. topology (geometry) of interconnected processing elements,
2. a method of encoding information, and
3. a method of recalling information.

10.2.1 Processing Element

The processing element (PE) is the unit analogous to the biological neuron. The PEs are also referred to as nodes, short term memory, neurons or threshold logic units. A processing element takes many input paths from either other processing elements, input elements (sensors), output elements or even from the element itself. Associated with each connected pair of PEs is referred to as connection strength or weight. The processing element combines the values of these input connection strengths generally through a weighted summation. The result is an internal activity level for the processing element. The combined input is then transformed by a threshold function $F(x)$ which, in turn, performs a sort of nonlinear normalization. The output of a processing element can be an input of other processing elements or can be one of the output signal of the neural network system provided that this PE happens to be one of the output elements of the system. The basic structure of a process element is shown in Figure 10.1.

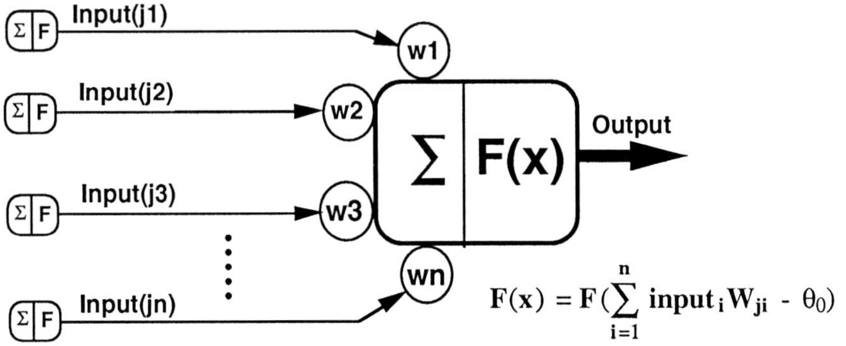

Figure 10.1: Basic structure of an artificial neuron (processing element)

10.2.2 Threshold Function

Threshold functions, also referred to as activation functions or signal functions, map PE's inputs domain to a prespecified range. A threshold function actually performs a nonlinear normalization on the weighed summation of input data. Four common threshold functions are linear function, step function, ramp function and sigmoid function as shown in Figure 10.2.

Among these, the sigmoid function is more realistic for most real-world applications and thus is the most popularly adopted threshold function. Three common types of sigmoid functions are used:

(1) logistic function

$$f(x) = (1 + e^{-x})^{-1} \tag{10.1}$$

(2) hyperbolic tangent function

$$f(x) = \tanh(x) \tag{10.2}$$

augmented ratio of squares

$$\begin{cases} x^2/(1+x^2), & \text{for } x \geq 0; \\ f(x) = 0, & \text{otherwise} \end{cases} \tag{10.3}$$

10.2.3 Training Procedures

A neural network must be trained (or a neural network must learn) to some extent before it is ready to solve problems. There are several types of training (or learning) procedures:

1. Supervised training which requires labeled training data and an external "teacher" to indicate whether the current output is correct or not. Examples

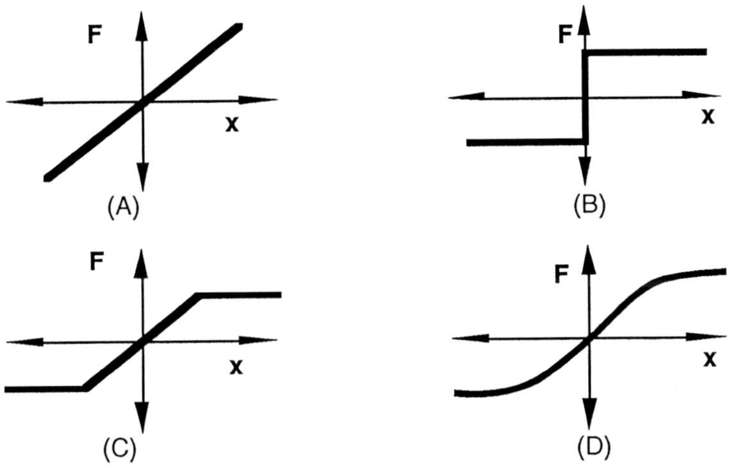

Figure 10.2: Common threshold functions (a) linear function, (b) step function, (c) ramp function and (d) sigmoid function

of supervised training algorithms are error-correction training, reinforcement learning, stochastic learning and hardwired systems.[16]

2. Unsupervised self-organization training which uses unlabeled training data and requires no external teacher. Data are presented and internal categories or clusters are formed which compress the input data that must be processed at higher levels without losing important information.

10.2.4 Network Topology

A typical neural network consists of an input layer, one or more hidden layers and an output layer as shown in Figure 10.3. However, a model with no hidden layers is not unusual. Patterns of connectivity between nodes (PEs) vary between neural network models. Nodes (processing elements) may be only locally connected to neighbors, fully connected to all other nodes, sparsely connected to a few distant nodes or randomly connected between randomly chosen nodes.

In addition, networks may be layered with exclusively feedforward connections from lower to higher layers as in the backpropagation network[15] or networks may be provided with recurrent feedback connections as in fully-connected discrete or continuous Hopfield networks. A variety of neural network topologies have been proposed. Each differs in the number and character of the processing nodes, the connections, the training procedures and the types (continuous, binary or discrete) of input and output values.

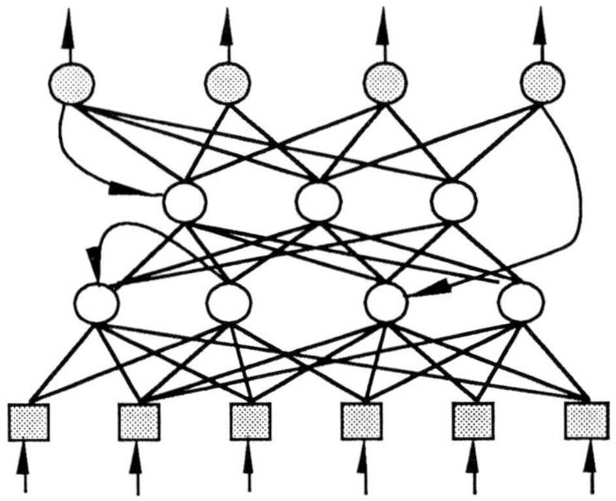

Figure 10.3: A typical multi-layer neural network with two hidden layers

10.3 CNC Machine Tool System Errors

Computer Numerical Controlled (CNC) machine tools have been extensively used all over the world. Although a CNC machine tool has numerous advantages over the traditional counterpart, a CNC machine tool always presents systematic errors which, in turn, significantly affect the dimensional accuracy and surface quality of the workpiece. For a manual-operated machine tool, system errors reflected on the workpiece can be adaptively rectified by the operator. For a CNC machine tool, system errors cannot be automatically and adaptively eliminated without thorough understanding and good modeling. Machine tool modelling is generally a difficult task due to the errors' nonlinear and time-varying nature as well as due to the difficulty of error data collection. Usually model needs to comprise between limited data availability and model accuracy.

The geometric variations observed on the finished parts in a machining process are the collective effect of several error sources. The error sources can be broadly classified as

1. high frequency domain (HFD) error (that is, dynamic error) and

2. low frequency domain (LFD) error.

The high frequency errors are associated with the machine tool dynamic behaviors which primarily include the spindle motion errors and machine tool structure vibration or chattering. The high frequency errors which are small in magnitude predominantly affect the workpiece surface texture (e.g., roughness) rather than the workpiece geometric correctness or dimensional accuracy. It can be avoided by select-

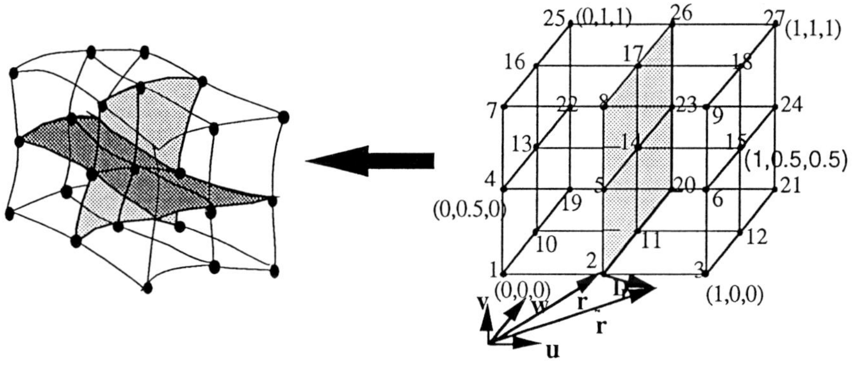

Figure 10.4: Distorted workspace and corresponding parametric ideal workspace

ing proper machining conditions in the finishing cut. Thus, the high frequency errors are not a major concern of this paper.

On the other hand, the low frequency domain errors, which are significant in magnitude, are much more critical to the finished parts' geometric correctness and dimensional accuracy. Low frequency domain errors consist of space and T-domain errors. A space domain error is defined as the error which is a function of its coordinates in 3D Euclidean space. Space domain errors are also referred to as geometric and quasi-static errors which result from machine structures deformation and unwanted motions of moving components. On the other hand, T-domain errors are referred to as either time dependent or temperature dependent errors (that is, thermal errors) which result from uneven thermal distribution and temperature gradient in the structural system of machine tools. Conceptually, space domain errors can be regarded as a slice of "frozen" T-domain errors. Or, on the other hand, T-domain errors can be regarded as a string of space domain errors.

10.4 Modeling Methodology

Machine system workspace distortion, shown in Figure 10.4, is a time-varying nonlinear process and directly affects the workpiece dimensional accuracy. The workspace distortion is in turn caused by the machine system low frequency domain (LFD) errors. In order to perform real-time error compensation, reliable as well as simple error models for both space and T-domain are required.

In terms of space domain error modeling, generally the methodologies can be categorized into two distinct classes. The first type of methods is the kinematic (or element) approach as seen in the work done by Love and Scarr,[13] Duffie and Malmberg.[2] The second method is the workspace approach, such as the works done by Leete[10] Jan, Chu and Liu.[6] Jan and Liu[7] present an integrated algorithm which correlate the kinematic and workspace approaches. The basic principles of the integrated algorithm are mathematically described in the following Eqs. (10.4)-(10.9). The integrated method is experimentally proven to be accurate and simple for practical application.

$$\tilde{r} = \vec{r} + \Delta\vec{r} \tag{10.4}$$

$$\Delta\vec{r} = (\Delta\vec{r}(u,v,w), \Delta y(u,v,w), \Delta z(u,v,w)) \tag{10.5}$$

$$\Delta x(u,v,w) = \begin{pmatrix} 1 & u & u^2 & \ldots & u^m \end{pmatrix} \begin{pmatrix} a_{00} & a_{01} & \ldots & a_{0n} \\ a_{10} & a_{11} & \ldots & a_{1n} \\ \vdots & \vdots & \ddots & \vdots \\ a_{m0} & a_{m1} & \ldots & a_{mn} \end{pmatrix} \begin{pmatrix} 1 \\ v \\ \vdots \\ v^n \end{pmatrix}$$

$$\begin{pmatrix} \alpha_1 & \alpha_2 & \ldots & \alpha_n \end{pmatrix} \begin{pmatrix} 1 \\ w \\ \vdots \\ w^k \end{pmatrix} =$$

$$\begin{pmatrix} N_1 & N_2, & \ldots & N_{kmn} \end{pmatrix} \begin{pmatrix} \delta x_1 & \delta x_2 & \ldots & \delta x_{kmn} \end{pmatrix}^T \quad m,n,k \in I \tag{10.6}$$

In compact forms,

$$\Delta x(u,v,w) = [U][A_{uv}][V]^T[A_w][W]^T = [N][\delta X]^T \tag{10.7}$$

Similarly, for the other axes,

$$\Delta y(u,v,w) = [U][B_{uv}][V]^T[B_w][W]^T = [N][\delta Y]^T \tag{10.8}$$

$$\Delta z(u,v,w) = [U][C_{uv}][V]^T[C_w][W]^T = [N][\delta Z]^T \tag{10.9}$$

where A, B and C are coefficient matrices of the x, y and z axes respectively. These coefficients define the space domain errors of the distorted workspace and must be determined by experimental data. In short, these coefficients serve as controlling points and therefore, once the coefficients are known, the space domain error at any location within the effective workspace can be calculated.

10.5 T-domain (Thermal) Errors

Thermal effects have far-reaching influences on every aspect of machining. The heat from both the internal and external sources cause the machine structural frame, hence, the workpiece, to distort under free thermal expansion or thermal stresses caused by constrained thermal strains. Much effort has been made to model the thermal errors. These approaches include heat transfer function with finite element analysis in the design phase[18,20] or employ hardware modification method to decrease the thermal effect in the application stage.[21] However, the current approaches are time consuming processes and do not meet the requirements: cost effectiveness and real-time response.

Thermal distortion is caused by temperature variation and is a time-varying nonlinear process. The interaction between the heat source location, heat source intensity, thermal resistance coefficient and the machine system configuration creates complex thermal errors. In response to such a situation, a learning approach (artificial neural network) is proposed to replace the classical analytical approaches like thermal elasticity modeling, multiple regression or even Group Method of Data Handling (GMDH).[5] Thermal error modeling and real-time tracking can be considered as a pattern classification problem. Artificial neural network modeling methodology is particularly useful when nonlinear mapping is required or the system of concern is too complicated to be modeled using classical analytical approaches, or even the underlying system character is unknown.

In addition, neural networks are capable to deduce the system's underlying property from given data as well as to perform multiple input to multiple outputs pattern classification. All these properties provide neural networks unique advantages to outperform the classical approaches for thermal errors tracking.

10.6 Neural Network Based Integrated Model

To the authors' knowledge, the space domain and T-domain errors have been modeled separately. No previous attempt was made to integrate both domains errors.

T-domain errors can be viewed as a continuous process of the space domain error. The space domain error, on the other hand, can be described as a "frozen" T-domain error at a certain time frame or thermal state. This paper thus presents an integrated methodology to unify both the domain errors simultaneously as follows.

As shown in Eq. (10.6), (10.7) and (10.8) the entire space domain errors are determined by a few observed errors, $\delta x_i, \delta y_i, \delta z_i$, thus, if these observed errors can be tracked accurately at any time frame, then the entire distorted workspace at any time frame can also be tracked accurately. That is, system error at any location at any time frame (or thermal state) within the workspace can be expressed as

$$\Delta = F(x, y, z, \delta_1, \delta_2, \delta_3, \ldots, \delta_n) \tag{10.10}$$

where x, y and z are nominal coordinates of Δ, Δ is the error to be determined, δ_i is the i-th observed error defined by:

$$\delta_i = G(x_i, y_i, z_i, T_1, T_2, T_3, \ldots, T_k) \tag{10.11}$$

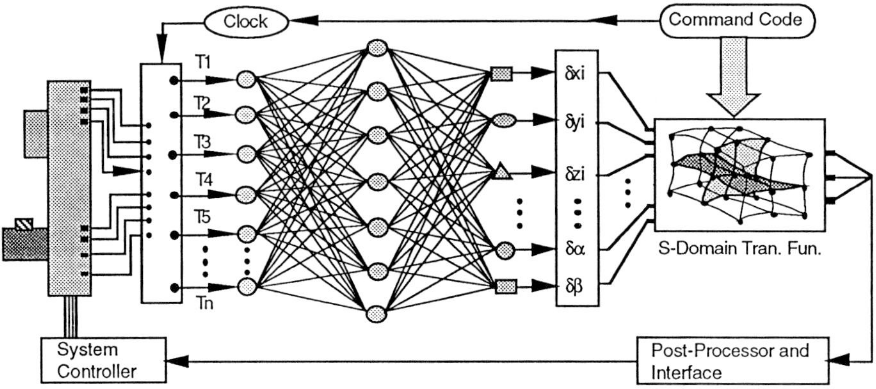

Figure 10.5: Neural network monitoring/control architecture in this research

and x_i, y_i, z_i are nominal coordinates of δ_i in space. $T_1, T_2, T_3, \ldots, T_k$ are temperature read-outs from the sensors array at prespecified locations throughout the system. Eqs. (10.7), (10.8) and (10.9) are used to establish the F function in Eq. (10.10). On the other hand, neural network learning approach, rather than classical analytical approach, is used to establish the G function in Eq. (10.11). The prespecified coordinates x, y and z in conjunction with temperature read-outs $T_1, T_2, T_3, \ldots, T_k$ from sensors are provided to the trained neural network. The outputs from the neural network are expected to give the values of δ_i in Eq. (10.11). Then δ_i's are substituted into Eqs. (10.7), (10.8) and (10.9) to obtain the entire workspace model at the specified time frame or thermal state.

In this research, a neural network with the backpropagation algorithm[15] is chosen. The network control architecture is shown in Figure 10.5.

The network used in this research initially has a 32-node input layer, a 5-node hidden layer and a 3-node output layer. Input layer with 5 to 32 nodes is also tested. The neural network training effectiveness, that is, the network's capability of generalization, is dependent on the distribution of the paired training data. Since neural network nonlinear mapping can be considered as an interpolation process in a multi-dimensional hyperspace, it is thus desired that the training sets contain information which is spread evenly throughout the entire normal service envelop of the system.[4]

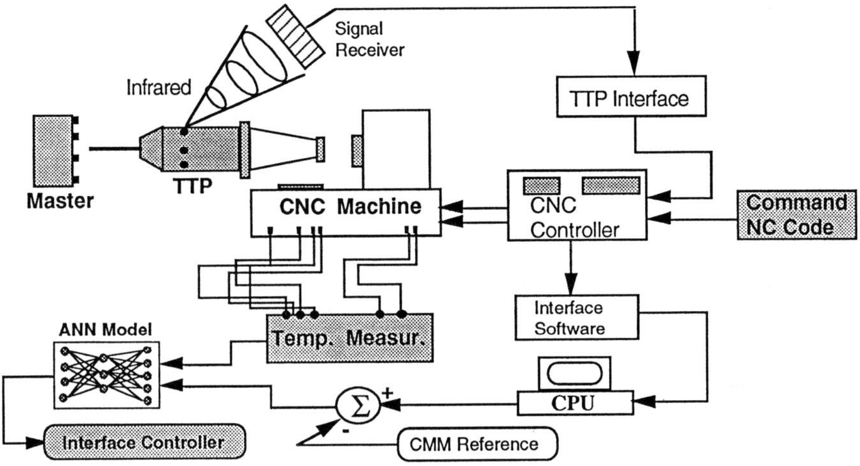

Figure 10.6: Machine error detection system

10.7 Sensory Systems and Experiments

A LVDT-type touch trigger probe is integrated with the machine control system and with a PC-based multi-channel temperature sensory system. This system, as shown in Figure 10.6, is used to:

1. collect data for artificial neural network training purpose in the off-line modeling phase and

2. provide real-time, on-line machine temperature fluctuation data for real-time monitoring and thermal-error tracking tasks.

A precision master plane stage gauge is also made for establishing coordinate frames. The combination of touch trigger probe and plane stage gauge can detect the thermal errors of the system. The temperature sensory system, as shown in Figure 10.7, consists of 32 channels of K-type metal-net shielded thermocouple wires whose ends contact with the machine at 32 different strategically selected locations on the machine tool system. Each thermocouple wire forms a single channel of thermal information. All 32 channels constitute a temperature spectrum generator.

Electronic noise initially posed severe problem to the experiment. Our experience reveals that the ground-loop noise and the cross-talk noise are the most significant sources of noise. The noise can be dramatically reduced by using proper grounding

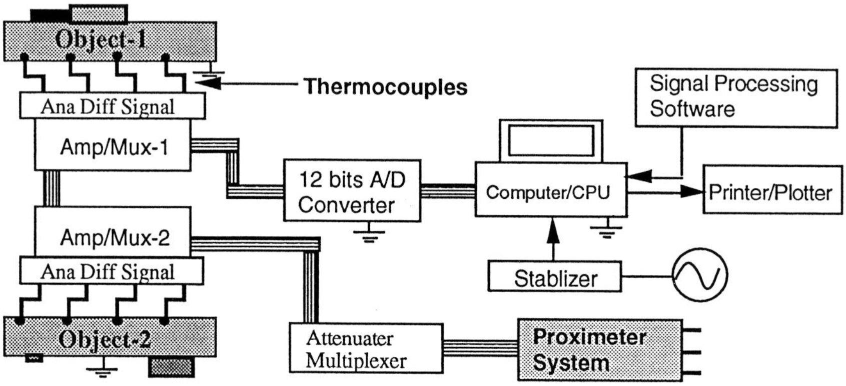

Figure 10.7: Thermocouple wires multiple channel temperature sensory system

and shielding (aluminum foil) simultaneously. More precise measurement can be achieved by further averaging out the residual noise using data acquisition/processing software. After proper signal noise reduction, the system is capable of detecting temperature variation of 0.2^o C or better.

Machine thermal errors are caused by various external and internal heat sources. Since thermal distribution is a continuous and highly coupled phenomenon, it is almost impossible to precisely control the temperature at certain locations without affecting the others. Thus the only way to obtain data is to actually run the machine system at various operation settings.

In the learning phase, temperature is generated by turning the spindle on and off with different RPM. The table, column and the saddle of the machine also travel back and forth to generate additional heat around the machine body. Meanwhile, system errors are detected by the on-board touch trigger probe at intervals of 4 or 6 minutes. The entire experiment lasts for about 100 hours and covers the machine service spectrum as much as possible. About 1200 sets of data are generated. Each data set contains 32 temperature readings from the thermal couple wires and several (depends on applications) corresponding error readings from the touch trigger probe. Three quarters of the data are used to train the neural network. The rest data are used for evaluating the effectiveness (prediction power) of the neural network model. The temperature profiles from some thermal couples in conjunction with the corresponding errors are shown in Figure 10.8. The data are used to train the network in a workstation. Several kinds of neural network topology are tested to find the feasible model.

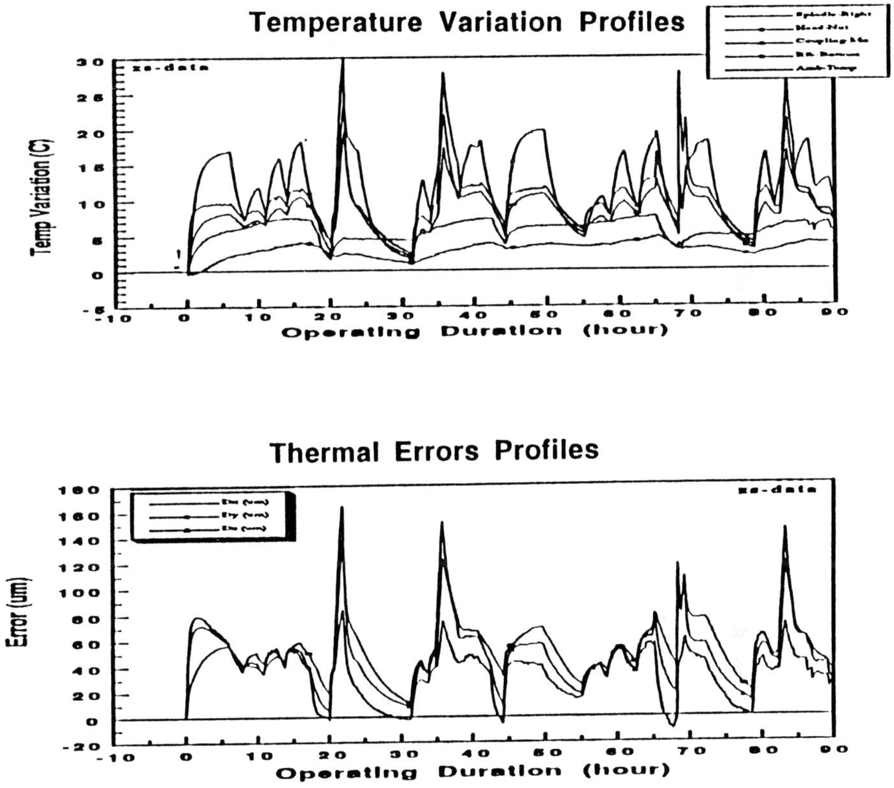

Figure 10.8: Measured (5 out of 32 sensors) machine system temperature variation profiles and the corresponding thermal error profiles

10.8 Results and Discussion

Disregarding the highly complicated machine system behaviors and the hostile manufacturing environment, Figure 10.9 shows that the neural network model is able to predict the system output (T-domain errors) effectively after the network is well trained. By substituting the neural network's outputs into Eqs. (10.7), (10.8) and (10.9), the entire workspace errors, that is, the manufacturing quality, can be calculated. Thus, as the neural network is incorporated with an appropriate control system, it can improve system performance and product quality in real-time through feed-back compensation. Since the entire workspace error, at any location at any time frame, can be predicted, the workpiece error virtually with any shape can thus be predicted by a simple transformation process. It provides an important advantage in an automatic, small batch production flexible system.

Note that the residual errors of the Y and Z axes in Figure 10.9 are literately on the order of the machine system's and measurement system's noise (random error). Thus, further improvement of the model is not possible for the Y and Z axes unless the system's random errors can be reduced. On the other hand, since the residual error of the X-axis is larger than system random error, it indicates that there is room for the current model to improve and a more sophisticated network configuration may be needed for better performance in the X-axis.

In addition, experiments show that the predictive power of the neural network is not sensitive to how the thermal couple wire contact points precisely distribute. As long as 32 wire contact points distribute reasonably over both the low and high temperature gradient area, the backpropagation network is able to correlate the error and the temperature read-outs and converge eventually to deliver a good predictive power.

Since the number of temperature sensors chosen is quite arbitrary, the fundamental guideline is not to miss important information. In practical application, it is desired to use as few sensors as possible. Effort is thus made to identify the minimum sensory information needed for developing a good neural network model. An effective graphical method, rather than more complicated ANOV statistical analysis, is developed for helping identify the major, moderate and the weak contributors to the total error. Table 10.1 shows how the prediction performance is affected as the number of sensors, (i.e., the number of input nodes), is reduced. Note that as the weak contributors are eliminated, the model predictive power is not affected. Model performance starts to degrade as one or more moderate contributors are eliminated. However, as experimentation indicates, the neural network must contain all major contributors' information in order to converge. This analysis provides a convenient method for sensory-system optimization.

Since all experiments are conducted in a full-scale workshop, input signals are subjected to noises and some sensor components occasionally malfunction over a long period of continuous operation. The robustness of the neural network model in such

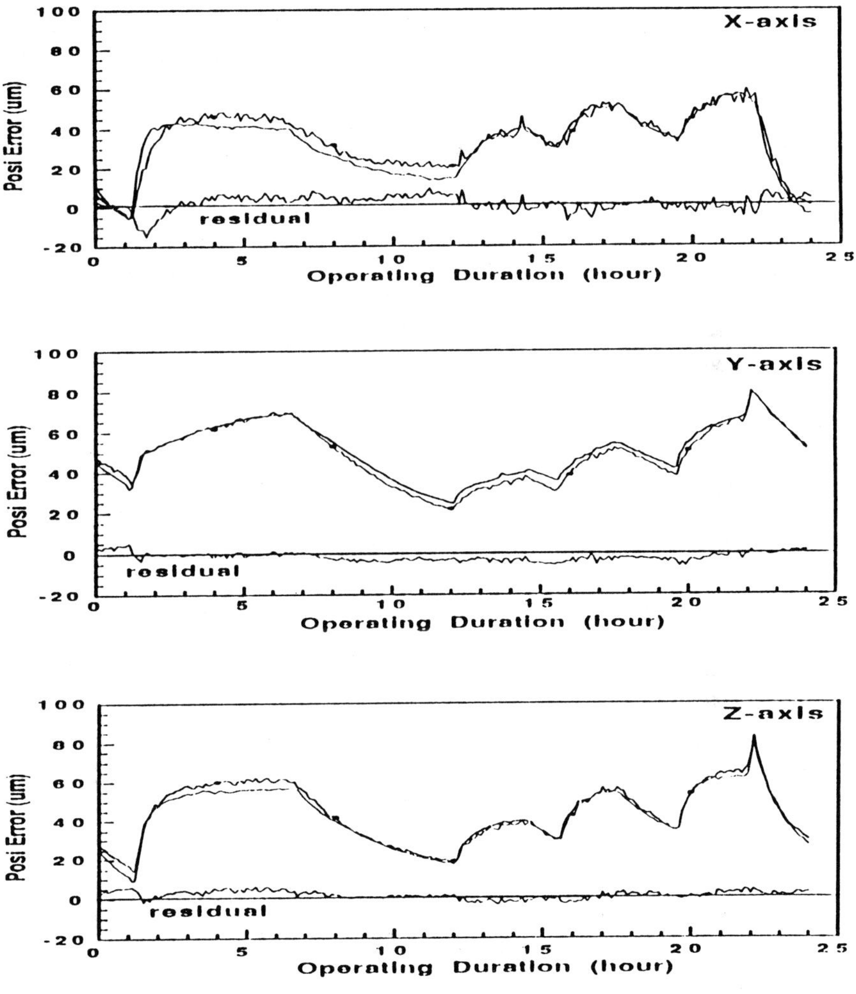

Figure 10.9: Model predictive power; comparison of model predicted T-domain errors and the actual errors

Table 10.1: Effect of sensor density

NEURAL NETWORKMODEL	(RMS-μm)	(RMS-μm)	(RMS-μm)
32-5-3	4.0	1.4	1.8
25-5-3	3.6	1.5	2.4
20-5-3	4.3	1.6	1.7
15-5-3	5.9	2.6	4
10-5-3	8.1	3.1	6.7
5-5-3		not converge	
5-10-3		not converge	

an environment is investigated. As shown in Figure 10.10, the results indicate that even one of the sensors in the major contributor category, for example, sensor No. 1 or No. 13, is disconnected, the neural network is still able to maintain fair predictive power. As two or more major sensors are disconnected, the predictive power degrades quickly. Also, if only one of the major sensors is contaminated by noisy signal (up to $\pm 2^o\ C$, that is, 20 times of the thermal sensor resolution), the neural network is not noticeably affected.

10.9 Angular Errors Prediction

Neural network models are also used to predict the machine head-stock angular errors at various temperature states. Head-stock angular error is a very significant signal error source. By the Abbe's principle, angular error will cause large positioning error at the cutting tool tip. The head-stock angular errors consist of the yaw (rotate about the vertical axis) and pitch (rotate about the horizontal axis) errors.

A set of proximeters are used to collect data of angular errors. The system is shown in Figure 10.11. Proximeter is a highly sensitive and fast response non-contact displacement measuring instrument. It is able to detect a displacement of 1 micrometer or better. For each type of angular error, a pair of proximeters are used. Two proximeters are placed about 300 mm apart. The difference between these two proximeters read-outs divided by the distance (300 mm) is the angular error which is measured in arc second.

The same temperature sensory system is used. Temperature system and proximeter system are synchronized to obtain data for training the neural network. As before, the machine temperature is generated by running the spindle on and off at different RPM for an extended period of operation. After the neural network is well trained, the predictive results are shown in Figure 10.12. Neural networks deliver a very good predictive power which is otherwise hard to achieve by classical approaches.

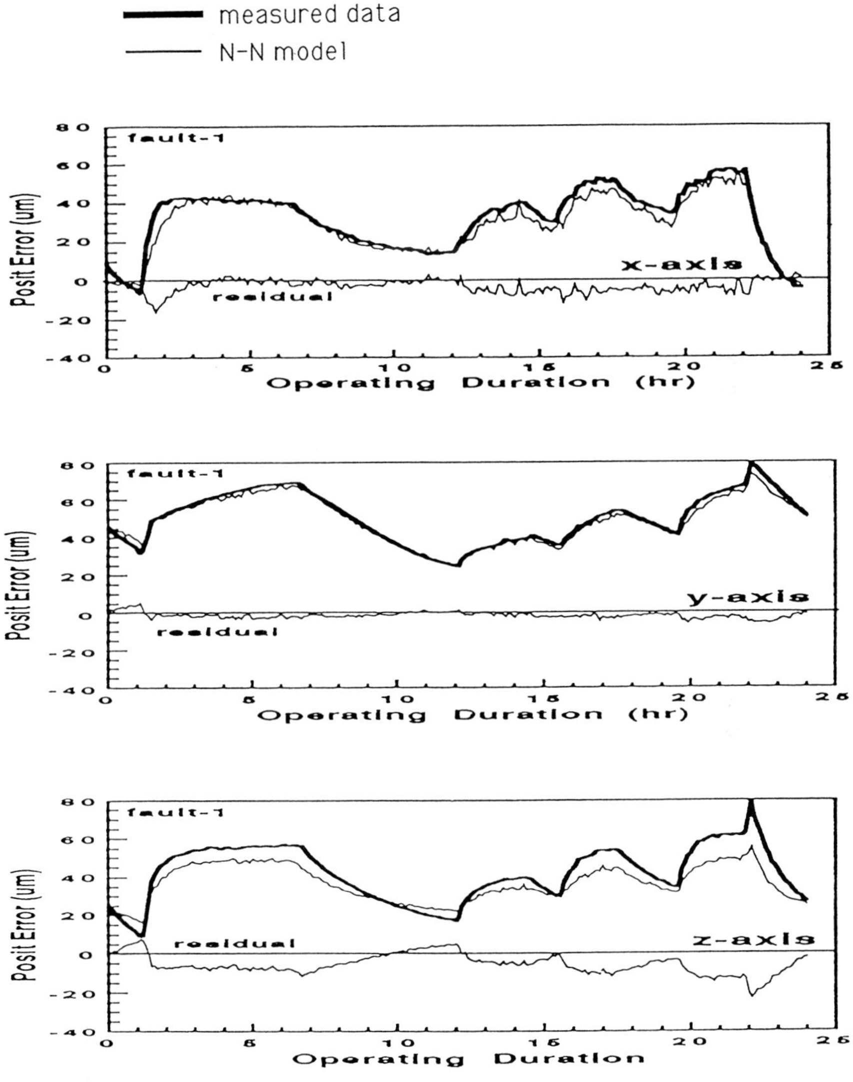

Figure 10.10: Neural networks fault tolerance (one of the major temperature sensor is damaged or disconnected

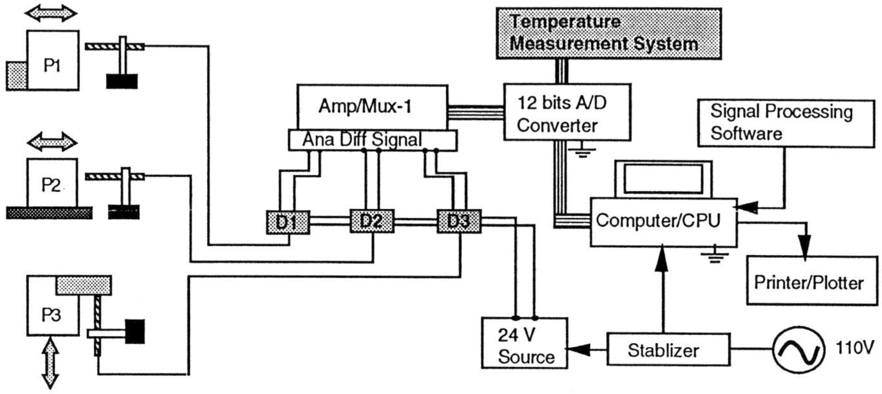

Figure 10.11: Multi-channel proximeter measurement system

10.10 Conclusion

The paper has discussed some results on the use of backpropagation neural networks for real-time tracking machine system's 3D distorted space as well as for machining quality evaluation. Artificial neural networks are particularly useful for modeling for a system whose underlying property is too complicated, too costly or too time-consuming to be modeled using classical methods or for a system whose underlying mechanism is not known at all. In many aspects, including fault and noise tolerant capability, the neural network approach outperforms the classical methods. Another main advantage of the neural network in this research is the representation of the entire workspace with both space and time domain errors with a single model. In this paper, the proposed neural network based hybrid methodology proves itself as a cost-justifiable and effective method for real-time accuracy and quality control in 3D machining process.

Acknowledgements

This work was supported by the NSF, Engineering Research Center of Purdue University. The senior author was partially supported by General Motor Corporation.

10.11 References

1. H. Boulard and C. Wellelens, "Multilayer perceptrons and automatic speech recognition," *Proceedings of the IEEE First International Conference on Neural Networks*, (San Diego, CA, 1987) **IV** 407-416.

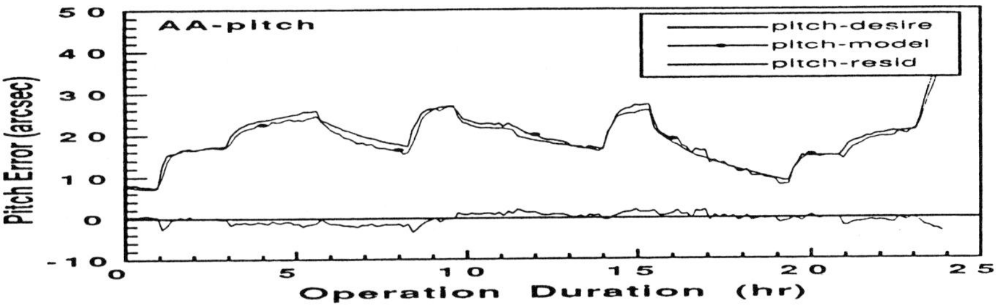

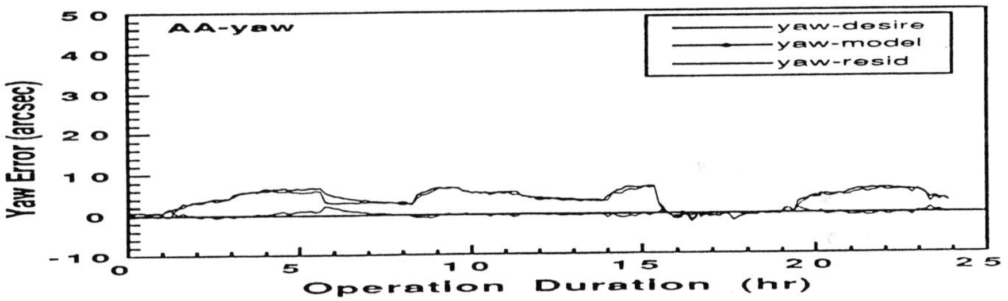

Figure 10.12: Model predictive power: comparison of model predicted angular (pitch and yaw) errors and the actual angular errors

2. N. A. Duffie and S. J. Malmberg, "Error diagnosis and compensation using kinematic model and position error data," *CIRP*, **36** (1) (1987) 355-358.

3. P. Gorman and T. Sejnowski, "Learned classification of sonar targets using a massively parallel network," *IEEE Transactions on Acoustic, Speech and Signal Processing*, **36** (1988) 1135-1140.

4. R. Hecht-Hielsen, *Neurocomputing*, (Addison-Wesley, Reading, MA, 1990).

5. A. G. Ivakhnenko, "Polynomial theory of complex systems," *IEEE Transactions on Systems on Systems, Man and Cybernetics*, **SMC-12** (1971) 364-378.

6. H. K. Jan, C. N. Chu, and C. R. Liu, "A configuration independent approach for modeling 3-D error map for machine system," *ASME 1990 Winter Annual Meeting, Symposium on the Accuracy, Dynamics and Control Modeling of Machine Systems*, Dallas, Texas), PED **45** (Nov. 25-30, 1990) 75-85.

7. H. K. Jan and C. R. Liu, "A parametric algorithm for characterizing the inaccuracy of multiaxial machine system," (November, 1990), *ASME Transactions, Journal of Engineering for Industry* (in review).

8. G. Josin, D. Charney, and D. White, "Robot control using neural networks," *Proceedings of the IEEE First International Conference on Neural Networks*, San Diego, CA, **II** (1987) 625-631.

9. R. Kuczewski, "Neural network approaches to multi-target tracking," *Proceedings of the IEEE First International Conference on Neural Networks*, San Diego, CA, **IV** (1987) 619-634.

10. D. L. Leete, "Automatic compensation of alignment errors in machine tools," *International Journal of Machine Tool Design and Research*, **1** (1961) 293-324.

11. Y. T. Lin, "Geometric adaptive control for accuracy and stability in machining cylindrical workpieces," Ph.D. Dissertation, Purdue University, W. Lafayette, Indiana (1985).

12. R. P. Lippmann, "An introduction to computing with neural nets" *IEEE Acoustic, Speech and Signal Processing (ASSP) Magazine*, (4) (1987) 4-22.

13. W. J. Love and A. J. Scarr, "The determination of the volumetric accuracy of multi-axis machines," *Proceedings of Machine Tools Design and Research Conference*, **14** (1973) 307-315.

14. F. Pourboghrat and M. Sayeh, "Neural Path Planning and Motion Control of Mobile Robots" *Neural Networks* (Abstracts Supplement, 1988) 460.

15. D. E. Rumelhart, G. E. Hinton, and Williams, R. J. , "Learning Internal Representations By Error Propagation," *Parallel Distributed Processing: Explorations in the Microstructure of Cognition*, **1**, Ed. E. Rumelhart, J. L. McClelland, (MIT Press, Cambridge, MA, 1986) 318-362.

16. P. K. Simpson, "Artificial Neural Systems -Foundations, paradigms, Applications and Implementations," (Pergamon Press, NY, 1990).

17. R. Schultschik, "Possibilities and Limits of error Feedback in Automatic Machining," *Annals of the CIRP*, **29** (1) (1981) 223-227.

18. R. Venugopal, and M. Barash, "Thermal Effect on the Accuracy of Numerically Controlled Machine," *Annals of the CIRP*, **35** (1) (1986) 255-258.

19. M. Watson, "A neural networks model for phoneme recognition using the generalized delta rule for connection strength modification," Proceedings of the IEEE First International Conference on Neural Networks, San Diego, CA, **IV** (1987) 389-396.

20. M. Weck and L. Zangs, "Computing the thermal behavior of machine tools using the finite element method -possibilities and limitations," *Proceedings of Machine Tools Design and Research Conference,* **16** (1975) 185-193.

21. H. Wiele, R. Mangelsdorf, and R. Heinke, "Permanent temperature Control is Securing Technological Processes in Machine Tools," *MTDR Conference Proceedings*, **23** (1982) 95-101.

Index